Secrecy, Law and Society

Commentators have shown how a 'culture of security' ushered in after the terrorist attacks of 11 September 2001 has involved exceptional legal measures and increased recourse to secrecy on the basis of protecting public safety and safeguarding national security. In this context, scholars have largely been preoccupied with the ways that increased security impinges upon civil liberties. While secrecy is justified on public interest grounds, there remains a tension between the need for secrecy and calls for openness, transparency and disclosure.

In law, secrecy has implications for the separation of powers, due process and the rule of law, raising fundamental concerns about open justice, procedural fairness and human rights. Beyond the counterterrorism and legal context, scholarly interest in secrecy has been concerned with the credibility of public and private institutions, as well as the legacies of secrecy across a range of institutional and cultural settings.

By exploring the intersections between secrecy, law and society, this volume is a timely and critical intervention in secrecy debates traversing various fields of legal and social inquiry. It will be a useful resource for academic researchers, university teachers and students, as well as law practitioners and policymakers interested in the legal and socio-legal dimensions of secrecy.

Greg Martin is a Senior Lecturer in Socio-Legal Studies at the University of Sydney. Among other things, his research interests are currently in: secret evidence and criminal law; social movements, law and policing; and cultural criminology. He is author of several titles including *Understanding Social Movements* (Routledge 2015).

Rebecca Scott Bray is Co-Director, Institute of Criminology, Sydney Law School, and Senior Lecturer in Socio-Legal Studies, Department of Sociology and Social Policy, University of Sydney. Her research interests lie at the intersections of law, criminology and culture, with a specific focus on issues around the dead.

Miiko Kumar is a Senior Lecturer in the Faculty of Law at the University of Sydney and a practising barrister at the NSW Bar. Her research interests include secrecy in procedure and evidence.

Secrecy, Law and Society

Edited by
Greg Martin,
Rebecca Scott Bray and
Miiko Kumar

Routledge
Taylor & Francis Group
a GlassHouse Book

First published 2015
by Routledge
2 Park Square, Milton Park, Abingdon, Oxfordshire OX14 4RN

and by Routledge
711 Third Avenue, New York, NY 10017

First issued in paperback 2016

Routledge is an imprint of the Taylor & Francis Group, an informa business

British Library Cataloguing in Publication Data
A catalogue record for this book is available from the British Library

Library of Congress Cataloging-in-Publication Data
Secrecy, law, and society / edited by Miiko Kumar, Greg Martin, Rebecca Scott Bray.
pages cm
Includes bibliographical references and index.
1. Secrecy—Law and legislation. 2. Privacy, Right of. 3. Human rights. 4. National security—Law and legislation. 5. Confidential communications. I. Kumar, Miiko. II. Martin, Greg. III. Bray, Rebecca Scott.
K3263.S39 2015
342'.0662—dc23
2014048730

ISBN 13: 978-0-415-79225-7 (pbk)
ISBN 13: 978-1-138-82650-2 (hbk)

Typeset in Baskerville
by Apex CoVantage, LLC

Contents

Acknowledgements

This book is the outcome of a workshop that was held in February 2014 at the University of Sydney, Australia. We would like to thank all who participated in the workshop, both those contributing to this volume and the other participants, all of whom gave their time and energy to the topic. For funding the workshop, we are extremely grateful to: the Sydney Institute of Criminology, Sydney Law School, University of Sydney; the Ross Parsons Centre of Commercial, Corporate and Taxation Law, Sydney Law School, University of Sydney; and the Law and Society Research Network, Faculty of Arts and Social Sciences, University of Sydney. For providing additional funds for editorial assistance, we are indebted to the Law and Society Research Network, and we thank Melanie Eslick for her painstaking editorial work. We are especially grateful to Colin Perrin and Rebekah Jenkins at Routledge for supporting this project, and we would like to thank the anonymous reviewers of the original book proposal for taking the time to provide insightful comments. Finally, we thank Professor Robert van Krieken for his support throughout the project.

Notes on contributors

Greg Martin is a Senior Lecturer in Socio-Legal Studies at the University of Sydney. Among other things, his research interests are currently in: secret evidence and criminal law; social movements, law and policing; and cultural criminology. He has published in these and related areas in a number of journals including *Crime Media Culture*; *Journal of Law and Society*; *Policing and Society*; and *Sydney Law Review*. He is author of *Understanding Social Movements* (Routledge 2015).

Rebecca Scott Bray is Co-Director, Institute of Criminology, Sydney Law School, and Senior Lecturer in Socio-Legal Studies, Department of Sociology and Social Policy at the University of Sydney. Her research interests lie in the intersections of law, criminology and culture, with a specific focus on issues around the dead. Areas include medico-legal and forensic criminology; photography, art and aesthetics; and coronial law and practice. Her monograph *Crime Scenes: Forensics and Aesthetics* is forthcoming from Routledge-Cavendish.

Miiko Kumar is a Senior Lecturer in the Faculty of Law at the University of Sydney and a practising barrister at the NSW Bar. Miiko has held positions at the Office of the Director of Public Prosecutions (NSW), Crown Solicitor (NSW) and the Australian Law Reform Commission. She was on the Advisory Committee for the Australian Law Reform Commission's review of the Evidence Act. Miiko is interested in secrecy in procedure and evidence and has published in this area. She is a co-author of several books on evidence and procedure. Miiko would like to thank Felicity Bell and Naomi Oreb for their assistance.

Rebecca Ananian-Welsh is a Lecturer at the TC Beirne School of Law at the University of Queensland. Prior to joining the TC Beirne School, Rebecca held positions with the Federal Attorney-General's Department, DLA Piper Sydney, and with the University of New South Wales' Gilbert + Tobin Centre of Public Law, where she was a member of the Laureate Fellowship Project 'Anti-Terror Laws and the Democratic Challenge'.

Gabrielle Appleby is an Associate Professor at UNSW Law. Gabrielle researches and teaches in Australian public law. Her publications include *Australian Public Law* (2nd edn., OUP 2014), *Public Sentinels* (Ashgate Publishing 2014) and *The Future of Australian Federalism* (CUP 2012). She is a chief investigator on an Australian Research Council Discovery Project entitled 'Law, Order and Federalism' (DP 140101218), and the research in her chapter is funded by this grant. Gabrielle would like to thank Greg Martin, Rebecca Scott Bray and Miiko Kumar for the invitation to be part of this project, and Alistair Sage and Nathan Deakes for excellent research assistance and their critical eyes.

Katherine Biber is a legal scholar, criminologist and historian in the Faculty of Law at the University of Technology Sydney. She is author of *Captive Images: Race, Crime, Photography* (Routledge 2007) and co-editor of *The Lindy Chamberlain Case: Nation, Law, Memory* (Australian Scholarly Publishing 2009). Her chapter in this volume derives from a funded project titled 'Open Justice and Open Secrets: The Cultural Afterlife of Criminal Evidence' supported by an Australian Research Council Discovery Grant (DP130102224). Katherine is grateful for assistance and support from the Melbourne Magistrates Court, Starla Hargita, Dean Biron, Isabella Alexander, Paul McCartan and the conveners and participants at the 'Secrecy, Law and Society' symposium.

Jessie Blackbourn is a lecturer in politics and human rights at Kingston University. Previously, she was a post-doctoral research fellow on the Australian Research Council Laureate Fellowship project 'Anti-Terror Laws and the Democratic Challenge' in the Gilbert + Tobin Centre of Public Law at the University of New South Wales. Her current research examines the way in which states review their national security and anti-terrorism laws with a particular focus on independent monitors. She is the author of *Anti-Terrorism Law and Normalising Northern Ireland* (Routledge 2015). Jessie would like to thank colleagues on Professor George Williams' ARC Laureate funded project 'Anti-Terror Laws and the Democratic Challenge' at the University of New South Wales for their discussion and comments on an earlier draft of her chapter.

Steven Churches is a barrister practising in Adelaide at Elliott Johnston Chambers. He has been writing and arguing about natural justice for many years. Dr Churches has been counsel in High Court cases such as *Bropho* (the presumption of Crown immunity from statutory provisions is not a rule); *Webster v Lampard* (officials covered by statutory protections are subject to cross-examination while establishing their immunity); *Teoh* (treaties may raise a legitimate expectation that they will be adhered to); and *McNamara v CTTT* (statutory bodies wanting to claim Crown status must have clear statutory authority). Steven gratefully acknowledges the assistance of Professor Charles Rickett, Dean, Auckland University of Technology Law School.

Thomas C. Ellington is Associate Professor of Political Science and Chair of the Department of History and Political Science at Wesleyan College, Macon, Georgia, USA. His research focuses on the tension between official secrecy and democracy, and has been published in journals such as *Public Integrity* and *Government and Opposition*. In 2014, he was a Fulbright Korea Senior Scholar and Visiting Professor at Ewha Womans University in Seoul. From 2007 to 2013, he served two terms as a member of the Macon, Georgia, City Council.

Ryan Goss is Lecturer in Law at the Australian National University (ANU), Canberra. Ryan's research and teaching focuses on public law and European human rights law, particularly fair trial rights. A Rhodes Scholar from Queensland, and previously Junior Research Fellow in Law at Lincoln College, Oxford, Ryan has been at ANU since mid-2013. Recent publications include *Criminal Fair Trial Rights: Article 6 of the European Convention on Human Rights* (Hart Publishing 2014) and '"To the Serious Detriment of the Public": Secret Evidence and Closed Material Procedures' in L Lazarus, C McCrudden and N Bowles (eds), *Reasoning Rights: Comparative Judicial Engagement* (Hart Publishing 2014).

Lawrence McNamara is Senior Research Fellow and Deputy Director at the Bingham Centre for the Rule of Law. The Bingham Centre is a part of the British Institute of International and Comparative Law, an independent research institute in London. Prior to joining the Bingham Centre in 2013, Lawrence was a Reader in Law at the University of Reading in the United Kingdom (2007–13), was awarded an ESRC Fellowship in Ideas and Beliefs (2009–2012) under which he ran the 'Law, Terrorism and the Right to Know' project, and held academic posts in Australia from 1997–2007. He has published and presented widely on matters relating to media law, security and the regulation of speech.

Brian Martin is Professor of Social Sciences at the University of Wollongong, Australia, and Vice President of Whistleblowers Australia. He is the author of 14 books and hundreds of articles on whistleblowing, non violence, scientific controversies, information issues, democracy and other topics. Brian thanks Suelette Dreyfus, Kathy Flynn and Steve Wright for valuable comments on drafts, and Greg Martin for suggesting several key references.

David Rolph is an Associate Professor at the University of Sydney Faculty of Law, specialising in media law. He is the author of two books, as well as many book chapters and journal articles, on all aspects of media law. From 2007 to 2013, Dr Rolph was the editor of the *Sydney Law Review*, one of Australia's leading law journals. He currently serves on the editorial boards of the *Media and Arts Law Review*, the *Communications Law Bulletin* and the *International Journal of the Semiotics of Law*.

Clive Walker is Professor Emeritus of Criminal Justice Studies at the School of Law, University of Leeds, where he has served as the Director of the Centre for Criminal Justice Studies (1987–2000) and as Head of School (2000–2005, 2010). He has been a visiting professor at many universities, including George Washington and Stanford Universities in the United States, and Melbourne and New South Wales in Australia. He has researched and written extensively on terrorism issues, with books such as *Terrorism and the Law* (Oxford University Press 2011). He is currently the special adviser to the Home Office's Independent Reviewer of Terrorism Legislation.

Chapter 1

Secrecy, law and society

Miiko Kumar, Greg Martin and Rebecca Scott Bray

Introduction

Secrecy intersects many areas of law and society. Prominent recent examples of such intersections include national security controversies connected to WikiLeaks, Chelsea Manning and Edward Snowden, and the United Kingdom's Leveson Inquiry into media ethics, which exposed clandestine relations between senior police, politicians and journalists. Typically, in cases such as these, secrecy is cast in a negative light because it is an affront to transparency, openness and accountability, which are values widely regarded as integral to the operation of government and public institutions in democratic societies.[1] In contrast, secrecy in the form of an individual right to privacy vis-à-vis intensified state monitoring and surveillance by private corporations[2] can be seen as positive, and is exemplified by the 'right to be forgotten', which enables people to request their removal from Internet search engine results; a right that was recognised by the European Court of Justice in May 2014.[3]

Notwithstanding cases of 'positive legal secrecy', secrecy in law tends to be viewed in terms of its negative implications for the separation of powers, due process, and the rule of law. This, in turn, raises concerns about open justice, procedural fairness, the right to a fair trial, and other human rights, including privacy rights. However, the law also recognises that, in certain circumstances, secrecy is required; for instance, to ensure the anonymity of vulnerable witnesses or to safeguard police surveillance operations and techniques. Indeed, the European Court of Human Rights has ruled that the right to disclosure of relevant evidence is not absolute, and that the protection of witnesses and the secrecy of police methods of investigation are among the factors to be balanced against an accused person's entitlement to disclosure.[4] Interrogation of the tension inherent in balancing seemingly mutually exclusive values has been particularly evident in the scholarly work conducted since the events of 11 September 2001, where much of the commentary has focused on the negative manifestations of secrecy.

In certain respects, what analysts have sought to explain here is an apparent contradiction: in developing counter-terrorism responses, liberal democratic societies have fostered a 'culture of security', which has not only impinged upon a range of human rights and civil liberties, but has also involved the introduction of exceptional legal measures – including increased recourse to secrecy – that have gradually become normalised.[5] Because the introduction of such measures has been justified on the grounds of protecting public safety and safeguarding national security, many commentators have been preoccupied with the theme of 'security versus liberty', although Adam Tomkins has argued recently that the 'security versus due process' dynamic is equally important.[6]

However, current scholarly concern with secrecy is not confined to developments in counter-terrorism and national security law. It also includes an examination of such matters as the legacies of secrecy across a range of institutional and cultural settings evidenced, for example, by the global exposure of historical child sexual abuse scandals.[7] Here, questions of secrecy go to the heart of the credibility of both public and private institutions. Accordingly, this chapter and this book examine secrecy not only in law but also in other areas of public and social life.

This chapter begins by exploring where and how secrecy manifests in the law. Secrecy in legal proceedings can arise, for instance, via the operation of various evidential privileges, through court orders for secrecy (such as closed court or non-publication orders), or in the use of secret (*ex parte*) evidence. The chapter then moves on to look at the operation of secrecy in law and society by exploring the secrecy–transparency dyad. Following that, the chapter examines sociological approaches to secrecy, considering, among other things, organisational secrecy, and some normative or ethical concerns with secrecy. The final section of the chapter sets out the structure of the book and provides brief summaries of each contribution, which are grouped into four parts, considering: secrecy and security; open justice and procedural fairness; the right to know; and secrecy and society.

Secrecy in law

A key area where secrecy exists in law is in evidential privileges, which can prevent the disclosure of information or exclude evidence. A successful claim of privilege maintains secrecy of information and creates unfairness because one litigant is unable to discover material and/or use it as evidence. Such information could be vital to a case. This means that the maintenance of privilege prevents a court from hearing all relevant evidence and potentially impacts on its ability to arrive at an accurate decision. Therefore, the interests of justice can be compromised or outweighed by the upholding of a privilege claim.

There are a number of recognised privileges that can maintain secrecy by resisting disclosure of information or the admission of evidence. For example, secrecy can protect communications made for the purpose of legal advice or for litigation. This privilege is one of the oldest of privileges for confidential communications.[8] In the common law, 'legal professional privilege' is a fundamental right or principle, which is essential to a properly functioning legal system. The civil law system also recognises the privilege as 'professional secrecy' or 'the law of the professional secret'.[9] The administration of justice in both common law and civil systems depends upon freedom of communication between lawyers and their clients.[10] It is seen as 'a practical guarantee of fundamental, constitutional or human rights',[11] which protects privacy[12] and ensures access to justice.[13] However, the privilege can frustrate justice when important evidence is withheld from the opposing party and the court.

Privilege is also raised to prevent the disclosure of information or the admissibility of evidence to protect a communication made in the context of another relationship that gives rise to confidentiality. For example, some jurisdictions recognise that privilege can be claimed in court by a journalist to keep the identity of a source secret, which ensures the important role that journalists contribute to the free flow of information.[14] There may also be protection of communications made in confidence in the context of a professional relationship (such as doctor and patient, rape counsellor and victim),[15] or claimed by a religious leader, such as a priest, to refuse to divulge a religious confession.[16] Privilege can protect communications made in an attempt to settle a civil dispute. The rationale for this privilege is to encourage settlement rather than costly litigation.[17]

In other circumstances, Crown privilege or public interest immunity is raised when an arm of government seeks to prevent the disclosure of information or to object to the admissibility of evidence. This is a substantive right raised by the state and is based on the harm that could be suffered if information were made public. For example, a government might seek to prevent the disclosure of cabinet minutes if it believes such disclosure could prejudice the functioning of government by preventing candour in cabinet discussions.[18] Privilege may also be claimed for documents that could reveal the identity of police informers whose safety may be compromised by disclosure, or on the basis that future sources of information could dry up, or that the police could be hindered in their duties of preventing and detecting crime.[19] Disclosure of documents containing confidential police methodology could also harm the proper conduct of future law enforcement.[20]

Unfairness can occur in the determination of public interest immunity claims because the party arguing against the immunity must do so without viewing confidential evidence tendered to the court in support of the claim, which includes the documents that are the subject of the claim. The introduction of special advocates, who represent the interests of the party objecting to the immunity, seeks to address procedural unfairness caused by the use of confidential evidence used to prove a public interest immunity claim. However, the use of special advocates has itself been controversial since, among other things, advocates may not take instructions or report to clients, which undermines the traditional lawyer/client relationship.[21]

The disclosure of confidential information held by governments has received increased focus due to leaks, such as those of WikiLeaks. These disclosures demonstrate the conflict between exposure of information that could reveal government abuse and the harm that may be caused to individuals and nations arising from the disclosure of sensitive information. In analysing criminal offences and legal protections in respect of disclosure in Australia, Keiran Hardy and George Williams note that the leaking of information could give rise to offences for terrorism, treason, espionage and/or statutory offences for persons who owe confidentiality as a result of their position, such as government employees.[22] Worryingly, they conclude, there are inadequate protections for whistleblowers in the Australian context.[23]

Secrecy in law also manifests in various intrusions upon the open justice principle. Open justice is a right to have a 'fair and public hearing'.[24] The principle of open justice is one of the most fundamental aspects of the justice system;[25] it means that a court is physically open to the public. A consequence of the open justice principle is that, absent any restriction ordered by the court (such as a non-publication or a suppression order), anyone may publish a fair and accurate report of the legal proceedings.[26] Reports about court proceedings are usually undertaken by media organisations, and 'publicity of proceedings is one of the great protections against the exercise of arbitrary power and a reassurance that justice is administered fairly and impartially'.[27] The purpose of open justice is to ensure integrity and the accountability of those who administer justice.[28] Furthermore, witnesses are more likely to tell the truth if they testify in public.[29] Open justice enhances the public's confidence in the justice system and perpetuates the rule of law.[30] The provision of reasons by the court for its decision is also an expression of the open justice principle.[31]

Given this, can secrecy in a hearing be fair? Secrecy in court proceedings requires a departure from the principle of open justice. A departure can occur when the court excludes the public from some part or all of a hearing,[32] or restricts access to information by making a suppression order restricting the disclosure of information in legal proceedings,[33] or by making pseudonym orders to prevent the disclosure of a witness's true identity,[34] or by ordering non-publication about information (usually evidence) raised in a legal proceeding. Pseudonym orders are also used to protect vulnerable persons, such as child offenders, victims or the subjects of family court litigation. More than one order can be made to protect information. For example, an undercover operative usually testifies with the protection of a pseudonym order, in closed court, with a non-publication order to protect publication of information that might identify the operative.

A fair hearing is one where the parties in the case hear and can test the evidence that is being led against them. Arguably, the principles of fairness and open justice are affected to the greatest extent by the use of 'secret evidence', defined as 'material adduced in judicial proceedings, but not disclosed to an affected party or their legal representative'.[35] In the United Kingdom, the use of such evidence has been most controversial when governments tender closed material or secret evidence in hearings to issue control orders against persons suspected of involvement in terrorism.[36] In these cases, 'questions of secrecy versus fairness are heightened by the liberty context within which control orders operate'.[37] Recently, however, the UK reduced the severity of control orders.[38]

By contrast, in Australia, control orders in the terrorism context have been extended to apply to serious organised crime, where the constitutional validity of 'criminal intelligence' provisions contained in legislation designed to control the activities of criminal organisations was upheld by the Australian High Court.[39] This legislation provides for a two-stage process where the initial court proceedings are to declare a criminal organisation, and the second stage is for an application to issue a control order against the members of the declared organisation. Significantly, the declaration can rely on secret criminal intelligence that is not revealed to the alleged members of the criminal organisation.[40] In an era where we appear to be witnessing the steady creep of secrecy in forensic settings, another contemporary issue in Australia, at least, is the use of secret compulsory hearings to question criminal suspects with a statutory abrogation of the right to silence.[41]

Secrecy in law and society

Whereas secrecy in the law appears in a set of established principles and rules, and exceptions to them, secrecy in the context of law and society highlights further sets of relations and processes that raise questions about justice, law enforcement and police accountability, to name but a few. As we have seen, a post-9/11 'culture of security' has yielded exceptional legal measures and increased recourse to secrecy, which have impacted upon due process and the rule of law, in turn raising fundamental concerns about open justice, procedural fairness and the right to a fair trial.[42] These concerns have become issues at the heart of contemporary democratic governance and institutional credibility, carrying cultural and moral weight, and falling either side of a fault line where 'secrecy comes to be associated with all that is nefarious (inefficiency, corruption, malfeasance, conspiracy) and transparency with all that is noble (efficiency, accountability, honesty, trustworthiness)'.[43]

Indeed, it has been argued that in modern democracies, secrecy has become the maligned half of a fraught secrecy–transparency dyad, where transparency is valorised for making possible the accountability of those in power, which is the 'real prize' that 'regulates a democracy'.[44] And while the 'ideal of open government and publicity, as one context for transparency' has existed since the emergence of representative politics and the Enlightenment, scholars such as Clare Birchall identify a particular 'modish inflection' to transparency in a profoundly technological era dominated by the Internet.[45] This is an era characterised not only by extraordinary levels of data storage, but also by possibilities for data access. These elements shape and yet also frustrate the pursuit of transparency in contemporary society.

Birchall notes that evidence abounds for the 'vogue for transparency', both within mainstream liberal democratic politics, buoyed by initiatives such as freedom of information legislation, and leftist activism that rails against neoliberalism by, for example, employing tactics such as surveillance at anti-capitalist protests to expose police practices.[46] From US President Barack Obama's championing of transparency through to WikiLeaks' investment in 'transparency in the service of accountability' via the mass release of classified documents,[47] the state of affairs is such that 'the ubiquitous notion' is 'that transparency is inherently more democratic than secrecy' and, in fact, that secrecy spoils democracy.[48] For example, in 2009, when the UK Government was introducing its second attempt in as many years to push for 'secret inquests' that would exclude the public – including family members – from inquest hearings involving sensitive information, the father of a man who died in the 7 July 2005 London terrorist bombings urged against the reform with the plea 'please do not discolour democracy with it'.[49] Operating in this way, a drive for secrecy is not merely undemocratic, it is seen to damage democracy.

For some commentators, the matter is far from uncomplicated whereby transparency can begin to resemble an agent of totalitarianism rather than democracy when there is no room for secrets.[50] Moreover, examples such as WikiLeaks highlight the paradox at the heart of both secrecy and transparency: the intractable relationship between the two, with which we must contend.[51] In the case of WikiLeaks, the irony is that secrecy is integral to its transparency project. It is a 'virtual, dispersed, non-statist, largely anonymous cyborg assemblage' that privileges secrecy by anonymising sources and membership,[52] leading to the recognition that opacity is an inescapable part of transparency. This 'force of transparency' that 'demands a level of secrecy equivalent to that practiced by the state' is what Birchall identifies as potentially the most radical aspect of the WikiLeaks project,[53] while the technological apparatus that enables the pursuit of transparency itself highlights the paradox inherent in the relationship between secrecy and transparency. For just as technology ensures 'we can be both objects and agents of intelligence', the bulk of information remains largely unaccounted for 'because of the sheer volume of data, the structure of databases, and the criteria of common search engines'.[54] It is in this way that 'extreme transparency . . . begins to have the same effect as secrecy'.[55]

Birchall identifies how tensions also exist, 'within the legislative and institutional framework of state power'.[56] At the same time that freedom of information statutes were drafted worldwide, permitting access to government documents, modern classification systems emerged and intelligence agencies were formalised. The goals of gathering and classifying, and thus protecting, intelligence information therefore operate simultaneously with techniques of liberating government information, thereby highlighting the uneasy coexistence of secrecy and transparency.[57] This uneasiness is reflected in other areas, such as the knowledge economy of business practices, where organisational strategy calls for transparency, but certain practices remain opaque to outsiders.[58]

It may be argued that, in part, there is good evidence for the promotion of transparency over secrecy. Eva Horn recounts the legitimate ambivalence over political secrecy, secrecy which, supported by or slipping past statute, 'opens up a universe of uncontained violence'.[59] By way of example, she posits:

> the world of aggressive secret operations, *coups d'état* and assassination plots, interventions in the domestic affairs of other states, secret police actions against potential terrorists, abductions and torture (as we have recently witnessed), and, last but not least, intrusive forms of surveillance, interception and other forms of invading citizens' privacy.[60]

State and state agent actions may be sanctioned, delimited or regulated by laws, but this says nothing about the 'shroud of non-communication, non-documentation and non-reporting' that withholds information from revelation and which escapes public as well as government scrutiny.[61] Other scholars have interrogated secrecy beyond the lens of democratic accountability to examine what else is at stake. Taking aim at secret law, Christopher Kutz argues that if law's function in the democratic project is to secure the state's legitimacy and morally orientate us as citizens, then law's secrecy 'hurts us existentially' by disrupting self-knowledge and membership in relation to the state, while also undermining the governor's right to rule.[62] In Kutz's thinking, legality and legitimacy are not the same.

For commentators such as Mark Fenster, in the end, secrecy is implausible. Information control ultimately fails; it fails because secrets (eventually) come to light by design, accident or mistake, even the 'deep secrets' or the 'unknown unknowns'.[63] That secrecy cannot be accomplished has the effect of making secrets more difficult to keep, as well as engendering public speculation about secrecy.[64] Consequently, the very 'practice of keeping secrets itself constitutes information', communicating 'important information about the state and its governance strategy' to a suspicious public.[65]

Writing on political secrecy, Horn distinguishes this decisively modern logic of secrecy from its pre-modern appreciation, where state secrecy constituted a 'legitimate part of governance',[66] operating as a 'stabilizing, defensive form of secrecy'.[67] Modern democracies instead are plagued by what Horn dubs the 'secrecy effect', where the 'secret is not so much a piece of withheld knowledge as a "secrecy effect" that binds the realm of secrecy to the public sphere by a dialectics of permanent suspicion and scandal'.[68] This modern logic 'tends to draw everything into the vortex of its secrecy effect – the secret as much as the public, political crimes as much as the rules of prudent discretion, an all-embracing suspicion as much as gullible belief in the power of revelation'.[69]

Recent revelations testify to the 'drama of concealment and revelation' that marks modern secrecy-as-scandal,[70] such as evidence given by undercover police officers in the UK, which has potentially led to miscarriages of justice,[71] the Leveson Inquiry into media ethics that has exposed clandestine relationships between senior police, politicians and journalists,[72] and the catalogue of concerns documented by the Hillsborough Independent Panel, including police altering of evidence following the 1989 Hillsborough football stadium disaster.[73] How might we reconcile the important work that comes of such disclosures when their secrecy is founded in corruption and deceit? While it is important, necessary and just that such (corrupt) secrets come to light, for many commentators their revelation and publicity need to be accompanied by responsibility and action.[74]

Nor might these events simply resolve the secrecy versus transparency debate on the side of transparency, as if greater transparency cures corruption and conspiracy. Instead, scholars call for other ways to approach the matter. As Fenster writes on government secrecy, presuming the state is either 'open and transparent or closed and opaque' is largely unproductive, and is a binary approach that rarely holds in reality as 'most events exist in a gray world of partial secrecy and partial disclosure'.[75] Considering national security leaks at the United States federal executive branch level, David Pozen places leaking within the 'larger ecosystem of presidential information control', arguing that leaks largely occupy a 'gray area between full authorization and no authorization',[76] where norms rather than leak laws organise disclosure and discipline.[77] Pozen concludes that, instead of frustrating governance, 'some substantial leaking is deeply valuable for the executive itself'.[78] Leaking, then, is more appropriately considered a 'feature, not a bug, of the system'.[79] Such a dynamic highlights how we need to 'deepen our understanding of . . . secrecy'.[80] Merely distinguishing between secrecy and transparency creates a simplistic or false dichotomy, as if transparency automatically eradicates secrecy and achieves accountability.[81] Instead, secrecy is constitutive and structures relations in civil society, which leads to more appropriate framing of secrecy as 'public secrecy'.[82]

Therefore, rather than choosing between secrecy and transparency, a more productive analysis might emerge from inhabiting the tension between the two.[83] For Horn, the crux of secrecy is that it is inescapably paradoxical, and finding a way through this uncomfortable truth is more worthwhile. A functional view of secrecy would reinstate its pragmatic value for state security but this view must be tempered by an acknowledgment of secrecy's 'irredeemable ambivalence'.[84] When secrecy's dilemma lies in its capacity to create a 'space of exception from the rule of law that breeds violence, corruption and oppression',[85] it seems much easier to insist on transparency. Moreover, for commentators such as Birchall, a radical rethink of our relationship with secrecy is required. Birchall even suggests rehabilitating the secret, using psychoanalysis and poetry as examples of sociocultural phenomena where something valuable can take place 'because of secrecy rather than (or as well as) transparency'.[86]

Teasing out secrecy's place in psychoanalysis, Birchall notes how the therapy relies on a mix of confidentiality, disclosure and non-disclosure in the analytical relationship between patient and analyst. Confidentiality ensures that the patient trusts in the analytical space; however, this trust not only enables revelation to occur, but also 'helps to create the analytic frame' by fostering a conducive atmosphere for unconscious patterns to emerge.[87] Yet this confidentiality does not result in total transparency. Analysis is achieved through the analyst being opaque and available to the patient only as a 'reflective figure' to enable transference.[88] In this way, the usual rules of social interaction do not apply, otherwise the analysis is compromised. Furthermore, the patient will falter at full self-disclosure, a resistance that actually signals 'the beginning of the therapeutic treatment'.[89] With this example, Birchall appreciates not only the productive aspects of secrecy but also its constitutive nature.

From this perspective, secrecy and transparency are not oppositional terms. To champion transparency above secrecy is to support a 'restrictive oscillation' between a false binary approach.[90] Instead, Birchall argues, a move towards 'post-secrecy' is needed, which disrupts the 'either/or' logic that pervades discussions of secrecy and transparency in the democratic project.[91] Why? Because ultimately, without a more nuanced appreciation of secrets, we face the choice not between 'lesser and greater democracy', but between democracy and totalitarianism.[92]

Secrecy in society

From the foregoing discussions, it is apparent that secrecy pervades numerous areas of social and public life. In this section of the chapter, we consider sociological interest in secrecy, which has existed for some time, although it could not be said that the field is at all coherent, or that it constitutes a disciplinary sub-field. One area where interest in secrecy has been relatively sustained, however, is in the sociology of organisations, where, early on, Max Weber recognised the importance of secrecy for bureaucratic forms of organisation. He observed that '[t]he concept of the "official secret" is the specific invention of bureaucracy, and few things it defends so fanatically as this attitude which . . . cannot be justified with purely functional arguments'.[93] According to Costas and Grey, Weber's comment that organisational secrecy is not a matter of pure functionality is not to say that functional reasons for secrecy do not exist, but that they coexist with secrecy's social and symbolic value.[94]

In contrast to the informational perspective that predominates in studies of organisational secrecy – which assumes that the significance of secrecy lies in the protection of valuable information – Costas and Grey focus on secrecy as a social process, rather than looking at the informational content of secrets.[95] Hence, they define organisational secrecy as 'the ongoing formal and informal social processes of intentional concealment of information from actors by actors in organisations'.[96] Accordingly, a focus on intentional concealment as a social phenomenon that is carried out by social actors in concert is likely to reveal a variety of symbolic and ritualistic practices.[97]

Costas and Grey's study draws on Erving Goffman's work on 'teams', which is a conceptual device intended to account for situations in which individuals cooperate with one another. Teams are also akin to secret societies, since members are 'in the know', whereas non-members are not.[98] Goffman's work on teams captures an interweaving of the informational and social aspects of secrecy, which can be placed in one of three types.

First, Goffman identifies what he terms 'dark' secrets, which 'consist of facts about a team which it knows and conceals and which are incompatible with the image of self that the team attempts to maintain before its audience'.[99] Second, there are 'strategic' secrets, which 'pertain to intentions and capacities of a team which it conceals from its audience in order to prevent them from adapting effectively to the state of affairs the team is planning to bring about'.[100] Examples include the strategic secrets employed in business or by the military when designing future actions against competitors or foes. As long as the team makes no pretence at having strategic secrets, those secrets do not constitute dark secrets. However, writes Goffman, even when strategic secrets are not dark, their discovery or disclosure will disrupt team performance, 'for suddenly and expectedly the team finds it useless and foolish to maintain the care, reticence, and studied ambiguity of action that was required prior to loss of its secrets'.[101] Finally, there are 'inside' secrets, which 'are ones whose possession marks an individual as being a member of a group and helps the group feel separate and different'. In other words, they make 'insiders feel distinct and special'.[102]

This sense of separateness and specialness is a recurrent theme in the sociology of secrecy. In his foundational essay on secrecy and the secret society, Georg Simmel talks about how the secret offers 'the possibility of a second world alongside the manifest world',[103] and how it 'gives one a position of exception'.[104] In the context of the secret society, isolation and specialness are tied to autonomy and, ultimately, freedom, whereby 'the society lives in an area to which the norms of the environment do not extend'.[105] Seclusion against the outside world functions to intensify cohesion within the secret society. Moreover, the sense of separateness and exclusiveness is reinforced through initiation rites and more generally via rituals. Here, Simmel cites the example of the vow of secrecy undertaken by Freemasons, which refers exclusively to the masonic ritual.[106]

Simmel's interest in secrecy is formalistic, rather than substantive or even normative. For him, the significance of the secret – which, he claims, 'is one of man's greatest achievements'[107] – to human relations 'must not be overlooked in view of the fact that the secret is often ethically negative; for, the secret is a general sociological form which stands in neutrality above the value functions of its contents'.[108] In this way, he argues, the secret has no immediate connection to evil, although it may constitute the sociological expression of 'moral badness'.[109] This leads to another key issue in sociological analyses of secrecy: the normative or ethical concern with secrecy.

As stated earlier, a typical view is that because secrecy runs counter to transparency and democratic accountability, it is undesirable and problematic.[110] For example, Warren and Laslett say '[s]ecrecy implies the concealment of something which is negatively valued by the excluded audience and, in some instances, by the perpetrators as well'.[111] Privacy, by contrast, 'protects behaviour which is either morally neutral or valued by society as well as by the perpetrators'.[112] Thus, for Warren and Laslett, 'privacy implies the legitimate denial of access, while secrecy in general implies that the denial of access is illegitimate'.[113] Citing as examples the privacy associated with the nuclear family and the secrecy of the homosexual world, Warren and Laslett argue that secrecy is an 'extreme form of denial of access to others'.[114] In what is now quite a dated study containing some rather antiquated thinking and expression, Warren and Laslett say that since homosexual acts are morally stigmatised, gay people often resort to secrecy to conceal their behaviour. Conversely, they argue, sexual interaction between heterosexual couples is seen as private, but not hidden, as in the case of homosexual couples.[115] Accordingly, to Warren and Laslett, the clandestine world of homosexuality constitutes a secret society in the sense intended by Simmel, since gay people inhabit a world that is based on norms the wider society prohibits.[116]

Bellman is critical of this characterisation of secrecy and secret societies as negative, non-consensual and illegitimate, which 'is contradicted by the existence of secrets and secret societies that are well integrated into the social and political institutions of the larger community'.[117] She shows how various fraternal organisations, including the Freemasons, which stress secrecy in their rites and rituals, are also 'highly considerate of and responsive to the outside community, and their activities are well within the normative control of the larger community'.[118] For Bellman, the depiction of secret societies and secrecy as negative partly has its origins in the view that because the secretive behaviour is seen to operate beyond the norms of the wider social environment, that necessarily means it is deviant in nature. However, the examples she gives:

> counter the usual negative description of secret societies and provide evidence of the way secrecy can be an integrating and legitimate basis for rendering social and political decisions in a society. They point to the way secret associations and secrecy can be either negative or positive, consensual or non-consensual, legitimate or illegitimate.[119]

In their ethnographic study of mushroom-collecting associations, Fine and Holyfield show how secrecy can have a positive social function, which is not incompatible with trust as a communal concern. They characterise mycological societies as voluntary organisations involved in 'dangerous leisure', or activities to which some measure of risk is attached;[120] that is, because harmful and sometimes fatal consequences can result if a person misidentifies a mushroom as edible. For Fine and Holyfield, the tension between solidarity (trust) and individualism (secrecy) is particularly evident in voluntary leisure groups, where 'force and moral compunction are absent'.[121] Hence, in mycological organisations, members must routinely trust the judgment of others to determine whether certain mushrooms are edible, yet secrecy is also crucial since members are highly competitive in finding mushrooms and keeping the location of their spots to themselves. However, in leisure organisations the two seemingly oppositional forces of trust and secrecy can also provide the basis for social cohesion and communal allegiance:

> To suggest that the combination of trust and secrecy provides the basis for the existence of voluntary organizations devoted to competitive, risky activities is to recognize a profound irony: that the tension between attachment (trust) and competition (secrecy) builds social order. Both attachment and competition require an arena to flourish: the leisure group provides this space.[122]

Fine and Holyfield show how mycological societies 'generate trust by supplying protective information to novices, who find themselves in an uncertain environment [and] must learn how to avoid the possibility of illness, or even death, from consuming "bad" mushrooms'.[123] On the other hand, secrecy is particularly evident, as the leisure world of mushroom collecting operates under conditions of scarcity and competition, where comparisons between participants are encouraged.[124] Fine and Holyfield show how the paradoxical relationship between secrecy and sociability is evident in humour, and provide the following example from field notes to show how joking permits the 'processing' of this ambivalence:

> Jerry, the club president, in adjourning a meeting at the end of a morel season, jokes: 'Why don't you share your favourite spots now that the season is over? We'll put them on slips and next year give everyone a slip. Don't give any bum spots'. Of course, nothing is done about either of the suggestions; spots are used by members from year to year.[125]

Fine and Holyfield's use of ethnographic techniques to investigate the operation of secrecy and trust in a social setting raises a final point about researching secrecy. Costas and Grey have said that '[e]mpirical investigations of organizational secrecy are by definition difficult'.[126] Nevertheless, social researchers have been able to gain access to secret worlds. For instance, Brian Rappert has conducted research into diplomatic and security communities. Such research, he says, raises at least two broad concerns: 'whether we as researchers can gain an adequate appreciation of the situations under study and to what extent we can (and should) discuss them in light of the disclosure rules, confidentiality agreements, and other such provisions in place'.[127]

In this area of qualitative social research, the telling of secrets is overwhelmingly couched in terms of research ethics and, in particular, the 'ethics of exposure'.[128] Issues here relate, for example, to maintaining the confidentiality and anonymity of research subjects as a deliberate act of concealment, as well as to ethical dilemmas associated with what to leave in and what to leave out of research accounts.[129] However, Rappert, attends to the absent in research accounts that focus on researchers' experiences by asking 'how what is absent could purposefully function as a creative aspect of qualitative writing; and specifically autobiographical-type writing'.[130]

Secrecy, law and society: the edited collection

Having addressed some of the diverse ways of framing secrecy in studies of law and society in the previous sections of this chapter, the final section provides a brief synopsis of each chapter contained in this edited volume. The book is organised into four parts, each of which considers an aspect of secrecy studies in legal and social inquiry.

Secrecy and security

Part 1 of the book focuses on secrecy and security. This part begins with a powerful critique in Chapter 2 by Clive Walker of the 'closed material procedure' in the UK's Justice and Security Act 2013, which imports radical changes into civil law proceedings by allowing the admission of evidence in hearings where litigant/s do not see 'closed material'. Walker explains the reason for the acute problems presented by national security disputes and considers the potential accommodations that were delivered by the 2013 Act within a framework of justice and respect for rights. In Chapter 3, Thomas C. Ellington analyses the legal basis of official secrecy in the United States, and examines some of the problems associated with its practice, including diminished accountability, increased opportunities for misconduct and compromise of judicial independence. Chapter 4 looks at secret evidence and closed material proceedings in the fair trial rights case law of the European Court of Human Rights and the British courts. Specifically, it considers the case law on 'gisting'. In this chapter, Ryan Goss examines the dialogue between the British courts and the European Court of Human Rights over gisting, and argues that the judgments dealing with gisting are in tension and are poorly explained. Goss argues that gisting's ability to act as a safeguard is easily hollowed out by arguments about overriding public interests.

Open justice and procedural fairness

Part 2 looks at the impact of secrecy on open justice and procedural fairness. This part asks whether fairness can exist without openness. In Chapter 5, Gabrielle Appleby considers an Australian High Court decision that confronted the question of how to balance the need for the secret exercise of security powers against the constitutionally guaranteed requirements of procedural fairness in judicial proceedings, and she explores the extent of the differences between the judicial approaches. In Chapter 6, Steven Churches questions whether there is a requirement for fair hearings in British and Australian courts. Churches observes that courts rest fundamentally on procedural fairness, but the demands of security following the events of 9/11 have seen progressive dismantling of natural justice from curial procedure, resulting in hybridisation whereby judges perform the task of responding to an allegation in respect of which the affected party is deprived of any knowledge. Chapter 7 looks at secrecy, procedural fairness and state courts in the context of recent Australian constitutional developments, challenging the use of secret 'criminal intelligence' evidence in Australian state court proceedings. In that chapter, Rebecca Ananian-Welsh considers the degree to which the separation of judicial power derived from the Australian Constitution limits the use of secret evidence in state courts, and critiques the High Court's approach to resolving the competing interests of secrecy and procedural fairness.

Right to know

Part 3 examines secrecy in the context of the 'right to know'. In Chapter 8, Lawrence McNamara examines how practices of information control and access in the UK affect the media. Drawing on confidential research interviews, he considers journalists' experiences and interactions with those who work within legal institutions and with Muslim communities. McNamara argues that journalists face difficult challenges and must not be hindered by the increasing tendency towards laws and practices that embed secrecy and distrust as the norm. In Chapter 9, Jessie Blackbourn evaluates the role that secret material has played in the process of reviewing both the content and use of anti-terrorism laws in Australia and Canada. Blackbourn focuses on the Australian Independent National Security Legislation Monitor and Inspector-General of Intelligence and Security, and also looks at the Canadian system of public inquiries. She questions whether those who have been tasked to review these contentious laws have managed to conduct their reviews in accordance with the principles of open justice. In Chapter 10, Miiko Kumar examines some of the evidential issues that arise from the use of evidence obtained from undercover policing, and how such issues are dealt with in Australia. The chapter asks whether the boundaries to the admissibility of evidence elicited by covert means have been extended, and considers the necessity for secrecy during court proceedings to protect the identity of operatives and police methods. In Chapter 11, David Rolph observes a trend towards plaintiffs seeking anonymity in defamation cases in England, Australia and Canada. Exploring the reasons for this phenomenon, he argues that the principle of open justice and factors particular to defamation litigation – most notably the concept of reputation and the need for vindication – militate significantly, if not decisively, against allowing plaintiffs in defamation proceedings to be anonymous. Rolph contends that the practice should be closely circumscribed. However, conceptual and practical challenges will be posed to this position with greater legal recognition of privacy, and the confluence of reputation and privacy.

Secrecy and society

Part 4 looks at secrecy in society. In Chapter 12, Brian Martin examines public interest leaking as a strategy for overcoming organisational secrecy. Martin notes that employers commonly use methods to reduce public outrage over activities exposed by leakers: hiding the activities (that is, relying on secrecy); discrediting leakers; reinterpreting their actions by lying, minimising the harm caused, blaming others and framing their activities favourably; using official procedures to give an appearance of justice; and intimidating leakers and their supporters. The US Government's actions against WikiLeaks and against Edward Snowden illustrate all these methods. Martin then suggests counter-strategies for WikiLeaks and for leakers in general. In Chapter 13, Katherine Biber considers the fate of photographic evidence. She asks what happens to intimate and criminal secrets in a regime of open justice. Biber argues against open justice and says that, in some instances, criminal evidence should not be disclosed or released publicly. The chapter focuses on photographic and other visual evidence, including images released by the court following the murder and sexual assault of Jill Meagher in Australia in 2012, and proposes a 'jurisprudence of sensitivity' for making decisions about material that is intimate, harmful, humiliating or secret. Finally, in Chapter 14, Greg Martin and Rebecca Scott Bray offer a sociological and criminological reading of the child abuse scandal that came to light on the Channel Island of Jersey from 2008, by relating the Jersey case to studies of institutional child sexual abuse scandals, and by exploring the operation of privacy and moral regulation in small communities. The chapter also attempts to make sense of some of the more outlandish explanations of cover-up and concealment in the Jersey case that connected it to the island's occupation by the Nazis during World War II, as well as its status as a tax haven.

Notes

1 Amy Gutmann and Dennis Thompson, *Democracy and Disagreement* (Harvard University Press 1996); Susan Maret (ed.), *Government Secrecy* (Emerald Group Publishing Limited 2011).
2 Kevin Haggerty and Richard Ericson, 'The Surveillant Assemblage' (2000) 51(4) *British Journal of Criminology*, 605.
3 Case C-131/12 *Google Spain SL, Google Inc v Agencia Española de Protección de Datos, Mario Costeja González* EU:C:2014:317.
4 *Edwards and Lewis* [2004] X Eur Ct HR 61, 77 [46].
5 See, for example, Kent Roach, *The 9/11 Effect: Comparative Counter-Terrorism* (Cambridge University Press 2011); David Cole, Federico Fabbrini and Arianna Vedaschi (eds.), *Secrecy, National Security and the Vindication of Constitutional Law* (Edward Elgar Publishing 2013); Aniceto Masferrer (ed.), *Post 9/11 and the State of Permanent Legal Emergency* (Springer 2012).
6 Adam Tomkins, 'National Security and the Due Process of Law' (2011) 64(1) *Current Legal Problems*, 215.
7 See, for example, Chris Greer and Eugene McLaughlin, 'The Sir Jimmy Savile Scandal: Child Sexual Abuse and Institutional Denial at the BBC' (2013) 9(3) *Crime Media Culture*, 243.
8 J. Wigmore, *A Treatise on the Anglo-American System of Evidence in Trials at Common Law* (3rd edn., Little, Brown and Co 1940) 547 [2290].
9 *AM & S Europe Ltd v Commission of the European Communities* [1983] EUECJ C-155/79, 1 QB 878, 730.
10 *Greenough v Gaskell* [1833] EngR 333; (1833) 39 ER 618, 621 (Lord Brougham). Lord Hoffman describes the privilege as 'a fundamental human right long established in the common law': *R (Morgan Grenfell) v Special Commissioner of Income Tax* [2002] UKHL 21, [2003] 1 AC 563 [7].
11 *AM & S Europe Ltd* (n. 9) 941.
12 *Hickman v Taylor* USSC 5 [1947]; 329 US 495, 510 (1946).
13 *General Mediterranean Holdings v Patel* [1999] 3 All ER 673, 688.
14 See, for example, s. 126K of the Evidence Act 1995 (NSW) and the Evidence Act 2008 (Vic.).
15 See, for example, s. 126B of the Evidence Act 1995 (NSW) and s. 10 of the Contempt of Court Act 1981 (UK).
16 See for example, s. 127 of the Evidence Act 1995 (Cth.); Evidence Act 2004 (NI); Evidence Act 1995 (NSW); Evidence (National Uniform Legislation) Act 2011 (NT); Evidence Act 2001 (Tas.); Evidence Act 2008 (Vic). These Acts together are collectively termed the Uniform Evidence Acts.
17 See *Rush & Tompkins Ltd v Greater London Council* [1989] AC 1280; see also s. 131 of the Uniform Evidence Acts.
18 Australian examples include: *Sankey v Whitlam* (1978) 142 CLR 1; *Commonwealth v Northern Land Council* (1993) 176 CLR 604; *New South Wales v Public Transport Ticketing Corporation* [2011] NSWCA 6 (23 March 2011).

19 English and Australian authorities include: *D v National Society for the Prevention of Cruelty to Children* [1978] AC 171, 218, 232, 241; *Cain v Glass (No 2)* (1985) 3 NSWLR 230, 232–3, 247; *Attorney-General (NSW) v Stuart* (1994) 34 NSWLR 667; *Director of Public Prosecutions v Smith* (1996) 86 A Crim R 308; *Gardiner v The Queen* (2006) 162 A Crim R 233.

20 *Young v Quin* (1985) 4 FCR 483, 494 (Beaumont J); *S v State of New South Wales (No 3)* [2009] NSWCA 248 [7] (5 August 2009); *New South Wales Commissioner of Police v Nationwide News Pty Ltd* (2007) 70 NSWLR 643, 648 [35].

21 *R v H and C* [2004] UKHL 3, 2 AC 134 [22] (Lord Bingham).

22 Keiran Hardy and George Williams, 'Terrorist, Traitor, or Whistleblower? Offences and Protections in Australia for Disclosing National Security Information' (2014) 37 *UNSW Law Journal*, 784.

23 Ibid. 815, discussing the *Public Interest Disclosure Act 2013* (Cth.).

24 See, for example, *International Covenant on Civil and Political Rights*, opened for signature 16 December 1966, 999 UNTS 171 (entered into force 23 March 1976) art. 14 (Australia is a party to this Covenant and it is scheduled and annexed to the Human Rights and Equal Opportunity Commission Act 1986 (Cth.)); *European Convention on Human Rights*, opened for signature 4 November 1950, 213 UNTS 222 (entered into force 3 September 1953) art. 6 (which is incorporated into English law by the Human Rights Act 1988 (UK)).

25 *John Fairfax Publications Pty Ltd v District Court of NSW* (2004) 61 NSWLR 344, 352 (Spigelman CJ).

26 *Hogan v Hinch* (2011) 243 CLR 506, 532 [22] (French CJ). This case concerned suppression orders.

27 *R v Richards* (1999) 107 A Crim R 318 (Spigelman CJ).

28 See generally Peter Wright, 'The Open Court: The Hallmark of Judicial Proceedings' (1947) 25 *Canadian Bar Review*, 721; Garth Nettheim, 'The Principle of Open Justice' (1984) 8 *University of Tasmania Law Review*, 25; J. J. Spigelman, 'Seen to be Done: The Principle of Open Justice – Part I' (2000) 74 *Australian Law Journal*, 290; Joseph Jaconelli, *Open Justice: A Critique of the Public Trial* (Oxford University Press 2002); New South Wales Law Reform Commission, *Contempt by Publication*, Report No. 100 (2003).

29 3 Bl Comm 373; Jeremy Bentham, *Judicial Evidence* (J. W. Paget 1825) 67–8. See also *J v L & A Services Pty Ltd (No 2)* [1995] 2 Qd R 10, 45 (Fitzgerald, P. and Lee, J.).

30 See generally J. J. Spigelman, 'Seen to be Done: The Principle of Open Justice – Part II' (2000) 74 *Australian Law Journal* 378; see also *Re S (A Child) (Identification: Restrictions on Publication)* [2005] 1 AC 593, 607–8; *R (Binyam Mohamed) v Secretary of State for Foreign and Commonwealth Affairs* [2010] EWCA Civ. 65 [39].

31 *Wainohu v New South Wales* (2011) 243 CLR 18, 215 [58] (French, CJ and Kiefel, J).

32 See, for example, *R v Richards* (n. 27).

33 See, for example, *Seven Network (Operations) Limited v Warburton (No 1)* [2011] NSWSC 385 (5 April 2011).

34 See, for example, *Witness v Marsden* (2000) 49 NSWLR 429.

35 Greg Martin, 'Outlaw Motorcycle Gangs and Secret Evidence: Reflections on the Use of Criminal Intelligence in the Control of Serious Organised Crime in Australia' (2014) 36(3) *Sydney Law Review*, 501, 503.

36 See Rebecca Scott Bray and Greg Martin, 'Closing Down Open Justice in the United Kingdom?' (2012) 37(2) *Alternative Law Journal*, 126.

37 Martin (n. 35) 520.

38 *Terrorism Prevention and Investigation Measures Act 2011* (UK). See Clive Walker, 'The Reshaping of Control Orders in the United Kingdom: Time for a Fairer Go, Australia' (2013) 37 *Melbourne University Law Review*, 143.

39 *Assistant Commissioner Michael James Condon v Pompano Pty Ltd* (2013) 295 ALR 638.

40 Martin (n. 35) 505.

41 *X7 v Australian Crime Commission* (2013) 248 CLR 92; *Lee v NSW Crime Commission* (2013) 251 CLR 196. In these hearings, the Crime Commission compelled witnesses for oral examination in order to conduct criminal investigations.
42 See n. 5.
43 Clare Birchall, 'Transparency, Interrupted: Secrets of the Left' (2011) 28(7–8) *Theory, Culture & Society*, 60, 66.
44 Clare Birchall, 'Introduction to "Secrecy and Transparency": The Politics of Opacity and Openness' (2011) 28(7–8) *Theory, Culture & Society*, 7, 8.
45 Birchall, 'Transparency, Interrupted: Secrets of the Left' (n. 43) 61.
46 Ibid. 62. See also Michael Welch, 'Counterveillance: How Foucault and the Groupe d'Information sur les Prisons Reversed the Optics' (2011) 15(3) *Theoretical Criminology*, 301; Andrew John Goldsmith, 'Policing's New Visibility' (2010) 50(5) *British Journal of Criminology*, 914; Kingsley Dennis, 'Keeping a Close Watch – The Rise of Self-surveillance and the Threat of Digital Exposure' (2008) 56(3) *The Sociological Review*, 347.
47 Birchall, 'Transparency, Interrupted: Secrets of the Left' (n. 43) 73.
48 Birchall, 'Introduction to "Secrecy and Transparency"' (n. 44) 19.
49 *INQUEST-LIBERTY-JUSTICE, Joint Briefing on the Return of 'Secret Inquests' in the Coroners and Justice Bill: Consideration of the House of Lords Amendments in the House of Commons* (November 2009) 3; see also Greg Martin and Rebecca Scott Bray, 'Discolouring Democracy? Policing, Sensitive Evidence and Contentious Deaths in the United Kingdom' (2013) 40(4) *Journal of Law and Society*, 624; Rebecca Scott Bray, 'Executive Impunity and Parallel Justice? The United Kingdom Debate on Secret Inquests and Inquiries' (2012) 19(3) *Journal of Law and Medicine*, 569.
50 Clare Birchall, 'The False Choice Between Secrecy and Transparency in US Politics' (2011) 7(1) *Cultural Politics*, 133, 149.
51 Birchall, 'Introduction to "Secrecy and Transparency"' (n. 44) 13.
52 Birchall, 'Transparency, Interrupted: Secrets of the Left' (n. 43) 73; see also Martha Merrill Umphrey, Austin Sarat and Lawrence Douglas, 'Transparency and Opacity in the Law: An Introduction' in Austin Sarat, Lawrence Douglas and Martha Merrill Umphrey (eds.), *The Secrets of Law* (Stanford Law Books 2012) 1–3.
53 Birchall, 'Transparency, Interrupted: Secrets of the Left' (n. 43) 73.
54 Birchall, 'Introduction to "Secrecy and Transparency"' (n. 44) 15–16.
55 Birchall, 'The False Choice Between Secrecy and Transparency in US Politics' (n. 50) 145.
56 Birchall, 'Introduction to "Secrecy and Transparency"' (n. 44) 13.
57 Ibid. 13–14.
58 Ibid. 14–15.
59 Eva Horn, 'Logics of Political Secrecy' (2011) 28(7–8) *Theory, Culture & Society*, 103, 116.
60 Ibid.
61 Ibid.
62 Christopher Kutz, 'Secret Law and the Value of Publicity' (2009) 22(2) *Ratio Juris*, 197, 200, 212.
63 Mark Fenster, 'The Implausibility of Secrecy' (2014) 65(2) *Hastings Law Journal*, 309, 313, 315, 331. On deep secrecy, see David E. Pozen, 'Deep Secrecy' (2010) 62(2) *Stanford Law Review*, 257; Kim Lane Scheppele, *Legal Secrets: Equality and Efficiency in the Common Law* (University of Chicago Press 1988).
64 Fenster (n. 63) 315, 332.
65 Ibid. 315.
66 Horn (n. 59) 104.
67 Ibid. 110.
68 Ibid. 103.

69 Ibid. 120.
70 Birchall, 'The False Choice Between Secrecy and Transparency in US Politics' (n. 50) 135.
71 Theresa May MP, 'Oral Statement to Parliament: The Ellison Review' (6 March 2014) <https://www.gov.uk/government/speeches/the-ellison-review> accessed 3 December 2014.
72 See 'The Leveson Inquiry: Culture, Ethics and Practice of the Press' (*The National Archives*, 29 November 2012) <http://webarchive.nationalarchives.gov.uk/20140122145147/http:/www.levesoninquiry.org.uk/> accessed 3 December 2014.
73 'Hillsborough Independent Panel: Disclosed Material and Report' (2012) <http://hillsborough.independent.gov.uk/> accessed 3 December 2014.
74 See, for example, Jeremy Gilbert, 'Public Secrets: "Being-with" in an Era of Perpetual Disclosure' (2007) 21(1) *Cultural Studies*, 22; Alasdair Roberts, *Blacked Out: Government Secrecy in the Information Age* (Cambridge University Press 2008); Jodi Dean, *Publicity's Secret: How Technoculture Capitalizes on Democracy* (Cornell University Press 2002).
75 Fenster (n. 63) 361.
76 David E. Pozen, 'The Leaky Leviathan: Why the Government Condemns and Condones Unlawful Disclosures of Information' (2013) 127 *Harvard Law Review*, 512, 515.
77 Ibid. 586.
78 Ibid. 634.
79 Ibid. 515.
80 Ibid. 634.
81 Birchall, 'The False Choice Between Secrecy and Transparency in US Politics' (n. 50) 147.
82 Michael Taussig, *Defacement: Public Secrecy and the Labor of the Negative* (Stanford University Press 1999).
83 Birchall, 'Introduction to "Secrecy and Transparency"' (n. 44) 12.
84 Horn (n. 59) 103.
85 Ibid. 120.
86 Birchall, 'Transparency, Interrupted: Secrets of the Left' (n. 43) 77.
87 Ibid. 68.
88 Ibid. 67.
89 Ibid. 68.
90 Birchall, 'The False Choice Between Secrecy and Transparency in US Politics' (n. 50) 141.
91 Ibid.
92 Ibid. 135.
93 Max Weber, *Economy and Society: Outline of Interpretative Sociology*, vol. 2 (University of California Press 1978) 992.
94 Jana Costas and Christopher Grey, 'Bringing Secrecy into the Open: Towards a Theorization of the Social Processes of Organizational Secrecy' (2014) 35(10) *Organization Studies*, 1423, 1429.
95 Ibid. 1424 (emphasis in original).
96 Ibid. 1423, 1426.
97 Ibid. 1426.
98 Erving Goffman, *The Presentation of Self in Everyday Life* (Penguin 1959) 88.
99 Ibid. 141.
100 Ibid.
101 Ibid. 142.
102 Costas and Grey (n. 94) 1429.
103 Georg Simmel, 'The Secret and the Secret Society' in Kurt H. Wolff (tr. and ed.), *The Sociology of Georg Simmel* (Free Press 1950) 330.

104 Ibid. 332.
105 Ibid. 360.
106 Ibid. 358.
107 Ibid. 330.
108 Ibid. 331.
109 Ibid.
110 Costas and Grey (n. 94) 1425.
111 Carol Warren and Barbara Laslett, 'Privacy and Secrecy: A Conceptual Comparison' (1977) 33(3) *Journal of Social Issues*, 43, 44.
112 Ibid.
113 Ibid. 45.
114 Ibid.
115 Ibid.
116 Ibid. 46.
117 Beryl L. Bellman, 'The Paradox of Secrecy' (1981) 4(1) *Human Studies*, 1, 6.
118 Ibid.
119 Ibid.
120 Gary Alan Fine and Lori Holyfield, 'Secrecy, Trust, and Dangerous Leisure: Generating Group Cohesion in Voluntary Organizations' (1996) 59(1) *Social Psychology Quarterly*, 22, 23.
121 Ibid.
122 Ibid. 24.
123 Ibid. 27.
124 Ibid. 30.
125 Ibid. 31.
126 Costas and Grey (n. 94) 1441.
127 Brian Rappert, 'Revealing and Concealing Secrets in Research: The Potential for the Absent' (2010) 10(5) *Qualitative Research*, 571, 571.
128 Ibid. 572.
129 Ibid.
130 Ibid. 574.

Part I

Secrecy and security

Chapter 2

Living with national security disputes in court processes in England and Wales

Clive Walker

Introduction

A subtitle for this chapter might be: 'It was the best of trials and the worst of trials'. The key issue is that the UK Government wants for itself 'the best of trials' and seeks to impose on those who oppose its interests 'the worst of trials'. This tendency is most evident in litigation that involves national security issues. One such response has been delivered in the UK by the Justice and Security Act 2013 (JSA 2013). This chapter will explain the background reasons for the acute and ongoing problems presented by national security issues within court processes. It will then consider the three solutions adopted in the JSA 2013. The chapter will then assess and criticise the legislation by reference to a framework of justice and respect for rights, and by contemplating the likely impact of the Act. Some conclusions will follow.

Problems arising from entertaining national security disputes in court processes

The policy paper behind the JSA 2013 is the UK Government's *Justice and Security Green Paper (Green Paper)*,[1] which set out proposals to change court procedures in civil cases involving national security information. The prime objective is to prevent damaging disclosures of national security-sensitive material. The changes are predicated on a sustained increase in the number and diversity of civil legal proceedings that are affected by national security considerations. These have become more frequent for various reasons. One relates to the more prominent role of the security services as the lead agency in countering terrorism (a position adopted in 1992).[2] In addition, counter-terrorism has expanded since 9/11 in terms of personnel and equipment held by the security agencies.[3] Next, prolonged foreign military campaigns in Afghanistan and Iraq have entailed intelligence-gathering against irregular forces, resulting in more personalised operations – against individuals rather than cohesive units. The final factor is the juridification of security disputes, according to which the courts are more willing than ever to entertain security disputes and less willing than ever to show deference to the state.[4]

The UK Government later quantified the scale of the problem:[5] national security considerations in 2011 affected 27 civil cases (mainly for damages) and over 60 judicial reviews concerning citizenship and naturalisation. An independent analysis was conducted by the Independent Reviewer of Terrorism Legislation (David Anderson QC),[6] who confirmed the presence of seriously intractable national security concerns if the litigation reached open court.

In contrast, the stated policy of the government in the field of terrorism, which has generated the most acute controversies, is to pursue whenever possible court proceedings against terrorists, particularly criminalisation.[7] Open justice is felt to be valuable as an encouragement towards honesty and accuracy, as an overt form of discipline on the state and as a form of public education.[8] However, some of the consequences of following this tack are unpalatable. In particular, the principle of open justice,[9] especially strong in criminal litigation, may demand the revelation of sensitive material. There may be three unpalatable outcomes.

The first is that a court, after carefully weighing the claims of both parties, may decide that sensitive evidence must nevertheless be disclosed to the other party on grounds of fairness, as illustrated by the claim of Binyam Mohamed about British collusion in US-directed rendition and torture.[10] That disclosure produced political controversy concerning the 'control principle', whereby a foreign intelligence partner provides intelligence to the UK on the strict condition that it is never passed any further. The disclosure left US Secretary of State Hillary Clinton 'deeply disappointed',[11] though the need for disclosure was underlined in the Court of Appeal's judgment in the comment by Lord Neuberger that 'some [Security Service] officials appear to have a dubious record when it comes to human rights and coercive techniques, and indeed when it comes to frankness about the United Kingdom's involvement with the mistreatment of Mr Mohammed by US officials'.[12] The *Green Paper* did not claim that the flow of intelligence from foreign agencies has been significantly harmed as a result of this or other court cases. However, David Anderson reported from his investigation some tangible adverse consequences.[13] The Intelligence and Security Committee also reported US disquiet about the actions of British courts,[14] while a witness statement on behalf of the Foreign & Commonwealth Office in *Belhaj v Secretary of State for Justice*[15] also underlined the assertion that harm is caused to foreign relations from litigation. The possibilities of discourtesy to foreign security interests have, however, been confined by the later decision in *R (Khan) v Secretary of State for Foreign & Commonwealth Affairs*.[16] Khan's father was killed by a drone in Pakistan. He alleged that the UK Government Communications Headquarters (GCHQ) had passed on location data to the US, amounting to the encouragement of murder. It was held to embody an arguable claim but it was blocked because it would primarily require a judgment on US governmental activities that would breach the principle that the courts will not sit in judgment on the sovereign acts of a foreign state. This view was less assuredly applied to the alleged breach of international humanitarian law under the International Criminal Court Act 2001, ss. 51 and 52.

A second problem arising from national security litigation is that the government may be able to convince a judge to suppress sensitive evidence by invoking the common law doctrine of public interest immunity (PII), but the government incurs some very important detriments from this 'victory'. The evidence subject to PII is suppressed for all purposes in the litigation, so that, whilst secrecy is protected, the Government is unable to adduce weighty evidence that may be crucial to winning its case, whether as a claimant or prosecutor or as a defendant (such as against Binyam Mohamed). The government wants to be able to avoid the normal balancing rule in PII[17] in favour of a heavier weighting towards the value of security and to reduce the standard of proof from the test of a 'real risk of serious prejudice to an important public interest'.[18] A final, less selfishly focused argument is that PII results in a diminished opportunity for the courts to scrutinise security activities and for the public thereby to be better informed.[19]

A third problem arises *in extremis* where the extent of non-disclosure (including through PII claims) renders the case non-justiciable:

> [W]here a large proportion of the sensitive material is of central relevance to the issues in the proceedings – judgments in these cases risk being reached based only on a partial and potentially misleading picture of the overall facts . . . justice seems barely to be served as the case is struck out for a lack of a mechanism with which to hear it.[20]

One of the rare cases where this outcome has been reported concerned police informant activity in *Carnduff v Rock*.[21] In *AHK v Secretary of State for the Home Department*,[22] claims for naturalisation were rejected on the ground of national security. The allegation was that PII claims made the appeal untriable, and the High Court accepted that the case was akin to *Carnduff* and that the applicants were bound to lose. Of course, non-justiciability may suit the interests of the government, but may not be in the interests of justice.

This point can be illustrated by two further cases. The first concerned Abdel Hakim Belhaj and his wife, who sued various state agencies and officials for false imprisonment, conspiracy to injure and trespass to person, misfeasance in public office and negligence, over their extraordinary rendition in 2004 from China to Libya. Government lawyers were reported to have indicated an intention to make a 'closed material procedure' (CMP) application.[23] However, their consciences were left untroubled. The High Court accepted the civil claim as 'well founded',[24] but dismissed it as both non-justiciable, since it mainly related to the activities of foreign authorities, and as an immune 'act of state' whereby the pursuit of litigation would harm national interests. The non-justiciability ground may be open to criticism as in this case there were allegations of torture which amount to international crimes as in *Re Pinochet*.[25] In addition, this absolute bar to litigation may breach art. 6 of the European Convention on Human Rights, though there are limits recognised to the right to litigate, including in the field of foreign relations.[26] Another concern about the act of state doctrine is that while it can empower the detention of foreigners[27] and can be pleaded as a defence against tortuous actions, the doctrine probably cannot apply against a British citizen or a friendly alien,[28] though there remains uncertainty as to whether the doctrine can apply against a British citizen abroad.[29]

A civil claim for collusion in torture was also successfully blocked by the government in *Salahuddin Amin v Director General of the Security Service*[30] and again without resort to CMPs. Amin was convicted at the Central Criminal Court (Old Bailey) in London in 2006 after being returned from Pakistan where he alleged that torture, with the collusion of British agents, had resulted in false confessions. The conviction expressly proceeded without any reliance on materials derived from Pakistan.[31] Amin subsequently sought to bring civil proceedings against the UK authorities, but the proceedings were halted as an abuse of process because they sought to undermine a sustained criminal conviction contrary to the doctrine of issue estoppel outlined in *Hunter v Chief Constable of West Midlands*,[32] which concerned an attempt by the Birmingham Six, a group of Irish men convicted of murderous terrorist bombings in 1974, to seek civil damages for their physical abuse by police and prison authorities. It is more than a little ironic that the fate of the Birmingham Six should figure so prominently as an argument to block civil process in the interests of justice, given that they were later acquitted when serious miscarriages of justice were revealed.[33] Furthermore, given that the prosecution had been at pains to assert (and the trial court had accepted) that the Pakistani events played no part in their evidence and had no impact on the criminal trial, how would it undermine the conviction now to litigate this wholly discarded and irrelevant evidence in civil proceedings?[34] Aside from the disconnect between the criminal and civil litigation in this case, there should also be a priority in public policy for the eradication of torture and abusive behaviour by officials – both national and international law require nothing less.

These problems would appear to be most acute in criminal cases where the burden rests on a state prosecutor and where proof must be sustained beyond reasonable doubt. Indeed, those requirements do sometimes result in the avoidance of criminal justice processes. Thus, in terrorism cases, resort is made to the Terrorism Prevention and Investigation Measures Act 2011 (UK), which allows restraints to be imposed on suspects without proof of criminal activity.[35] Four 'terrorism prevention and investigation measures' (TPIMs) have been issued against individuals who have been before the criminal court but not convicted.[36] The 2011 Act allows for CMPs during hearings about TPIMs.[37] However, it was regular civil litigation that prompted the JSA 2013. That Act seeks to alleviate the difficulties arising in civil damage claims where government wrongdoing is alleged (such as collusion in torture) or where executive decisions taken by the government (such as deportations or employment dismissals based on security concerns) are challenged. The real inconvenience is that the government is forced to concede or settle civil cases regardless of their merits (when viewed with the benefit of the undisclosed national security evidence) and must then pay substantial compensation. These problems became more acute after the UK Supreme Court ruled in *Al*

Rawi v Security Service that, in the absence of clear statutory authority, a court cannot develop a CMP in common law.[38]

Another related problem addressed by the JSA 2013 is the application of the *Norwich Pharmacal* doctrine to national security information.[39] This doctrine allows a claimant to apply to the civil courts for an order for disclosure of information about alleged wrongdoing so that the materials can be put by the applicant to use as claimants or defendants in proceedings involving third parties, including third parties overseas, where the information is held by a person within the jurisdiction (whether implicated in the wrongdoing or not). That case involved unlicensed importation into the UK of a chemical compound for which Norwich Pharmacal owned the patent. Norwich Pharmacal was unable to identify the importers but the Customs and Excise Commissioners held such information for revenue purposes. The House of Lords recognised a legal discretion to issue an order to compel the third party to assist the party to litigation and affected by the wrongdoing by giving them that information. The power was established in 1974 but was commonly used against non-governmental, commercial parties. However, on nine occasions since 2008, *Norwich Pharmacal* applications have been made by individuals seeking to obtain disclosure of Government-held sensitive information, including sensitive intelligence information shared by foreign partner governments on a confidential basis.[40] The most important case involved Binyam Mohamed, who sought disclosure of information about his treatment by the UK and US authorities, which was needed to resist any attempts to try him before a US military commission. The willingness of the Court of Appeal to disclose the information resulted in a rapid settlement of Binyam Mohamed's case and those of five others.[41] An inquiry was set up under Sir Peter Gibson, but was later suspended pending criminal investigations into the collusion in torture by UK security officials.[42] A truncated publication, *The Report of the Detainee Inquiry*, appeared in 2013 and indicated ominously that 27 issues merited further examination. These points have been referred to the Intelligence and Security Committee.[43]

The dangers to national security information from the *Norwich Pharmacal* jurisdiction were substantially abridged by the decision in 2013 in *Omar v Secretary of State for the Foreign & Commonwealth Office*.[44] A request was made for disclosure of documents held by the UK Government for use in litigation concerning alleged terrorist attacks involving the applicants, who claimed to have been irregularly rendered from Kenya to Uganda with UK agency complicity. The application failed on the sweeping ground that any available statutory mechanisms that 'respect a sovereignty limit'[45] should be invoked in priority. This litigation fell within the category of criminal proceedings, and so the Crime (International Cooperation) Act 2003 (UK) should be applied. Under sch. 1 para. 5 of that Act, any application would fail since there are clear exemptions relating to national security materials and the compulsion of Crown Officers. In addition, the Court of Appeal ventured that, even if this first interpretation was wrong, it would not have granted a *Norwich Pharmacal* order because of the applicants' failure to apply for disclosure in the Ugandan courts, the circumvention of which by the English courts would undermine international comity.

The uncomfortable position of the courts in these cases is evident, though it is notable that more respect was arguably shown to Uganda in this case than to the mighty United States in the case of Binyam Mohamed, where the statutory point was said not to be raised (though not *per incuriam*). On the basis of *Omar*, the chances of success for many litigants who seek *Norwich Pharmacal* relief have been diminished. Therefore, it could be argued that any need for reform does not reside in limiting *Norwich Pharmacal* relief, but rather in according greater attention to the 2003 Act and to its equivalent within civil litigation, the Evidence (Proceedings in Other Jurisdictions) Act 1975. Under the 1975 Act, relief is again at hand for the government-defendant under s. 3(3), by which:

> a person shall not be compelled by virtue of an order under section 2 above to give any evidence if his doing so would be prejudicial to the security of the UK; and a certificate signed by or on behalf of the Secretary of State to the effect that it would be so prejudicial for that person to do so shall be conclusive evidence of that fact.

For both the 1975 and 2003 Acts, it may be asked whether the relief for national security matters should be set in absolute terms and whether a balancing test might be applied or at least some form of inquiry (if necessary through a CMP) undertaken.

Solutions

Part II of the JSA 2013 answers at least some of these manifold problems in three stages.

Adopted solution I

The first solution is piecemeal reform to specific and specialist tribunal jurisdictions that operate akin to existing CMP-affected jurisdictions. The Special Immigration Appeals Commission Act 1997, allowing CMPs to deal with deportation or the refusal of asylum on national security grounds, was the first example of a statutory CMP,[46] and it has been copied for other purposes such as the Terrorism Prevention and Investigation Measures Act 2011. There are reckoned to be 21 such schemes in total.[47] Section 15 of the JSA 2013 extends the CMP under the Special Immigration Appeals Commission Act 1997 to cover reviews of cases where the Secretary of State has decided to exclude on public good grounds a non-EEA national from the UK and the direction is personally certified by the Secretary of State as one that was made wholly or partly in reliance on information which, in the opinion of the Secretary of State, should not be made public in the interests of national security, foreign relations, or otherwise for the purposes of the public interest. The other dispute affected concerns a refusal of a certificate of naturalisation under s. 6 of the British Nationality Act 1981[48] or a refusal to grant an application of the kind mentioned in s. 41A of that Act (such as an application to register an adult or young person as a British citizen) where the decision is certified as involving national security, foreign relations, or is otherwise in the public interest. The person affected can apply to the Special Immigration Appeals Commission for judicial review (there is no appeal), but may encounter the application of CMPs under s. 15. Next, the JSA 2013, s. 16, amends the Regulation of Investigatory Powers Act 2000 to permit admission of intercept evidence in another instance of CMPs, here in employment tribunal cases involving dismissal on security grounds.[49]

Adopted solution 2

The most controversial remedy by which the *Green Paper* seeks an accommodation is by extrapolating from the experience of CMPs applying within these specialist statutory jurisdictions and applying them more generally to civil court proceedings.[50] Sections 6–14 of the JSA 2013 provides for CMPs, but they are confined by s. 6(11) to non-criminal proceedings only before the High Court, the Court of Session (in Scotland), the Court of Appeal or the Supreme Court, and only in relation to national security materials. Aside from these cases, normal rules of disclosure must apply under s. 10, and PII is unaffected under s. 14. The invocation of CMPs involves two stages, subject under s. 11(1) to an overriding court duty to ensure that disclosures of information are not made where they would be damaging to national security (but not to other state interests, as originally proposed in the Bill).[51] In this way, and in contrast to PII claims, there is no balancing of party interests as arises under PII. Even if the risk to national security is small, the court must still consider an application, thereby giving a litigation advantage to the government.[52] In addition, there is some return to claims to privilege based on classes of documents, rather than their precise content.[53] However, the litigation remains within the jurisdiction of the higher courts, and the *Green Paper* rightly shows little enthusiasm for a specialist national security court to handle sensitive material in civil legal proceedings.[54] It concludes that:

> proposals to establish a specialist court carry significant risks and unclear benefits. Establishing such a structure would represent a significant cultural upheaval for many members of the judiciary and would unnecessarily distinguish cases involving sensitive material from other types of proceedings, against the usual case management practices of our courts.[55]

The first stage of the application under pt. II is that the Secretary of State or (and, departing from the exclusivity originally specified in the Bill) any other party to the case[56] may apply to the court to make a declaration under s. 6 that the proceedings are ones in which a CMP application may be made. In addition, the court may grant a declaration on its own motion. Furthermore, s. 6(9) provides for any party, or the court itself, to notify the Secretary of State that a CMP may be needed, especially when the government is not a party to the proceedings, thereby affording an opportunity to make an application for a declaration or to be joined to any proceedings for an application for a declaration. At this stage, the declaration is an 'in principle' decision about availability. However, a CMP application or action on the court's own motion can also be undertaken at this interim stage under s. 11(4) so that the court can determine the substantive claim without disclosing the existence of the process.[57] Otherwise, there must normally be notice under s. 6(10) to every other person entitled to make an application in relation to the case of the intention to make an application for a declaration.

An application can be granted provided the following grounds are met (set out in s. 6); the court does retain discretion unlike in the original designs.[58] First, the court must be satisfied that the Secretary of State has considered instead an application for PII. Public interest immunity could be viewed as preferable since it explicitly balances the interests of all parties, but there is no court power to order the making of a PII application even if it is viewed as a preferable solution (though the shunning of PII may raise questions under s. 6(5) below). Certainly, CMPs need not be a 'last resort'.[59] Second, the applicant must persuade the court that there is relevant material (not necessarily all relevant material under s. 6(6)) the disclosure of which would damage national security. Third, under s. 6(5), the applicant must show why CMPs would be 'in the interests of the fair and effective administration of justice'. This point may be based on factors such as the degree of 'the relevance of the sensitive material to the issues in the case'[60] and whether it would be fair to present the case without it or to exclude the other party from direct knowledge of it. As indicated above, there is no balancing act between conflicting interests of the parties as under PII, though it remains to be seen what weight the courts might give to general public considerations such as 'open justice'.

If a declaration is made under s. 6, a CMP application may then be made by any party to the proceedings not to disclose specific pieces of material (whether held by the parties to the case or another identified person), except to the court, a special advocate or the Secretary of State. Under s. 7, the court may at any stage, on application or on its own motion, review or revoke a declaration made under s. 6 if it is no longer in the interest of the fair and effective administration of justice, and the court is obliged to undertake a review as part of the pre-trial disclosure exercise.

The second stage of the process falls under s. 8, which prescribes the requirements for detailed rules of court. Once a declaration has been made under s. 6, a relevant person must make a further application under s. 8 for specified pieces or tranches of sensitive material to be heard in a CMP. The court must again consider (always within a CMP to protect the material) whether there would be damage to national security if disclosure were ordered. The court must further consider whether a non-damaging summary of the material should be provided (in open proceedings). If the court does not give permission to withhold material and considers that the material in question might undermine the relevant person's case or assist the case of another party to the proceedings, the court must then under s. 8(2) and (3) direct that the applicant does not rely on these materials in the litigation or make any concessions or other steps set out by the court. One apparent omission is that there is no restatement in s. 8 that the CMP must be considered by the court to be in the interest of the fair and effective administration of justice. This formula was proposed during the legislative passage, but was rejected by the government as part of a bundle of rejected amendments during the House of Lords report stage late in the parliamentary day.[61] All is not lost, for s. 7 arguably requires continuing review on the basis of the interest of the fair and effective administration of justice.[62]

The details of what a CMP involves are set out in s. 11(2). Rules of court may be made about the mode of proof and evidence, to enable or require proceedings to be determined without a hearing, to restrict the details of reasons for decisions, and to exclude persons from hearings. In cases where a CMP applies, either in interim applications or in the trial itself, there will always be disclosure to the government and there will also be an appointment under s. 9 of a special advocate. The special advocate is a security-cleared lawyer appointed by the Attorney-General, the Advocate General for Scotland or the Advocate General for Northern Ireland, who represents the interests of an excluded party in a CMP by challenging the need for the CMP and also by advocacy on the evidence introduced in the CMP. Special advocates are not responsible to the person whose interests they represent, and there has been a prolonged debate as to whether their role is effective, especially as special advocates cannot take instructions from the excluded party once the sensitive evidence has been disclosed to them.[63] The courts are instructed under s. 14(2) not to act inconsistently with due process requirements under art. 6 of the European Convention on Human Rights. Whether this requirement means that at least a 'gist' of the issues being alleged, sufficient to allow a party to give effective instructions to counsel, should be disclosed[64] will depend on the nature of the dispute; when personal liberty is at stake, then 'gisting' is required, but perhaps not otherwise.[65]

This extraordinary intrusion by CMPs into rights to due process means that they should be subjected to special scrutiny. Therefore, s. 12 provides for an annual report to parliament by the Secretary of State. In addition, s. 13 requires that a reviewer be appointed to cover the operation of the legislation for five years from commencement with a report to the Secretary of State that must be presented to parliament.[66]

Adopted solution 3

The third part of pt. II of the JSA 2013 amends the common law disclosure doctrine under *Norwich Pharmacal* (or indeed any residual common law disclosure jurisdiction). Section 17 removes that jurisdiction if the information being sought is 'sensitive'. Under s. 17(3), 'sensitive' information means any information, or alleged information, that is held by or for, or obtained from, an 'intelligence service' (meaning the security agencies or defence intelligence units) or the disclosure of which the Secretary of State has certified would damage the interests of national security or the UK's international relations. 'Sensitive' here has a much wider meaning than elsewhere in pt. II of the Act.[67] In relation to such information, the Secretary of State may then issue a certificate on consideration that it would be contrary to the interests of national security or the international relations of the UK[68] to disclose the information, whether or not the information exists and whether or not the information is held. This formula preserves the practice of 'neither confirm nor deny' (also known in US law as the Glomar response).[69] Under s. 17(7), a certificate may be issued whether the information is being sought from the Secretary of State or from another person and is without prejudice to claims to PII, which allows the courts to consider this alternative.[70] The jurisdiction to order disclosure of non-sensitive information under *Norwich Pharmacal* relief can still be invoked.

Any party to the proceedings may apply under s. 18 to the court to set aside a certificate issued by the Secretary of State on the ground that the Secretary of State was wrong to determine that disclosure would be damaging on the specified grounds. The court will consider the application on judicial review principles under s. 18(3), and such consideration may involve a CMP as if under ss. 6–11 of the Act (except that wider grounds for a certificate are allowed in terms of the information to be protected).

Commencement and implementation

The JSA Act commenced on 25 June 2013.[71] Its further implementation involved the passage of new rules of court (Civil Procedure Rules, pt. 82) which were almost as controversial as the Act itself.[72] These rules amend what is known as the overriding objective in r. 1.2 (to do justice), making it subject to r. 82.2(2): 'The court must ensure that information is not disclosed in a way which would be damaging to the interests of national security'. However, this drastic statement, couched in terms of 'must' rather than 'may' apply, as in s. 6 of the 2013 Act, was stated in debates to be still subject to s. 14(2) (requiring respect for art. 6 of the European Convention on Human Rights).[73]

Overall assessment

In principle

The UK Government claims that the pt. II scheme for CMPs in civil litigation is consistent with principles of justice and fairness, transparency, the protection of security, and maximising evidence before an open court.[74] Though CMPs have been endorsed by the European Court of Human Rights in the context of terrorism prevention and surveillance special jurisdictions,[75] and the sole empowerment of the trial judge in all aspects of process has not been insisted upon,[76] these claims may be contested on three grounds.

First, the assumption that because various statutory versions of CMPs are well established and have proliferated they are therefore acceptable as a model of justice and fairness represents an assertion that overreaches in two respects. One aspect of overreach is the signal that CMPs are bound to be fair since they have been already tried and tested. However, that testing has resulted in CMPs being condemned as unfair in given circumstances, with challenges being especially prominent in the field of anti-terrorism prevention orders.[77] The view that the terrorism prevention procedures are on the cusp of basic fairness is reflected by the rejection of any extension of CMPs at common law in *Al Rawi v Security Service*[78] and the assertion of common law natural justice standards in cases such as *Bank Mellat v HM Treasury*[79] in England and Wales. Therefore, the UK Government can at best claim that CMPs are 'capable of satisfying the requirements of the ECHR [European Convention on Human Rights]'.[80]

The other aspect of overreach is the crossing of a boundary that may damage the legitimacy of the regular justice system. Thus, the *Green Paper* gives no consideration as to whether the CMPs already in operation in specialist statutory procedures (often tribunals)[81] represent desirable precedents for mainstream litigation. On the contrary, it might be argued that these specialist instances of CMPs are acceptable since they are confined to extraordinary processes which handle narrow disputes where rights claims are highly attenuated because the rights at stake are diminished (in the case of aliens) or because the obligations imposed produce no more than a temporary detriment (in the case of terrorism suspects). In this way, the impact upon rights is limited.[82] In addition, these processes are fundamentally different in kind to normal litigation in that they are inquisitorial, rather than adversarial. For example, under Special Immigration Appeals Commission (Procedure) Rules 2003, r. 4(3), and the Civil Procedure Rule 80.2(3) (applicable to TPIMs), the relevant tribunal 'must satisfy itself that the material available to it enables it properly to determine proceedings'. In the light of these fundamental distinctions, it is disingenuous for the *Green Paper* to claim simply that 'CMPs have been a part of the framework of the courts of the UK since 1997'.[83] The prior CMP jurisdictions are highly divergent from normal legal processes, a feature signalled by special rules of court. The resulting special system is also viewed as distinctly second rate by some judges, notably by Lord Kerr in *Al Rawi v Security Service*:

> The [government's] second argument proceeds on the premise that placing before a judge all relevant material is, in every instance, preferable to having to withhold potentially pivotal evidence. This proposition is deceptively attractive – for what, the [government] imply, could be fairer than an independent arbiter having access to all the evidence germane to the dispute between the parties? The central fallacy of the argument, however, lies in the unspoken assumption that, because the judge sees everything, he is bound to be in a better position to reach a fair result. That assumption is misplaced.

> To be truly valuable, evidence must be capable of withstanding challenge. I go further. Evidence which has been insulated from challenge may positively mislead. It is precisely because of this that the right to know the case that one's opponent makes and to have the opportunity to challenge it occupies such a central place in the concept of a fair trial. However astute and assiduous the judge, the proposed procedure hands over to one party considerable control over the production of relevant material and the manner in which it is to be presented. The peril that such a procedure presents to the fair trial of contentious litigation is both obvious and undeniable.[84]

In short, there is a threat to the public standing and legitimacy of the regular courts as well as a threat to the dignity of the individual. The performance of the judges in scrutinising terrorism prevention orders may have demonstrated their independence and expertise, but it has hardly accorded to those systems an unequivocally clean bill of health. It is likely that civil proceedings subject to CMPs will likewise suffer denigration from time to time both in court and beyond. Though there is some recognition in the *Green Paper* that existing CMPs within their limited statutory contexts are criticised (not least by special advocates themselves), the range and depth of those criticisms are not addressed.

Aside from overreach, a second ground for principled criticism relates to limited public benefit. Any supposed benefits to stakeholders other than the government are far from clear. It is claimed that the facilitation of more litigation will educate and inform the public,[85] but how this will occur through secret evidence and secret hearings, in breach of the principle of open justice, remains a mystery since the impact of CMPs is to shift security affairs 'inexorably into the shadows'.[86]

The third criticism relates to the principle of proportionality, which demands that other, less intrusive or more balanced avenues of redress should be considered as a priority. Public interest immunity has been canvassed in this regard.[87] Existing statutory mechanisms include postponement and suppression orders under the Contempt of Court Act 1980, ss. 4 and 11,[88] with more extensive anonymity rules for juveniles under the Children and Young Persons Act 1933, s. 39.[89] Criminal trials *in camera* can arise under the Official Secrets Act 1920, s. 8.[90] Another power to inhibit the publication of information is to sit *in camera* under common law.[91] It may be concluded that the legal reform undertaken by the JSA 2013 is very limited. It does not consider the reform, systemisation or adaptation of these existing options.

Aside from the possibility of other remedies, the modest scale of the problem arguably makes the pt. II response excessive. Most problem cases have been resolved by the relatively non-contentious measures under 'Solution 1' detailed earlier. Given that only 27 cases were identified in 2011 for 'Solution 2' (and with only nine awaiting 'Solution 3'), and given that several of the most prominent cases have related to various excesses within the 'war on terror' and have since been settled (leaving an estimated 20 cases in 2013),[92] the mischief being addressed appears very confined. More effective and desirable strategies of attenuation might be pre-emptive, such as the development of UK standards for UK officers on service abroad so as to reduce the risk that they might become complicit in the excesses (including torture) of foreign agencies. Thus, the Foreign & Commonwealth Office has issued documentation giving guidance and warnings to officers carrying on, or assisting with, investigations abroad.[93] Assuming this documentation is observed and therefore that the alleged wrongdoing giving rise to civil litigation, such as in the paradigm case of *Binyam Mohamed*, is less likely to arise, the mischief behind the act should fade in the future by the suppression of these underlying misdeeds. These arguments might be less forceful if the government could show the generation of new cases that relate to a wide variety of new circumstances. The government has stated that there were six civil claims between November 2010 and mid-2012 where sensitive material will be centrally relevant. However, no indication is given as to the nature of those claims or whether they are quite distinct from the pre-existing 'war on terror' cases.[94]

In practice

It is contended that CMPs have been used 'sparingly'.[95] A report on the first year of operation (up to 24 June 2014) revealed just five applications for CMPs.[96] There were grants against three claimants in two separate cases under the JSA Act pt. II. Two claimants, Mohamed Ahmed Mohamed, and CF,[97] made an abuse of process application that related to the involvement of the UK security agencies in their arrest and detention in Somaliland. The third applicant is undisclosed, but further grants arising from the five applications after the anniversary have included litigation involving the Islamic Republic of Iran Shipping Lines (contesting financial sanctions)[98] and Martin McGartland[99] (a former Provisional Irish Republication Army 'supergrass' (informant) from the 1980s who was tracked down and attacked in England in 1999 and seeks damages for negligent police protection).[100] An unspecified number of other cases have arisen in tribunals, such as *R (Ignaoua) v Secretary of State for the Home Department*,[101] concerning a Tunisian who had been extradited to Italy, and challenged by judicial review his exclusion from the UK on national security grounds and failure to deal with his asylum claim. The proceedings were terminated and transferred to the Special Immigration Appeals Commission under the JSA 2013, s. 15. Aside from this limited report, a database of usage was promised for use by the special advocates, but is available only through the Special Advocate Support Office.[102] Warnings against invocation to dampen inquiries into torture allegations have been issued by the UN Committee Against Torture.[103]

Criminal process

Before coming to some final conclusions, further consideration should be given to whether the *Green Paper* represents an apt pathway for the problems caused by the ventilation of security information in criminal process. The *Green Paper* emphatically disclaims any seepage into criminal proceedings:

> Civil and criminal proceedings in England and Wales are fundamentally different. In civil cases, the courts adjudicate on disputes between parties under

> the civil law. In criminal cases, it is usually the state which prosecutes individuals for the commission of criminal offences; where defendants are convicted, they face criminal sanctions including imprisonment. Due to the understandably more onerous requirements of the right to a fair trial in criminal cases, the rules concerning the use and protection of sensitive evidence are different to those in civil cases.[104]

These are important and valid distinctions. There are also strong statements of support for open justice in criminal trials. In 2007, the then Director of Public Prosecutions, Sir Ken Macdonald, stated that 'we can't have secret courts, we can't have vetted judges, and we can't have secret justice'.[105] This stance chimes with the warning of Lord Diplock, given at the height of terrorism conflict in Northern Ireland in 1972, that:

> The minimum requirements that we have adopted as the criterion for criminal trial by a court of law, permit of hearings *in camera* where, *inter alia*, the interests of public order or national security so require. But even where the hearing takes place *in camera* they call for the accused to be informed *in detail* of the nature of the accusation against him and to examine or have examined witnesses against him.[106]

Yet, given that CMPs already represent decisive seepage from special process into normal process, who can guarantee that there will not be another, and arguably lesser, degree of seepage from civil to criminal? There are already, as noted earlier, devices such as PII and *in camera* hearings, authorisations under the Contempt of Court Act 1980, and witness anonymity is allowed under pt. III of the Coroners and Justice Act 2009.[107]

Though CMPs are not presently on the agenda for the criminal courts, that system has already been tainted by the influence of state security. Juries largely survive in national security cases in Britain, aside from the isolated examples of the special non-jury Scottish trial (in the Netherlands) of those accused of the Lockerbie bombing,[108] and aside from the allowance in England and Wales of judge-only criminal trials (not confined to terrorism) when there is a high level of proof of jury intimidation under the Criminal Justice Act 2003, s. 44.[109] However, a state security court does exist in Northern Ireland in the shape of juryless 'Diplock' courts, which were instituted following the Diplock Report in 1972 as a bespoke shift toward the criminalisation of terrorism suspects.[110] Another disturbing aspect of secrecy in criminal trials concerns the occasional willingness of the courts to restrict public access and reporting, illustrated by the almost blanket suppression (at least until the trial is over) in *Guardian News and Media Ltd v Incedal and Bouhadjar*,[111] where the court accepted that a trial of terrorist charges could largely proceed *in camera* pursuant to common law powers, together with those contained in ss. 4(2) and 11 of the Contempt of Court Act 1981 (UK).

Conclusions

Recourse to sensitive evidence is increasing in forensic settings and that trend has resulted in legal anomalies, challenges and obscurities. However, the UK Government must recognise that the main cause of this trend is not an increase in the amount of, or aggression within, litigation brought by aggrieved private litigants, nor even is the Human Rights Act 1998 to blame. Rather, the underlying cause is the spread of functions and size of the intelligence agencies and their deployment against individuals rather than state officials. This point is recognised briefly in the *Green Paper*,[112] but is not followed by any reflection upon the consequences of the impact of intelligence agencies on everyday lives; rather, it focuses on the remote and exotic machinations of espionage. Thus, the prime deficits in accountability, powers, and processes reside not with courts, but with intelligence agencies.[113]

Until systematic review and reform is undertaken, the UK Government will continue to suffer discomfiture from the contemporary orientation of security services that have been designed with inter-state espionage in mind. Unfortunately, the subsidiary role of litigation in bringing the intelligence agencies to account may have been blunted by the JSA 2013, but it has certainly not been as emasculated as portrayed by some critics. It may therefore be predicted that the UK's increasingly assertive judges will, with occasional lapses, continue to be heard above the muffle of secret justice.

Notes

1 Ministry of Justice, *Justice and Security Green Paper* (Cm. 8194, 2011) (*Green Paper*). See further Ministry of Justice, *Response to the Public Consultation on Justice and Security* (Cm. 8364, 2012). During legislative passage, various parliamentary inquiries were held: House of Lords Select Committee on the Constitution, *Justice and Security Bill* (HL 2012–13, 18 and 31) and *Government Response to the House of Lords Select Committee on the Constitution, Justice and Security Bill* (Cm. 8460, 2012); Joint Committee on Human Rights, *Legislative Scrutiny: Justice and Security Bill* (2012–13 HL 59, HC 372) and the *HM Government Response to the Joint Committee on Human Rights Fourth Report of Session 2012–13: Legislative Scrutiny: Justice and Security Bill* (Cm. 8533, 2013); Joint Committee on Human Rights, *Legislative Scrutiny: Justice and Security Bill* (2012–13, HL 128, HC 1014).

2 HC Deb 8 May 1992, vol. 207, col. 297. See further Security Service Act 1996; Anti-terrorism, Crime and Security Act 2001, s. 116.

3 C. Walker and A. Staniforth, 'The Amplification and Melding of Counter-terrorism Agencies: from Security Services to Police and Back Again' in A. Masferrer and C. Walker (eds.), *Counter-Terrorism, Human Rights and the Rule of Law* (Edward Elgar 2013).

4 C. Walker, 'The Threat of Terrorism and the Fate of Control Orders' [2010] *Public Law*, 3; C. Walker, 'The Judicialisation of Intelligence in Legal Process' [2011] *Public Law*, 235; *Green Paper* (n. 1) para. 1.51.

5 *Response to the Twenty-Fourth Report from the Joint Committee on Human Rights Session 2010–12: The Green Paper* (Cm. 8365, 2012) 2.

6 Supplementary Memorandum to the Joint Committee on Human Rights, *The Justice and Security Green Paper* (2010–12, HL 286, HC 1777) JS12A.

7 HC Deb 21 February 2008, vol. 472, col. 561, Tony McNulty. See C. Walker, 'Terrorism Prosecution in the United Kingdom: Lessons in the Manipulation of

Criminalization and Due Process' in O. Gross and F. ni Aolain, *Guantanamo and Beyond* (Cambridge University Press 2013).

8 J. Resnik, 'Bring back Bentham' (2011) 5 *Law and Ethics of Human Rights*, 1.

9 See *Scott v Scott* [1913] AC 417; *R v Secretary of State for the Home Department; Ex parte Simms* [2000] 2 AC 115; *R v Central Criminal Court; Ex parte A* [2006] EWCA Crim 4.

10 *R (Binyam Mohamed) v Secretary of State for the Foreign & Commonwealth Office* [2008] EWHC 2048, 2100, 2519, 2549, 2973 (Admin), [2009] EWHC 152 (Admin), [2010] EWCA Civ. 65. See also A. Tomkins, 'National Security and the Due Process of Law' (2011) 64 *Current Legal Problems*, 215. Nine other similar cases were reported in *Government Response to the House of Lords Select Committee on the Constitution, Justice and Security Bill* (Cm. 8460, 2012) 4.

11 'US Disappointed at UK Appeal Court Torture Ruling' (*BBC News*, 11 February 2010) <http://news.bbc.co.uk/1/hi/uk/8509787.stm> accessed 16 September 2014.

12 [2010] EWCA Civ. 158 [17].

13 Supplementary Memorandum to the Joint Committee on Human Rights, *The Justice and Security Green Paper* (2010–12, HL 286, HC 1777)JS12A, para. 24. The point is also made by the government *Response to the House of Lords Select Committee on the Constitution, Justice and Security Bill* (Cm. 8460, 2012) 4.

14 See Intelligence and Security Committee, *Annual Report 2010–2011* (Cm. 8114, 2011) para. 230; Intelligence and Security Committee, *Annual Report 2011–2012* (Cm. 8403, 2012) para. 157.

15 [2013] EWHC 4111 (QB) (*Belhaj*); see also Witness Statement of Laurie Bristow, 7 June 2013 (see <http://www.reprieve.org.uk/media/downloads/2013_10_23_PUB_Belhaj_Preliminary_Issues_Skeleton_FINAL.pdf>, accessed 1 October 2014) paras. 31, 42, 43.

16 [2014] EWCA Civ. 24.

17 *R v Chief Constable of West Midlands Police; Ex parte Wiley* [1995] 1 AC 274.

18 *R v H and C* [2004] UKHL 3 [36]. See further CPS, *Disclosure Manual*, para. 13.3 <http://www.cps.gov.uk/legal/d_to_g/disclosure_manual/> accessed 16 September 2014.

19 *Green Paper* (n. 1) para. 1.5.

20 Ibid. para. 1, 52.

21 [2001] EWCA Civ. 680.

22 [2013] EWHC 1426 (Admin).

23 I. Cobain, 'Libya Case May be First Test of Secrecy Law' *The Guardian* (London, 22 May 2013) 9.

24 *Belhaj* (n. 15) [151].

25 [1999] UKHL 1.

26 See *A v United Kingdom* App No 35373/97 (ECHR, 17 December 2002); *Colombani v France* App No 51279/99 (ECHR 2002-V, 25 June 2002); *Jones v United Kingdom* App. Nos. 34356/06 and 40528/06 (ECHR, 14 January 2014). Compare *Zollman v United Kingdom* App. No. 62902/00 (ECHR 2003-XII, 27 November 2003).

27 *R v Vine St Police Station; Ex parte Liebmann* [1916] 1 KB 268.

28 *Johnstone v Pedlar* [1921] 2 AC 262.

29 *Nissan v AG* [1970] AC 179.

30 [2013] EWHC 1579 (QB).

31 *R v Khyam* [2008] EWCA Crim 1612.

32 [1982] AC 529.

33 See C. P. Walker and K. Starmer (eds.), *Miscarriages of Justice* (Blackstone Press 1999) ch. 2.

34 Compare on similar facts *R v Rangzieb Ahmed* [2011] EWCA Crim 184 [68], [69].

35 See C. Walker and A. Horne, 'The Terrorism Prevention and Investigation Measures Act 2011' [2012] *Criminal Law Review* 421.

36 D. Anderson, *First Report of the Independent Reviewer on the Operation of the Terrorism Prevention and Investigation Measures Act 2011* (Home Office 2013) para. 7.9.
37 See Civil Procedure Rules 2012 pt. 80 (Civil Procedure (Amendment No 3) Rules 2011 SI 2011/2970).
38 [2011] UKSC 34 (*Al Rawi*). In *R (Maya Evans) v Secretary of State for Defence* [2013] EWHC 3068 (Admin.), concerning the transfer of prisoners to the Afghan authorities, the hearings had partly been in closed proceedings, but it was later recognised that no such power existed. Compare *Bank Mellat v HM Treasury* [2013] UKSC 38.
39 *Norwich Pharmacal Co v Customs and Excise Commissioners* [1974] AC 133. See *Green Paper* (n. 1) paras. 2.83–2.97.
40 Explanatory Notes on the Justice and Security HL Bill (2012–13) [16].
41 See HC Deb 16 November 2010, vol. 518, col. 752.
42 See HC Deb 6 July 2010, vol. 513, col. 175; HC Deb 18 January 2012, vol. 538, col. 751; *The Detainee Inquiry* <http://www.detaineeinquiry.org.uk/> accessed 16 September 2014; HC Deb 17 July 2012, vol. 548, col. 132WS.
43 Intelligence Services Act 1994, s. 10. For the referral for further inquiry, see Intelligence and Security Committee, 'Detainee Inquiry' (Press release, 19 December 2013) <http://isc.independent.gov.uk/files/20131219_ISC_statement_Detainee_Inquiry.pdf> accessed 16 September 2014.
44 [2013] EWCA Civ. 118 (*Omar*).
45 Ibid. [20].
46 It responded to *Chahal v United Kingdom* App. No. 22414/93 (ECHR 1996-V, 15 November 1996).
47 Joint Committee on Human Rights, *Counter-Terrorism Policy and Human Rights (Seventeenth Report): Bringing Human Rights Back In* (2009–10, HL 86, HC 111) para. 58. See also JUSTICE, *Secret Evidence* (London 2009) pt. 2.
48 Close material procedure was previously not allowed in that context: *AHK v Secretary of State for the Home Department* [2012] EWHC 1117 (Admin.), [2013] EWHC 1426 (Admin.).
49 A further exception is added to the Regulation of Investigatory Powers Act 2000, s. 18.
50 *Green Paper* (n. 1) para. 1.28. For other ideas, see paras. 2.24–2.82.
51 See Joint Committee on Human Rights, *The Justice and Security Green Paper* (2010–12, HL 286, HC 1777) para. 45; see also Intelligence and Security Committee, *Annual Report 2011–12* (Cm. 8403, 2012) para. 151; Joint Committee on Human Rights, *Legislative Scrutiny: Justice and Security Bill* (2012–13, HL 59, HC 372) paras. 30, 31.
52 House of Lords Select Committee on the Constitution, *Justice and Security Bill* (HL 2012–13 18) para. 22.
53 Following the *Report of the Inquiry into the Export of Defence Equipment and Dual-Use Goods to Iraq and Related Prosecutions* (HC 1995–96 115) vol. 4 s. K ch. 6 (Scott Report), the government announced it would no longer make PII claims for classes of information (such as national security), but would confine itself to specific content: see HC Deb 18 December 1996, vol. 287, col. 949; HL Deb 18 December 1996, vol. 596, col. 1507.
54 *Green Paper* (n. 1) paras. 2.53–2.62.
55 Ibid. para. 2.60.
56 This reciprocity point arose in *W v Secretary of State for the Home Department* [2010] EWCA Civ. 898 under Special Immigration Appeals Commission (Procedure) Rules 2003 SI 2003/1034, r. 39.
57 See HL Deb 23 July 2012, vol. 739, col. 514, Baroness Stowell.
58 Joint Committee on Human Rights, *The Justice and Security Green Paper* (2010–12, HL 286, HC 1777) para. 103.
59 Compare HL Deb 26 March 2013, vol. 744, col. 1018.
60 PBC Deb (Bill 27) 31 January 2013, col. 127, James Brokenshire.
61 See HL Deb 21 November 2012, vol. 740, col. 1885.

62 In later debates on court rules, the government claimed that both ss. 6(5) and 7 applied to s. 8: HC Delegated Legislation Committee, 15 July 2013, col. 8, James Brokenshire; HL Deb 29 July 2013, vol. 747, cols. 1615, 1628, Lord Wallace.
63 See Constitutional Affairs Committee, *The Operation of the Special Immigration Appeals Commission (SIAC) and the Use of Special Advocates* (HC 2004–05 323–I); JUSTICE (n. 47) pt. 4; J Ip, 'Al Rawi, Tariq and the Future of Closed Material Procedures and Special Advocates' (2012) 75 *Modern Law Review*, 606.
64 See *Re AF (No 3)* [2009] UKHL 28; *A v United Kingdom*, App. No. 3455/05 (ECHR, 19 February 2009).
65 See *Home Office v Tariq* [2011] UKSC 35 [83]; *IR v United Kingdom*, App. Nos. 14876/12 and 63339/12 (ECHR, 28 January 2014). The government had originally considered the possibility of enshrining gisting in the legislation (*Green Paper* (n. 1) paras. 2.10–2.46), but then changed its policy, a point on which it was criticised: Joint Committee on Human Rights, *Legislative Scrutiny: Justice and Security Bill* (2012–13, HL 59, HC 372) para. 77 and Joint Committee on Human Rights, *Legislative Scrutiny: Justice and Security Bill* (2012–13, HL 128, HC 1014) para. 96; *HM Government Response to the Joint Committee on Human Rights Fourth Report of Session 2012–13: Legislative Scrutiny: Justice and Security Bill* (Cm. 8533, 2013) 15.
66 Joint Committee on Human Rights, *Legislative Scrutiny: Justice and Security Bill* (2012–13, HL 128, HC 1014) para. 99 called for annual review.
67 The breadth was criticised by the Joint Committee on Human Rights, *Legislative Scrutiny: Justice and Security Bill* (2012–13, HL 59, HC 372) paras. 101, 103.
68 United Kingdom interests may extend to the security of an ally: *Secretary of State for the Home Department v Rehman* [2001] UKHL 47.
69 See *Baker v The Information Commissioner and the Cabinet Office* (EA/2006/0045); *DIL v Commissioner of Police of the Metropolis* [2014] EWHC 2184 (QB).
70 Compare *Green Paper* (n. 1) para. 2.7.
71 Justice and Security Act 2013 (Commencement, Transitional and Saving Provisions) Order 2013, SI 2013/1482.
72 See Civil Procedure (Amendment No. 5) Rules 2013, SI 2013/1571. See also Rules of the Court of Judicature (Northern Ireland) (Amendment) 2013, SR 175; Act of Sederunt (Rules of the Court of Session Amendment No. 5) (Miscellaneous) 2013, SSI 2013/238.
73 HC Delegated Legislation Committee, 15 July 2013, col. 5, James Brokenshire; HL Deb 29 July 2013, vol. 747, col. 1615, Lord Wallace.
74 *Green Paper* (n. 1), xii.
75 *A v United Kingdom* (n. 64); *Kennedy v United Kingdom* App. No. 26839/05 (ECHR, 18 May 2010).
76 *McKay v United Kingdom* App. No. 543/03 (ECHR, 3 October 2006); *Botmeh and Alami v United Kingdom* App. No. 15187/03 (ECHR, 7 June 2007).
77 See C. Walker, *Terrorism and the Law* (Oxford University Press 2011) ch. 7.
78 *Al Rawi* (n. 38) [93].
79 [2013] UKSC 39.
80 *Green Paper* (n. 1) para. 1.29.
81 The Investigatory Powers Tribunal, set up under the Regulation of Investigatory Powers Act 2000, s. 65, is in a class of its own since the Investigatory Powers Tribunal Rules 2000, SI 2000/2665 allow for secret processes going well beyond CMP in part to preserve the 'neither confirm nor deny' approach. This system was upheld as compliant with ECHR, art. 6 in *Kennedy v United Kingdom* (n. 75) para. 188. The *Green Paper* did not view the Tribunal as an acceptable model for mainstream civil litigation: *Green Paper* (n. 1) paras. 2.53–2.71.
82 Compare the epistemic factors adduced by J. Jackson, 'Justice, Security and the Right to a Fair Trial' [2013] *Public Law*, 720.

83 *Green Paper* (n. 1) para. 2.3.
84 *Al Rawi* (n. 38).
85 *Green Paper* (n. 1) vi.
86 C.R.G. Murray, 'Out of the Shadows' (2013) 18 *Journal of Conflict & Security Law*, 193, 232.
87 Compare the view of the Joint Committee on Human Rights, *The Justice and Security Green Paper* (2010–12, HL 286, HC 1777) paras. 72, 122, 192, 216.
88 See C. P. Walker, I. G. Cram and D. Brogarth, 'The Reporting of Crown Court Proceedings and the Contempt of Court Act 1981' (1992) 55 *Modern Law Review*, 647; J. Jaconnelli, *Open Justice: A Critique of the Public Trial* (Oxford University Press 2002); *Borrie and Lowe: Law of Contempt* (4th edn., LexisNexis 2010) ch. 7.
89 See *JC and RT v Central Criminal Court* [2014] EWHC 1041 (QB).
90 See Security Commission, *Report of the Security Commission on the Case of Michael John Bettany* (Cmnd. 9514, 1985) App. A.
91 See *R v Khyam* (n. 31); *R v Rangzieb Ahmed* [2010] EWCA Crim 1551; *Guardian News & Media v AB and CD* [2014] EWCA Crim 1861.
92 Explanatory Notes to the Civil Procedure (Amendment No. 5) Rules 2013, SI 2013/1571, para. 7.1.
93 See Foreign & Commonwealth Office, *Overseas Security Justice Assistance (OSJA) Human Rights Guidance 2011*; Foreign & Commonwealth Office, *Torture and Mistreatment Reporting Guidance 2011*.
94 *Response to the Twenty-fourth Report from the Joint Committee on Human Rights, Session 2010–2012: The Green Paper* (Cm. 8365, 2012) 2. There were seven by the end of October 2012: Explanatory Notes to the Civil Procedure (Amendment No. 5) Rules 2013, SI 2013/1571, para. 7.1
95 T. Cohen, 'Ministers Demand Five Trials in Secret: New Powers Used to Block Access to Court Cases' *Daily Mail* (23 July 2014) <www.dailymail.co.uk/news/article-2702166/Ministers-demand-five-trials-secret-New-powers-used-block-access-court-cases.html> accessed 16 September 2014.
96 HC Deb 22 July 2014, vol. 584, col. 123WS. An application in *Youssef v Secretary of State for Foreign and Commonwealth Affairs* [2013] EWCA Civ. 1302 was not proceeded with.
97 *CF & Mohamed v Secretary of State for the Home Department* [2013] EWHC 3402 (QB).
98 *R (Sarkandi) v Secretary of State for Foreign and Commonwealth Affairs* [2014] EWHC 2359 (Admin.).
99 *McGartland v AG* [2014] EWHC 2248 (QB).
100 Pending cases are *Terence McCafferty v Secretary of State for Northern Ireland* (2012 No. 360: revocation of licence of a convict) and *Margaret Keeley v Chief Constable of the Police Service of Northern Ireland* (2008 No. 133645: false imprisonment related to the protection of an informant).
101 [2013] EWHC 2512 (Admin.).
102 HC Delegated Legislation Committee, 15 July 2013, col. 20, James Brokenshire.
103 UN Committee Against Torture, *Concluding Observations on the Fifth Periodic Report of the United Kingdom, Adopted by the Committee at its Fiftieth Session (6–31 May 2013)*, UN Doc CAT/C/SR.1160 and 1161, para. 12.
104 *Green Paper* (n. 1) 7.
105 Quoted in JUSTICE (n. 47) para. 252.
106 *Report of the Commission to Consider Legal Procedures to Deal with Terrorist Activities in Northern Ireland* (Cmnd. 5185, 1972) para. 20.
107 The court may also use its common law power to appoint a special advocate to cross-examine the witness claiming anonymity on a *voir dire*: see *R v Nazir* [2009] EWCA Crim 213; *R v Chisholm* [2010] EWCA Crim 258.
108 See High Court of Justiciary (Proceedings in the Netherlands) Order 1998, SI 1998/2251; *HM Advocate v Al-Megrahi* 2002 JC 99, [2008] HCJAC 15, [2008] HCJAC 58.

109 See *R v Twomey* [2009] EWCA 1035; *R v JSM* [2010] EWCA Crim 1755; *R v KS* [2010] EWCA Crim 1756. The system was upheld as in accordance with European Convention on Human Rights art. 6 in *Twomey, Cameron and Guthrie v United Kingdom* App. Nos. 22226/12, 67318/09 (ECHR, 28 May 2013).
110 See now Justice and Security (Northern Ireland) Act 2007. Their history and practice is discussed in Walker (n. 77) ch. 11.
111 [2014] EWCA Crim 1861.
112 *Green Paper* (n. 1) vii.
113 See further C. Walker, 'Intelligence and Anti-terrorism Legislation in the United Kingdom' (2006) 44 *Crime, Law and Social Change*, 387; K. Starmer, 'Setting the Record Straight: Human Rights in an Era of International Terrorism' [2007] *European Human Rights Law Review*, 123.

Chapter 3

Secrecy law and its problems in the United States

Thomas C. Ellington

Introduction

After years of significant growth, the United States system for keeping national security secrets has come to be the focus of both popular and scholarly attention. This is in part due to the presidency of Barack Obama, who has lived up only partially to his promise to have 'the most transparent administration in history', and partly due to high-profile failures by the US to keep its secrets, notably with regard to WikiLeaks[1] as well as the ongoing disclosures by Edward Snowden. As a very early adopter of a freedom of information statute,[2] the US has an information policy that at least theoretically defaults to openness and disclosure. However, a web of statutes, administrative policies and judicial practices creates an environment in which official secrecy flourishes in the US. The legal bases for American secrecy are outlined in this chapter, as is the resulting damage to democracy and the rule of law.

The foundations of American secrecy law rest in several places: in statutes (including the Freedom of Information Act[3] and its exemptions, the Atomic Energy Act of 1954,[4] the Espionage Act of 1917[5] and the Intelligence Identities Protection Act[6]); in a string of executive orders on classification dating back to World War II (the most recent being issued by President Obama in 2009); and in judicial doctrine (for example, the state secrets doctrine and the Glomar response). While some legal mechanisms for keeping secrets are necessary for a modern state, the American system is also subject to some significant problems. These problems include interference with citizens' ability to hold their government accountable, inhibition of legitimate activities by whistleblowers and working journalists, and the creation of a legal/political culture that treats already disclosed information as if it were still secret.

Statutory bases for secrecy

The US has kept secrets since the Revolutionary War. George Washington maintained a spy ring that operated behind British lines and used rudimentary cryptography and invisible ink.[7] In Federalist No. 64, John Jay argues for the necessity of secrecy in diplomacy, writing: 'It seldom happens in the negotiation of treaties, of whatever nature, but that perfect *secrecy* and immediate *despatch* are sometimes requisite'.[8] And in Federalist No. 70, Hamilton describes the utility of a unitary executive partly in terms of the value of secrecy: 'Decision, activity, secrecy, and despatch will generally characterize the proceedings of one man in a much more eminent degree than the proceedings of any greater number; and in proportion as the number is increased, these qualities will be diminished'.[9]

However, American secrecy law is rooted less in the founding than in a complex set of statutes, executive orders and judicial doctrine that developed in the twentieth century. The Freedom of Information Act (FOIA), passed in 1966 and amended significantly in 1974, created a general presumption that state-held or state-generated documents would be publicly accessible. Unlike some other states, the US has never had an Official Secrets Act, which would create a presumption against disclosure. In fact, the most recent serious effort to enact an American version of the Official Secrets Act in 2000 ended with a presidential veto.[10]

The FOIA includes nine exemptions: Exemption 1, which is of particular interest here, shields national defence and foreign policy information from disclosure, provided that it is properly classified pursuant to executive order. American courts have been very reluctant to evaluate the propriety of any particular classification decision,[11] and a general deference to the executive in this area has led to a so-called 10th exemption under the Glomar doctrine (discussed further below).[12] Other exemptions deal with matters such as privacy, personnel policies, trade secrets, some law enforcement files and geophysical data. Together, the exemptions to the FOIA create a significant sphere within which a regime of secrecy can and does flourish.

Contemporary legal protections for secrecy in the US begin with the Espionage Act. Enacted shortly before the US entered into World War I, the Espionage Act criminalises the dissemination of national defence information, a category that may overlap with classified information but that is not synonymous with it. Specifically, the Espionage Act makes it a crime to obtain 'information respecting the national defense with intent or reason to believe that the information is to be used to the injury of the United States, or to the advantage of any foreign nation'.[13] Generally, the Espionage Act has been used for the prosecution of people accused of engaging in traditional acts of spying. However, in recent years, it has been used to prosecute people engaged in public interest disclosures, for example, leakers and whistleblowers.[14] It has also been suggested that Eric Lichtblau and James Risen from the *New York Times* should have been prosecuted for the initial 2005 disclosures about the National Security Agency's (NSA's) warrantless wiretapping program[15] and, more recently, Julian Assange[16] and Glenn Greenwald.[17]

While the Espionage Act is significant, much of the American system of keeping secrets developed in the years immediately after World War II. The National Security Act of 1947[18] reorganised the military and intelligence establishments, but it did not set criminal penalties for unauthorised disclosures or give specific guidance on what information was to be protected from disclosure. Other than information covered specifically by the Atomic Energy Act and the Intelligence Identities Protection Act, official secrets in the US are kept based on a series of executive orders, rather than by statutory mandate. Those statutes, along with the Espionage Act's provisions regarding national defence information, are the laws of general application criminalising disclosure in the American system.

The Atomic Energy Act created a category of 'restricted data' that comprises all atomic energy–related information. Unlike national security secrets created under the classification system, atomic energy secrets are presumed 'born classified' and only subject to disclosure via positive state action.[19] The Atomic Energy Act was subsequently amended in 1954 and 1981 and now includes a category of 'unclassified nuclear information' that requires authorisation by the Secretary of Energy for legal disclosure.[20]

In 1982, the US enacted the Intelligence Identities Protection Act, which makes it a crime to identify a US covert agent. This statute was a reaction to actions by Philip Agee, a former officer with the Central Intelligence Agency (CIA), who revealed the names of covert operatives.[21] American officials, including former Director of Central Intelligence, George H. W. Bush, attributed the 1975 assassination of Athens, Greece Station Chief Richard Welch to Agee's revelations.[22] Agee's passport was revoked in 1979, and he died in exile in Havana in 2008.[23] This statute is unusual in substance and has resulted in only two prosecutions. Former CIA clerk Sharon Scranage accepted a plea bargain and pleaded guilty to violating the Act in 1985, after initially being charged with violating the Espionage Act in connection with US operations in Ghana;[24] and, in 2011, John C. Kiriakou was convicted of violating the Act for providing a freelance reporter with the name of a covert CIA operative. The reporter did not publish the name, and Kiriakou was not charged until after a televised interview in which he was interviewed regarding waterboarding.[25]

The Intelligence Identities Protection Act is probably best known for a prosecution that did not occur. In July 2003, columnist Robert Novak wrote a column in which he named Valerie Plame as a CIA operative.[26] Plame's husband, Joseph C. Wilson, had travelled to Niger to investigate allegations that Iraq had attempted to purchase yellowcake uranium, and his report was subsequently cited by President George W. Bush as evidence that Iraq had an active nuclear weapons programme. Wilson subsequently wrote an op-ed column in which he refuted Bush's claims.[27] Novak suggested that Plame had improperly influenced the decision to send her husband to Niger as part of an effort to discredit Wilson's claims. Because of her status with the CIA, the claim was made that Novak's source or perhaps Novak himself had violated the law in naming her. Despite the appointment of a special prosecutor and the ultimate revelation that the Deputy Secretary of State, Richard Armitage, was Novak's primary source, no one was ever charged.[28]

While Plame insisted that her position was covert and protected under the statute, Novak and his defenders claimed that her position was neither covert nor unknown publicly. 'Wilson's wife is a desk jockey and much of the Washington cocktail circuit knew that already,' claimed *National Review* writer Jonah Goldberg.[29]

Under 50 USC § 422(a), naming a covert agent is not a crime if the US has publicly acknowledged that person's identity, but there is no provision for a 'common knowledge' defence. This is not an argument in favour of prosecution, but rather points out a problem with a law that may make private individuals responsible for keeping secrets that the government itself has proved unable or unwilling to keep. This problem of 'open secrets' is a recurring theme in American secrecy policy. While the Act appears to be on solid ground in barring 'insiders' from naming names, it slips into unconstitutional territory in penalising people without access to classified information for disclosing information found in open sources.[30]

Executive orders and policy directives

The current national security classification system in the US began with Executive Order 8381 issued by Franklin D. Roosevelt in March 1940, essentially granting presidential imprimatur to existing practices by the US military. Presidents since Roosevelt have commonly issued executive orders on classification, altering and updating the system, but the underlying framework remains much the same.[31] With the stated goal of increasing transparency, President Obama issued Executive Order 13526 in December 2009, which is still in force. It set up the National Declassification Center and established a general rule that documents would automatically be declassified after 25 years – with significant exceptions.

In addition to secrets protected by statute or under the national security classification system, a number of categories of 'sensitive but unclassified information' (SBU) have developed. By 2009, there were '107 unique markings and over 130 different labeling or handling processes and procedures for SBU information'.[32] This type of information exists in a twilight zone in which it is not officially secret, but its release is also not officially sanctioned. In a telling example from 2009, a declaration to the International Atomic Energy Agency of US nuclear sites was inadvertently published online by the Government Printing Office:

> Nuclear experts said it was theoretically possible that the document could benefit terrorists contemplating an attack on one of the facilities. Still, because the information was unclassified and most of it is publicly available through other sources, the release generally was deemed more embarrassing than harmful.[33]

Nevertheless, the report, which contained neither restricted nor classified information, was taken down. David Albright, President of the Institute for Science and International Security, did tell a *Washington Post* reporter that the release was a violation of the law, but it is not clear which law he had in mind.[34]

Judicial doctrine

The US court system is adversarial and generally open in character. The Sixth Amendment to the US Constitution, for instance, guarantees a defendant the right to 'a speedy and public trial . . . and to be informed of the nature and cause of the accusation; to be confronted with the witnesses against him; to have compulsory process for obtaining witnesses in his favor'. The courts are not strangers to secrecy in a limited set of circumstances (for example, grand jury hearings), and not every proceeding sees two opposing sides presenting arguments (for example, a search warrant application). Nevertheless, governmental efforts to keep secrets and even requirements for secret proceedings can present problems for a legal system like that of the US.

In criminal prosecutions, a defendant's right to discovery of potentially exculpatory information can come into conflict with the government's legitimate interest in protecting national security information that has been properly classified, creating a 'disclose or dismiss dilemma' that is sometimes referred to as 'graymail'.[35] Congress acted to resolve many of the problems presented by graymail in enacting the Classified Information Procedures Act (CIPA).[36] The CIPA provides for clearance of defence counsel (and prohibitions on disclosure of classified information, including with clients), as well as unclassified summaries and redactions of classified evidence and *in camera* review of classified evidence:

> CIPA contains numerous mechanisms to guard against such dilemmas: notification requirements prohibiting unilateral defense disclosures of classified information; protective orders prohibiting cleared counsel from sharing classified information with their clients; redactions, summaries, admissions, and substitutions; in camera and ex parte hearings.[37]

Ideally, the CIPA protects the due process rights of criminal defendants while still allowing the government to protect its legitimate national security interests. In practice, defendants, such as the recently acquitted Thomas Drake, 'complain they are rarely given access to the government's classified evidence or permitted to submit their own classified evidence',[38] even as the government may argue that some rulings under the CIPA provide for inappropriate disclosures. Whatever its vices, the great virtue of the CIPA is that it recognises a role for the judiciary in handling national security secrets in the context of a trial. Rather than assuming or demanding deference to a party to a controversy, the CIPA sets up a procedural mechanism by which judges may grapple with legitimate concerns of national security and due process.

This is a far cry from the practice of judicial decision-making in other areas of the law. As noted above, while Exemption 1 to the FOIA does not require the disclosure of *properly classified* information, American courts have been reluctant to make independent judgments on the propriety of particular classification decisions, even in the face of evidence of rampant over-classification[39] and specific examples of plainly absurd classification decisions, such as the classification of published newspaper articles.[40] The CIPA provides a mechanism for the use of properly classified information at trial, but does not address the problem of information that is classified *improperly*.

Judicial deference at its most extreme, however, is found in the application of the state secrets privilege, under which the government withholds evidence by claiming that revealing it to a judge or opposing counsel would tend to endanger national security. Accordingly, '[b]ecause successful invocation of the privilege involves no independent judicial review of the evidence, critics worry that it opens the door to abuse by the executive branch'.[41] Louis Fisher provides the definitive account of the origins of state secrets privilege and some of the problems in its underlying doctrine.[42] Two things are worth noting:

1 the state secrets privilege has its origins in a case in which the government has since been shown definitely to have mischaracterised the nature of the evidence it was withholding; and
2 the US Government has increasingly invoked the state secrets privilege in recent years as a way of shutting down civil litigation in cases involving such subjects as extraordinary rendition and blanket eavesdropping by the NSA.[43]

What had once been a moribund piece of judicial doctrine has found new life under the Bush and Obama administrations. Laura K. Donohue counts more than 100 instances in which the Bush administration invoked the state secrets privilege.[44] Despite setting a new policy that is supposed to limit the circumstances in which the state secrets privilege is invoked,[45] the Obama Justice Department continues to use this flawed doctrine extensively. The Federation of American Scientists maintains an ongoing list of state secrets claims.[46]

> Courts, almost unanimously, have cast their lot with national security, granting considerable deference to government assertions of the state secrets principle. This deference to state secrets shows no signs of abating; indeed, the growing trend is for courts to dismiss these legal challenges pre-discovery.[47]

In an exemplary case carried over from the Bush administration, a federal appeals court dismissed a lawsuit alleging that the CIA had contracted with a private company to transport victims overseas for the purpose of torturing them. The dismissal, on state secrets grounds, came '*before defendant had answered the complaint*'.[48] Clearly, part of the problem lies with a Justice Department that has chosen to aggressively use the state secrets privilege. However, part of the problem also lies with the courts, which have continued to recognise this privilege. Especially in cases of alleged government misconduct, 'Judges need to look',[49] rather than simply taking the word of one of the litigants.

In other instances, judges are looking, but outside the adversarial context. In 2013, *The Guardian* (and a number of other news outlets) published stories indicating that the NSA was engaged in wide-ranging surveillance of telephone calls, emails and other electronic communications of both US and non-US persons. The initial stories, based on leaks from former NSA contractor, Edward Snowden, showed the existence of a secret court order for US telecommunications provider, Verizon, to provide information to the NSA as follows: '[T]he numbers of both parties on a call are handed over, as is location data, call duration, unique identifiers, and the time and duration of all calls'.[50] Subsequent stories in a variety of outlets showed the scope of surveillance was not limited to Verizon, nor simply to metadata involving voice transmissions. One programme purported to be authorised under s. 215 of the Uniting and Strengthening America by Providing Appropriate Tools Required to Intercept and Obstruct Terrorism Act of 2001 (known commonly as the Patriot Act) involves the sweeping collection of electronic metadata;[51] another related to s. 702 deals specifically with the content of electronic communications. Hints of this capability had come earlier. As early as 4 May 2013, a former FBI counter-terrorism agent suggested, in the wake of the Boston Marathon bombings, that all telephone conversations are recorded and available to the US Government,[52] and the existence of a Bush-era warrantless wiretapping programme, seemingly in violation of the Foreign Intelligence Surveillance Act of 1978 (FISA), had been revealed in December 2005 after *The New York Times* held the story for more than a year.[53]

What was new with the 2013 revelations is that this time the surveillance had the imprimatur of a court order. Of course, it was an unusual court and an unusual kind of order. As a response to plainly abusive activities by the US intelligence community in the 1960s and 1970s, Congress passed the FISA in 1978 in an effort to prevent a repetition of the worst abuses. The FISA distinguished between 'US Persons' and 'non-US persons', with the latter receiving minimal statutory protection, but the former – US citizens and foreign citizens in the US – to be protected from surveillance in the absence of a court order. The FISA also created a special court to hear requests for warrants for intelligence surveillance. The Foreign Intelligence Surveillance Court meets *ex parte*, with the subjects of warrants generally never learning that their communications had been subject to surveillance, even after the fact. From the court's first sitting in 1979 until 2004, it approved 18,748 warrants and rejected just five.[54] While at least one FISA court judge is reported to have bristled at the description of the court as a 'rubber stamp',[55] its procedures and the government's success rate in obtaining surveillance warrants suggest that is a fair characterisation.

The FISA court did not rubber stamp the initial Bush NSA programme. Rather, Bush ordered the programme without any court supervision or authorisation, based on a theory of presidential power, which held that the president's role as commander-in-chief, as well as inherent powers of the presidency, made judicial authorisation unnecessary. Once the programme was revealed, Congress amended the FISA in 2008 to bring the so-called Terrorist Surveillance Program under the purview of the court, while also granting retroactive immunity to telecommunications companies that had co-operated with the previous iteration of the NSA programme.[56] It was in this context that the Snowden revelations occurred, with the court order (repeatedly renewed) authorising the communications dragnet being finally declassified in November 2013.[57] The Snowden revelations brought condemnations from allied governments who believed their trust had been abused,[58] as well as domestic civil libertarians who claimed that Americans' privacy had been invaded wholesale and without due process.[59] The Snowden revelations also called many Americans' attention to the existence of a secret court issuing secret orders in a process so tilted towards the government that it could quite accurately be called a rubber stamp.

Foreign and domestic reactions have been significant, with some indications of American companies losing business as part of the backlash.[60] There is no general prohibition in international law against electronic surveillance of the sort engaged in by the NSA. In fact, the US, the UK, Canada, Australia and New Zealand have a longstanding agreement to share electronic intelligence.[61] Nevertheless, there is a reasonable political question as to whether a policy likely to antagonise allies when revealed is a wise one. One does not have to take former Secretary of State Henry L. Stimson's position that 'Gentlemen do not read each other's mail'[62] to conclude that such a policy may not be in the best interests of the US.

On the domestic side, the NSA's programme appears to be on much shakier ground. Despite a veneer of legality provided by the 2008 amendments to the FISA, the fact remains that the burden of proof for a FISA warrant is far lower than the 'probable cause' of the Fourth Amendment, and the lack of any adversarial character to the process leaves it open to unchecked abuse – a concern that is more than merely theoretical.[63]

US courts have been divided on the constitutionality of the NSA's sweeping domestic surveillance efforts. In December 2013, District Judge Richard J. Leon ruled that the NSA's programme, 'infringes on "that degree of privacy" that the founders enshrined in the Fourth Amendment', but, less than two weeks later, District Judge William H. Pauley III ruled in favour of the programme, calling it a 'counterpunch' to Al-Qaeda and finding that its sweeping character was crucial to its success.[64] Higher courts will certainly rule on this issue, even as Congress and the Obama administration consider revisions to the NSA's statutory powers. Arguments in favour of the programme's constitutionality hinge on the 1979 case *Smith v Maryland*,[65] in which it was concluded that a 'pen register' does not violate citizens' reasonable expectations of privacy. For the NSA's domestic spying activities to be found unconstitutional, either *Smith* will have to be overturned or the courts will have to find that the metadata collected today is so much broader in scope than that related to old landlines that it has privacy implications unimagined by the *Smith* court.

One final oddity of American secrecy law bears noting: the Glomar response, sometimes referred to as the FOIA's 10th exemption. The Glomar response takes its name from the *Glomar Explorer*, a ship built by Howard Hughes, which the CIA used as part of an effort to reach a sunken Soviet submarine. In a case decided in 1976 (*Phillipi v CIA and Bush*[66]), a federal appeals court refused to force the CIA to release documents related to the *Glomar Explorer* or even to force the agency to issue a standard denial under the FOIA citing the relevant exemption. Under the Glomar response, a federal agency may simply reply that it can neither confirm nor deny the existence of requested materials under the claim that either confirmation or denial would be harmful to national security.[67]

The Glomar response has been used to block disclosure regarding programmes that are already publicly known. For instance, in April 2012, the CIA used the

Glomar response regarding an inquiry into its use of drones. This successful use of the Glomar response came despite widespread reporting on the programme in the popular press and a public statement by White House counter-terrorism adviser, John Brennan.[68] Since 11 September 2001, the government has radically increased its use of the Glomar exception. While some uses have been towards noble ends, it is also frequently used 'to conceal information related to programs that no longer feel secret to the general public'.[69] In some instances, the government has simultaneously leaked information and invoked Glomar on the same topic.

Under what is known as the 'official acknowledgment doctrine', the Glomar response cannot be used for documents that have already been acknowledged to exist. However, what constitutes acknowledgment can be problematic. Michael D. Becker argues that 'using the Glomar response to conceal documentation that undoubtedly exists undermines not only the spirit of the FOIA but also the public's trust in the federal government.[70] This 'widely acknowledged' standard would encompass a great deal more than 'official' acknowledgment, which has proved to be tremendously narrow. As it now stands, the Glomar response (and the courts' acquiescence to its abuse) encourages the political/legal fiction of 'open secrets'.

Problems of secrecy in American law

While some level of secrecy is unavoidable for a modern nation-state, official secrecy presents a number of challenges for democracy and the rule of law. The American experience shows that secrecy covers up lies and abuses of power; secrecy hampers citizens in making informed judgments about policies carried out on their own behalf; efforts to keep secrets harm institutions dedicated to accountability, as shown by recent prosecutions of leakers and threats to prosecute journalists for engaging in normal news-gathering activities; and excessive secrecy may also perpetuate a culture of 'open secrets' by which already disclosed information is treated as if it were secret.

In particular, the NSA's unprecedented collection of 'metadata' both domestically and internationally has enormous implications for privacy. The use of secrecy to conceal this programme also points to a broader problem with official secrecy. Secrets can bolster lies that are used to conceal either corruption or embarrassing information, as when Senator Ron Wyden (D-Oregon) asked Director of National Intelligence, James Clapper, in an open congressional hearing: 'Does the NSA collect any type of data at all on millions or hundreds of millions of Americans?' Clapper's response: 'No sir . . . not wittingly'.[71] If not lying outright, Clapper was channelling Humpty-Dumpty from *Alice in Wonderland*, when he said: 'When I use a word . . . it means just what I choose it to mean – neither more nor less'.[72] The problem is this: 'When it comes to discussing government surveillance, US intelligence officials have been using a vocabulary of misdirection – a language that allows them to say one thing while meaning quite another'.[73] With a secret programme and esoteric vocabulary for protection, it is not difficult for officials to lie while appearing to be co-operative and forthright.

The previous and current US administrations have also been extraordinarily aggressive about keeping secrets, not only in terms of what is classified, but also in efforts to maintain secrecy after it has been established. This pattern has been seen in the increasing use of the state secrets privilege, as well as in an unprecedented number of criminal prosecutions against leakers. To date, the Obama administration has brought, or carried forward, Espionage Act charges against eight individuals who were not engaged in any activity traditionally recognised as espionage.[74] Former NSA officer, Thomas Drake, was prosecuted after revealing problems in a programme that ultimately wasted more than $1 billion. While Drake did plead guilty to mishandling government information, he was sentenced to no time incarcerated, and the judge condemned prosecutors for putting him through 'four years of hell', describing its actions as 'unconscionable'.[75] Drake's experience is emblematic of the problems with using a law ill-suited to the purpose for the general maintenance of secrets.

Official secrecy interferes with citizens' ability to evaluate government policy and implementation. For instance, while operational secrecy surrounding particular drone strikes may be necessary and justifiable, secrecy about targeting policies leaves citizens unable to judge whether the US is generally using drones appropriately (as defenders claim) or whether their use is illegal, immoral or even simply counter-productive. The problem is compounded when US officials act as though facts that are already public knowledge are somehow still secret, as when the CIA successfully used the Glomar response regarding drones, even after public acknowledgement of the programme by White House counter-terrorism adviser, John Brennan.[76]

It is remarkable that a high-ranking official can speak openly about a widely known and debated programme, while others in that same government can continue to act as if it is secret – and demand that others do likewise. Remarkable, but not unusual; parts of the Atomic Energy Act are predicated on the idea that certain principles of basic physics are secret and only discoverable through Department of Energy archives. When WikiLeaks released its first major dump of diplomatic cables, the Air Force Materiel Command responded by ordering employees and their families not to look at the documents, or risk being prosecuted.[77] Even if this order were followed perfectly, it did nothing to protect American interests. It prevented neither Al-Qaeda members nor interested foreign governments from gaining access to the formerly secret documents. It is difficult to imagine a more futile gesture. While absurd, this logic of open secrets can have serious consequences. It is the same logic that would leave journalists open to Espionage Act prosecutions – for failing to keep the same secrets that government itself has already failed to keep.

Conclusion

Some use of secrecy is a state imperative, even for democratic states that rely on a level of citizen engagement with public policy for their legitimacy. In the US, a complex system of keeping secrets has evolved. The FOIA has created a system that, in theory at least, defaults to disclosure, albeit with some specifically named exemptions. However, other statutes and executive orders outline categories of information that can be withheld. Furthermore, the American judiciary generally is so deferential to executive judgments on secrecy and disclosure that it does not function well as a check in this particular policy area, particularly regarding claims of the state secrets privilege, as well as the Glomar response.

What would it take to create a more balanced system of keeping essential secrets in the US? For starters, there must be genuine recognition that an informed public, which can hold its government accountable for its actions, is essential to democracy. This necessarily entails providing citizens with the tools they need to make reasonable judgments about what is being done on their behalf. There is some evidence of progress on this front: the Obama administration did slash the number of individuals holding original classification authority and did issue an executive order early on to require agencies to construe FOIA exemptions narrowly in responding to requests from the public.[78] For 2013, the Information Security Oversight Office reported just 58,794 original classification decisions, the lowest number on record.[79] However, the Obama administration's extraordinarily aggressive use of the flawed state secrets privilege, as well as its novel (and dangerous) interpretation of the Espionage Act against leaks by whistleblowers, shows that serious reforms are still needed.

Some of these reforms are possible within the executive. Agencies could cease treating already disclosed information as if it were still secret. It is within the power of the Justice Department to stop invoking the state secrets privilege, although this is a policy decision that certainly could be reversed by future administrations. The US Attorney-General could likewise announce that prosecutors will henceforth bring charges under the Espionage Act only in cases of genuine espionage, as was the general practice until very recently. Criminal charges under the Espionage Act should only be brought in cases in which there is clear intent by the person or persons in question to harm the US or aid its adversaries – and in which cases they had reason to believe that the information they disclose is likely to cause harm. The restoration of such a standard would provide the required protection to whistleblowers and journalists.

The judiciary also has a role to play. The state secrets privilege should no longer be recognised, especially given that the initial precedent was set thanks to fraudulent representations by the federal government. While there is certainly information relevant to trial that might not be prudent to reveal in open court, judges themselves should decide on that, just as they do on other issues, as guided by arguments made by litigants. Accepting state secrets claims amounts to tilting the scales too heavily in favour of the federal government in ways that are potentially subject to abuse. The role of the judiciary also extends to reining in the NSA, which is engaging in domestic surveillance in a manner well beyond what is contemplated by the US Constitution. It is also appropriate for courts to evaluate the propriety of classification decisions, as contemplated in the original text of the FOIA. Finally, appropriate legislation, properly enforced, could solve some of the problems described here, but given the current situation of legislative sclerosis in the US, the prospects for that in the near future appear to be slight at best.

Notes

1 Thomas C. Ellington, 'The Most Transparent Administration in History? An Assessment of Official Secrecy in the Obama Administration's First Term' (2013) 15 *Public Integrity*, 133.
2 David Banisar, *Freedom of Information around the World 2006* (Privacy International 2006).
3 5 USC § 552 (FOIA).
4 42 USC § 2011 (Atomic Energy Act).
5 18 USC § 792 (Espionage Act).
6 50 USC § 421.
7 Alexander Rose, *Washington's Spies: The Story of America's First Spy Ring* (Bantam Books 2007).
8 John Jay, 'Federalist #64' in *The Federalist Papers* (The Library of Congress THOMAS, Project Gutenberg, 6 June 1992) <http://thomas.loc.gov/home/histdox/fed_64.html> para. 7, accessed 17 September 2014.
9 Alexander Hamilton, 'Federalist#70' in *The Federalist Papers* (The Library of Congress THOMAS, Project Gutenberg, 6 June 1992) <http://thomas.loc.gov/home/histdox/fed_70-2.html> para. 7, accessed 17 September 2014.
10 William J. Clinton, 'Intelligence Authorization Act for Fiscal Year 2001: Veto Message from the President of the United States' *Congressional Record* (Government Printing Office 2000) H11852.
11 'Keeping Secrets: Congress, the Courts and National Security Information' (1990) 103 *Harvard Law Review*, 906.
12 Michael D. Becker, 'Piercing Glomar: Using the Freedom of Information Act and the Official Acknowledgment Doctrine to Keep Government Secrecy in Check' (2012) 64 *Administrative Law Review*, 673.
13 18 USC 3.
14 Richard E. Moberly, 'Whistleblowers and the Obama Presidency: The National Security Dilemma' (2012) 16 *Employee Rights and Employment Policy Journal*, 51.
15 Gabriel Schoenfeld, *Necessary Secrets: National Security, the Media, and the Rule of Law* (W. W. Norton and Co. 2010).
16 Dianne Feinstein, 'Prosecute Assange Under the Espionage Act' *The Wall Street Journal* (New York, 7 December 2010) A19.
17 Erik Wemple, 'What Would It Take to Nail Glenn Greenwald Under the Espionage Act?' *The Washington Post* (Washington, 25 June 2013) <http://www.washingtonpost.com/blogs/erik-wemple/wp/2013/06/25/what-would-it-take-to-nail-glenn-greenwald-under-the-espionage-act/> accessed 14 September 2014.
18 50 USC ch. 15.
19 Harold P. Green, '"Born Classified" in the AEC: A Legal Perspective' (1981) 37[10] *Bulletin of the Atomic Scientists*, 28.
20 Allan Adler, 'Unclassified Secrets' (1985) 41[3] *Bulletin of the Atomic Scientists*, 26.
21 Joe Holley, 'Philip Agee, 72; Agent Who Turned against CIA' *The Washington Post* (Washington, 10 January 2008) B7.
22 Jesse Walker, 'Agee's Revenge: It's Past Time to Kill the Intelligence Identities Protection Act' (*Reason*, 14 July 2005) <http://reason.com/archives/2005/07/14/agees-revenge> accessed 14 September 2014.
23 Holley (n. 21).
24 Steven Aftergood, 'New Leak Case Relies on 1982 Law on Intelligence Identities' (*Secrecy News*, 25 January 2012) <http://blogs.fas.org/secrecy/2012/01/kiriakou_iipa/> accessed 14 September 2014.

25 Scott Shane, 'From Spy to Source to Convict' *The New York Times* (New York, 6 January 2013) A1.
26 Robert D. Novak, 'Mission to Niger' *The Washington Post* (14 July 2003) <http://www.washingtonpost.com/wp-dyn/content/article/2005/10/20/AR2005102000874.html> accessed 14 September 2014.
27 Joseph C. Wilson 4th, 'What I Didn't Find in Africa' *The New York Times* (New York, 6 July 2003) 8.
28 Michael Isikoff and David Corn, *Hubris: The Inside Story of Spin, Scandal, and the Selling of the Iraq War* (Broadway Books 2006).
29 David Corn, 'Plame's Role at the CIA' *The Nation* (25 September 2006) 6.
30 Susan D. Charkes, 'The Constitutionality of the Intelligence Identities Protection Act' (1983) 83 *Columbia Law Review*, 727.
31 Arvin S. Quist, *Security Classification of Information: Volume 1: Introduction, History, and Adverse Impacts* (Oak Ridge Classification Associates 2002) <http://www.fas.org/sgp/library/quist/index.html> accessed 14 September 2014.
32 Barack Obama and Office of the Press Secretary, 'Classified Information and Controlled Unclassified Information' (Presidential Memorandum, 27 May 2009) <http://www.whitehouse.gov/the_press_office/Presidential-Memorandum-Classified-Information-and-Controlled-Unclassified-Information/> accessed 14 September 2014.
33 Joby Warrick, 'List of US Nuclear Sites Inadvertently Posted Online' *The Washington Post* (Washington, 3 June 2009) A3.
34 Ibid.
35 Karen H. Greve, 'Graymail: The Disclose or Dismiss Dilemma in Criminal Prosecutions' (1980) 31 *Case Western Reserve Law Review*, 84.
36 18 USC App. III Sections 1–16 (CIPA).
37 David E. Pozen, 'The Leaky Leviathan: Why the Government Condemns and Condones Unlawful Disclosures of Information' (2013) 127 *Harvard Law Review*, 513, 552.
38 Ibid. 552.
39 Lanie D'Alessandro, 'Evaluation of the National Reconnaissance Office Classification Management Under Public Law 111–258, the Reducing Over-Classification Act (Project 2013–001 S)' (Office of Inspector General, 30 September 2013) <http://fas.org/sgp/othergov/intel/nro-roca.pdf> accessed 14 September 2014; Steven Aftergood, 'National Security Secrecy: How the Limits Change' (2010) 77 *Social Research*, 839.
40 Steven Aftergood, 'What Is Overclassification'? (*Secrecy News*, 21 October 2013) <http://blogs.fas.org/secrecy/2013/10/overclass/> accessed 14 September 2014.
41 Ellington (n. 1) 42.
42 Louis Fisher, *In the Name of National Security: Unchecked Presidential Power and the Reynolds Case* (University Press of Kansas 2006).
43 Dan Froomkin, 'Obama's State Secrets Overreach' *The Washington Post* (9 April 2009) <http://voices.washingtonpost.com/white-house-watch/obamas-state-secrets-overreach040909.html> accessed 14 September 2014.
44 Laura K. Donohue, 'The Shadow of State Secrets' (2010) 159 *University of Pennsylvania Law Review*, 77.
45 Carrie Johnson, 'Obama to Set Higher Bar for Keeping State Secrets' *The Washington Post* (Washington, 23 September 2009) A1.
46 Federation of American Scientists, 'The State Secrets Privilege: Selected Case Files' (16 September 2014) <http://www.fas.org/sgp/jud/statesec/> accessed 16 September 2014.
47 Timothy Bazzle, 'Shutting the Courthouse Doors: Invoking the State Secrets Privilege to Thwart Judicial Review in the Age of Terror' (2012) 23 *Civil Rights Law Journal*, 29.
48 D. A. Jeremy Telman, 'On The Conflation of the State Secrets Privilege and the Totten Doctrine' (2012) 3 *National Security Law Brief*, 1 (emphasis in original).

49 Louis Fisher, 'Judges Need to Look: In FOIA Cases over National Security, Courts Should Examine the Documents' (2008) 31[47] *Legal Times*, 34.

50 Glenn Greenwald, 'NSA Collecting Phone Records of Millions of Verizon Customers Daily' *The Guardian* (6 June 2013) <http://www.theguardian.com/world/2013/jun/06/nsa-phone-records-verizon-court-order> accessed 16 September 2014.

51 The Privacy and Civil Liberties Oversight Board has described the s. 215 programme as having 'minimal value', adding '[W]e have not identified a single instance involving a threat to the United States in which the program made a concrete difference in the outcome of a counterterrorism investigation': Privacy and Civil Liberties Oversight Board, *Report on the Telephone Records Program Conducted under Section 215 of the USA PATRIOT Act and on the Operations of the Foreign Intelligence Surveillance Court* (PCLOB 2014).

52 Glenn Greenwald, 'Are All Telephone Calls Recorded and Accessible to the US Government?' *The Guardian* (4 May 2013) <http://www.theguardian.com/commentisfree/2013/may/04/telephone-calls-recorded-fbi-boston> accessed 16 September 2014.

53 James Risen and Eric Lichtblau, 'Bush Lets US Spy on Callers Without Courts' *The New York Times* (16 December 2005) A1.

54 Carol D. Leonnig, 'Secret Courts Judges Were Warned About NSA Spy Data' *The Washington Post* (9 February 2006) <http://www.washingtonpost.com/wp-dyn/content/article/2006/02/08/AR2006020802511.html> accessed 16 September 2014.

55 Carol D. Leonnig, Ellen Nakashima and Barton Gellman, 'Secret-Court Judges Upset at Portrayal of "Collaboration" with Government' *The Washington Post* (30 June 2013) <http://www.washingtonpost.com/politics/secret-court-judges-upset-at-portrayal-of-collaboration-with-government/2013/06/29/ed73fb68-e01b-11e2-b94a-452948b95ca8_story.html> accessed 16 September 2014.

56 Glenn Greenwald, 'GOP and Feinstein Join to Fulfill Obama's Demand for Renewed Warrantless Eavesdropping' *The Guardian* (28 December 2012) <http://www.theguardian.com/commentisfree/2012/dec/28/fisa-feinstein-obama-democrats-eavesdropping> accessed 16 September 2014.

57 Spencer Ackerman, 'Fisa Court Order that Allowed NSA Surveillance Is Revealed for First Time' *The Guardian* (19 November 2013) <http://www.theguardian.com/world/2013/nov/19/court-order-that-allowed-nsa-surveillance-is-revealed-for-first-time> accessed 16 September 2014.

58 Colum Lynch, Shane Harris and John Hudson, 'Exclusive: Germany, Brazil Turn to UN to Restrain American Spies' *Foreign Policy* (25 October 2013) <http://thecable.foreignpolicy.com/posts/2013/10/24/exclusive_germany_brazil_turn_to_un_to_restrain_american_spies> accessed 16 September 2014.

59 American Civil Liberties Union, 'Why the FISA Amendments Act Is Unconstitutional' <http://www.aclu.org/files/images/nsaspying/asset_upload_file578_35950.pdf> accessed 16 September 2014.

60 Mark Scott, 'Irked by NSA, Germany Cancels Deal With Verizon' *The New York Times* (New York, 27 June 2014) B2; Carola Hoyos and Joe Leahy, 'Saab Shares Soar on $4.5bn Brazil Defence Deal' *The Financial Times* (19 December 2013) <http://www.ft.com/cms/s/0/c93d30dc-6821–11e3–8ada-00144feabdc0.html> accessed 16 September 2014.

61 Richard Norton-Taylor, 'Not So Secret: Deal at the Heart of UK-US Intelligence' *The Guardian* (25 June 2010) <http://www.theguardian.com/world/2010/jun/25/intelligence-deal-uk-us-released> accessed 16 September 2014.

62 Henry L. Stimson and McGeorge Bundy, *On Active Service in Peace and War* (Harper 1948) 188.

63 Barton Gellman, Julie Tate and Ashkan Soltani, 'In NSA-Intercepted Data, Those Not Targeted Far Outnumber the Foreigners Who Are' *The Washington Post* (Washington, 6 July 2014) A1; Spencer Ackerman, 'Fisa Court Documents Reveal Extent of NSA Disregard for Privacy Restrictions' *The Guardian* (19 November 2013) <http://www.

theguardian.com/world/2013/nov/19/fisa-court-documents-nsa-violations-privacy> accessed 16 September 2014.

64 Sari Horwitz, 'NSA Collection of Phone Data is Lawful, Federal Judge Rules' *The Washington Post* (27 December 2013) <http://www.washingtonpost.com/world/national-security/nsa-collection-of-phone-data-is-lawful-federal-judge-rules/2013/12/27/4b99d96a-6f19-11e3-a523-fe73f0ff6b8d_story.html> accessed 16 September 2014.

65 442 US 735 (1979).

66 46 F 2d 1009 (DC Cir., 1976).

67 The CIA's first tweet upon joining Twitter played on the Glomar response: 'We can neither confirm nor deny that this is our first tweet': Erik Wemple, 'Want to Talk to the CIA? Tweet @CIA' *The Washington Post* (6 June 2014) <http://www.washingtonpost.com/blogs/erik-wemple/wp/2014/06/06/want-to-talk-to-the-cia-tweet-cia/> accessed 16 September 2014.

68 Becker (n. 12) 679.

69 Ibid. 677.

70 Ibid. 678.

71 Fred Kaplan, 'Fire James Clapper' (*Slate.com*, 11 June 2013) <http://www.slate.com/articles/news_and_politics/war_stories/2013/06/fire_dni_james_clapper_he_lied_to_congress_about_nsa_surveillance.html> accessed 16 September 2014.

72 Lewis Carroll, *The Annotated Alice: Alice's Adventures in Wonderland and Through the Looking Glass.* (CN Potter 1960) 266.

73 Jameel Jaffer and Brett Max Kaufman, 'How to Decode the True Meaning of What NSA Officials Say' (*Slate.com*, 31 July 2013) <http://www.slate.com/articles/news_and_politics/politics/2013/07/nsa_lexicon_how_james_clapper_and_other_u_s_officials_mislead_the_american.html> accessed 16 September 2014.

74 Jamie Tarabay, 'Obama and Leakers: Who Are the Eight Charged Under the Espionage Act?' (*Al Jazeera America*, 5 December 2013) <http://america.aljazeera.com/articles/2013/12/5/obama-and-leakerswhoaretheeightchargedunderespionageact.html> accessed 16 September 2014.

75 Scott Shane, 'No Jail Time in Trial over NSA Leak' *The New York Times* (New York, 16 July 2011) A13.

76 Becker (n. 12).

77 Ewan MacAskill, 'US Air Force Backtracks Over WikiLeaks Ban' *The Guardian* (8 February 2011) <http://www.theguardian.com/world/2011/feb/08/us-air-force-wikileaks-families-banned-classified-material> accessed 16 September 2014.

78 Ellington (n. 1).

79 Information Security Oversight Office, *2013 Report to the President* (2014) <http://fas.org/sgp/isoo/2013rpt.pdf> accessed 16 September 2014.

Chapter 4

Balancing away Article 6 in *Home Office v Tariq*

Fair trial rights in closed material proceedings

Ryan Goss

Introduction

This chapter considers how dialogue between the British courts and the European Court of Human Rights (European Court) has led to an undermining of fair trial rights and an undermining of the judicial safeguards put in place in an attempt to minimise infringements of those fair trial rights.

Under art. 6 of the European Convention on Human Rights (ECHR),[1] anyone involved in civil or criminal proceedings has the benefit of a number of fair trial guarantees. Some of those guarantees are explicit in the text of art. 6 (for example, the right to a hearing within a reasonable time). Other guarantees have been recognised by the European Court as implicit in art. 6 (for example, the right 'that criminal proceedings . . . should be adversarial and that there should be equality of arms between the prosecution and defence').[2] Despite the fact that art. 6 is among the most heavily litigated provisions of the ECHR,[3] there is considerable uncertainty about how best to interpret its interlocking guarantees. This uncertainty takes many forms.[4] It is not always clear from the Court's case law, for example, whether the various guarantees falling under the art. 6 umbrella should be treated as independent stand-alone rights,[5] or whether they are better understood as being desiderata of a single holistic right.[6]

Significantly, there is also uncertainty about the circumstances in which the European Court will countenance taking broader public interests into account in justifying an art. 6 infringement. Unlike some other provisions of the ECHR, the text of art. 6 contains no indications about the extent to which infringements may be justified, if at all, on the basis that the infringement is 'necessary in a democratic society'.[7] This omission of an express indication has contributed to significant ambiguity in the European Court's case law about the appropriate way to frame public interest arguments in the context of art. 6. Indeed, in some cases, any hint of public interest balancing in the art. 6 context is regarded as wholly inappropriate.[8] In others, public interest considerations are enthusiastically embraced by the Court,[9] and in yet others, public interest considerations are said to be capable of justifying infringements only where that infringement does not affect 'the very essence' of the relevant right.[10] This uncertainty about whether art. 6 is properly or usefully regarded as a 'qualified' right or an 'absolute' right, or something in between, also has the potential to affect how we conceptualise the broader ECHR system of human rights.[11]

It is against this background that the European and British debate about closed material proceedings generally, and gisting specifically, takes place. The debate is a tricky one in any jurisdiction,[12] but particular textual and case law factors in the ECHR system, such as those foreshadowed above, add to the complexity of the controversy in Europe and the UK. We must consider not only whether national security ought ever to trump procedural fairness as a question of policy, but also whether the ECHR or the case law of the European Court provide a jurisprudential mechanism whereby such a question may even be asked and answered.

This chapter critically analyses recent attempts by the European and British courts to ask and answer that question. It argues that the place of gisting in assessing infringements of fair trial rights is tenuous and that the judgments dealing with gisting are in tension and poorly explained. Moreover, in examining decisions such as *Home Office v Tariq*,[13] this chapter will argue that gisting's ability to act as any form of safeguard is all too easily hollowed out by arguments about overriding public interests. This may have broader consequences for those who rely on counter-balancing as a safeguard against infringements of art. 6 process rights.

The European and British dialogue that led to gisting

The story of gisting is the story of dialogue between European and British institutions. In order to explain the current controversy over gisting, and the current contours of that debate, it is necessary to track the ways in which those lines of dialogue developed over time in the case law of the European and British courts.

For current purposes, the starting point is *Chahal v United Kingdom*.[14] In that case, the European Court considered an alleged violation of ECHR art. 5(4)'s right of any person deprived of their liberty to have the lawfulness of their detention decided by a court. In seeking to challenge the lawfulness of his detention, the applicant noted that 'national security' concerns had meant he had been unable to have access to confidential material against him, and argued that this meant that the domestic courts had been unable to review his detention adequately, in violation of art. 5(4). (In considering the fairness of hearings under art. 5(4), the European Court has effectively imported a similar approach to that which it adopts when considering the art. 6 guarantees.)[15] In agreeing with the applicant's arguments, the European Court noted that the use of confidential material may sometimes be 'unavoidable,' but 'attache[d] significance to the fact that' Canadian legislation provided for security-cleared counsel to step into cases of this sort.[16] Thus, while *Chahal* did not explicitly require the adoption of a special advocate system, the UK subsequently introduced a special advocate system, at first in the immigration appeals context.[17] Similar passing references were made, several years later, in *Rowe and Davis v United Kingdom*.[18]

Rowe and Davis concerned an art. 6 application arising from criminal proceedings in which the applicants were convicted of murder, assault occasioning grievous bodily harm, and three counts of robbery.[19] In the European Court, the applicants argued that the prosecution's withholding of evidence on public interest grounds amounted to a violation of their art. 6 rights, and that they ought to have enjoyed greater rights protection, such as that which would have been provided by a special advocate system.

The Court began its analysis by emphasising the importance of the rights at stake:

> The right to an adversarial trial means, in a criminal case, that both prosecution and defence must be given the opportunity to have knowledge of and comment on the observations filed and the evidence adduced by the other party. In addition . . . prosecution authorities should disclose to the defence all material evidence in their possession.[20]

The difficulty that the European Court faces in cases such as this is, as foreshadowed above, that the text of art. 6 gives no indication about whether the public interest might *ever* be capable of justifying an infringement of fair trial rights. The Court's reasoning in resolving this difficulty is worth disaggregating. The Court articulated the particular public interests that might justify an infringement of the art. 6 right:

> the entitlement to disclosure of relevant evidence is not an absolute right. In any criminal proceedings there may be competing interests . . . In some cases it may be necessary to withhold certain evidence from the defence so as to preserve the fundamental rights of another individual or to safeguard an important public interest.[21]

The Court then imposed limits on the extent to which those public interests might be capable of justifying an infringement of the right, requiring that any restrictions be 'strictly necessary' and that 'any difficulties caused to the defence by a limitation on its rights must be *sufficiently counterbalanced* by the procedures followed by the judicial authorities'.[22]

This analytical framework, resting on strict necessity and counter-balancing, is crucial to understanding subsequent cases about special advocates and gisting. But it must also be joined up with, and read together with, another stream of case law.

In that other stream of art. 6 cases, the European Court has frequently referred to 'the very essence' of art. 6, or 'the very essence' of a particular art. 6 right.[23] Sometimes, these references appear to be little more than a rhetorical flourish,[24] but in other cases the Court uses the essence of a right as an additional way in which to constrain the use of public-interest balancing. More precisely, the Court will often state that it will countenance allowing public interest considerations to justify infringements of art. 6 rights, but only if any infringement does not go so far as to infringe upon 'the very essence of the right'. So, for example, in *Bykov v Russia*, the European Court stated that '[p]ublic-interest concerns cannot justify measures which extinguish the very essence of an applicant's defence rights'.[25]

Two points should be made about the Court's case law in this area. First, the Court's understanding of 'the very essence' of a right is often opaque and difficult to decipher (for example, the Court rarely identifies a non-essential aspect of the right to a fair trial).[26] This, as will be demonstrated, leads to difficulties. Second, despite uncertainty over what constitutes the very essence of the right, it is plain that the European Court regards infringements upon the very essence of the right as incapable of justification by reference to public interest considerations.[27]

Applying the more general art. 6 principles to secret evidence and gisting

In the UK, the use of 'the very essence' in the secret evidence context appears to have begun with reference to a 'core, irreducible minimum entitlement' in *R (Roberts) v Parole Board*.[28] Two years later, this was picked up by Lord Bingham in *Home Secretary v MB*,[29] a case concerning control orders sought against two persons suspected of links to extremist groups. The reasoning in *MB* was not always crystal clear. Lord Bingham indicated his understanding that 'the concept of fairness imports a core, irreducible minimum of procedural protection'.[30] Lord Bingham did not identify *non-core* aspects of procedural protection, but it seemed clear that, whatever the core was, it was 'irreducible'. Lord Bingham did, however, state that:

> I do not understand any of my noble and learned friends [in *Roberts*] to have concluded that the requirements of procedural fairness under domestic law or under the Convention would be met if a person entitled to a fair hearing, in a situation where an adverse decision could have severe consequences, were denied such knowledge, in whatever form, of what was said against him as was necessary to enable him, with or without a special advocate, effectively to challenge or rebut the case against him.[31]

Both appellants in *MB*, Lord Bingham concluded, had had 'the very essence of the right to a fair hearing . . . impaired':[32] the first appellant had, for example, been 'confronted by a bare, unsubstantiated assertion which he could do no more than deny'.[33] Lord Brown regarded it as decisive that, for both appellants in *MB*, the trial judge had regarded 'the disclosure made (or capable of being made consistently with the public interest) as insufficient *to allow of any effective challenge*'.[34] The 'basic requirement,' said Lady Hale, 'is to know the case against one and to have an opportunity of meeting it'.[35] Her Ladyship went on to say that:

> It is quite possible for the court to provide [a person subject to control order proceedings] with *a sufficient measure of procedural protection* even though the whole evidential basis for the basic allegation, which has been explained to him, is not disclosed.[36]

Lady Hale's language here, and the House of Lords' reasoning in *MB* generally, generated considerable ambiguity.[37] To some extent, this ambiguity was a product of the more general uncertainty about the extent to which the public interest may justify infringements of art. 6, and the extent to which art. 6 rights are properly regarded as 'qualified', 'absolute' or something else altogether. Importantly, aspects of this general ambiguity, and the specific gisting ambiguity relevant to *MB* – concerning, among other things, precisely *what* was required by 'core, irreducible minimum of procedural protection' or by the 'sufficient measure of procedural protection' – continue to this day.

The litigation about the use of control orders in secret evidence matters returned to the House of Lords in 2009. Two weeks before the House of Lords heard that case (*AF (No 3)*), however, the European Court's Grand Chamber handed down its decision in *A v United Kingdom*.[38] *A* concerned the detention without trial of non-citizens suspected of involvement with terrorism,[39] and involved a number of ECHR violations. This chapter focuses solely on the secret evidence issue. The Court began by noting the importance of the right to adversarial proceedings characterised by 'equality of arms'. Next, the Court went on to consider the circumstances in which an infringement of those rights might be capable of justification, emphasising that any restrictions must be 'strictly necessary in the light of a strong countervailing public interest' and that 'any difficulties caused to the defendant . . . [must be] sufficiently counterbalanced'.[40] In the circumstances of this case, which included a 'dramatic impact . . . on the applicants' fundamental rights', the European Court stated that:

> it was essential that as much information about the allegations and evidence against each applicant was disclosed as was possible without compromising national security or the safety of others. Where full disclosure was not possible, Article 5(4) required that the difficulties this caused were counterbalanced in such a way that *each applicant still had the possibility effectively to challenge the allegations against him.*[41]

The Court then applied this counter-balancing test: would the use of a special advocate scheme be sufficient to counter-balance the difficulties faced by the defence? Could the applicants here effectively challenge allegations against them?

> The Court further considers that the special advocate could perform an important role in counterbalancing the lack of full disclosure and the lack of a full, open, adversarial hearing by testing the evidence and putting arguments on behalf of the detainee during the closed hearings. However, the special advocate could not perform this function in any useful way *unless the detainee was provided with sufficient information about the allegations against him to enable him to give effective instructions* to the special advocate.[42]

Having emphasised the importance of providing an individual with 'sufficient information', the Court considered what this might mean in practice:

> While this question must be decided on a case-by-case basis, the Court observes generally that, where the evidence was to a large extent disclosed and the open material played the predominant role in the determination, it could not be said that the applicant was denied an opportunity effectively to challenge the reasonableness of the Secretary of State's belief and suspicions about him.[43]

The Court gave other examples as it sought to explain its approach, including that:

> Where . . . the open material consisted purely of general assertions and [the] decision to uphold the certification and maintain the detention was based solely or to a decisive degree on closed material, the procedural requirements of Article 5(4) would not be satisfied.[44]

This form of reasoning provided further support for the notion that some form of gist or summary would be a necessary counter-balancing safeguard in order to comply with the ECHR. These explanations, however, left uncertainty about the circumstances in which a gist would be required, as will be seen.

The dialogue continues: *AF (No 3)*

Soon after the Grand Chamber's decision in *A*, the question of gisting came before the House of Lords in the control orders case of *AF (No 3)*. The House of Lords faced at least two tasks in this case: first, it had to interpret and apply *A*'s approach to secret evidence in the UK context. Second, it had to attempt to resolve some of the uncertainty about gisting that had been generated by the decision in *MB*. The importance of the reasons in *AF (No 3)* means that they warrant particularly close analysis. As Lord Hope put it at the beginning of his concurring judgment, *AF (No 3)* brought into focus 'the acute tension that exists between the urgent need to protect the public from attack by terrorists and the fundamental rights of the individual'.[45]

In his speech, Lord Phillips considered the government's argument that 'a less stringent standard of fairness was applicable in respect of control orders' than in respect of criminal proceedings.[46] His Lordship concluded that while this might be true as a general proposition, it was not the case that this meant *minimum disclosure requirements* would differ.[47] Importantly, therefore, Lord Phillips explicitly rejected the government's argument that gisting requirements might differ depending on the nature of the case. Lord Phillips summarised the effect of *A v United Kingdom*, and especially para. [220] of *A*, as establishing 'that the controlee must be given sufficient information about the allegations against him to enable him to give effective instructions in relation to those allegations'.[48]

Later in his judgment, Lord Phillips said that 'non-disclosure cannot go so far as to deny a party knowledge of the essence of the case against him, at least where he is at risk of consequences as severe as those normally imposed under a control order'.[49] Lord Hope put it thus:

> The controlled person must be given sufficient information about the allegations against him to give effective instructions to the special advocate. This is the bottom line, or the core irreducible minimum . . . a denunciation on grounds that are not disclosed is the stuff of nightmares. The rule of law in a democratic society does not tolerate such behaviour. The fundamental principle is that *everyone is entitled to the disclosure of sufficient material to enable him to answer effectively the case that is made against him*.[50]

Lord Scott dealt with the issue in a matter-of-fact way, holding that an 'essential requirement of a fair hearing is that a party against whom relevant allegations are made is given the opportunity to rebut the allegations'.[51] And in her judgment, Lady Hale stated that:

> Strasbourg has now, in *A* . . . made it entirely clear what the test of a fair hearing is. The test is whether the controlled person has had the possibility effectively to challenge the allegations against him . . . he has to have sufficient information about those allegations to be able to give effective instructions to his special advocate.[52]

The language of Lord Brown was emphatic:

> In short, Strasbourg has decided that the suspect must *always* be told sufficient of the case against him to enable him to give 'effective instructions' to the special advocate, notwithstanding that sometimes this will be impossible and national security will thereby be put at risk . . . Strasbourg has . . . [stipulated] the need in all cases to disclose to the suspect enough about the allegations forming the sole or decisive grounds of suspicion against him to enable him to give effective instructions.[53]

The general rule was, it seemed, not in doubt: 'An essential requirement of a fair hearing is that a party against whom relevant allegations are made is given the opportunity to rebut the allegations'; 'This is . . . the core irreducible minimum'. There are, perhaps, hints that the general rule might not be easily applied outside the context of control orders,[54] but there are also strong indications that the general rule is a broadly applicable interpretation of art. 6 and that some form of gisting would be required in all cases.[55] Furthermore, the reasoning underlying the judgments also lends itself to the view that a gist would be required in all cases.

Indeed, from the *AF (No 3)* judgments it seemed clear that the rule of law required at least some level of disclosure to those who were the subject of allegations,[56] that the disclosure requirement was 'essential' to a fair hearing,[57] and that, although the manifestation of some procedural protections might differ depending on the subject matter, there was no reason to think that disclosure requirements might differ from one type of case to another.[58] Given all of this, surely that which was required by the rule of law could not be overborne by a competing public interest?

Moreover, as discussed above, the European Court's case law had given clear indications that public interest considerations could only justify restrictions on art. 6 rights where those restrictions did not infringe 'the very essence' of art. 6. At this point, it is worth noting that both the European Court and the House of Lords have indicated that providing a person involved in proceedings with the evidence against them, or at least with a gist of that evidence, is 'essential' and a 'core irreducible minimum'.[59] Surely, then, faithful application of European and UK case law would regard as impermissible attempts to use the public interest to justify infringements of this essential core element of the right to a fair trial?

Tariq: The consensus breaks down?

In *Tariq*, the claimant was employed by the UK Home Office as an immigration officer, a post for which he required, and was granted, a security clearance.[60] In August 2006, the claimant's brother and cousin were arrested as part of a counter-terrorism investigation. Nine days later, the claimant was suspended from work, and his security clearance was subsequently withdrawn. In proceedings in the Employment Tribunal, Tariq claimed that the withdrawal of the security clearance resulted from 'direct or indirect discrimination on grounds of race and/or religion':

> [H]e had been advised that his suspension and the withdrawal of his security clearance were because of his perceived association with certain relatives or associates of relatives suspected of association with terrorist activities and the risk of their attempting to exert influence on him.[61]

No information suggested that Tariq had been involved in any terrorist plot.[62] In the Employment Tribunal, the Home Office denied the alleged discrimination, and maintained that 'it acted throughout to protect national security'.[63]

Of interest here is the way in which the closed material procedure was deployed in the Employment Tribunal. The Employment Tribunal ordered that a closed material procedure be utilised; on appeal to the Employment Appeal Tribunal and the Court of Appeal, it was held that art. 6 '"requires [Mr Tariq] to be provided with the allegations being made against him in sufficient detail to enable him to give instructions to his legal team so that those allegations can be challenged effectively" (a requirement that can conveniently be described as 'gisting'), even if this put the Home Office "in the invidious position of having to make difficult decisions about disclosure and whether or how a claim is to be defended"'.[64]

Tariq's case, in many ways, seemed precisely that described by the European Court in *A* as warranting a gist: 'the open material consisted purely of general assertions' and the relevant decision was seemingly 'based solely or to a decisive degree on closed material'.[65]

In the Supreme Court, the Home Office appealed against the Court of Appeal's conclusion.[66] By a majority of 8:1, the Supreme Court held that no gist was required. The reasoning of the Supreme Court is worthy of close analysis.

The majority's reasons in *Tariq*

The majority's reasons are characterised by a willingness to allow public interest considerations to justify what would otherwise be infringements of art. 6 rights, (including rights previously recognised as being part of the very essence of art. 6), and by the use of older, more general authorities in preference to the more recent and more specific guidance of *A* as interpreted in *AF (No 3)*.

Lord Mance wrote the lead judgment for the majority. In questioning the need for a gist in this case, Lord Mance began by noting that 'cases where the state is seeking to impose on the individual actual or virtual imprisonment [such as the control orders in cases like *AF (No 3)*] are in a different category to the present, where an individual is seeking to pursue a civil claim'.[67]

In adopting this starting point, Lord Mance relied on those portions of the European Court judgment in *A*, which emphasised the drastic impact of deprivation of liberty on the individual.[68] In further support of this proposition, Lord Mance relied on three decisions of the European Court. Remarkably, two of these decisions predated the Grand Chamber's decision in *A* and had been dismissed as unhelpful or outdated by the Court of Appeal in *Tariq*,[69] while the third was a chamber decision that failed to make any reference to those portions of *A* dealing with gisting.[70]

Lord Mance went on to note that, in this case, the claimant had been provided with information about 'the general nature of the Home Office's case' and that what was in issue was whether art. 6 required that he 'be provided with the allegations being made against him in sufficient detail to enable him to give instructions to his legal team so that those allegations can be challenged effectively'.[71] Lord Mance framed the question as being:

> whether there is an absolute requirement that a claimant should himself or herself see and know the allegations forming the basis of the state's defence in sufficient detail to give instructions to the defence legal team to enable the allegations to be challenged effectively.[72]

Extraordinarily, just 25 months after the House of Lords' decision in *AF (No 3)*, Lord Mance concluded that a 'clear line of jurisprudence' supported the view that there was no such gisting requirement.[73] Given the authorities discussed above, the important national security considerations, and the fact that Tariq had been given general information about the case against him, Lord Mance held that there was no need for a gist.[74]

Seven judges agreed.[75] Lord Hope, framing the question as one about 'the very essence of his right to a fair trial', concluded that the risk which a gist posed to the public interest in having an effective security vetting system was too great.[76] Tariq's case was 'entirely different' to that in *AF (No 3)* and there could not, Lord Hope said, 'be an absolute rule that gisting must always be resorted to whatever the circumstances'.[77] Intriguingly, just 25 months earlier, Lord Hope had said that 'everyone is entitled to the disclosure of sufficient material to enable him to answer effectively the case that is made against him'.[78]

Likewise, Lord Brown said that it would be 'absurd' to apply *AF (No 3)* as though art. 6 required a gist in all cases; 25 months previously Lord Brown had stated that a 'suspect must always be told sufficient of the case against him to enable him to give "effective instructions"' and that *A* set down 'a rigid principle . . . in all cases'.[79]

In Lord Dyson's judgment, his Lordship was willing to accept that the general rule was 'that an applicant should enjoy the full panoply of art. 6 rights, including full disclosure of all relevant material, and that any limitation on the ordinary incidents of art. 6 requires careful justification'.[80] However, Lord Dyson indicated that it was 'clear' that *A* did not provide for an absolute gisting requirement; in support of that proposition, his Lordship cites a passage drawn from *A*'s general comments about procedural fairness and omits reference to *A*'s specific treatment of gisting.[81] Lord Dyson considered that, whatever the general rule might be, different considerations applied in surveillance and security-vetting cases. This view was supported, Lord Dyson argued, by the cases relied upon by Lord Mance, as well as another case decided 30 years before *A*.[82] Summarising his view of the law, Lord Dyson stated: 'The cases show, in particular, that there is no right to be given the gist of relevant information if and to the extent that this would jeopardise the efficacy of the surveillance or security vetting regime'.[83]

The public interest, Lord Dyson held, thus overwhelms the art. 6 rights of the claimant in such cases. In his conclusion, he reflected on the nature of human rights law:

> [M]uch of the content of the European Convention . . . is about striking balances. This is sometimes very difficult and different opinions can reasonably be held. As a consequence, outcomes are sometimes difficult to predict. This is inevitable. But it is not a reason for striving to devise hard and fast rules and rigid classifications.[84]

At least in this respect, Lord Dyson may rest assured: whatever other criticisms may be made of *Tariq*, it certainly cannot be said that the post-*Tariq* case law suffers from hard and fast rules or rigid classifications.

Lord Kerr's dissent in *Tariq*

Lord Kerr's dissent began by articulating a concern about the policy considerations underlying the arguments of the Home Office, and the reasoning of the majority.

The state, Lord Kerr noted, was faced with a dilemma in cases like Tariq's: reveal 'the information on which it relies to defeat the claim and compromising national security by doing so' or 'be forced to settle the case'.[85] Rather than pursue either of these unpalatable options, the state seeks a solution 'founded not on principle but on pragmatism': 'the state should be allowed to deploy the information on which the claim can be defeated but be absolved from the need to disclose it to the claimant'.[86] Drawing on British and European authority, Lord Kerr then offered a summary of the orthodox view, noting that restrictions on the art. 6 right to equality of arms must be 'strictly necessary and proportionate', in response to 'a strong countervailing public interest', and 'sufficiently counterbalanced'.[87] Moreover, 'the restrictions must not be such as effectively to extinguish the very essence of the right'.[88]

Lord Kerr then went on to offer a robust argument in support of the view that what is required by art. 6 in this context cannot vary depending on the nature of the proceedings or the nature of the public interest implicated by those proceedings:

> A function of the counterbalancing measures is to ensure that the very essence of the right is not impaired. . . . If equality of arms lies at the heart of a fair trial, the essence of the right must surely include the requirement that sufficient information about the case which is to be made against him be given to a party so that he can give meaningful instructions . . . if the essence of the right is to be regarded . . . as the indispensable and necessary attributes of the right as opposed to those which it may or may not have, its essence cannot alter according to the circumstances in which it falls to be considered.[89]

Tellingly, unlike the majority's reasons, Lord Kerr's judgment went on to include detailed analysis of the *Klass/Leander/Esbester* and the *A* and *AF(No 3)* cases.[90] With respect, Lord Kerr's judgment is commendable for the way in which his Lordship draws on authority, makes principled arguments on the basis of that authority, and engages with the European Court's approach to gisting even where that approach is not necessarily crystal clear.

Assessing the majority judgment: the risk of the gist

Ultimately, there are two points to be made in assessing the majority's judgment in *Tariq*: a narrow point and a broader point. The narrow point is that the judgment is, at the very least, in some considerable tension with the decisions in *A* and *AF (No 3)*. The impression that there may be an outright contradiction between *A* and *Tariq* is strengthened by the *Tariq* Court's apparent reluctance to engage directly with the most relevant passages of the *A* judgment.

The broader point is that, regardless of how the relationship between the various recent authorities is interpreted, the logic of *Tariq* is that the public interest can justify what would otherwise be an infringement of art. 6 rights, especially where the rights at stake in the relevant proceedings are regarded as not particularly 'fundamental'. This is so even though, as previously held in *AF (No 3)*, the relevant art. 6 right is a right regarded as forming part of the very essence of a fair trial. These conclusions are not, and should not be seen as, uncontroversial.

At the level of authority, these conclusions run contrary to a vast body of case law, which has indicated that infringements of art. 6 may never be justified on public interest grounds, or may only be justified to the extent that any infringement does not affect the very essence of the right.[91] If the public interest is allowed to justify infringements even where those infringements affect the very essence of the right to a fair trial, the European Court's elaborately constructed analytical architecture falls away.

But even if one leaves the question of authority to one side, and considers the *Tariq* majority judgments at a principled level, their conclusions raise questions about how to conceptualise art. 6's place within the ECHR framework. Specifically, judgments like that in *Tariq* raise questions about the extent to which art. 6 should essentially be regarded as a qualified right, similar to arts 8–11, despite the lack of textual support in the ECHR itself for such an approach.[92] The more that art. 6 is treated as a qualified right, for which a proportionality analysis is entirely appropriate, the more likely it is that the public interest will be able to be used to whittle down process rights, and to whittle down the counter-balancing safeguards that past courts have erected in an attempt to minimise the damage done to process rights in the name of the public interest. In this sense, perhaps putting faith in special advocates and gisting gives the game away: if the public interest can be deployed to justify infringements of rights, provided that safeguards are in place, then the public interest can also be deployed to justify infringements of those safeguards. The state will usually be willing to emphasise the important public interest in keeping information secret;[93] if that public interest can overwhelm process rights, then, as *Tariq* bears out, it can also overwhelm attempts to counter-balance infringements. From this perspective, *Tariq* may even be regarded not so much as an anomalous decision inconsistent with previous authority, but rather as the logical product of introducing public interest balancing into the art. 6 context at all.

Conclusion

If this area of the law is to be marked by clarity and coherence, there is a need for a robust judicial articulation of the extent to which (if at all) the public interest may justify infringements of art. 6, and faithful application of the standard set in that articulation. In the UK, this will be increasingly important as judges begin to interpret the Justice and Security Act 2013 (UK), which provides for considerable expansion of the availability of closed material proceedings in civil matters. Section 8(1) of that Act, which will have to be interpreted consistently with European human rights law,[94] requires that courts in any closed material proceedings 'consider' requiring a gist.[95] Interpreting this provision in accordance with European human rights law will almost certainly create new opportunities for the British courts, and for the European Court, to consider afresh whether there is an absolute gisting requirement, and the extent to which the public interest may justify infringements of art. 6.

Notes

1 *Convention for the Protection of Human Rights and Fundamental Freedoms*, opened for signature 4 November 1950, 213 UNTS 221 (entered into force 3 September 1953), as amended by Protocol No 14 bis to the *Convention for the Protection of Human Rights and Fundamental Freedoms*, opened for signature 27 May 2009, CETS No. 204 (entered into force 1 September 2009) (ECHR).

2 *Rowe and Davis v United Kingdom* (2000) 30 EHRR 1 [60].

3 European Court of Human Rights, *The European Court of Human Rights: Some Facts and Figures: 1959–2009* (Council of Europe 2009) 6. See D. Harris, M. O'Boyle and C. Warbrick, *Law of the European Convention on Human Rights* (2nd edn., Oxford University Press 2007) 202.

4 See Ryan Goss, *Criminal Fair Trial Rights: Article 6 of the European Convention on Human Rights* (Hart 2014).

5 See, for example, *Pakelli v Germany* (1984) 6 EHRR 1 [42], citing *DeWeer v Belgium* (1979–80) 2 EHRR 439 [56].

6 See, for example, *Bonisch v Austria* (1987) 9 EHRR 191 [29]; *Barbera, Messegue and Jabardo v Spain* (1989) 11 EHRR 360 at [67]; *Salduz v Turkey* (2009) 49 EHRR 19 [50]; *Al-Khawaja and Tahery v United Kingdom* (2012) 54 EHRR 23 [145].

7 Compare art. 6 with arts. 8–10.

8 See, for example, *Kostovski v Netherlands* (1990) 12 EHRR 434 [44]; *Saidi v France* (1994) 17 EHRR 251 [44]; *Saunders v United Kingdom* (1997) 23 EHRR 313 [74]; *Ramanauskas v Lithuania* [2008] Crim LR 639 [53]–[54].

9 See, for example, *Janosevic v Sweden* (2004) 38 EHRR 22 [101]–[104]; *Jussila v Finland* (2007) 45 EHRR 39 [43] (cf, [O-II 2]); *Marcello Viola v Italy* App. No. 45106/04 (ECtHR, 5 October 2006) [71]–[77]; *Jalloh v Germany* (2007) 44 EHRR 32 [117]; *Heglas v Czech Republic* (2009) 48 EHRR 44 [87].

10 See, for example, *Grayson and Barnham v United Kingdom* (2009) 48 EHRR 30 [49]; *Bykov v Russia* App. No. 4378/02 (ECtHR, 10 March 2009) [93].

11 Andrew Ashworth, 'Security, Terrorism and the Value of Human Rights' in B. Goold and L. Lazarus (eds.), *Security and Human Rights* (2nd edn., Hart 2007).

12 See Ryan Goss, '"To the Serious Detriment of the Public": Secret Evidence and Closed Material Procedures' in Liora Lazarus, Christopher McCrudden and Nigel Bowles (eds.), *Reasoning Rights: Comparative Judicial Engagement* (Hart 2014).

13 [2011] UKSC 35; [2012] 1 AC 452, subsequently cited in, for example, *Condon v Pompano* [2013] HCA 7 [63] (French CJ) (*Tariq*).

14 (1997) 23 EHRR 413 (*Chahal*).

15 See, for example, *A v United Kingdom* (2009) 49 EHRR 29 [203], [217] (*A*).

16 *Chahal* (n. 14) [131]; see also [144].

17 See, for example, *Tinnelly & Sons Ltd and McElduff v United Kingdom* (1998) 27 EHRR 24 [52]; *Rowe and Davis* (n. 2) [46]. For subsequent expansion of the special advocate system see, for example, *Rowe and Davis* (n. 2) [49]; *Justice and Security Act 2013* (UK).

18 *Rowe and Davis* (n. 2) [46]–[49].

19 Ibid. [22]–[33].

20 Ibid. [60]. An example of a more recent articulation of this principle is *Zahirović v Croatia* App. No. 58590/11 (ECtHR, 25 April 2013).

21 Ibid. [61].

22 Ibid. (emphasis added). Requirements of strict necessity and counter-balancing do not appear in the text of art. 6.

23 On similar German terminology, see D. Grimm, 'Proportionality in Canadian and German Constitutional Jurisprudence' (2007) 57 *University of Toronto Law Journal*, 383, 384–7; David Currie, *The Constitution of the Federal Republic of Germany* (University of Chicago Press 1994) 178.
24 See, for example, *John Murray v United Kingdom* (1996) 22 EHRR 29 [49].
25 *Bykov* (n. 10) [93]. See also *Eliazer v Netherlands* (2003) 37 EHRR 45 [30]; *Heaney and McGuinness v Ireland* (2001) 33 EHRR 12 [58]; *Jalloh* (n. 9) [97]; *Omar v France* (2000) 29 EHRR 210 [34].
26 See Yutaka Arai-Takahashi, *The Margin of Appreciation Doctrine and the Principle of Proportionality in the Jurisprudence of the ECHR* (Intersentia 2002) 36; cf. Julian Rivers, 'Proportionality and Variable Intensity of Review' (2006) 65 *Cambridge Law Journal*,174, 187.
27 As always with art. 6 jurisprudence, there are exceptions: see Ryan Goss, *Criminal Fair Trial Rights: Article 6 of the European Convention on Human Rights* (Hart 2014) pt. E.
28 [2005] UKHL 45; [2005] 2 AC 738 (*Roberts*).
29 [2007] UKHL 46; [2008] 1 AC 440 [34], [43] (*MB*).
30 Ibid. [43].
31 Ibid. [34].
32 Ibid. [41], [43].
33 Ibid. [41]; cf, Lord Hoffmann at [45]–[55].
34 Ibid. [92] (emphasis added).
35 Ibid. [58].
36 Ibid. [75] (emphasis added).
37 See, on the ambiguity, *Home Secretary v AF (No 3)* [2009] UKHL 28; [2010] 2 AC 269 [17] (Lord Phillips), [100]–[106] (Lady Hale) (*AF (No 3)*).
38 *A* (n. 15).
39 See also *A v Home Secretary (Belmarsh)* [2004] UKHL 56; [2005] 2 AC 68.
40 *A* (n. 15) [205].
41 Ibid. [218] (emphasis added).
42 Ibid. [220] (emphasis added).
43 Ibid. The application of this approach to the facts in *A* led to four violations of art. 5(4) and five non-violations. See also Steve Foster, 'The Fight against Terrorism, Detention without Trial and Human Rights' (2009) 14(1) *Coventry Law Journal*, 4.
44 Ibid. [220].
45 *AF (No. 3)* (n. 37) [76].
46 Ibid. [57].
47 Ibid.
48 Ibid. [59].
49 Ibid. [65] (Lord Phillips). It is not quite clear if, or how, the inclusion of the final phrase here modifies the remarks made by Lord Phillips at [57] earlier in the same judgment.
50 Ibid. [81]–[85] (Lord Hope) (emphasis added).
51 Ibid. [96] (Lord Scott).
52 Ibid. [101]–[103] (Lady Hale).
53 Ibid. [116], [119] (emphasis in original).
54 For example, Lord Phillips and Lady Hale both frame the rule as applicable to a 'controlee' or a 'controlled person': Ibid. [59], [103].
55 See, for example, Lord Phillips [57]; Lord Scott [96]; Lord Brown [116]–[119].
56 *AF (No. 3)* (n. 37) [81]–[85] (Lord Hope).
57 Ibid. [96] (Lord Scott).
58 Ibid. [57].
59 *A* (n. 15) [219]; *AF (No. 3)* (n. 37) [81]–[85] (Lord Hope), [96] (Lord Scott).
60 *Tariq* (n. 13) [4].
61 Ibid. [6].
62 Ibid. [5]–[6].

63 Ibid.
64 Ibid. [3]; see *Home Office v Tariq (CA)* [2010] EWCA Civ 462 (4 May 2010) [5], [50].
65 *A* (n. 15) [220]. Lord Mance acknowledged that Tariq had only been provided with the general case: *Tariq* (n. 13) [63].
66 *Tariq* included consideration of EU law *and* European human rights law. This chapter restricts its focus to the latter.
67 *Tariq* (n. 13) [27].
68 Ibid. [25]–[27]; cf. Lord Phillips in *AF (No. 3)* (n. 37) [57] and the discussion above. See also *Tariq* (n. 13) [120]–[121] (Lord Kerr).
69 *Leander v* Sweden (1987) 9 EHRR 433; *Esbester v United Kingdom (Admissibility)* App. No. 18601/91 (ECtHR, 2 April 1993); cf. *Home Office v Tariq (CA)* (n. 64) [50].
70 *Kennedy v United Kingdom* App no 26839/05 (ECtHR, 18 May 2010), which referred to *A* only in passing ([109],[184]), but made no reference to those passages of *A* that dealt with gisting in detail and were the subject of close attention in, for example, *AF (No. 3)* (n. 37).
71 *Tariq* (n. 13) [63]–[64].
72 Ibid. [65].
73 Ibid. [67]–[69].
74 Ibid.
75 Ibid. [163]–[164].
76 Ibid. [77]–[82].
77 Ibid. [80], [83].
78 *AF (No. 3)* (n. 37) [81]–[85] (Lord Hope) (emphasis added).
79 *Tariq* (n. 13) [87]–[88].
80 Ibid. [146].
81 Ibid. [145].
82 See discussion of *Klass v Germany* (1979–80) 2 EHRR 214; *Leander* (n. 69); *Esbester* (n. 69); *Kennedy* (n. 70); *Tariq* (n. 13) [148]–[158].
83 *Tariq* (n. 13) [158].
84 Ibid. [161].
85 Ibid. [106].
86 Ibid.
87 Ibid. [113].
88 Ibid.
89 Ibid. [118]–[119]
90 Ibid. [120]–[135].
91 See, for example, *Kostovski* (n. 8) [44]; *Ciulla v Italy* (1991) 13 EHRR 346 [41]; *Funke v France* (1993) 16 EHRR 297 [44]; *Saunders v United Kingdom* (1997) 23 EHRR 313 [683]; *Teixeira de Castro v Portugal* (1999) 28 EHRR 101 [36]; *Edwards and Lewis v United Kingdom* (2005) 40 EHRR 24 [49]; *Hulki Gunes v Turkey* (2006) 42 EHRR 27 [96]; *Shannon v United Kingdom* (2006) 42 EHRR 31 [38]; *Heaney and McGuinness* (n. 25) [56]–[58]; *Papon v France* (2004) 39 EHRR 10 [98], citing *Koch v Germany* App. No. 1270/61 (Commission Decision, 8 March 1962); *Ramanauskas* (n. 8) [53]–[54]; *Hanzevacki v Croatia* App. No. 17182/07 (ECtHR, 16 April 2009) [23]; *Aleksandr Zaichenko v Russia* App. No. 39660/02 (ECtHR, 18 February 2010) [39]; *Bannikova v Russia* App. No. 18757/06 (ECtHR, 4 November 2010) [33]–[35]; *Quinn v Ireland* App. No. 36887/97 (ECtHR, 21 December 2000) [48]; *Jalloh* (n. 9) [97], [101].
92 cf. Ashworth, above.
93 See, for example, *MB* (n. 29) [66] (Lady Hale).
94 Section 3 of the Human Rights Act 1998 (UK).
95 See especially s. 8(1)(d)–(e).

Part 2

Open justice and procedural fairness

Chapter 5

Protecting procedural fairness and criminal intelligence

Is there a balance to be struck?

Gabrielle Appleby

Introduction

In political theory, security is intimately connected to political power.[1] In the eighteenth century, political economist Adam Smith observed that the state must meet three 'duties' to attain a 'system of natural liberty':

> [F]irst, the duty of protecting society from the violence and invasion of other independent societies; secondly, the duty of protecting . . . every member of the society from the injustice or oppression of every other member of it . . . and thirdly, the duty of erecting and maintaining certain publick works and certain publick institutions, which it can never be for the interest of any individual . . . to erect and maintain.[2]

Smith's first two duties emphasise the state's role in protecting the nation, community and individual from violence, invasion, injustice and oppression. These duties are the correlative of the individual's right to security as part of a society.[3] It is in pursuit of these duties that the state requires its most extensive, coercive and intrusive powers: powers to undertake surveillance within and outside the community; powers to search, seize and question foreign nationals and its own citizens; powers to detain those suspected of criminal activity and, increasingly, those suspected of possible future criminal activity. In exercising these powers, the executive necessarily intrudes on the liberties and private lives of individuals within and outside of the community. The right to security exists in tension to other rights and liberties. Powers exercised to protect security justifiably make us nervous. Such powers must often be exercised in secret. The secret exercise of such powers justifiably makes us even more nervous.

This chapter examines government invocation of state secrecy in legislation aimed at organised crime in Australia. The High Court of Australia has recently confirmed that procedural fairness – and specifically the right of parties to be informed of the case and material brought against them – in curial processes is an essential characteristic of an Australian court. As such, it is protected with respect to Australian state courts under the *Kable* doctrine[4] and with respect to Commonwealth courts under the *Boilermakers'* doctrine.[5] Nonetheless, the High Court has, on several occasions, upheld legislative provisions that make serious incursions into this right where these incursions are justified by reference to broader 'public interest' objectives, including security objectives, such as maintaining the secrecy of police operations and protecting police operatives and others from harm.[6]

This chapter considers how the High Court balances the protection of procedural fairness in curial proceedings against other public interest objectives that are invoked to maintain state secrecy. It examines the approaches evident in the High Court's 2013 decision, *Condon v Pompano*,[7] and is informed by the High Court's previous understandings of the constitutional protection of procedural fairness.

This chapter introduces a number of different legislative forms that protect state secrecy in administrative and curial proceedings, drawing predominantly on the Australian states' anti-organised crime legislation. Next, it explains the difference between these contemporary provisions – through which the government attempts both to maintain state secrecy and use the information against individuals in curial proceedings – and traditional invocation of state secrecy in public interest immunity claims. It goes on to consider the concept of procedural fairness, as distinct from natural justice, as the High Court's now preferred conception of process requirements in both administrative and constitutional law. This discussion demonstrates that by adopting procedural fairness as a preferred concept, the High Court may be signalling its acceptance that procedural rights must yield to other objectives (including state secrecy), and their content may be removed when circumstances require. Finally, it considers the High Court's approach to balancing the protection of procedural fairness against state secrecy in *Pompano*.[8] Two approaches emerge from the judgments: one in which the need to achieve the ideals of procedural fairness are weighed against competing public interests; and the other, in which procedural fairness is deemed 'immutable', but with varying content. While acknowledging the attraction of the latter approach, this chapter argues that it is disingenuous and may lead to loss of public confidence in the judicial process. It is preferable for judges to be transparent in identifying incursions and failures of procedural fairness that are justified on the basis of competing objectives.

In a practical sense, little necessarily differentiates the approaches in their application. Both require 'balancing' in some form of the benefits of maintaining procedural fairness rights against the benefits of maintaining state secrecy. In judicial application, *Pompano* reveals two approaches to this balancing process. The first focuses on whether procedural safeguards provided within a legislative scheme are sufficient to achieve the necessary balance. The second places trust in the individual judge's ability to maintain fairness in a process where serious incursions into the fundamental rights associated with procedural fairness exist. The second approach leaves the balancing necessary to maintain fairness in the hands of the trial judge.

The final part of the chapter explores the limitations of both approaches, particularly their failure to articulate the balancing test that the judges are asked to undertake at either level. By failing to explain the nature and mechanics of this test, the extent to which judges will exercise restraint or deference in the course of the balancing process is unclear. This part of the chapter argues that it is necessary for the High Court to adopt a test at both levels that stresses the priority of individual rights to counter-balance the criminal intelligence schemes' inherent bias towards state secrecy which has, to date, been granted judicial support.

Using criminal intelligence in the courts: an overview

Legislative provisions that allow government parties to rely upon material in court proceedings and also in administrative processes, but where that material is not provided to the other side, have spread across Australian jurisdictions over the last decade.[9] Australia's criminal intelligence and closed hearings framework is not unique. In the United Kingdom and Canada, for instance, closed hearings to receive security intelligence have been provided for by legislation in both immigration and terrorism control-order proceedings.[10] Two aspects of the overseas experience are notable. First, their national security context is distinguishable from the *organised* crime context of many of our criminal intelligence provisions. If the magnitude or nature of the threat is relevant to the question of whether such laws legitimately displace procedural fairness, the existential danger of terrorism (or at least the perception thereof) is conceivably far greater than that of organised criminal enterprise. Conversely, however, it could be argued that those international provisions require greater procedural fairness because the consequences of their application are more significant than many of ours – including deportation and near-house arrest.[11] Second, in both the UK and Canada, the courts have exercised considerable vigour in scrutinising such provisions and, on occasion, have found them to be in violation of their respective rights protection instruments.[12]

South Australia

In South Australia, such provisions are found in the Casino Act 1997 (SA),[13] Firearms Act 1977 (SA),[14] Gaming Machines Act 1992 (SA),[15] Liquor Licensing Act 1997 (SA),[16] Summary Offences Act 1953 (SA),[17] Security and Investigation Industry Act 1995 (SA),[18] Hydroponics Industry Control Act 2009 (SA),[19] Serious and Organised Crime (Unexplained Wealth) Act 2009 (SA),[20] Serious and Organised Crime (Control) Act 2008 (SA),[21] and most recently beyond the organised crime arena in amendments to the Child Sex Offenders Registration Act 2006 (SA).[22]

The ubiquity of criminal intelligence provisions is not replicated in commonality of form across Australian jurisdictions. A single form of process has been rolled out across the South Australian legislation, modelled on the provision upheld as constitutional in *K-Generation v Liquor Licensing Court*.[23] An example of the South

Australian approach can be taken from s. 5A of the Serious and Organised Crime (Control) Act 2008 (SA) (SOCCA):

5A – Criminal intelligence

(1) In any proceedings under this Act before a court, the court:

(a) must, on the application of the Commissioner, take steps to maintain the confidentiality of information properly classified by the Commissioner as criminal intelligence, including steps to receive evidence and hear argument about the information in private in the absence of the parties to the proceedings and their representatives; and
(b) may take evidence consisting of or relating to information so classified by the Commissioner by way of affidavit of a police officer of or above the rank of superintendent.

(2) The duties imposed on a court by subsection (1) in relation to proceedings under this Act apply to any court dealing (whether on an appeal under this, or another, Act or otherwise) with information properly classified under this Act as criminal intelligence or with the question of whether information has been properly classified under this Act by the Commissioner as criminal intelligence.

Criminal intelligence is defined as:

> information relating to actual or suspected criminal activity (whether in this State or elsewhere) the disclosure of which could reasonably be expected to prejudice criminal investigations, to enable the discovery of the existence or identity of a confidential source of information relevant to law enforcement or to endanger a person's life or physical safety.[24]

There are three important dimensions of the South Australian provision. The first is the absence of a mandatory interlocutory hearing to determine whether material is properly classified as criminal intelligence. In the second dimension, and despite the first dimension, the court maintains the power to review whether the Commissioner has properly classified information as criminal intelligence (this power of review was key to the provision's constitutional validity, as explained by the majority in *K-Generation*).[25] As such, there remains the possibility (anticipated by s. 5A(3)) that there will be a judicial investigation into whether information has been properly classified as criminal intelligence. The third dimension is the absence of any express provision for a non-government party advocate to appear in proceedings, either where criminal intelligence is being used (for instance, in a substantive control order hearing under the SOCCA) or in proceedings where the question of whether information has been properly classified as criminal intelligence is agitated.

Western Australia has introduced provisions that share the dimensions identified in the South Australian provisions detailed above.[26]

Queensland and Victoria

In contrast to the South Australian and Western Australian provisions are those found in the anti-organised crime control order legislation in Victoria, Queensland and New South Wales (drafted, in almost its entirety, based on the Queensland provision). Queensland's Criminal Organisation Act 2009 was the first Australian control order regime to adopt, first, a mandatory separate hearing for determining whether information was criminal intelligence under the scheme; and second, the requirement for a statutorily appointed advocate (the 'criminal organisation public interest monitor') to attend these hearings, together with other substantive closed hearings in which criminal intelligence is submitted.[27] The advocate's role is to test and make submissions to the court about the appropriateness and validity of the application.[28] After the constitutional validity of the Queensland control-order regime was upheld in *Pompano*,[29] New South Wales adopted provisions in relation to the use of criminal intelligence in its regime in substantially the same form.[30]

This regime, French CJ explained in *Pompano*, shares many characteristics with the system of special advocates adopted in Canada and the UK. However, it adopts 'a fairly minimalist approach to the protection of the respondent's interests' in comparison to those international regimes, where the special advocate represents the interests of the respondent rather than functions only to test the appropriateness and validity of the application.[31]

The regime adopted in Queensland's control-order legislation is not replicated in other Queensland legislation,[32] which instead make use of a model more akin to that in South Australia and Western Australia.[33]

Victoria, which had for many years publicly stood against the policing need for control order legislation, introduced statutory requirements for a special advocate to be appointed where criminal intelligence would otherwise close the court.[34] The current Victorian criminal-intelligence regime in its control-order legislation is drawn from provisions introduced early in 2009 in a number of other pieces of Victorian legislation.[35] These 2009 amendments preceded the Queensland regime, and created the first Australian scheme providing for the mandatory appointment of special advocates.

The Victorian model differs in a fundamental respect from the regime in Queensland in that the special advocate is appointed to represent the interests of the affected party, not simply to test the appropriateness and validity of the application. Furthermore, in both applications for determining whether information is criminal intelligence and substantive applications for control orders, the court is required to be closed, *unless the court otherwise provides*.[36] This discretion to order an open (or partially open) hearing is not narrowly confined – the court may exercise it whenever 'it considers it appropriate to do so'.[37] Section 79 of the Criminal Organisations Control Act 2012 (Vic), which provides for special counsel in an application for classification of material as criminal intelligence, states that the court may appoint a special counsel 'to represent the interests of the respondent to the substantive application in relation to which the protection application was made at the hearing of the protection application'. Special counsel is given permission under the provision to communicate with the respondent or the respondent's representative for the purpose of obtaining information necessary for the special counsel to represent the interests of the respondent, but may not provide the respondent with the information or any information that would compromise its confidentiality.

The Victorian provisions reflect the European standard for compatibility with art. 6 of the European Convention on Human Rights.[38] That article guarantees the right to a 'fair hearing', and judicial interpretation makes clear that special advocates, appointed to represent the non-government respondent in security-sensitive situations, must be able to communicate robustly with the respondent and the respondent's legal representatives.[39] In *Home Secretary v AF (No. 3)*,[40] the House of Lords concluded that non-disclosure obligations on special advocates must not go so far as to preclude the respondent being made aware of the 'essence of the case against him, at least where he is at risk of consequences as severe as those normally imposed under a control order'.[41] While the Victorian law does not go so far as to permit the advocate to disclose the 'essence of the case' expressly (whether in a protection application or a substantive application), it goes some way to vitiating the procedural unfairness inherent in the criminal intelligence scheme by allowing the special advocate to seek further information from the respondent.

Commonwealth

At the Commonwealth level, the focus moves from the protection of criminal intelligence in the pursuit of organised crime, to terrorism. This is outside the immediate scope of this chapter, but it is informative in terms of providing for an alternative, comparator regime addressing state-secrecy issues in judicial proceedings, and also in regard to the directive it contains to the judiciary in the balancing process.

A detailed regime with respect to maintaining the confidentiality of information that poses a threat to national security in civil and criminal proceedings is provided for in the National Security Information (Criminal and Civil Proceedings) Act 2004 (Cth.). The scheme is invoked only when the Attorney-General considers that information or the evidence of a witness is likely to prejudice national security. At that point, the Attorney-General may issue a certificate describing the information and ordering that the parties must not, except in permitted circumstances, disclose the information. An Attorney-General's certificate will trigger a court hearing at which the court may confirm or vary the Attorney-General's orders.

If the court confirms that information must not be disclosed, the information is still admissible if, apart from the order, it is admissible. In determining the order to be made, the court is directed to the interests it must consider and how it must balance those interests when there is conflict:

(a) whether, having regard to the Attorney-General's certificate, there would be a risk of prejudice to national security if:

    (i) where the certificate was given under subsection 26(2) or (3) – the information were disclosed in contravention of the certificate; or
    (ii) where the certificate was given under subsection 28(2) – the witness were called;

(b) whether any such order would have a substantial adverse effect on the defendant's right to receive a fair hearing, including in particular on the conduct of his or her defence;
(c) any other matter the court considers relevant.

Unlike the state regimes, the Commonwealth legislation directs the court to give paragraph (a) the 'greatest weight'.[42] This has been interpreted judicially as a balancing direction to give national security comparatively 'greater weight' than the considerations in either paragraphs (b) or (c), rather than as a direction to treat national security as of paramount and overriding concern.[43]

A disclosure hearing must be closed and if, in the court's opinion, the information may be disclosed to the defendant or the defendant's legal representatives who do not hold security clearance at the level considered appropriate in relation to the information concerned, the court can order that the disclosure hearing take place in their absence.[44] Despite this exclusion, a defendant maintains a right to be heard on the question of non-disclosure.[45] This may be in the absence of hearing the case for non-disclosure if he or she and his or her legal representatives have been excluded from the hearing. There is no express provision for an appointed special advocate to attend a closed hearing in the event that the defendant and his or her legal representatives are excluded. However, in first instance proceedings involving the Act, Whealy J concluded that such an advocate may be appointed to represent the interests of the defendant, consistent with the legislative secrecy scheme.[46] His Honour accepted that the preponderance of authority 'demonstrate[d] . . . that a statutory basis is not required for the appointment of special counsel'.[47] In 2013, the Council of Australian Governments *Review of Counter-Terrorism Legislation* recommended the introduction of a national system of special advocates,[48] together with a form of 'gisting', where the respondent must be provided with a sufficient amount of information to ensure that effective instructions can be provided.[49]

In addition to this general scheme, the Commonwealth's anti-terrorism control order provisions provide for the non-disclosure of material to the respondent of information likely: to prejudice national security; to be protected by public interest immunity; to put at risk ongoing operations by law enforcement agencies or intelligence agencies; or to put at risk the safety of the community, law enforcement officers or intelligence officers.[50] There is no separate hearing to determine the validity of the national security claims, nor a regime for the appointment of special advocates in the event that such non-disclosure occurs.

Summary

This brief survey of provisions protecting state secrecy in curial processes demonstrates that, in Australia, there are a number of different legislative approaches to balancing the public interest in protection of secrecy against incursions on the right to a fair trial for the party seeking the information. Under each of the regimes, the courts must be the ultimate assessors of whether material is properly classified as secret, although in some regimes there is no mandated procedure for this to occur. The regimes provide for different levels of respondent input into the court's decision-making process both in terms of determining whether material is properly classified and in its use in a substantive application. In the Commonwealth regime, in determining whether material should be disclosed, the courts are directed to give greater weight to potential prejudice to national security than to the individual's right to a fair trial.

Public interest immunity compared

The advent of criminal intelligence provisions marks a distinct break from traditional public interest immunity claims made by the state to protect police operations and operatives and national security.[51] As Gummow, Hayne, Heydon and Kiefel JJ observed in *Gypsy Jokers* of a Western Australian criminal intelligence provision: '[T]he operation of this legislative regime has an outcome comparable with that of the common law respecting public interest immunity, but with the difference that the Court itself may make use of the information in question'.[52]

The significance of this difference remained unexplored in the remainder of the majority's reasons. Crennan J, with whom Gleeson CJ agreed on this point, explained that, in her view, this difference was irrelevant to the question of incursions into procedural fairness:

> The statutory modification of procedural fairness achieved by s 76(2) (including any effect on the giving of reasons) is indistinguishable from the modification of procedural fairness which can arise from the application of the principles of public interest immunity.[53]

As the High Court stresses in the more recent decision of *Pompano*, the key difference between the two (and that alluded to by the joint judgment in *Gypsy Jokers* – except its significance was glossed over) is the consequences. Under public interest immunity, the state may resist the production of documents; under criminal intelligence provisions, the state seeks to use the information against the other party.[54] Crennan J overlooks the importance of this difference in determining the allowable modifications of procedural fairness under the two regimes.

In *Pompano*, French CJ emphasises this distinction between traditional balancing of interests as achieved by public interest immunity and that in criminal intelligence provisions. However, in terms of procedural fairness, he argues that there is an important analogy. French CJ argued that the provisions in the Queensland control order legislation that require a hearing to be conducted to determine whether information is criminal intelligence closed to the other side is analogous to the inherent powers of the court to inspect privately any documents that are the subject of a claim for public interest immunity.[55] He explained the similarities by reference to the power of the court to determine the question of immunity:

> The party resisting production will know what is in the documents. The party calling for them will not. The court will decide. Sometimes, but not always, the court will decide, with the assistance of the legal representative of the party calling for production, subject to directions or undertakings as to non-disclosure.[56]

This analogy is relied upon in part by French CJ to uphold the validity of the Queensland regime despite its incursions into normal procedural fairness protections.[57]

The court's continued use of the immunity as an analogy and justification of incursions into procedural rights is inherently flawed and makes it necessary to emphasise, again, the differences between public interest immunity and these criminal intelligence provisions. These differences have an impact on the procedural fairness that must be accorded to the respondent under the different regimes. It is well established that the content of procedural fairness is determined partly by reference to the consequences that flow from a decision.[58] The repercussions of a finding of justified state secrecy are fundamentally different in the two cases. The outcome of how the information is used means that the original analogy drawn in *Gypsy Jokers*, but somewhat retreated from in *Pompano*, is flawed. It also means that French CJ's analogy is flawed. Granted, hearings in which public interest immunity claims are tested may be examples of where the court must make a decision, in a closed setting, as to whether material would prejudice the public interest if disclosed. But the repercussions of such a decision are remarkably less serious. The repercussions of a successful claim for public interest immunity are simply that a government party can resist production, as opposed to when a government party can rely upon secret information in a proceeding where an individual's livelihood or liberty is at stake. The fairness that must be accorded to the individual in this considerably higher-stake process must be more extensive.

Procedural fairness as a defining characteristic of an Australian court

Case law elaborating the content of procedural fairness predominantly relates to administrative decision-making. The modern preference for the term 'procedural fairness' over 'natural justice' was adopted by Mason J in *Kioa v West*[59] as arising from the close association of natural justice with curial processes, and as not always appropriate for application to administrative decision-making. Mason J deliberately separated the two:

> The developing application of the doctrine of natural justice in the field of administrative decision-making has been very largely achieved by reference to the presence of characteristics which have been thought to reflect important characteristics of judicial decision-making. . . . The emphasis given . . . to the presence and absence of these characteristics diverted attention from the need to insist on the adoption in the administrative process of fair and flexible procedures for decision-making, procedures which do not necessarily take curial procedures as their model. . . . In this respect the expression 'procedural fairness' more aptly conveys the notion of a flexible obligation to adopt fair procedures which are appropriate and adapted to the circumstances of the particular case.[60]

The High Court seems now to have adopted the administrative law nomenclature in the *Kable* analysis of whether legislation impairs the 'essential characteristics' of a state Supreme Court.

The adoption of 'procedural fairness' as the appropriate test to ascertain whether proceedings before a Ch. III court contravene the *Kable* principle may be explained by the continued insistence of the High Court that the principle must still accord the states 'procedural and institutional flexibility' to repose powers in their courts outside the ordinary judicial function.[61] In French CJ's judgment in *K-Generation*, his Honour noted the 'institutional and procedural flexibility' granted to the state parliaments.[62] The argument, then, can be put that procedural fairness, rather than curial natural justice, is the appropriate test of repugnancy under *Kable* because the separation of powers does not apply at state level. On this line of reasoning, it would be to apply (wrongly) the separation of powers doctrine to the states to require that state courts exercise natural justice, strictly construed; instead, the *Kable* doctrine of repugnancy could only ensure that courts are held to a 'duty to act fairly', flexibly understood.[63]

This would distinguish the essential characteristics of state courts from those of federal courts, a distinction compatible with the orthodoxy that the *Boilermakers'* doctrine is a stricter protection of judicial independence and impartiality than the *Kable* doctrine. It is also congruent with earlier statements as to the federal requirements. Dicta by Mason CJ, Dawson and McHugh JJ in *Leeth v Commonwealth* suggests that the touchstone for federal courts is natural justice: 'It may well be that any attempt on the part of the legislature to cause a court to act in a manner contrary to natural justice would impose a non-judicial requirement inconsistent with the exercise of judicial power'.[64]

Gaudron J's oft-quoted early statement in *Nicholas v The Queen*[65] – that a statute compelling a federal court to follow procedures contrary to the normal judicial process would be unconstitutional – invoked neither natural justice nor procedural fairness directly. It was, however, prescriptive:

> In my view, consistency with the essential character of a court and with the nature of judicial power necessitates that a court not be required or authorised to proceed in a manner that does not ensure equality before the law, impartiality and the appearance of impartiality, *the right of a party to meet the case made against him or her*, the independent determination of the matter in controversy by application of the law to facts determined in accordance with rules and procedures which truly permit the facts to be ascertained and, in the case of criminal proceedings, the determination of guilt or innocence by means of a fair trial according to law.[66]

This was also the case in *Bass v Permanent Trustee Co Ltd*,[67] where Gleeson CJ, Gaudron, McHugh, Gummow, Hayne and Callinan JJ observed judicial power as involving the application of relevant law to facts as found in proceedings conducted in accordance with judicial process, which requires 'that the parties be given an opportunity to present their evidence and to challenge the evidence led against them'.[68]

However, the early judicial attempts to demarcate the limits applicable to federal courts as opposed to those applicable to state courts have largely fallen away. This is attributable to the focus of the High Court on the minimum constitutional requirements of a 'court', a requirement common to federal and state institutions. Certainly, the more recent *Kable* cases considering the defining characteristics of state courts have readily drawn on the statements, set out above, that relate to judicial process in federal courts, without drawing a distinction between the requirements of natural justice and the requirements to accord procedural fairness. In *International Finance Trust Co v New South Wales Crime Commission*, French CJ stated, after considering the federal cases:

> Procedural fairness *or natural justice* lies at the heart of the judicial function. . . . It requires that a court be and appear to be impartial, and provide each party to proceedings before it with an opportunity to be heard, to advance its own case and to answer, by evidence and argument, the case put against it. According to the circumstances, the content of the requirements of procedural fairness may vary.[69]

Gageler J stated that 'procedural fairness' is 'an immutable characteristic of a Supreme Court *and of every other court in Australia*'.[70]

Through its *Kable* and *Boilermakers'* principles, the High Court has constitutionalised the requirements of procedural fairness as an essential incident of the judicial function. It is therefore an essential characteristic that must be exhibited by both state and federal courts. By adopting the concept of procedural fairness, the High Court is signalling that what is required is not rigid application of predetermined rules of process, but a 'notion of a flexible obligation to adopt fair procedures which are appropriate and adapted to the circumstances of the particular case'.[71] This flexibility was first required when the curial notions of fairness and justice were transposed into administrative decision-making. Its return to the judicial context undermines the protection offered by the stricter rules of natural justice as previously understood to apply in judicial proceedings.

In relation to administrative decision-making, the High Court explained the process of giving content to procedural fairness in any given case in the seminal decision of *Kioa*.[72] In that case, the appellants argued that they had not been accorded procedural fairness when the minister cancelled their visas. Brennan J's judgment is particularly instructive with respect to determining the content of procedural fairness (referred to by him as 'natural justice'). He states: 'The principles of natural justice have a flexible quality which, chameleon-like, evokes a different response from the repository of a statutory power according to the circumstances in which the repository is to exercise the power'.[73]

Brennan J quotes from the seminal judgment of Tucker LJ in *Russell v Duke of Norfolk*:

> The requirements of natural justice must depend on the circumstances of the case, the nature of the inquiry, the rules under which the tribunal is acting, the subject-matter that is being dealt with, and so forth. Accordingly, I do not derive much assistance from the definitions of natural justice which have been from time to time used, but, whatever standard is adopted, one essential is that the person concerned should have a reasonable opportunity of presenting his case.[74]

Brennan J goes so far as to accept that the requirements of procedural fairness may in effect recede to nothingness (that is, have no content) if the circumstances require it. Performing some deft mental twists, he distinguishes the concept of no procedural fairness being according in these circumstances, and the idea that procedural fairness is attracted but its content is reduced to 'nothingness':

> It must therefore be accepted, as one commentator points out that 'the contents of natural justice range from a full-blown trial into nothingness'.[75] Yet Tucker LJ said in *Russell v. Duke of Norfolk*, that there is an irreducible minimum required by the principles of natural justice, namely, that 'the person concerned should have a reasonable opportunity of presenting his case'. If his Lordship's view be right, it would be necessary to hold that if, in some circumstances, perhaps unusual circumstances, a power may need to be exercised peremptorily, no exercise of that power is conditioned on observance of the principles of natural justice. But it would be wrong to attribute to a legislature such an intention. Rather, the intention to be implied when the statute is silent is that observance of the principles of natural justice conditions the exercise of the power although in some circumstances the content of those principles may be diminished (even to nothingness) to avoid frustrating the purpose for which the power was conferred. Accepting that the content of

> the principles of natural justice can be reduced to nothingness by the circumstances in which a power is exercised, a presumption that observance of those principles conditions the exercise of the power is not necessarily excluded at least where, in the generality of cases in which the power is to be exercised, those principles would have a substantial content.[76]

Brennan J's position in *Kioa* can be further understood by examining the Full Federal Court decision in *Leghaei v Director-General of Security*.[77] This case concerned the issue of an adverse security assessment against Mr Leghaei, which formed the basis for the cancellation of his residency. The facts on which the assessment were based were not released to Mr Leghaei. He argued that he was owed procedural fairness and that such fairness had not been provided.

The court, both at first instance and on appeal, held that a duty to provide procedural fairness did exist, but that in practical terms it amounted to 'nothingness' – at least insofar as giving the appellant a chance to respond to allegations. All it required was that the respondent decision-maker *give genuine consideration to whether information could be disclosed to the respondent for comment*. On the evidence in the case, the decision-maker had done so. The government's argument that there was no procedural fairness required, given the sensitive national security context, was rejected on the basis that the parliament had not evinced a clear intention to override common law fairness. However, the content of that fairness was severely restricted by the national security context of the case. Indeed, it was restricted to such an extent that the outcome for the other side was the same as if it had been abrogated.

The High Court's *Boilermakers'* and *Kable* jurisprudence in the last decade has, like its administrative law jurisprudence, emphasised the flexible nature of the procedural fairness principle, rather than fixating on absolute procedural rules that inform minimum content.[78] How this has manifested in the latest decision of *Pompano*[79] and the dangers of adopting the approach of Brennan J in *Kioa*[80] are discussed below.

Procedural fairness meets state secrecy

The High Court's flexible approach to fairness is readily apparent in the Court's 2013 *Kable* decision, *Pompano*. In *Pompano*, the High Court considered the constitutionality of Queensland's control order legislation, the Criminal Organisation Act 2009 (Qld.), and specifically the procedure for determining whether information was criminal intelligence and the regime established for submitting criminal intelligence in substantive hearings (see the outline of this scheme, discussed above).

French CJ's opening paragraph emphasises the importance of procedural fairness principles:

> Antithetical to [the common law] tradition is the idea of a court, closed to the public, in which only one party, a government party, is present, and in which the judge is required by law to hear evidence and argument which neither the other party nor its legal representatives is allowed to hear.[81]

But French CJ observes that the answer is not 'black and white' when considering criminal intelligence regimes. Rather, he acknowledges:

> The deeply rooted common law tradition of the open court, presided over by an independent judge according procedural fairness to both parties, is adapted to protect the public interest in cases such as those involving national security, commercially sensitive documents and the protection of police informants. Similarly, the constitutional limits do not prevent parliaments from making laws for the protection of the public interest in such areas.[82]

What French CJ proposes then is a constitutional limit in which procedural fairness requirements can be reduced (perhaps to 'nothingness' if Brennan J's position in *Kioa* is adopted, although French CJ does not address this possibility) where it is justified in the achievement of competing public interest concerns. His judgment accepts that what results in these cases is an element of procedural unfairness: 'The greater the degree of procedural unfairness and of curial secrecy which is mandated by a statute, the greater the risk that the statute will impair defining characteristics of the court required to implement that unfairness and secrecy'.[83]

He explains that the defining characteristics of courts 'are not and cannot be absolutes':[84]

> Procedural fairness, manifested in the requirements that the court be and appear to be impartial and that the parties be heard by the court, is defined by practical judgments about its content and application which may vary according to the circumstances. Both the open court principle and the hearing rule may be qualified by public interest considerations such as the protection of sensitive information and the identities of vulnerable witnesses, including informants in criminal matters.[85]

French CJ's approach would thus appear to acknowledge incursions into procedural fairness, and the 'unfairness' that results can still be constitutional, provided they are justified by public interest considerations. This is a break from the position adopted by Brennan J in *Kioa*,[86] where he rejected the position that the rules of natural justice were excluded, explaining that even where their content may be diminished to 'nothingness', procedural fairness is still said to apply.

The judgment of Hayne, Crennan, Kiefel and Bell JJ also rejects the constitutionalised requirements of procedural fairness as 'absolute'.[87] However, they go on to explain their position in a way that accords with the position of Brennan J in *Kioa*, and Gageler J's position in *Pompano*, rather than that of French CJ. They explain that '[t]he rules of procedural fairness do not have immutably fixed content'.[88] This is echoed by Gageler J:

> Ch. III of the Constitution mandates the observance of procedural fairness as an *immutable characteristic* of a Supreme Court and of every other court in

> Australia. Procedural fairness has a variable content *but admits of no exceptions. A court cannot be required by statute to adopt a procedure that is unfair.* A procedure is unfair if it has the capacity to result in the court making an order that finally alters or determines a right or legally protected interest of a person without affording that person a fair opportunity to respond to evidence on which that order might be made.[89]

There is a strong attraction to the definitive statements of constitutional principle in Gageler J's judgment. The distinction and principle that Gageler J attempts to establish, however, is more elusive later in his judgment. He explains:

> Suggestions that there are exceptions to procedural fairness in the common practices of courts are unfounded. The suggested exceptions are more apparent than real.[90]
>
> . . .
>
> Procedural fairness can be provided by different means in different contexts and may well be provided by different means in a single context. The legislative choice as to how procedural fairness is provided extends to how procedural fairness is accommodated, in a particular context, to competing interests.[91]

By employing what is, in effect, some form of balancing test to determine the content of procedural fairness, it is difficult to see whether there is a distinction between the approaches of French CJ and Gageler J. Gageler J may very well be making a point of high principle. In Australia, courts *will always* exercise their power in accordance with procedural fairness. This is a very attractive constitutional proposition and holds great symbolism. It becomes less attractive when it is placed against the background of what Brennan J was prepared to accept in *Kioa*, and the full federal court in *Leghaei*, that while procedural fairness may be accorded, this may amount, for all intents and purposes, to 'nothingness' for the respondent. Indeed, in the case of criminal intelligence proceedings under the Criminal Organisation Act 2009 (Qld.), it appears that Gageler J accepted that procedural fairness may still be accorded in circumstances that have been described in other jurisdictions as 'the stuff of nightmares'.[92]

Such an approach carries with it a real risk that procedural fairness may become an empty facade. As such, Gageler J's position is more damaging to public confidence in the institutional integrity of the judiciary than that taken by French CJ. There is something compelling in the frankness of French CJ's approach. He wrestles with the difficult collision between procedural fairness requirements and state secrecy. It is a dilemma for French CJ that may result in a degree of 'unfairness', even if it is unfairness that might be justified in certain instances where another legitimate public interest consideration requires it. A layperson reviewing the outcome of the court's decision, or a future litigant, would have less difficulty understanding French CJ's struggle and his outcome than comprehending a statement that procedural fairness is an immutable concept but one that could be reduced if the circumstances require it. Where is the fairness in that?

Balancing secrecy and fairness

Now we turn from the different conceptualisations of the collision between state secrecy and curial requirements of procedural fairness to how the judges approached the question of balancing in these formulas. In this respect, French CJ's approach accorded more closely with that of Gageler J, in contradistinction to the joint judgment of Hayne, Crennan, Kiefel and Bell JJ, although there are areas of overlap.

Both approaches accept that there is a balancing involved in the question of determining whether procedural fairness requirements have been impermissibly infringed, or their content impermissibly reduced. That is, the courts must go beyond simply accepting government claims of secrecy on national security grounds, both in process and in substance. Procedurally, courts must do more than simply accept at face value government submissions that national security prevents disclosure. Substantively, even if the government's claim of state secrecy holds up under judicial scrutiny, the court should not immediately conclude that the public interest in continued secrecy trumps natural justice.

The difference in the judgments of interest at this point lies in the 'safeguards' that were considered sufficient to counter-balance intrusions into the ordinary rules of procedural fairness.

Hayne, Crennan, Kiefel and Bell JJ

The joint judgment's focus is on the procedural safeguards contained within the legislative scheme. Thus, for the joint judgment, under the Criminal Organisation Act 2009 (Qld.), two features of the scheme meant that, despite the respondent's incapacity to be present and respond at hearings in which criminal intelligence was being assessed or in substantive applications where it was being used, the court maintained the capacity to act 'impartially and fairly'. The first feature was the provision that expressly permitted the Supreme Court, in exercising its discretion to declare information to be criminal intelligence, to have regard to whether the considerations underpinning secrecy 'outweigh any unfairness to a respondent'.[93] Second, the scheme may have denied the respondent knowledge of how the Commissioner would prove an allegation (that is, the evidence that will be submitted), but it requires the Commissioner to disclose particulars of the allegation.[94] Also relevant is the judges' assumption that, within the scheme at the point of a substantive hearing, the respondent's inability to contest criminal intelligence would be taken into account by the court.[95] This approach is primarily focused on the procedural mechanisms contained within the scheme that counter-balance incursions into fair process, although some of those mechanisms necessarily rely on the discretionary intervention of a trial judge.

French CJ and Gageler J

The second approach relies upon the supervision of the trial judge and the court's inherent jurisdiction to avoid an abuse of process that arises in circumstances of manifest unfairness. This approach is most starkly apparent in Gageler J's judgment, with French CJ adopting an approach that is, in some respects, also similar to the joint judgment. As did the joint judgment, French CJ also assesses the statutory scheme, noting a number of factors that support its validity,[96] including, for example, some of those relied upon by the joint judgment. In addition, French CJ relies upon the maintenance of the Supreme Court's 'discretion to refuse to exercise its power to make a declaration even if satisfied of the matters which enliven the power'.[97]

Under Gageler J's approach, constitutionality is entirely reliant upon the maintenance of the inherent jurisdiction of the Supreme Court to stay a substantive application in a case where practical unfairness becomes manifest.[98] Indeed, Gageler J rejects the argument that the scheme is saved by the existence of counter-balancing features, such as the presence of the Criminal Organisation Public Interest Monitor, or the ability of the Court to determine the weight to be accorded to declared criminal intelligence. Presumably, Gageler J's approach does not require a stay to be issued whenever criminal intelligence is led in a substantive hearing; to do so would be to deny any scope to the legislation's intended operation.

Another failure to explain the nature and mechanics of balancing

Both approaches require the courts, at some stage in the process, to engage in a balancing exercise. In the joint judgment, the focus on the structural features of the scheme requires an exercise of balancing to determine constitutionality: whether the public interest in maintaining confidence justifies the incursions into traditional rules of procedural fairness and whether, in all the circumstances, the scheme nonetheless maintains sufficient judicial impartiality and fairness. Under Gageler J's approach, balancing is also required: by relying on the individual judge's discretion to stay proceedings where unfairness becomes manifest, Gageler J emphasises the role of the individual judge, balancing the competing interests in any given case and determining whether the incursions into fairness are outweighed by the other public interest considerations that would maintain state secrecy. Faith is placed in the judgment of the individual judge in each instance.

But both approaches suffer from a failure by the judges to articulate the nature and mechanics of the balancing test to be undertaken. As an avid observer of the High Court, this failure is nothing new – the High Court has, for decades, struggled with clear and consistent articulation and application of any sort of balancing principle across a number of subject areas. This is most apparent in the area of constitutional rights and limitations, where the court is often required to resolve conflicts between individual rights and liberties and governmental objectives through a balancing exercise. The failure is not limited to Australia. Aileen McHarg has observed of the jurisprudence from the European Court and Commission of Human Rights that it fails 'to develop a coherent set of tests for determining when rights prevail over the public interest and *vice versa*'.[99]

Regardless of which of the High Court justices' approaches is preferred, greater clarity around the nature and mechanics of the balancing test is required. Failure to articulate the process of deliberation required within a balancing test reduces it to a rhetorical device that obscures, rather than clarifies, the judicial reasoning process. With no explicit process associated with 'balancing', the weighing up is unpredictable and indefensible as a step within rational judicial decision-making. Here, the chapter will consider these dangers first in relation to balancing as part of determining the constitutionality of a scheme, before turning to Gageler J's approach, where the balancing is undertaken on a case-by-case basis.

There are a number of indications that the High Court's approach to proportionality analyses in constitutional law draws only on the requirements of 'necessity', as understood in the more developed European proportionality test. The test of necessity follows a test of suitability. The suitability test asks whether the measure is rationally connected with the objective it is designed to meet. The necessity test then asks whether the measure is necessary to meet the objective, in the sense that there is no less restrictive way of achieving it. Under a full European proportionality analysis, the Court would go further, asking whether the objective is a legitimate government objective, and whether the measure has a disproportionate effect on rights in its pursuit of that objective. This is where 'balancing' in the European sense comes in. Robert Alexy explains that the first two analyses of suitability and necessity in fact involve no balancing at all and are factual issues only,[100] whereas the proportionality test requires a normative judgment.[101]

The Australian courts, and particularly the High Court, seem reluctant to engage in the third 'balancing' step. Instead, as in other areas of the High Court's constitutional jurisprudence,[102] it is increasingly common to see the High Court conduct a necessity analysis, even if it is not referred to as such. For example, in *Wainohu v New South Wales*, Gummow, Hayne, Crennan and Bell JJ considered 'what other course was available to the legislature' in determining the constitutionality of the New South Wales control-order legislation.[103] In *International Finance Trust Co v New South Wales Crime Commission*, the majority relied heavily on the lack of a subsequent opportunity for a restraining order made *ex parte* to be challenged by the respondent in determining that the New South Wales civil confiscation of assets scheme was unconstitutional.[104] The judges thus compared the New South Wales scheme to possible alternatives that had a lesser effect on infringing the traditional rules of procedural fairness. In *Pompano*, the judges rejected alternatives to the scheme as feasible, efficient or less burdensome. French CJ considered the alternative options put forward by the applicant to deal with criminal intelligence,[105] and rejected these options as viable alternatives since they each 'involved some prejudice to somebody'.[106] Hayne, Crennan, Kiefel and Bell JJ also rejected an alternative scheme whereby the respondent's lawyers may be provided with details of the criminal intelligence as failing to meet the procedural fairness concerned raised by the original scheme.[107]

The necessity analysis that is evident in these decisions is a more restrained analysis than the European balancing test. It will often operate to over-protect state secrecy. This is so because it accepts *without qualification* that, provided a measure is necessary for achieving a legitimate state objective, its incursions into individual liberties are justified. By adopting a test of necessity, the High Court's approach to date has been to emphasise the need for restraint in assessing the incursions into procedural fairness in the name of state secrecy. It conducts no normative analysis as to whether the gains to the public achieved by state secrecy justify the interference with the right to procedural fairness.

As mentioned, in Gageler J's approach, the balancing is performed by the individual judge on a case-by-case basis. Relying on the individual trial judge's assessment of whether practical injustice has become manifest requires significant guidance if it is to be applied consistently and in a way that achieves fairness. Without guidance, there is a real danger that this will result in the judge, in practice, exercising restraint, not wanting to stay proceedings unless it is absolutely clear to him or her that intervention is required, and exercising deference to the government's claims to secrecy for security objectives.[108] The 'status quo' of the scheme is that the secrecy is justified; intervention requires the vigilance and conscientiousness of the individual judicial officer. To avoid this position, greater clarity as to the balancing process must be provided. Further, and as discussed below, that balancing should favour the protection of procedural fairness, not the status quo, which favours the protection of state secrecy.

As has been argued elsewhere,[109] where there is limited guidance as to the mechanics of a balancing test in the criminal and defence context, there is a potential danger that judges will subconsciously tend to defer to the executive in determining state secrecy claims, which necessarily comes at the cost of the right to fair process. This is explicable by reference to the limited expertise and material available to a judge in assessing the veracity and strength of claims to state secrecy and also the potential consequences of releasing information for national security and police operations. Denise Meyerson argues that judges are:

> not archangels, immune to popular sentiment and fear. They might therefore be subjectively predisposed to underestimate the strength of rights when they come into conflict with governmental goals, especially in areas like preventing crime and protecting national security.[110]

There is also a danger that when judges are asked to engage in the weighing up of competing interests in a closed setting in which they are provided with evidence and submissions by a government party only (or, in the case of the Queensland regime, the submissions of a public interest monitor but not the legal representative of the respondent), the judges can be captured by the institutional imperatives pressed upon them to maintain state secrecy. Rahul Sagar has explained:

> [I]s it prudent to assume that judges will remain disinterested for long once they are drawn into the business of substantively evaluating whether secret information ought to be disclosed to the public? On the contrary, it is likely that vesting such politically significant authority in the courts will make appointments to the relevant benches a point of strong contention. And since the appointed judges will need to keep the grounds for their decisions secret, it will be difficult for the public to ascertain that they have *not* been influenced by partisan or ideological considerations.[111]

The greater weight accorded to state secrecy objectives over individual rights to a fair trial is also explicable by reference to the fact that the protection of procedural fairness is a fundamentally deontological exercise, where the consequences of breach are not readily apparent and can be more easily dismissed if considered unlikely to change the final result. In contrast, the protection of state secrecy is a fundamentally consequential exercise, where the courts can focus on the potentially disastrous consequences of failing to protect national security or police operations for the community.

Conclusion

The current Australian approach to balancing, where procedural fairness requirements come up against imperatives of state secrecy, is restrained and deferential. The criminal intelligence regimes proliferated across Australia create a status quo in which secrecy is granted to criminal intelligence unless the courts exercise a discretion to prevent unfairness to the other side. In this context, even more than in others where competing interests may be on more level playing fields to begin with,[112] there is an imperative for individual rights to procedural fairness to be given greater weight than the interests of state secrecy. If the High Court is serious about the constitutional imperative of maintaining fairness in curial processes, even in the face of claims to state secrecy, it must make explicit the need to accord proper weight fairness in any balancing exercise.

Notes

1 Liora Lazarus, 'The Right to Security' in Rowan Cruft, Matthew Liao and Massimo Renzo (eds.), *The Philosophical Foundations of Human Rights* (Oxford University Press 2015).

2 Adam Smith, *An Inquiry into the Nature and the Causes of the Wealth of Nations* (R. H. Campbell and A. S. Skinner (eds.), first published 1776, Clarendon Press 1976) 687. See also Hobbes' assurance of security in Thomas Hobbes, *Leviathan* (first published 1651, reprint Clarendon Press 2012) ch XII § 9.

3 See, for example, 3 Bl Comm 129.

4 *Kable v DPP (NSW)* (1996) 189 CLR 51 (*Kable*).
5 *R v Kirby; Ex parte Boilermakers' Society of Australia* (1956) 94 CLR 254 (*Boilermakers*).
6 See, for example, *Gypsy Jokers Motorcycle Club Inc v Commissioner of Police* (2008) 234 CLR 532 (*Gypsy Jokers*); K-Generation Pty Ltd v Liquor Licensing Court (2009) 237 CLR 501 (*K-Generation*); *Condon v Pompano* (2013) 228 A Crim R 237 (*Pompano*).
7 *Pompano* (n. 6).
8 Ibid.
9 See further explanation of the history of this 'creep' in Gabrielle Appleby and John Williams, 'The Anti-Terror-Creep: Has South Australia adopted a Culture of Control?' in Andrew Lynch, Nicola McGarrity and George Williams (eds.), *Counter-Terrorism and Beyond: The Culture of Control of Law and Justice after 9/11* (Routledge-Cavendish 2010) 150.
10 See, for example, Prevention of Terrorism Act 2005 (UK), c. 2 and Immigration and Refugee Protection Act 2001 (Can), c. 27. For an overview of the intertwined history, legislative and judicial, of the British and Canadian schemes, see David Jenkins, 'There and Back Again: The Strange Journey of Special Advocates' (2011) 42 *Columbia Human Rights Law Journal*, 279.
11 See, for example, *Tariq v Home Office* [2012] 1 AC 452, which upheld closed proceedings in an employment context under a less stringent test than was applied elsewhere because the liberty of the respondent was not in issue.
12 See, for example, in the UK, *A v United Kingdom* (2009) 49 EHRR 29; *Home Secretary v AF (No 3)* [2010] 2 AC 269 (*AF (No 3)*); and, in Canada, *Charkoui v Canada (Minister for Citizenship and Immigration)* [2007] 1 SCR 350.
13 Barring orders and the general jurisdiction of the licensing authority (ss. 45A, 66A, 69).
14 Grant or revocation of firearms licences or the making of prohibition orders by the Registrar of Firearms – the Commissioner of Police – and subsequent review (ss. 10, 10B, 12, 20, 26B, 26C).
15 Liquor Commissioner's jurisdiction to grant licences or take disciplinary action against licensees (ss. 12, 70A).
16 Licensing authority's jurisdiction to grant licences and approvals and take disciplinary action against licensees (s. 28A).
17 Various provisions to do with firearms possession, production and the removal of fortifications (ss. 21F, 21H, 21J, 66B, 66J, 74BGA).
18 Grant of licences and approvals in relation to the security industry (s. 5B).
19 Police Commissioner's jurisdiction to grant/revoke/vary licences (s. 7).
20 Making of unexplained wealth orders by the court on application by the Crown Solicitor (s. 6).
21 Making of criminal organisation declarations (ss. 5A, 9).
22 Made by the Child Sex Offenders Registration (Miscellaneous) Amendment Act 2013 (SA). Decisions made by the Commissioner under the Act generally (see ss. 4, 5 of the Amending Act).
23 *K-Generation* (n. 6).
24 See, for example, SOCCA, s. 3 (interpretation of 'criminal intelligence').
25 *K-Generation* (n. 6) 531–2 [92]–[99] (French CJ), 542–3 [143]–[149] (Gummow, Hayne, Heydon, Crennan and Kiefel JJ).
26 See, for example, Criminal Organisations Control Act 2012 (WA), pt. 5.
27 Criminal Organisation Act 2009 (Qld.), ss. 62, 70, 78 and pt. 7 div. 2.
28 Ibid. s. 86.
29 *Pompano* (n. 6).
30 Crimes (Criminal Organisations Control) Act 2012 (NSW), pt. 3B.
31 *Pompano* (n. 6) [65].

32 Nor in New South Wales: see, for example, Explosives Act 2003 (NSW) – jurisdiction to grant/revoke licenses and security clearances under the Act (s. 24A); Combat Sports Act 2013 (NSW) – making security determinations in relation to participants in the combat sports industry and taking disciplinary action against them.
33 See, for example, Tattoo Parlours Act 2013 (Qld.).
34 Criminal Organisation Control Act 2012 (ss. 71, 79), providing for appointment of special counsel to represent the interests of the respondent.
35 Introduced by the Major Crime Legislation (Amendment) Act 2009 (Vic.).
36 Criminal Organisations Control Act 2012 (Vic.) ss. 73, 81.
37 Ibid. ss. 73(2), 81(2).
38 *Convention for the Protection of Human Rights and Fundamental Freedoms*, opened for signature 4 November 1950, 213 UNTS 221 (entered into force 3 September 1953) (ECHR). For further discussion of the cases that have articulated these standards, see ch. 4 of this volume.
39 See *A v United Kingdom* (n. 15).
40 AF (No 3) (n. 15).
41 Ibid. [65] (Lord Phillips of Worth Matravers).
42 National Security Information (Criminal and Civil Proceedings) Act 2004 (Cth.), s. 31(7) and (8).
43 *Lodhi v The Queen* (2007) 179 A Crim R 470, 482–3 [33]–[38] (Spigelman CJ); see also *R v Lodhi* (2006) 199 FLR 364, 383 [108] (Whealy J).
44 National Security Information (Criminal and Civil Proceedings) Act 2004 (Cth.), s. 29(3).
45 Ibid. s. 29(4).
46 *R v Lodhi* (2006) 163 A Crim R 475, 483–5 [28]–[42]. In an interlocutory decision on application for appointment of special counsel, Whealy J found it too early to determine whether such an appointment would be necessary (at 485–7 [43]–[48]).
47 Ibid. 485 [39].
48 Council of Australian Governments, *Review of Counter-Terrorism Legislation* (Attorney-General's Department, Commonwealth of Australia 2013) [237].
49 Ibid. [238]. See further discussion in Greg Martin, 'Outlaw Motorcycle Gangs and Secret Evidence: Reflections on the Use of Criminal Intelligence in the Control of Serious Organised Crime in Australia' (2014) 36 *Sydney Law Review* 505.
50 See, for example, Criminal Code Act 1995 (Cth.) s. 104.12A(3).
51 Appleby and Williams (n. 9) 150.
52 *Gypsy Jokers* (n. 6) 559 [36] (Gummow, Hayne, Heydon and Kiefel JJ).
53 Ibid. 596 [183] (Crennan J).
54 See, for example, *Pompano* (n. 6) 282 [148] (Hayne, Crennan, Kiefel Bell JJ).
55 Ibid. 255 [46].
56 Ibid. 264 [74].
57 Ibid. 265 [78].
58 See, for example, *Gribbles Pathology (Vic) Pty Ltd v Cassidy* (2002) 122 FCR 78, 100 [117]; *New South Wales v Canellis* (1994) 181 CLR 309, 330; *Plaintiff M47/2012 v Director-General of Security* (2012) 86 ALJR 1372, 1472 [497].
59 (1985) 159 CLR 550, 583–4 (Mason J) (*Kioa*).
60 Ibid.; see also at 585 (Mason J).
61 *K-Generation* (n. 6) 529–30 [88] (French CJ).
62 Ibid.
63 Mason J uses the 'duty to act fairly' interchangeably with a 'duty to accord procedural fairness' in *Kioa* (n. 62), for instance at 583–5.
64 (1992) 174 CLR 455, 470 (Mason CJ, Dawson and McHugh JJ). See also Gaudron J in *Re Nolan; Ex parte Young* (1991) 172 CLR 460, 496.

65 (1998) 193 CLR 173.
66 Ibid. 208–9 (emphasis added).
67 (1999) 198 CLR 334.
68 Ibid. 359 [56].
69 (2009) 240 CLR 319, 354 [54] (emphasis added) (*International Finance Trust*).
70 *Pompano* (n. 6) 289 [177] (emphasis added).
71 Mason J in *Kioa* (n. 62).
72 Ibid.
73 Ibid 612 [15].
74 (1949) 1 All ER 109, 118 (Tucker LJ) referred to in *Kioa* (n. 62) 612. Brennan J also endorses the position taken in *Mobil Oil Australia Pty Ltd v Federal Commissioner of Taxation* (1963) 113 CLR 475, 504 (Kitto J); and *National Companies and Securities Commission v New Corporation* (1984) 52 ALR 417, 427–8 (Gibbs CJ).
75 G Johnson, 'Natural Justice and Legitimate Expectation in Australia' (1985) 15 *Federal Law Review*, 39, 71.
76 *Kioa* (n. 62) 615–16 [19].
77 (2007) 241 ALR 141 (*Leghaei*).
78 See, for example, outcomes in *Thomas v Mowbray* (2007) 233 CLR 307, and *Gypsy Jokers* (n. 6) and *K-Generation* (n. 6), particularly French CJ at 512 [10]).
79 *Pompano* (n. 6).
80 *Kioa* (n. 62).
81 *Pompano* (n. 6) 242 [1].
82 Ibid. 243 [5].
83 Ibid. 260 [64].
84 Ibid. 262 [68].
85 Ibid.
86 *Kioa* (n. 62).
87 *Pompano* (n. 6) 275 [119].
88 Ibid. 259–60 [62].
89 Ibid. 274–5 [117] (emphasis added).
90 Ibid. 292–3 [192].
91 Ibid 293 [195].
92 *Secretary of State for the Home Department v AF (No. 3)* [2009] UKHL 28 [83] (Lord Hope).
93 *Pompano* (n. 6) 285–6 [162].
94 Ibid. 286 [163].
95 Ibid. 286–7 [166]. In this respect the joint judgment was very similar to the approach taken by the Court in *K-Generation* in determining that the South Australian model of criminal intelligence provisions was constitutional.
96 Ibid. 267–8 [87].
97 Ibid. 267 [87](2).
98 Ibid. 289 [178].
99 Aileen McHarg, 'Reconciling Human Rights and the Public Interest' (1999) 62 *Modern Law Review*, 671, 695.
100 Robert Alexy, *A Theory of Constitutional Rights* (Julian Rivers tr., 2nd edn., Oxford University Press 2002) 397–9.
101 Ibid. 67–8.
102 And specifically s. 92 and implied freedom jurisprudence.
103 *Wainohu v New South Wales* (2011) 243 CLR 181, 229; see also *North Australian Aboriginal Legal Aid Service Inc v Bradley* (2004) 218 CLR 146, 158–9.
104 *International Finance Trust* (n. 67) 366–7 [97] (Gummow and Bell JJ), 385 [154] (Heydon J).
105 *Pompano* (n. 6) 267 [85].
106 Ibid.

107 Ibid. 285 [160]–[161].

108 For a discussion of the difference between restraint and deference, see Julian Rivers, 'Proportionality and Variable Intensity of Review' (2006) 65(1) *Cambridge Law Journal* 174, 203.

109 Denise Meyerson, 'Why Courts Should not Balance Rights against the Public Interest' (2007) 31 *Melbourne University Law Review* 873.

110 Ibid.

111 Rahul Sagar, *Secrets and Leaks: The Dilemma of State Secrecy* (Princeton University Press 2013) 71.

112 Although see Meyerson's argument that this reweighting ought to apply across the board: Meyerson (n. 112).

Chapter 6

Is there a requirement for fair hearings in British and Australian courts?

Steven Churches

Introduction

As in so many areas of the law, Sir Edward Coke set the markers for natural justice as integral in the operation of courts in the early seventeenth century. His report of *Boswell's case*[1] and his decision in *Bagg's case*[2] both quoted the first century CE Roman playwright, Seneca, who had Medea say in the eponymous play: 'He who decides something without hearing the other side is not just, even if he makes a just decision'.[3] But the general principles enunciated in the early seventeenth century would be tried in the fire of a very different modern world in which sovereign parliaments exercised a relentless intervention affecting common law values.

The position in the second half of the twentieth century on open fair hearing in courts

Britain

Lord Goddard CJ was very clear in the post-World War II period as to the necessity of natural justice in courts, admonishing the magistrates at Bodmin for taking evidence from a witness in chambers in the absence of the other party: 'Time and again this court has said that justice must not only be done but must manifestly be seen to be done. If justices interview a witness in the absence of the accused, justice is not seen to be done, because the accused does not and cannot know what was said'.[4]

Despite this simplicity, cases concerning child welfare impelled the English courts to place the concept of 'justice' ahead of the necessity for natural justice, and the arguments for administrative bodies having a more relaxed regime in the provision of fair hearings[5] were extended to courts performing family law functions.

Upjohn LJ's leading judgment in *Re K (Infants)*,[6] assuming that procedural fairness was a *sine qua non* for judicial proceedings, was unanimously overturned on appeal.[7] In the context of the ancient Chancery jurisdiction over the welfare of children, described as partially administrative, Lord Evershed (Lord Reid agreeing) relied on the fluctuating parameters theory advanced for tribunals and administrative bodies by Tucker LJ in *Russell v Duke of Norfolk*[8] to permit a decision-maker to deny basic procedural fairness to a party whose interests were at stake in the proceedings.[9] The theory was advanced that procedure was merely the handmaiden of justice and, as such, should not impede the achievement of justice.[10]

The claims for an absolute requirement of open fair hearing in the procedure of courts was thus undercut by *K's case*, but for the best possible motive: the welfare of children. And *K's case* went off on the capacity of courts to determine, entirely at their own discretion, the rare occasions on which a supervening principle, such as child welfare, should displace the assumption of natural justice in all court proceedings.

The temptations involved in judicial discretion appeared in 1977, and provided another illustration of a weighing up of competing interests that did not see natural justice as the necessary *sine qua non* of judicial proceedings. A brush with the problem of protecting the identity of 'informers' in *D v National Society for the Prevention of Cruelty to Children*[11] took the law lords down the path of discretionary undermining of natural justice, and did so by analogy with public interest immunity (PII) – a false analogy as PII involves a judicial determination that certain material should not be admitted into evidence, and so is not to be part of the judicial decision-making process.

To the close of the twentieth century: Australia

Australian jurisprudence paralleled the British experience, with earlier twentieth-century cases making clear that natural justice was required procedure in superior courts: see *Cameron v Cole*[12] and *Commissioner of Police v Tanos*,[13] both dealing specifically with superior court judges bearing powers under statute. The former case concerned the byzantine world of bankruptcy proceedings, while the latter provided a touching tale of petticoat government as a wife cleaned up the illegal liquor practices of her husband in the restaurant they jointly owned. Dixon CJ and Webb J[14] quoted *Medea*[15] (with citation), and observed the fundamental role of natural justice in the work of a court, but then noted that parliaments had the capacity to dismantle the requirements of procedural fairness. This capacity was stated in general terms, but the question of whether an Australian Parliament could dispel natural justice from the working of a court under Ch. III of the Australian *Commonwealth of Australia Constitution Act* was a question that would only arise for adjudication nearly a half century later.[16]

In 1986, a case emerged that raised the issue of natural justice in a superior court, concerning both the open fair hearing arm and the rule against bias: *Re RJL; Ex parte CRL*.[17] The facts of this case are remarkable and deserve attention, noting also that the High Court split 3:2.

In the course of proceedings in the Family Court of Australia, a court counsellor attended on the judge hearing a matter in private chambers during the luncheon adjournment. After conversation between them, the judge called counsel for the parties to her chambers. It then became known that the counsellor was a clinical psychologist, that she favoured the wife's position, and that she had discussed the conduct of the proceedings with the judge. When the hearing resumed, counsel for the husband applied to the judge to disqualify herself. The judge refused. The husband then sought relief in the High Court to restrain the judge from proceeding in the matter. This was a replay of the Bodmin justices interviewing a witness in private.[18] The majority of the court found for the husband, Mason J (in the majority) saying: 'It would be inconsistent with basic notions of fairness that a judge should take into account, or even receive, secret or private representations on behalf of a party or from a stranger with reference to a case which he has to decide'.[19]

Dawson J, in dissent, relied on the special jurisdiction of the family court as prescribed by statute, being primarily concerned with the welfare of children. Accordingly, he rested on the authority of the House of Lords in *K's case*.[20] The case law in Australia from that point, at least at High-Court level, emerges in the context of arguments that legislation (usually state in origin) has improperly impinged on the independent operation of Ch. III courts (usually state courts) and has thus infringed the principle in *Kable v DPP (NSW)*,[21] allowing for a determination that is constitutionally defective. Thus in *Kable* itself, McHugh J said in dicta: 'N[o] Parliament, for example, can legislate in a way that permits [a State] Supreme Court while exercising federal judicial power to disregard the rules of natural justice'.[22]

Little did McHugh J know what another generation of High Court judges could do to that assumption,[23] but his assertion had been anticipated by a joint judgment with Mason CJ and Dawson J in *Leeth v Commonwealth*, which stated:

> It may well be that any attempt on the part of the legislature to cause a court to act in a manner contrary to natural justice would impose a non-judicial requirement inconsistent with the exercise of judicial power, but the rules of natural justice are essentially functional or procedural and, as the Privy Council observed in the *Boilermakers' Case* [*Attorney-General of the Commonwealth of Australia v The Queen*],[24] a fundamental principle that lies behind the concept of natural justice is not remote from the principle that inspires the theory of separation of powers.[25]

Gaudron J provided powerful dicta on the subject of an open fair hearing in courts in *Nicholas v The Queen*:

> In my view, consistency with the essential character of a court . . . necessitates that a court not be required or authorised to proceed in a manner that does not ensure equality before the law, impartiality and the appearance of impartiality, the right of a party to meet the case made against him or her, the independent determination of the matter in controversy by application of the law to facts determined in accordance with rules and procedures which truly permit the facts to be ascertained and, in the case of criminal proceedings, the determination of guilt or innocence by means of a fair trial according to law.[26]

The following year, six members of the High Court said that the judicial process 'requires that the parties be given an opportunity to present their evidence and to challenge the evidence led against them'.[27] Note that these late-twentieth-century High Court assertions were not uttered in anodyne terms that might be shaded at a later date. They were clear that affected parties in judicial proceedings had the right to know the case against them, and meeting that case involved them being able to put on their own evidence and challenge that advanced against them. Note also that these observations came in the context of the special place of Ch. III courts in the Australian constitutional pantheon: such courts were marked by the fact that they, unlike administrative bodies that might be statutorily empowered to act without procedural fairness, were constitutionally bound to act in accordance with natural justice, and that involved, *inter alia, audi alteram partem* (hear the other side).

The position in the twenty-first century on open fair hearing in courts

Britain

The new century opened with natural justice under sustained attack throughout the common law world. Concern for the security of operational evidence and the witnesses that could testify to it motivated both judges and legislators, and this concern was sharpened by the century's new war, that on terror, in the wake of 9/11. The anti-terror statutes that emerged after the events in September 2001 accentuated assumptions that had been lurking as to appropriate processes for dealing with standard issue criminal law problems, such as the protection of prosecution witnesses from interference by defendants. However, in the United Kingdom, the Human Rights Act 1998 had come into force in 2000, bringing into play art. 6 of the European Convention on Human Rights (ECHR).[28] Relevantly, art. 6(3) provides:

> 3. Everyone charged with a criminal offence has the following minimum rights:
>
> . . .
>
> (d) to examine or have examined witnesses against him and to obtain the attendance and examination of witnesses on his behalf under the same conditions as witnesses against him;

These assumptions led politicians in common law legislatures to move with speed into areas of curial conduct that had always been assumed to be sacrosanct from legislative intrusion and capable of variation only by courts themselves; the open fair hearing rule was just such a matter that now faced being swept away by legislative fiat. But at the same time, the courts themselves had taken to shielding witnesses with protective orders, cloaking them in anonymity, in the interests of witness protection and attempting to obtain evidence untainted by the threat of violence.

Cases of courts exercising a 'self-denying ordinance' where natural justice would not be available

R v Davis[29] involved an appeal against the ruling of a trial judge who had ordered the suppression of witness identities in the interest of witness protection in a very serious homicide trial. The appellant argued that this made for a fundamentally unfair trial, offensive both to common law precepts, and to art. 6 of the ECHR.

The House of Lords was unanimous that the trial process had resulted in unfairness that led to injustice, and upheld the appeal. Lord Bingham delivered a speech detailing the case law throughout the common law world, including in the United States, on this matter, noting that appeal courts in the Australian states of Queensland and Victoria had differed by degrees as to what constituted fairness.[30] Where particular evidence was crucial to the result, the discretion in the court to weigh up competing interests had to be exercised in favour of the accused, who must be entitled to confront the accusing witness. Lord Bingham observed that policy considerations to the contrary had inspired both the Spanish Inquisition and the Court of Star Chamber, and noted the passing of the latter.[31] This speech is a primer on the issues involved in natural justice, and the extent to which its precepts are flexible in court procedure. Lord Bingham was clear that, in a criminal law context, ECHR art. 6 went hand in hand with the common law requirements of natural justice, a thread in all the speeches in *Davis*.

Lord Mance turned to proceedings in the International Criminal Tribunal for the former Yugoslavia (ICTY) to illustrate the primal importance of open fair hearing. The ICTY had conducted what amounted to a *voir dire* in the matter of *Tadic*[32] as to whether witnesses to a murder prosecution should remain anonymised (for their protection). In a three-judge bench, Judge Sir Ninian Stephen alone opined that there had to be proper confrontation with key witnesses. When the trial proper in *Tadic* was underway, fresh evidence made clear how dangerous it was to allow proceedings to progress using anonymised witnesses. Lord Mance said:

> Judge Stephen's dissent received retrospective support, when during the trial in *Tadic* the identity of one of the anonymous witnesses was eventually discovered by the defence. The witness had asserted that he had seen Mr Tadic execute 30 males including the witness's own father. After managing to identify the witness, the defence were able to produce his father, still alive, and only then did the witness admit that he had been trained by Bosnian Government authorities to give his evidence against Mr Tadic.[33]

Judge Stephen relied, *inter alia*, on the appeal division decision in *Jarvie*,[34] which had allowed a trial to proceed with witnesses retaining the false names they had adopted as undercover police informants; this was said to be a very different matter from failing to allow the defence to cross-examine at all.

The care for securing the evidence of the 'authorities' was revealed a few months prior to 9/11 in *Carnduff v Rock*,[35] in which a majority of the Court of Appeal thought proceedings taken by a police informer under an alleged contract to supply information should be struck out. This approach at least protected the operational evidence without it being relied on in a one-sided manner by the bench. The plaintiff was merely non-suited, as, in the words of Jonathan Parker LJ in the majority:

> In my judgment, [counsel for the police] was right to recognise an overriding public interest in not requiring the police to disclose information or material for the purposes of a civil trial where such disclosure would be contrary to the public interest. It seems to me to follow that if a fair trial of the issues in the case would necessarily involve the disclosure by the authorities of information or material which is sensitive or confidential and the disclosure of which is not in the public interest, and if that in turn means that it would be contrary to the public interest that the trial should take place, then the case should not be allowed to proceed. As soon as it becomes apparent that that is the position, then in my judgment it is open to the court, in the exercise of its inherent jurisdiction, to strike the action out.[36]

R (Roberts) v Parole Board[37] involved a determination by the parole board to withhold the identity of witnesses who had given information used to deny parole to the appellant. The House of Lords determined 3:2 that the rules promulgated under the relevant statute allowed for graded natural justice and that included a trade-off between the interests of the prisoner and the public interest (the appellant had been convicted for the murder of three police officers, and sentenced to a minimum of 30 years imprisonment). But Lords Bingham and Steyn were in the minority, and Lord Steyn observed:

> [A] prisoner against whom unfounded allegations have been made is in a Kafkaesque situation. [The] reference [is] to *The Trial* (1925), the masterpiece of Franz Kafka. A passage in *The Trial* has a striking resonance for the present case. Joseph K was informed '. . . the legal records of the case, and above all the actual charge-sheets, were inaccessible to the accused and his counsel, consequently one did not know in general, or at least did not know with any precision, what charges to meet in the first plea; accordingly it could be only by pure chance that it contained really relevant matter. . . . In such circumstances the Defence was naturally in a very ticklish and difficult position. Yet that, too, was intentional. For the Defence was not actually countenanced by the Law, but only tolerated, and there were differences of opinion even on that point, whether the Law could be interpreted to admit such tolerance at all. Strictly speaking, therefore, none of the Advocates was recognized by

the Court, all who appeared before the Court as Advocates being in reality merely in the position of hole-and-corner Advocates'.[38]

This was not the last occasion on which Kafka and *The Trial* would be advanced; there is an unnerving sense that the work of the paranoid Czech in writing *The Trial* in the first year of World War I had deep insight into the likely ends of the bureaucratic process. Lord Bingham's concern to maintain the impartiality of British courts shows in his reasoning in *Brown v Stott*,[39] in which he pursued the 'equality of arms' principle, in accordance with which the parties in court should be armed equally and the judge should be equidistant from them. If one party (an arm of government) is to introduce evidence into a court on a secrecy basis so that the judge sees the material but the affected party does not, equality of arms is immediately destroyed. His Lordship raised this metaphor by reference to decisions of the European Court of Human Rights on art. 6 of the ECHR, adopted in the UK from 2000 pursuant to the Human Rights Act 1998 (UK).

The impact in Britain of legislatively prescribed closed material procedures

Control orders were made pursuant to post-9/11 statutes that provided for the Home Secretary to order the incarceration of an individual, or other restraint such as effective house arrest – considerable inroads into personal liberty. Furthermore, such orders were made on the basis that crucial evidence leading the Home Secretary to such a decision might be withheld from the affected party in the public interest (that is, in the interest of national security), but that the affected party's position would be secured by a special advocate, who would, however, not be allowed to discuss with his client what was alleged against him.

The House of Lords sat a bench of nine in *Home Secretary v AF (No 3)*,[40] and the history of control orders and the path of A's litigation is set out in the speech of Lord Phillips of Worth Matravers, presiding. The decision in June 2009 had been preceded by the ruling of the Grand Chamber of the European Court of Human Rights in *A v United Kingdom*[41] in February 2009, which determined that the statutory process provided for obtaining a control order at the behest of the Home Secretary, when contested curially, was unfair and in breach of art. 6 of the ECHR.

The House of Lords felt obliged to follow the ruling of the European Court (the most grudging assent coming from Lord Hoffmann, who only ruled in favour of A because he felt obliged by the February ruling).[42] Suffice to say, the House of Lords required that if special advocates were to be employed pursuant to 'closed material procedures' (CMPs), they must be empowered at least to reveal to their clients what the 'gist' of the accusation was against them, so that the affected party would be in a position to give the special advocate material that might rebut the government evidence. To that extent, CMPs were made potentially fairer, although later cases would have to reflect on the situation in which governmental materials were so sensitive that not even a gist with any real utility could be released to the affected party. Lord Hope of Craighead summed up the ruling in *AF (No. 3)* as follows:

> The principle that the accused has a right to know what is being alleged against him has a long pedigree. As Lord Scott of Foscote observed in *A v Secretary of State for the Home Department* [2005] 2 AC 68, para 155, a denunciation on grounds that are not disclosed is the stuff of nightmares. The rule of law in a democratic society does not tolerate such behaviour. The fundamental principle is that everyone is entitled to the disclosure of sufficient material to enable him to answer effectively the case that is made against him.[43]

The thinking of the House of Lords on the practical necessity for fairness in a trial, allowing that the gist of the adverse case might be sufficient, coupled with the policy reasons for ensuring an open fair hearing, may be seen in the speech of Lord Phillips:

> There are, however, strong policy considerations that support a rule that a trial procedure can never be considered fair if a party to it is kept in ignorance of the case against him. The first is that there will be many cases where it is impossible for the court to be confident that disclosure will make no difference. . . . Next there [are] the . . . feelings of resentment that will be aroused if a party to legal proceedings is placed in a position where it is impossible for him to influence the result.[44]

Even more recently, the UK Supreme Court simultaneously decided *Tariq v Home Office*[45] and *Al Rawi v Security Service*.[46] The former case involved an appeal flowing from the removal of the appellant's security clearance, which had resulted in his suspension from work as an immigration officer, a suspension upheld by the employment tribunal. Seven Supreme Court Judges found that a closed hearing in a tribunal did not necessarily offend s. 6 of the Human Rights Act 1998 obligations for natural justice: the common law in respect of court procedure could be, and was, more demanding than the terms of the ECHR. The majority looked to issues of balance between public interest and the needs of an adversely affected litigant. This avoided the thorny issue of what a court was going to do at the point that CMPs blocked any meaningful material coming to the affected party – few judges were comfortable with the idea of generally deploying the *Carnduff v Rock*[47] precedent for courts rendering themselves irrelevant, as incapable of performing their functions in order to avoid inherent unfairness.[48] Lord Kerr of Tonaghmore JSC alone dissented, averring that it was not good enough to balance information passing to the affected party down to nothing:

> Where, as in this case, the challenged decision is the subject of factual inquiry or dispute and the investigation of the disputed facts centres on an individual's actions or, to bring the matter directly to the circumstances of this case, his

> supposed vulnerability, that individual is the critical source of information needed to discover the truth; in many cases he may be the only source. If he is denied information as to the nature of the case made either directly against him or, as seems more likely here, against others whose presumed relationship with the claimant renders it unsuitable for him to retain security clearance and if he is thereby forced to speculate on the content of the defendant's case, no truly adversarial proceedings are possible. As Upjohn LJ put it in *In re K* [1963] Ch 381, the proceedings are not judicial.
>
> [208] The withholding of information from a claimant which is then deployed to defeat his claim is, in my opinion, a breach of his fundamental common law right to a fair trial.[49]

As seen above, Upjohn LJ was overruled in *K's case*,[50] but on the basis that the court in question was performing more than merely a 'curial' function. The Upjohn test for what passes as 'judicial' remained sound. *Al Rawi*,[51] like *Tariq*, a civil case with heavy security overtones, was an appeal (via the Court of Appeal, affirming) from the decision of a High Court judge to accede to the request from the security service for a CMP. This litigation arose from a civil claim brought by British Guantanamo Bay detainees against the British Government. They were greeted with a closed court in which they could not see or hear some of the evidence, withheld on the basis that the security service needed to keep the evidence covert in the interest of national security. A majority of the eight bench[52] determined that a court could not dispense with natural justice of its own volition; whether Parliament could so order was another matter, reflected on in dicta.[53] Only Lord Clarke of Stone-cum-Ebony JSC, dissenting, disallowed the appeal. Lord Hope DPSC said that 'absolutely fundamental principles such as the right to a fair trial, the right to be confronted by one's accusers and the right to know the reasons for the outcome [were concepts in respect of which] . . . [t]he court has for centuries held the line as the guardian'.[54]

It is noteworthy that the litigation in *Al Rawi* culminated in uncertainty as to whether a CMP could be agreed between the parties, and the matter was settled for an undisclosed sum. It was again Lord Kerr JSC who was most trenchant in defence of pure natural justice theory, and with the keenest eye to the heresies that might be employed to undermine it. He observed that one of the Government arguments:

> proceeds on the premise that placing before a judge all relevant material is, in every instance, preferable to having to withhold potentially pivotal evidence. This proposition is deceptively attractive for what, the defendants imply, could be fairer than an independent arbiter having access to all the evidence germane to the dispute between the parties? The central fallacy of the argument, however, lies in the unspoken assumption that, because the judge sees everything, he is bound to be in a better position to reach a fair result. That assumption is misplaced. To be truly valuable, evidence must be capable of withstanding

> challenge. I go further. Evidence which has been insulated from challenge may positively mislead. It is precisely because of this that the right to know the case that one's opponent makes and to have the opportunity to challenge it occupies such a central place in the concept of a fair trial. However astute and assiduous the judge, the proposed procedure hands over to one party considerable control over the production of relevant material and the manner in which it is to be presented. The peril that such a procedure presents to the fair trial of contentious litigation is both obvious and undeniable.[55]

The British position in 2014 reveals sound theory under intense pressure from events. The necessity for open fair hearing is standard rhetoric, particularly for curial procedure, but the demand for secrecy of governmental materials may be met in various ways in court proceedings. A court might declare that since it cannot order the police or security services to produce evidence to the other side, there can be no fair trial, and so dismiss the matter. This self-abnegation approach is not warmly regarded amongst the senior judiciary, but in the light of *Al Rawi* seems to be accepted as a last resort. If there is no statutory demand for the withholding of evidence from the other side, but the governmental body relies on such evidence in court on the basis that the court will withhold it from the affected party, British courts until 2013 had no power to proceed with a trial without, at the very least, providing a gist as prescribed in *AF (No. 3)*.[56] However, under s. 8 of the Justice and Security Act 2013 (UK), 'gisting' is now required to be dealt with in rules of court, and seems to depend on judicial discretion arising from authorisations to courts. Special advocates are now entrenched (under s. 8 of the Act) as a 'solution' to the growth of CMPs, now authorised by the Act for civil matters, despite the special advocates themselves flaying their own utility as a sop to natural justice.[57]

The matter becomes more complicated if statutory provisions provide for governmental materials to be given to the court on a one-sided basis. At that point, the case law highlights the amount of discretionary power vested in common law judges, as they weigh up various factors, particularly whether the proceedings are criminal (attracting the highest need for some form of open fair hearing); the public interest in keeping particular evidence closed, as well as other public interest such as preserving open justice; and the interests of the affected party. But it seems that if the governmental evidence is too sensitive to be allowed into the possession of the affected party even in gist form, and that material is critical to the determination of the matter, it may be that the matter will need to be struck out as incapable of fair curial determination.

The conundrum of natural justice and executive care for confidentiality in the public interest may be seen in the latest case in the line of child welfare litigation, *Re A (A Child) (Disclosure of Third Party Information)*,[58] concerning the question of whether the evidence of a child third party to allegations in a custody struggle should be suppressed, such evidence involving alleged sexual assault. The interest at stake was that of the child third party, alleging sexual assault by the father involved in the custody dispute (she was not a child of the family involved). The Supreme Court (Baroness Hale of Richmond JSC; with Lord Neuberger of

Abbotsbury PSC, Lord Clarke of Stone-cum-Ebony, Lord Wilson and Lord Reed JJSC agreeing) performed the complex weighing up of relevant factors and determined that the child's evidence should be taken in court, unless medical evidence as to her condition was to the contrary, but Baroness Hale's opening line sums up the conflicting claims now afloat in British jurisprudence: 'We are asked in this case to reconcile the irreconcilable'.[59]

The position in the twenty-first century on open fair hearing in courts

Australia

The arrival of *Kable*[60] in 1996 might have quickened the pulse of the proponents of natural justice. They could have anticipated that legislating for courts to behave in manner antithetical to common law standards (as had been the case in *Kable*) would face a considerable constitutional inhibition in the shape of the separation of powers. That separation focused particularly on the preservation of the judiciary from legislative and executive interference with the fundamental structure of Ch. III courts.

The legislative assault on natural justice in courts took off in earnest in the twenty-first century, fuelled by fear of terrorism after the terror attacks of 11 September 2001.[61] Both Commonwealth and state governments passed a considerable amount of anti-terror legislation, and the states compounded the anti-terror search for evidence that could be tendered in secret with a statutory barrage aimed at domestic targets, principally 'criminal bikie gangs'. Wars were declared on such gangs, along with wars on drugs, and Premier Rann of South Australia even declared war on upstream users of Murray-Darling water.

The Queensland Court of Appeal rose to the challenge in *Re Criminal Proceeds Confiscation Act 2002*[62] when it was confronted with anti-bikie gang/anti-drug dealing provisions.[63] These provided for a court to take evidence on the basis that the affected party, facing the expropriation of his or her property, was not to be present (in person or through counsel), and neither was anyone else other than court officers and the prosecution team, and the affected party was not to even know the proceedings were underway. Williams JA, for the court, explained the difference between what the Criminal Proceeds Confiscation Act 2002 (Qld.) proposed and the acceptable process of *ex parte* applications.[64] He then determined that s. 30 of the Act 'clearly abrogated the audi alteram partem rule'.[65]

The Western Australian Corruption and Crime Commission Act 2003 (WA Act) was the focus of the first High Court case in the field in the twenty-first century. In *Gypsy Jokers Motor Cycle Club Inc v Commissioner of Police*[66] the subject of scrutiny was s. 76(2) of the WA Act, providing for review by the Supreme Court of a notice of intent to remove a 'bikie gang's' fortified premises. Subsection 76(2) states:

> The Commissioner of Police may identify any information provided to the court for the purposes of the review as confidential if its disclosure might

> prejudice the operations of the Commissioner of Police, and information so identified is for the court's use only and is not to be disclosed to any other person, whether or not a party to the proceedings, or publicly disclosed in any way.

The joint judgment of Gummow, Hayne, Heydon and Kiefel JJ observed that the sort of material that an affected party might seek by way of subpoena for the review process could be expected to be met by a claim for PII.[67] The joint judgment then noted that the outcome of a successful PII application would be that neither the applicant nor the court could refer to the immunised material. The result was that the decision of the court would be made on less than the entirety of the relevant materials,[68] but the inference was clear: this was not the same thing as allowing evidentiary material to pass to the bench on an *ex parte* basis. The siren call of PII, however, sounded loudly in the decision of Crennan J, who observed that in a claim for PII a court may look at information that is not revealed to the non-supplying party, but then, relying on *Alister v The Queen*,[69] her Honour pronounced that 'a court may resolve a claim finally without one of the parties being shown certain material relied on for determination of a proceeding'.[70]

It needs to be said that, far from *Alister* standing for the destruction of natural justice (as her Honour's summary would have it), at the pages referenced, it was a brief addendum, in which the four justices reflected on further intelligence materials that had come to light since the principal litigation. The material being discussed was not present when the trial was being run, and so in no way was relied upon for the determination of that proceeding. Furthermore, the justices reflected on the generally adverse view of a trial proceeding without all the relevant information being available to the court, but they noted that such perfection was impossible where security information subject to PII was involved. The material referred to was never part of the court's determining process.

The joint judgment in *Gypsy Jokers* was content to find that s. 76(2) of the WA Act did not constitutionally offend on the basis of statutory interpretation (the Supreme Court would not be dictated to by the Commissioner as s. 76(5) provided for the court to be able to review the reasonableness of the Commissioner classifying the information as confidential). However, Crennan J (Gleeson CJ agreeing) persisted with the PII analogy and determined that s. 76(2) was not constitutionally offensive, as: 'The statutory modification of procedural fairness achieved by s 76(2) (including any effect on the giving of reasons) is indistinguishable from the modification of procedural fairness which can arise from the application of the principles of public interest immunity'.[71]

But all Australian States were about to embark on the use of a rubric plainly designed to stifle open fair hearing. The unspoken issues involved whether such suppression was intended to occur in courts, as opposed to in executive tribunals and committees, and whether it would be used in criminal proceedings. The stifling rubric arrived principally in the form of the legislative device of 'criminal intelligence', which phrase became a code for material that the police and other agencies could determine required protection from publication, and which could be led in court for the purpose of being relied on by the bench, on the express basis that the court would preserve the confidentiality of the evidence. Plainly, criminal intelligence as a concept was intended to defy accepted standards of procedural fairness. An early example of the definition and intended operation of 'criminal intelligence' may be seen in the original provisions of the Liquor Licensing Act 1997 (SA), set out below in the form in which they were litigated in *K-Generation v Liquor Licensing Court*:[72]

> **Section 4**
>
> ***criminal intelligence*** means information relating to actual or suspected criminal activity (whether in this State or elsewhere) the disclosure of which could reasonably be expected to prejudice criminal investigations, or to enable the discovery of the existence or identity of a confidential source of information relevant to law enforcement.
>
> . . .
>
> **Sub-s 28A(1)**
>
> No information provided by the Commissioner of Police to the [Liquor] Commissioner may be disclosed to any person (except the Minister, a court or a person to whom the Commissioner of Police authorises its disclosure) if the information is classified by the Commissioner of Police as criminal intelligence.
>
> . . .
>
> **And sub-s 28A(5)**
>
> In any proceedings under this Act, the [Liquor] Commissioner, the Court or the Supreme Court –
>
> (a) must, on the application of the Commissioner of Police, take steps to maintain the confidentiality of information classified by the Commissioner of Police as criminal intelligence, including steps to receive evidence and hear argument about the information in private in the absence of the parties to the proceedings and their representatives; and
> (b) may take evidence consisting of or relating to information classified by the Commissioner of Police as criminal intelligence by way of affidavit of a police officer of or above the rank of superintendent.

K-Generation Pty Ltd and its principal, Genargi Krasnov, applied for a liquor licence. The application was refused by the Licensing Commissioner on the basis of criminal intelligence supplied by the police under the Liquor Licensing Act (LL Act). The Liquor Licensing Court affirmed the decision of the Liquor Licensing Commissioner, and then K-Generation attacked the constitutionality of the 'criminal intelligence' provisions in the South Australian Full Court as *Kable* defective for destruction of the Liquor Court's independence and impartiality. Having lost 2:1 in the full court, K-Generation appealed to the High Court, where it lost unanimously. French CJ provided a fair summary of the reasoning in *K-Generation* when he said of the LL Act that it:

> infringes upon the open justice principle that is an essential part of the functioning of courts in Australia. It also infringes upon procedural fairness to the extent that it authorises and effectively requires the Licensing Court and the Supreme Court to consider, without disclosure to the party to whom it relates, criminal intelligence information submitted to the Court by the Commissioner of Police. However, it cannot be said that the section confers upon the Licensing Court or the Supreme Court functions which are incompatible with their institutional integrity as courts of the States or with their constitutional roles as repositories of federal jurisdiction. Properly construed the section leaves it to the courts to [1] determine whether information classified as criminal intelligence answers that description. It also leaves it to the courts to [2] decide what steps may be necessary to preserve the confidentiality of such material. The courts may, consistently with the section, disclose the material to legal representatives of the party affected on conditions of confidentiality enforced by undertaking or order. It leaves it open to the courts to decide whether to accept or reject such material and to decide what if any weight shall be placed upon it.[73]

French CJ followed up on point 2, saying: 'The better view, which is permitted by the language of the statute, is that the Court is authorised but not required to exclude legal representatives from . . . the proceedings'.[74]

This approach, symptomatic of the approach of all the justices, simply ignored the existence of LLA Act sub-s. 28A(1), which is a point-blank requirement that criminal intelligence supplied to the Liquor Commissioner not be revealed to any unauthorised persons, and those authorised are the relevant minister and courts. Gaudron J's concern that curial unfairness not even be authorised[75] (and her Honour was particularly concerned that an affected party have the right 'to meet the case against him or her') was abandoned (and see also Kirby J in *K-Generation*[76] for further abandonment). *Nicholas*, particularly the portion quoted from Gaudron J, was quoted in argument to the High Court, but received not one reference save for a glancing blow as being amongst those cases in the train of *Kable*.

The joint judgment of Gummow, Hayne, Heydon, Crennan and Kiefel JJ provided in two paragraphs the 'machinery' for discounting this particular legislative attack on open fair hearing as required for a Ch. III court:

> [147] The steps which are taken may go so far as to involve the reception of evidence and the hearing of argument by the Licensing Court in private and in the absence of the parties and their representatives. However, the phrase 'including steps' in para. (a) of s 28A(5) does not mandate the taking of such

> steps. Rather, the phrase appears in s 28A(5) to mark out the limits of the range within which the Licensing Court may act in particular cases when determining how to maintain the confidentiality of the information.
>
> [148] Further, the Licensing Court is not bound to accept in its terms the 'criminal intelligence' upon which the Police Commissioner relies. The Court itself may question the evidence in closed session. Evidence led by other parties, and any limited form of cross-examination on the affidavits supplied under para. (b) of s 28A(5), must be taken into account. The potential that the s. 28A(5) procedure has for injurious effects is reduced by the fact that a decision by the Police Commissioner to make a s 28A(5)(a) application itself may greatly reduce the chance of the 'criminal intelligence' being decisive, because, in at least some cases, the Licensing Court may feel disinclined to place weight on material which the Police Commissioner's application has prevented the applicant for a licence being able to test, or even see.[77]

The material concerning 'taking steps' in para. 147 simply defies the plain meaning of s. 28A(5), particularly when read in the light of the general direction in s. 28A(1). The joint judgment makes claim for judges to be able to ascertain 'the truth' in closed session; that is, without the presence of, let alone input from, the affected party. Kirby J was equally delinquent in his view[78] that the court could perform the cross-examination of a witness that the court had summoned of its own volition.[79] This is precisely the position that Lord Kerr JSC has inveighed against repeatedly[80] in the years since *K-Generation.*

It should also be noted that the legislation under review in *K-Generation* involved not criminal law sanctions, but rather the formation of status, in this case the status of a person 'not allowed to be a holder of a liquor licence'. Most of such legislation around the Australian States is aimed at bikie gangs: members of such gangs are to be placed in a 'status' in which they can be pre-emptively controlled, so that the ordinary *ex post facto* processes of police investigation and prosecution are not required. The provisions of the LL Act were amended specifically to restrict 'bikies' from controlling licensed premises.[81] To that extent, *K-Generation* reflected the tendency in the UK to Anti-Social Behaviour Orders (ASBOs): pre-emptive status strikes, but not strictly criminal process.

The remaining case concerned with open fair hearing in Australian courts is *Assistant Commissioner Condon v Pompano Pty Ltd*,[82] in which none of the justices struck down the Queensland Criminal Organisation Act 2009 (Qld.) (CO Act), although Gageler J reasoned in a manner antithetical to the remainder of the court and ruled that if the legislation, aimed at providing for a closed court barring the affected party, were relied on in court, the affected and barred party should immediately obtain a stay from the Supreme Court. *Pompano* was another 'bikie gang' case, involving criminal intelligence, where a court was authorised by the CO Act to move into closed mode, with the affected party and all representatives of such a party excluded from the court. The litigation also involved a 'criminal organisation public interest monitor' (COPIM), whose functions were not intended to mimic the British special advocate, but who could cross-examine witnesses in the closed hearing anticipated by the CO Act.

French CJ found the CO Act constitutionally inoffensive, referring to *K-Generation* as an example of legislation that was permissive of 'imposing a disadvantage on one party',[83] which is to say that the Gaudron J line from *Nicholas*[84] forbidding even legislative authorisation (that is, permission) in a court's discretion to depart from the lineaments of natural justice, was yet again jettisoned. French CJ found for the validity of the CO Act on (*inter alia*) the following grounds:

> 6. The COA does not prevent the Supreme Court from having regard to degrees of unfairness to the respondent in determining whether or not to accept criminal intelligence tendered in the course of the substantive hearing.
> 7. The COPIM provides a limited measure of redress for the imbalance between the parties in respect of the use of criminal intelligence.
> 8. The Supreme Court in a special closed hearing, during the hearing of a substantive application, may call witnesses and the COPIM may examine or cross-examine them.[85]

The same criticism that was mounted regarding *K-Generation*[86] and the false assumption that third parties or the court can take the place of an affected party pertains here. The joint judgment of Hayne, Crennan, Kiefel and Bell JJ kept well away from *Nicholas* and *Leeth*. Relying on *Gypsy Jokers* and *K-Generation*, the joint judgment reasoned to acceptance of the closed court scheme:

> As the trade secrets cases show, however, the general rule is not absolute. There are circumstances in which competing interests compel some qualification to its application. And, if legislation provides for novel procedures which depart from the general rule described, the question is whether, taken as a whole, the court's procedures for resolving the dispute accord both parties procedural fairness and avoid 'practical injustice'.[87]

The acceptance of a broad and vague generalised 'practical injustice' test reveals a complete withdrawal from the field of contest on which natural justice was being fought over. The reference by Lord Kerr JSC to Upjohn LJ on the defining quality of the judicial function[88] by reference to an open fair hearing seems a distant thing. Lord Kerr JSC specifically referred to the consequence of withholding evidence from a party and consequently forcing that party to speculate on the case against it. How conducive is a closed court room door to an affected party being able to engage with litigation in a manner that reflects a judicial process, as understood by Lord Kerr JSC and Upjohn LJ?

Gageler J took a refreshingly different approach to the CO Act. In a judgment laced with the use of 'fair' and 'fairly' and derivatives, his Honour cited *Leeth*[89] and *Bass*[90] and reasoned as to the inherent unfairness of the CO Act, 'because the appearance of a fair hearing in a court and the maintenance of confidence in the curial process are constitutionally mandated'.[91] The utility of the COPIM was dismissed: '[I]t cannot cure a want of procedural fairness'.[92] In his conclusion, leading to his 'solution' (orders might be made staying any attempted use of the closed court CO Act procedure), Gageler J said, in terms that resonate back to what Lord Kerr JSC said about the mirage of courts making up for excised natural justice:[93]

> To attempt to overcome a want of procedural fairness in a court by relying on the court to compensate in the way the court reasons to a decision is, in the long run, self-defeating. The attempted resolution leverages off the institutional integrity of the court. The problem is that the appearance, if not the actuality, of that institutional integrity will not endure if there is manifest unfairness in the procedure of the court.[94]

In the midst of the cheese paring, less exalted courts around Australia still proclaim *audi alteram partem* as a fundamental principle. See, for example, Fryberg J in the Queensland Court of Appeal in *Greig v Stramit Corporation Pty Ltd*,[95] where his Honour quoted the lines from *Medea*[96] in the context of the necessity of open fair hearings in courts. But adherence to that standard in the face of legislative incursion is the difficulty, and the High Court has been most reluctant to assert the necessity for realistic, unencumbered fair hearing as fundamental to court procedure. There is a grim irony that, while the High Court is anaemic in its response to legislative incursions into open fair hearings in Ch. III courts, privative clauses enacted to make tribunals review proof if they perform without natural justice are circumvented by the federal court on the basis that procedure absent natural justice does not provide a 'hearing' or 'review' as the relevant legislation requires.[97] A subordinate court is working to keep natural justice alive in executive decision-making, while realistic open fair hearings dwindle in Ch. III courts.

Conclusion

British courts will accept a legislated regime that provides a special advocate who receives otherwise covert evidence, but only on condition that the special advocate receive at least a gist of the adverse evidence in a form that can be discussed with the affected party. British courts are also clear that they will not, absent legislative command, dispense with natural justice on the application of a (governmental) party. Curial discretion is wide, and allows for weighing of competing aspects of the public interest, but the wholesale rolling-up of natural justice would, on the British analysis, remove the quintessence of a court. Whether British courts would accept a legislative command for the destruction of effective confrontation with the moving party's evidence in court proceedings is not yet clear. However, the strength of common law tradition for most of the senior judges, together with the existence of art. 6 of the ECHR, indicates an unlikely meek acceptance of a proposal that would reduce British courts to mere administrative bodies.

The Australian position seems much weaker regarding the necessity of open fair hearings in courts, which is surprising in the light of the constitutional separation of Ch. III courts, which separation indicates a necessary bright-line boundary between them and administrative decision-makers. That bright line had always seemed to be the necessity for natural justice in curial proceedings, a procedure that could be whittled away from tribunals and similar bodies. The High Court of Australia appears (with the exception of Gageler J in *Pompano*) to accept legislative tinkering with court procedure, on the general thread that the courts concerned retain sufficient autonomy about their procedure to provide some kind of interaction with the moving party's charge and evidence. But the interaction imagined in *K-Generation* and *Pompano* is not that of the affected party, and such a state of affairs is not even a poor man's open fair hearing. The reasoning of Gageler J in *Pompano* reveals the inappropriate nature of the hope that courts will find a way in the face of increasingly clear statutory provisions intending to destroy fair hearings.

As Lord Kerr JSC and Gageler J understand, in adversarial common law courts it is not feasible for the court to provide the 'missing link' in court proceedings: if a party does not know what is alleged against him or her and has no opportunity to counter the allegation with his or her own evidence and a cross-examination based in knowledge of what is at stake (as opposed to merely pushing against credibility), the proceedings are not fit to be called court proceedings.

The twenty-first century arrived with grave security problems arising from the activities of terrorists and, in Australia, the political perception of the danger of bikie gangs. The legislative response is still being worked out in Britain and Australia. In the former, senior judges are prone to weighing up the public interest factors at stake, even in the absence of legislative direction, and the voice of a dissenter reminding others of basic common law values is important: hence the references to Lord Kerr JSC. In Australia, senior judges have been much more compliant in the face of legislative commands, exercising every interpretive technique to stretch meaning to an acceptable possibility of the retention of the shell of natural justice. That seems a long way from fidelity to the common law's insistence on realistic and effective interaction by an affected party with his or her accuser's material in the procedure of a court.

Notes

1 (1605) 6 Co Rep 48b, 77 ER 326.
2 (1615) 11 Co Rep 93b, 77 ER 1271, also reported at 1 Rolle 224, 81 ER 448.
3 The actual Latin may be noted at this stage, as it is frequently quoted by common law judges of a later date: 'Quicunque aliquid statuerit, parte inauditâ alterâ, aequum licet statuerit, haud æquus fuerit'.
4 *R v Justices of Bodmin* [1947] 1 KB 321, 325 (*Bodmin*).
5 *Russell v Duke of Norfolk* [1949] 1 All ER 109, 118 (Tucker LJ).
6 [1963] Ch 381, 405–6 (Upjohn LJ).
7 *Official Solicitor to the Supreme Court v K* [1965] AC 201 (*K's case*).
8 *Russell* (n. 5).
9 *K's case* (n. 7) 218–9, and see Lord Devlin at 238.

10 Ibid. 218.
11 [1978] AC 171.
12 (1944) 68 CLR 571, particularly Rich J at 589.
13 (1958) 98 CLR 383.
14 Ibid. 395–6.
15 See n. 3.
16 See text at n. 72ff. Ch. III of the Australian Constitution marks the federal judiciary (and state courts capable of carrying federal jurisdiction) as severed from the legislative and executive branches of the Commonwealth government, and the case law on this subject, beginning with *Kable v DPP (NSW)* (1996) 189 CLR 51, calls for such courts to be independent of the other arms of government, displaying integrity and impartiality. Sir William Deane, who had been junior counsel for Mrs Tanos, had just left the High Court when *Kable* came to be argued nearly 40 years later, laying the basis for the challenge in *K-Generation v Liquor Licensing Court* (2009) 237 CLR 501.
17 (1986) 161 CLR 342 (*Re RJL*).
18 *Bodmin* (n. 4).
19 *Re RJL* (n. 17) 350.
20 *K's case* (n. 7).
21 (1996) 189 CLR 51 (*Kable*).
22 Ibid. 116.
23 See text at n. 72ff.
24 (1957) 95 CLR 529, 542.
25 (1992) 174 CLR 455, 470 (*Leeth*).
26 (1998) 193 CLR 173, 208–9 [74] (*Nicholas*).
27 *Bass v Permanent Trustee Co Ltd* (1999) 198 CLR 334, 359 [56] (*Bass*).
28 Convention for the Protection of Human Rights and Fundamental Freedoms, opened for signature 4 November 1950, 213 UNTS 221 (entered into force 3 September 1953) (ECHR).
29 [2008] 1 AC 1128 (*Davis*).
30 Ibid. 1141. The cases were *R v Stipendiary Magistrate at Southport; Ex parte Gibson* [1993] 2 Qd R 687 and *Jarvie v Magistrates Court of Victoria at Brunswick* [1995] 1 VR 84 (*Jarvie*). The second plays a circuitous hand in the jurisprudence of *Davis*.
31 *Davis* (n. 29) 1138, 1148.
32 *Prosecutor v Tadic* (Case No ICTY-94–1) (10 August 1995). (Separate Opinion of Judge Stephen on the Prosecutor's Motion Requesting Protective Measures for Victims and Witnesses.)
33 *Davis* (n. 29) 1171 [93].
34 *Jarvie* (n. 30).
35 [2001] 1 WLR 1786 (CA) (*Carnduff*).
36 Ibid. 1798 [49].
37 [2005] 2 AC 738.
38 Ibid. 787 [95].
39 [2003] 1 AC 681, 695ff.
40 [2010] 2 AC 269 (*AF (No. 3)*).
41 (2009) 49 EHRR 625 (GC).
42 *AF (No 3)* (n. 40) 356–8 [70]–[74].
43 Ibid. 359 [83]. 'Sufficient material' is the heart of the 'gist' concept: the condition is that it be sufficient to allow effective answer.
44 Ibid. 355 [63]. The idea of the gist being sufficient is attacked by M. Aronson et al., *Judicial Review of Administrative Action* (5th edn., Thomson Lawbook Co 2013) 607 fn. 739 on the ground of ultimate inutility. The concern for public perception of justice not merely being done, but being seen to be done, was reflected by John Jackson in 'Justice, Security and the Right to a Fair Trial: Is the use of Secret Evidence Ever Fair?' [2013]

PL 720, 732–3. Gisting is no longer mandatory, having been overtaken by the Justice and Security Act 2013 (UK).
45 [2012] 1 AC 452 (*Tariq*).
46 [2012] 1 AC 531 (*Al Rawi*).
47 *Carnduff* (n. 35).
48 See, for example, Lord Mance JSC at *Tariq* (n. 45) 489 [40] suggesting that while a prosecution might have to be dropped for gross unfairness, a civil action could proceed because: 'The rule of law must, so far as possible, stand for the objective resolution of civil disputes on their merits by a tribunal or court which has before it material enabling it to do this'. Which is to say, some material, and not necessarily the affected party's rebutting material, since the evidence before such a court might be seen only by the proffering party and the bench, not the affected party, but that could be sufficient to sustain a curial decision.
49 *Tariq* (n. 45) 514 [107]–[108]. This chapter agrees with the view expressed by Jackson (n. 44) 723 that, at the very least, a gist (what Jackson calls '*A* type disclosure') must be produced to the affected party: Lord Kerr's dissent is to be preferred to the potential vacuum of evidence allowed in the other judgments.
50 See *K's case* (n. 7)ff.
51 *Al Rawi* (n. 46).
52 Lord Rodger of Earlsferry JSC died after argument but before judgment in both *Tariq* and *Al Rawi*, although Lord Phillips PSC indicated in the latter (*Al Rawi* (n. 46) 620 [198]) that he would have sided with the majority in that case. The majority five were Lords Hope DPSC and Brown, Kerr and Dyson JJSC, Lord Phillips PSC agreeing briefly.
53 *Al Rawi* (n. 46) 587 [74] (Lord Hope DPSC).
54 Ibid. 587 [72].
55 Ibid. 592–3 [93].
56 *AF (No. 3)* (n. 40)ff.
57 Special Advocates, 'Justice and Security Green Paper: Response to Consultation from Special Advocates', 16 December 2011.
58 [2013] 2 AC 66.
59 Ibid. 81 [1].
60 *Kable* (n. 21).
61 David Bennett referred in argument to 'September 10 thinking': Transcript of Proceedings, *Thomas v Mowbray* [2007] HCATrans 76 (20 February 2007) 9235.
62 [2004] 1 QdR 40.
63 Section 30 of the Criminal Proceeds Confiscation Act 2002 (Qld.).
64 [2004] 1 QdR 40, 48–9 [31].
65 Ibid.
66 (2008) 234 CLR 532 (*Gypsy Jokers*).
67 Ibid. 556 [23].
68 Ibid. [24].
69 (1984) 154 CLR 404, 469–70 (Gibbs CJ, Wilson, Brennan and Dawson JJ) (*Alister*). This case arose from the Sydney Hilton bombing, which occurred in February 1978 in a hotel in Sydney that was hosting the Commonwealth Heads of Government Regional Meeting, and had a large input from the Australian Security Intelligence Organisation.
70 *Gypsy Jokers* (n. 66) 595 [180].
71 Ibid. 596 [183]. Crennan J followed these observations with analogy to patent cases: the inapposite nature of that comparison is dealt with at n. 87.
72 (2009) 237 CLR 501 (*K-Generation*). The provisions were slightly altered after that litigation.
73 Ibid. 512 [10] (numbering inserted).
74 Ibid. 526 [73].

75 *Nicholas* (n. 26).
76 *K-Generation* (n. 72) 577–8 [257] fifth bullet point.
77 Ibid. 542–3 [147]–[148].
78 *K-Generation* (n. 76).
79 Just how this would work, when the court could have no idea what particular issues would attract the eye of the affected party, what particular inaccuracies (known only to the affected party) were exposed in the criminal intelligence, is a matter of conjecture.
80 See *Tariq* (n. 49)ff.
81 There is no public record of Genargi Krasnov, the principal in K-Generation Pty Ltd, having any links to bikie gangs, nor any other criminal involvement. A senior officer of South Australia Police told a senior criminal solicitor in Adelaide (not the instructor in *K-Generation*) that the criminal intelligence reflected Krasnov having married into a Lebanese criminal family. This was simple misinformation, as a glance at the public record would have shown that Krasnov, who was of Chinese/Russian descent, was married to a woman of Chinese background (with no criminal record).
82 (2013) 295 ALR 638 (*Pompano*).
83 Ibid. 665 [86].
84 *Nicholas* (n. 26).
85 *Pompano* (n. 82) 665 [87].
86 See *K-Generation* (n. 72)ff.
87 *Pompano* (n. 82) 682 [157]. The reference to 'trade secrets cases' goes back to *Scott v Scott* [1913] AC 417, 443 and, in Australia, *ABC v Parish* (1980) 43 FLR 129 (Full Fed Ct), going to the assumption of an open court. Patent litigation involves the conundrum that if the party holding the device in contention is forced to make full discovery of the working to the party claiming a patent, valuable intellectual property may be surrendered. Courts have inherent power to make orders that will go some way to restricting an open fair hearing on 'machinery' aspects, determining the need for a party, driven to litigation by a rival claimant, to be protected from having to reveal the workings of its machinery, to be greater than the public interest in open fair hearings. These cases make a poor analogy for criminal intelligence cases, in which the party driven to litigation is defending itself, and discovers that its inability to receive realistic natural justice is validated by the High Court, while, in trade secrets cases, the party driven to defend itself is the party given protection by the court restricting the ambit of an open fair hearing.
88 See *Tariq* (n. 49).
89 *Leeth* (n. 25).
90 *Bass* (n. 27).
91 *Pompano* (n. 82) 693 [209].
92 Ibid. [208].
93 See *Al Rawi* (n. 55).
94 *Pompano* (n 82) 694 [211].
95 [2004] 2 QdR 17, 48–9 [135]–[136].
96 See n. 3.
97 Aronson et al. (n. 42) 964, citing *Minister for Immigration and Citizenship v Li* (2012) 202 FCR 387.

Chapter 7

Secrecy, procedural fairness and state courts

Rebecca Ananian-Welsh

Introduction

The Australian Constitution contains no explicit protection for fair process in judicial proceedings. It does, however, give rise to fairly robust implied protections for judicial independence and impartiality. The manner and extent to which the constitutional separation of judicial power protects procedural fairness is one of the most uncertain aspects of an already fraught area of law. This uncertainty arises in part from the High Court's failure to adopt a clear or consistent approach in interpreting constitutional protections for fair process.

In recent years, however, the High Court has faced a string of constitutional challenges to secret evidence in state court proceedings, and has adopted a clear approach to resolving the tension between secrecy and procedural fairness. In the most recent of these cases, *Assistant Commissioner Condon v Pompano Pty Ltd*,[1] Gageler J suggested that the Constitution provides a robust protection for procedural fairness in proceedings in state courts: 'Chapter III of the Constitution mandates the observance of procedural fairness as an immutable characteristic of a Supreme Court and of every other court in Australia'.[2] His Honour went on to say that '[s]uggestions that there are exceptions to procedural fairness in the common practices of courts in Australia are unfounded. The suggested exceptions are more apparent than real'.[3]

This chapter discusses the cases on secret 'criminal intelligence' evidence in state court proceedings and considers the degree to which the separation of judicial power limits its use. It critiques the High Court's approach, highlights some of its key weaknesses and argues that Gageler J's statements hold true if they are read in a particular light.

The chapter concludes by discussing some possible broader implications of the High Court's approach to resolving the competing interests of secrecy and procedural fairness. Ultimately, the cases on secret evidence provide a degree of proof that the separation of judicial power is an imperfect, even inadequate, tool for the protection of fair process in judicial proceedings.

Ch. III, fair process and state courts

In the absence of a national Bill or Charter of Rights, Ch. III of the Constitution has become a key mechanism by which rights, particularly fair process rights, may be protected from legislative incursion.[4] This separation of judicial power is strict in respect of federal courts. These Ch. III courts are restricted to the exercise of judicial (and ancillary non-judicial) powers, and judicial powers may only be vested in Ch. III courts.[5]

State courts are beyond the direct reach of the Commonwealth Constitution. However, these courts are vested with limited federal jurisdiction and, to that extent, their independence and integrity is entitled to constitutional protection.[6] Similarly, state courts form part of an integrated national court system, which further justifies their entitlement to a degree of constitutional protection.[7] On these bases, the High Court has interpreted the Constitution, first, to prohibit the conferral of powers on state courts and judges that are 'incompatible' with their fundamental independence and impartiality[8] and, second, to require that state courts meet the definition of a court; that is, that they maintain the defining or essential features of courts.[9]

The strict formalist separation of judicial power at federal level tends to render more principled considerations of fair process tangential to the central, definition-focused Ch. III analysis.[10] The flexible, functionalist test that governs the permissible powers of state courts seems to have considerably greater potential in this respect.[11] As procedural fairness is central to judicial independence and impartiality, it follows that a scheme that compromises fairness by, for instance, involving secret evidence, may be incompatible with those values and, therefore, constitutionally repugnant.

Secret evidence and constitutional values

The term 'secret evidence' refers to material adduced in judicial proceedings that is not disclosed to an affected party or his or her legal representative. It may be heard in closed hearings from which the affected party and his or her representative may be excluded, or it may be in the form of documentary evidence that is not made available to the party or his or her representative in whole or in part.

Courts and the adversarial system of justice are built upon the values of a fair trial, open justice, equality of arms, and the capacity for parties to meet the case against them. In an oft-quoted statement, Gaudron J described the general features of fair process arising from Ch. III of the Constitution as 'open and public enquiry (subject to limited exceptions), the application of the rules of natural justice, the ascertainment of the facts as they bear on the right or liability in issue and the identification of the applicable law, followed by an application of that law to those facts'.[12]

Secret evidence poses a stark challenge to many of these values. This much was acknowledged by French CJ in the opening paragraph of his judgment in *Condon*:

> At the heart of the common law tradition is a 'method of administering justice'. That method requires judges who are independent of government to preside over courts held in public in which each party has full opportunity to present its own case and to meet the case against it. Antithetical to that

> tradition is the idea of a court, closed to the public, in which only one party, a government party, is present, and in which the judge is required by law to hear evidence and argument which neither the other party nor its legal representatives is allowed to hear.[13]

Despite secret evidence standing at odds with traditional notions of fair process and judicial independence and impartiality, legal institutions are familiar with secret evidence in judicial proceedings. This is particularly the case in circumstances where it is necessary to protect national security information and intelligence-gathering methods and sources.

Secret evidence need not, in all instances, challenge constitutional values. Secret evidence against a party presented in respect of a claim of public interest immunity is an example of this. Applications for public interest immunity typically occur in open court, although the content of the information is not disclosed to the other party. Significantly, while the court receives this secret evidence, a successful claim of public interest immunity will result in that material being excluded from the body of evidence that may be adduced at trial and, therefore, secret evidence is not used to prove the substantive case.[14]

The criminal intelligence provisions considered in this chapter are distinct from information subject to public interest immunity.[15] In short, criminal intelligence provisions generally involve a claim for secrecy being heard in closed proceedings from which the other party and his or her representatives are excluded. If the application is successful, then the information will be admitted as evidence and may thus form a basis for the judge's determination, but it will still be withheld from the other party and his or her representatives. Provisions of this kind strike the balance between the competing interests of secrecy and procedural fairness more heavily in favour of secrecy as, in effect, a party is no longer able to know or test significant aspects of the case against him or her.

'Criminal intelligence' evidence in state courts

In recent years, a trend has emerged towards withholding evidence from a party to proceedings and his or her legal representatives on the basis of its identification as 'criminal intelligence' information. This has occurred most commonly in control order proceedings (discussed below) but also in liquor licensing and other contexts. A number of these schemes have been challenged on the basis that they compromise fair process and, therefore, impermissibly undermine the actual and perceived independence and integrity of the national judicature. The remainder of this chapter outlines the kinds of criminal intelligence provisions that have come before the High Court and discusses how the High Court has resolved to settle the tension between secrecy and procedural fairness posed by these provisions.

The withholding of criminal intelligence evidence first came before the High Court in *K-Generation Pty Ltd v Liquor Licensing Court*.[16] *K-Generation* concerned provisions requiring the South Australian Licensing Court to maintain the confidentiality of information classified as criminal intelligence by the Commissioner of Police. Criminal intelligence was defined under these provisions as:

> [I]nformation relating to actual or suspected criminal activity (whether in this State or elsewhere) the disclosure of which could reasonably be expected to prejudice criminal investigations, or to enable the discovery of the existence or identity of a confidential source of information relevant to law enforcement.[17]

Following *K-Generation*, in which the constitutional validity of these provisions was upheld for reasons explained below, these kinds of criminal intelligence provisions have become increasingly common across Australian jurisdictions. In particular, they have become a regular feature of control order schemes.

Australia's first control order scheme was introduced as part of the Commonwealth's suite of anti-terrorism measures enacted in the years following the terrorist attacks of 11 September 2001. These orders were adapted from the UK.[18] The control order provisions of the Commonwealth Criminal Code empowered federal courts to impose a wide variety of potentially onerous obligations and restrictions on persons for the purpose of protecting the community from the threat of terrorism.[19] A court issuing a control order on a person was also required to be satisfied that imposing the order would substantially assist in preventing a terrorist act or that the person had been involved in training with a listed terrorist organisation.[20]

Following the High Court's validation of the Commonwealth control order scheme in the 2007 case of *Thomas v Mowbray*,[21] the Australian states began to develop orders that were similarly focused on the prevention of future harm divorced from any necessary wrongdoing on the part of the controlee. These orders were touted as 'bikie laws' and politically marketed as part of states' efforts to combat outlaw motorcycle gangs.[22] However, the laws were aimed at serious organised crime generally.

The state control order schemes drew upon two elements of the Commonwealth's national security laws: control orders for individuals were made once their membership of a 'declared organisation' was established, and the declaration processes resembled, to varying degrees in each state, the federal law enabling proscription of terrorist organisations.[23] There were important differences between each jurisdiction's processes of declaring organisations and issuing control orders, but the general effect of the latter was to restrict individuals from associating with other members of the organisation, or from carrying on certain activities.[24] Breach of the association restrictions of a control order carried heavy penalties, including criminal prosecution and imprisonment.[25]

Increased reliance on secret evidence has been identified as an inevitable consequence of the intelligence-led approach adopted by many governments to meeting the threat of transnational terrorism following 9/11.[26] The utility of the kinds of preventive orders introduced to combat terrorism depended greatly upon the ability of the state to adduce intelligence-based evidence, such as intercepted communications, which may support a claim that the person ought to be restrained in order to prevent future harm. As state control orders aimed at serious organised crime were adapted from the federal national security context, it is little surprise that secret evidence played an integral part in both the declaration and control order stages of these schemes. That said, removed from the national security context it is less apparent why information of this nature could not simply be governed by the well-established principles of public interest immunity.

South Australia was the first state to enact serious organised crime control orders with the Serious and Organised Crime (Control) Act 2008 (SA) (SOCCA). Under the SOCCA, organisations were declared by the South Australian Attorney-General on application by the Commissioner of Police.[27] The basis of the declaration was a finding that 'members of the organisation associate for the purpose of organising, planning, facilitating, supporting or engaging in serious criminal activity' and 'the organisation represents a risk to public safety and order in this State'.[28] The Attorney-General was not required to provide reasons for the decision to declare an organisation.[29] Once a declaration had been made by the Attorney-General, control order proceedings could be commenced in the Magistrates Court, seeking orders in respect of members of the declared organisation.

Under the SOCCA, information provided to the Attorney-General that was classified by the Commissioner as criminal intelligence was not to be disclosed except to specifically authorised persons.[30] Criminal intelligence had an identical definition to the provisions upheld in *K-Generation*, with the additional inclusion of 'information relating to actual or suspected criminal activity . . . the disclosure of which could reasonably be expected . . . to endanger a person's life or physical safety'.[31]

Once the Commissioner had classified information as criminal intelligence, the court was empowered to assess whether the information was 'properly' so classified. If properly classified, the court was obliged to maintain the confidentiality of the information throughout the control order proceedings,[32] including by removing criminal intelligence information from the statement of the grounds on which the control order was issued.[33]

Highly similar control order schemes were introduced in other states and territories. Like the South Australian SOCCA, the New South Wales and Queensland control order schemes would be subject to constitutional challenge. Under the Crimes (Criminal Organisations Control) Act 2009 (NSW) (CCOCA) and the Criminal Organisation Act 2009 (Qld.) (COA), the basis of declaring organisations and the nature of control orders was much the same as the SOCCA.[34] Likewise, the provisions concerning 'criminal intelligence' were effectively identical under all three Acts.[35] The key difference between the schemes existed at the declaration stage.

Under the CCOCA, organisations were declared by 'eligible judges', being judges of the New South Wales Supreme Court acting in a personal capacity.[36] The role of the eligible judge was akin to that of the Attorney-General under the SOCCA, although proceedings before an eligible judge had the appearance (albeit superficial) of open court proceedings.[37] The rules of evidence did not apply to declaration proceedings before an eligible judge and reasons or grounds for the decision did not have to be given.[38] The confidentiality of criminal intelligence information was maintained during proceedings before an eligible judge as well as in any subsequent control order proceedings in the Supreme Court.[39] Under Queensland's COA, both declaration and control order proceedings were conducted by the Queensland Supreme Court.[40]

In summary, the South Australian, New South Wales and Queensland schemes were largely identical insofar as they provided for secret criminal intelligence evidence. The primary distinction between the schemes is that the decision to declare an organisation – and thus any decisions as to criminal intelligence information at the declaration stage – was made by the Attorney-General in South Australia, by an eligible judge in New South Wales, and by the Supreme Court in Queensland.

Under all three of these control order schemes, information could be withheld at the declaration or control order stages of proceedings, provided that the body responsible for issuing that order was satisfied that the information was criminal intelligence.[41] Under Queensland's COA, the Criminal Organisation Public Interest Monitor (COPIM) could be involved in any preliminary hearings held to determine whether information qualified as criminal intelligence. However, the COPIM was in no way acting as a representative of the respondent person or organisation in these proceedings.[42]

The schemes outlined above provide the focus of the present discussion. They also suggest a trend towards the standard inclusion of provisions for the withholding of criminal intelligence information in proceedings aimed at crime prevention. There are clear policy reasons behind provisions of this kind. It is of course in the government's interests to be able to keep information of this kind secret from the other party and from the public, without losing the capacity to rely on it in court. However, this trend is no doubt also facilitated by the High Court's repeated affirmation and legitimation of the use of secret evidence in state court proceedings.

The High Court on secrecy

The Commonwealth Constitution limits parliaments' abilities to confer functions on state courts that are incompatible with institutional independence or integrity, or that compromise the essential or defining features of a court. Throughout the case law interpreting these limitations, the High Court has consistently affirmed that fair process is central to judicial independence and impartiality, and is entitled to a degree of constitutional protection.[43] The repeated challenges to the constitutional validity of secret evidence provisions provide a relatively rare opportunity to clearly identify and assess the High Court's approach to protecting an aspect of fair process in judicial proceedings.

The High Court first tackled a constitutional challenge to secret evidence in a state court before the criminal intelligence cases described above. *Gypsy Jokers Motorcycle Club Inc v Commissioner of Police*[44] concerned the issue of fortification removal notices by the Commissioner of Police to bikie gang premises, and the review of those notices by the Supreme Court of Western Australia. The relevant legislation provided that:

> The Commissioner of Police may identify any information provided to the court for the purposes of the review as confidential if its disclosure might prejudice the operations of the Commissioner of Police, and information so identified is for the court's use only and is not to be disclosed to any other person, whether or not a party to the proceedings, or publicly disclosed in any way.[45]

Despite the apparent plain meaning of the section automatically preventing disclosure of information following the Commissioner's classification, a majority of the High Court accepted that the Supreme Court retained the ability to review the Commissioner's classification of the material.[46] By reading down the provision to allow for independent judicial review of the restricted classification, the High Court was able to avoid the affront to the independence and integrity of the Supreme Court that would have resulted from legislation that 'purported to direct the courts as to the manner and outcome of the exercise of their jurisdiction'.[47] This ruling provided the foundation for the High Court's subsequent decisions concerning secret evidence.

In *K-Generation*, the first constitutional challenge to state criminal intelligence provisions, the High Court ruled that the independence and integrity of the licensing court was maintained on two bases. First, the licensing court was not required to accept the classification of criminal intelligence assigned to the evidence by the Commissioner of Police – the crucial factor that had maintained constitutional validity in *Gypsy Jokers*. Second, the licensing court was not forced to take particular steps to maintain the confidentiality of the information, thus avoiding any potential usurpation of decisional independence and maintaining fundamental judicial control of the proceedings.[48] This second basis for the court's decision to uphold the Act was developed further in *Condon*, discussed further below.

In 2010 and 2011, the South Australian SOCCA and the New South Wales CCOCA, respectively, were struck down on the bases that they were (in whole or in part) repugnant to the constitutional separation of judicial power. The High Court's reasons for striking down these laws did not, however, relate to the schemes' provisions for secret criminal intelligence evidence.

In *South Australia v Totani*,[49] the High Court held that s. 14(1) of the SOCCA was invalid on the basis that it obliged the Magistrates Court of South Australia to issue a control order against a person effectively at the behest of the executive government. Specifically, once the court had determined that the person was a member of the declared organisation, the latter classification having been made by the Attorney-General, the legislation required the court to make a control order in respect of that person. According to the High Court, this obligation effectively rendered the Magistrates Court an instrument of the executive government.[50]

Notwithstanding the absence of any similar obligations being placed on the eligible judge or the Supreme Court under the New South Wales CCOCA, in *Wainohu v New South Wales*[51] the High Court struck down that Act on Ch. III grounds. The basis of this decision was fairly narrow. Section 13(2) of the CCOCA removed the requirement that the eligible judge provide reasons for his or her decision to declare an organisation. A majority of the High Court held that this provision damaged the institutional integrity of the judge, and ultimately of the Supreme Court, to the point that the scheme as a whole was repugnant to the separation of judicial power.[52]

The withholding of criminal intelligence information from the person or organisation, or their legal representatives, had provided one strand of the full court of the Supreme Court of South Australia's reasons for finding that the SOCCA was constitutionally invalid – a decision that was overturned on appeal in *Totani*.[53] The criminal intelligence provisions had also been a primary subject of the constitutional challenge to the New South Wales scheme.[54] Despite this, the High Court in *Totani* and *Wainohu* gave little attention to the secret evidence provisions. In both cases, the court simply emphasised the strong similarities between the criminal intelligence provisions at hand, and those upheld as constitutionally valid in *Gypsy Jokers* and *K-Generation*.[55] In short, as the provisions closely resembled one another, and the same degree of independent review and judicial discretion was preserved in each of the secret evidence schemes, the court simply applied its reasons in *Gypsy Jokers* and *K-Generation* to the SOCCA and CCOCA, and moved on to what it considered to be the more problematic aspects of those Acts.[56]

This set of cases indicates that secret evidence is constitutionally permissible, provided that the court is given the chance to independently review the classification of the material as criminal intelligence and is not forced to take particular steps in respect of that information.

Of the three state control order cases to date, only in the 2013 case of *Condon* has the High Court squarely faced the issue of secret evidence. The case for invalidity in *Condon* rested upon the assertion that withholding criminal intelligence evidence from the respondent amounted to a breach of procedural fairness and was, therefore, incompatible with the independence and integrity of the Supreme Court of Queensland. This argument failed.

In *Condon*, the High Court affirmed its earlier findings in *Gypsy Jokers*, *K-Generation*, *Totani*, and *Wainohu* and built on those authorities. The constitutional validity of the COA not only rested on the Supreme Court's capacity to independently review the secret classification of the evidence, and the lack of any obligations as to the use of that evidence, but on a further, crucial finding. Validity in *Condon* was based on the Supreme Court's retention of sufficient independence in declaration and control order proceedings to enable it to remedy any potential unfairness arising from the secret evidence.

French CJ suggested that the Supreme Court's existing discretion could enable the court to 'refuse to rely upon the criminal intelligence where to do so would give rise to a degree of unfairness in the circumstances of the case'.[57] In a joint judgment, Hayne, Crennan, Kiefel and Bell JJ suggested that the Supreme Court could remedy potential unfairness by attributing less weight to the secret, and hence unchallenged, evidence.[58] Gageler J adopted the same general approach, but concluded that the only effective means by which the Supreme Court could potentially counter any unfairness arising from the secret evidence would be to order a stay of proceedings.[59] Therefore, for Gageler J, it was the Supreme Court's capacity to order a stay of proceedings that preserved the validity of the COA.

For the High Court as a whole, the Queensland Supreme Court retained sufficient discretion to effectively preserve the fairness of proceedings before it – whether through exercising its discretion to attribute less, or even no, weight to the evidence, or to order a stay of proceedings. Precedent played a significant role in the court's reasons in *Condon*. The court was careful to maintain a consistent position on the constitutional validity of secret criminal intelligence evidence. The disagreement between the justices came in the details of just which discretionary mechanism will successfully overcome potential unfairness arising from secret evidence.

A relatively clear overall position on how the tension may be resolved between secret evidence and procedural fairness arises from the string of criminal intelligence cases. Secret evidence is constitutionally permissible, provided that the court is able to independently review the classification of the criminal intelligence material, and then deal with the evidence as it sees fit – by determining the weight attributable to the evidence or, according to Gageler J, by ordering a stay of proceedings for want of fairness.

The High Court's approach resolves the tension between secrecy and procedural fairness in a manner that will almost always result in the scheme being upheld. It appears that the usurpation or control of a fundamental aspect of a state court's decisional independence will be required before a scheme for secret evidence will fall foul of Ch. III.

Secrecy and the separation of powers: fairness without openness?

The outset of this chapter referred to two statements by Gageler J in *Condon*. His Honour said that 'Ch. III of the Constitution mandates the observance of procedural fairness as an immutable characteristic of a Supreme Court and of every other court in Australia'[60] and that '[s]uggestions that there are exceptions to procedural fairness in the common practices of courts in Australia are unfounded. The suggested exceptions are more apparent than real'.[61] Having discussed the principles and authorities to which his Honour was referring, it can be seen that, in order to hold true, these statements must be read in a particular light. Gageler J suggests that procedural fairness is an immutable characteristic of courts that admits of no exceptions. Yet secret evidence is generally permissible in judicial proceedings. If secret evidence is indeed 'antithetical' to procedural fairness, how can it be true that secret evidence is permissible *and* procedural fairness admits of no exceptions?

The High Court has resolved this apparent contradiction by reasoning that no court can be *required* to adopt a procedure that is unfair. That is, a legislative scheme may be unfair, but if the court has any mechanism at its disposal that would enable it to avoid the unfairness, then constitutional validity will be preserved. As Gageler J put it: 'If a procedure cannot be adopted without unfairness, then it cannot be required of a court'.[62] Anything less than a complete and unavoidable requirement that a court implement an unfair process will, it appears, survive a challenge on Ch. III grounds. Thus, it seems that the court is willing to find that a process is 'fair', even if it completely lacks openness.

Jurisprudence concerning the fair process protections arising from Ch. III has been sparse. The High Court's approach to secret evidence does not bode well for the evolution of a substantive set of fair process rights from Ch. III – even at the State level where the principles governing the separation of judicial power are more flexible and, arguably, more substantive than the strict formalist principles governing federal courts. Rather, the criminal intelligence cases suggest that constitutional invalidity on procedural fairness grounds will be a rare finding, requiring complete usurpation or control of an element of the court's decisional independence.

The High Court's approach to secret evidence demonstrates that, in considering questions of fairness and constitutional validity, the court will focus narrowly on the independence with which the judge fulfills his or her role. As a result, judicial control of court proceedings and the basic independence of the court from the executive branch are maintained. However, there are some flaws in this approach. Ultimately, these weaknesses highlight the imperfect nature of Ch. III as a tool for effectively protecting fair process from legislative incursion.

First, the approach adopted by the High Court in the criminal intelligence cases undervalues the importance of the perceived independence and impartiality of state courts.[63] The importance of perceived impartiality to Ch. III has been acknowledged by the High Court in its references to the need to maintain public confidence in the independent judicature.[64] Public confidence in this context cannot mean actual public perception;[65] rather, it must be understood as an objectively assessable standard. In *Nicholas v The Queen*,[66] Gaudron, McHugh and Kirby JJ emphasised the role of fair process in this context, observing that courts' power to protect their own processes and thus maintain public confidence in the administration of justice is central to the constitutional conception of judicial power.[67] Wendy Lacey has surmised that, following *Nicholas*, courts bear a power to protect their processes, rather than to protect their reputation.[68] The capacity for each party to effectively meet the case against himself or herself in open court is fundamental to maintaining public confidence in the impartial administration of justice. Closed hearings and secret evidence are sharply at odds with these traditional facets of judicial independence and impartiality. Thus, by indicating that fairness may exist where openness is absent, the High Court's approach arguably undervalues the impact of secrecy and closed proceedings on public confidence in the impartial administration of justice.

Second, by focusing narrowly on the question of judicial independence and impartiality, the High Court has failed to address the clearer problem arising from secret evidence: fairness to the parties. Discussion of principles such as open justice, equality of arms and due process has been overshadowed by the emphasis on judicial functions, traditions and decisional independence. No guiding principles with respect to disclosure have been developed, beyond ensuring the court is capable of independently reviewing the basis of non-disclosure. Thus, despite the High Court facing so many constitutional challenges to secret evidence, it has not once suggested that a minimum standard for disclosure exists in order to ensure a fair hearing. This stands in contrast to jurisprudence in, for example, the UK and Europe, where these issues have received far greater judicial attention and development.[69]

From one perspective, party rights are tangential, even separate, to the considerations of judicial independence and impartiality arising from Ch. III. However, an alternative view places greater weight on the principles underpinning the separation of judicial power. The core purpose of the separation of judicial power is the achievement of independent and impartial courts. This is not an end in itself, but a means by which deeper constitutional aims are achieved. These aims can be said to include equality, limited government, open justice and the rule of law.[70] Secret evidence and closed proceedings compromise these aims and, therefore, challenge the values underpinning the separation of judicial power.

The flexible, principled incompatibility test, which governs the permissible powers of state courts and that was applied in the cases discussed, has the potential to provide substantive protection to the fair process and rule of law values that underpin the separation of judicial power.[71] However, in the criminal intelligence cases, the High Court has shied away from broader considerations of fairness, instead focusing closely on the independence with which the court exercises its functions. Again, this demonstrates that even a principled, functionalist approach to protecting the separation of judicial power may not be particularly effective at preserving constitutional values such as fair process.[72] This suggests that the weakness in Ch. III's capacity to protect fair process may not arise from the character of the interpretive model being applied, but from the fact that fairness is being achieved through the lens of the separation of judicial power. A clear and direct fair trial protection, a common feature of other constitutions, would perhaps serve better than even a more principled interpretation of Ch. III.

Finally, the validity of secret evidence schemes has hinged entirely on the state court's capacities to weigh secrecy and fairness in each case. But how well equipped is a judge to fulfil this task? Australian courts are unassisted by statutory systems such as special advocates.[73] In the context of state control order schemes, there is nothing comparable to the procedures available in the national security setting, in particular those set down by the National Security Information (Criminal and Civil Proceedings) Act 2004 (Cth.) for hearings in which a non-disclosure certificate issued by the Attorney-General may be challenged.[74] This places considerable pressure on the judge to make independent assessments of evidence and fairness where aspects of the hearing no longer fit the mould of adversarial justice.

In these circumstances, it is important to recognise that the courts' ability to question the untested claims of the executive may not always be effective.[75] In his Honour's dissenting opinion in the federal control orders case, *Thomas*, Hayne J summarised the impact of secret evidence on the integrity of the issuing court in a lengthy, but valuable, passage. After emphasising the crucial importance of expert evidence to predictive decisions (such as those that may be involved in issuing a control order), Hayne J said:

> In cases where [intelligence information] could not be tested [by expert evidence] . . . (and such cases would be the norm rather than the exception) the court, and any party against whose interests the information was to be provided, would be left with little practical choice except to act upon the view that was proffered by the relevant agency.
>
> These difficulties are important, but not just because any solutions to them may not sit easily with common forms of curial procedure. They are important because, to the extent that federal courts are left with no practical choice except to act upon a view proffered by the Executive, the appearance of institutional impartiality and the maintenance of public confidence in the courts are both damaged.[76]

Hayne J's observations highlight that the mere preservation of judicial discretion is not the whole story when it comes to preserving the independence of courts from the executive or the fairness of judicial proceedings. His Honour's reasons relate to federal courts, but are applicable to state courts presiding over similar control order schemes.

The High Court's approach to resolving the tension between secret evidence and procedural fairness goes a considerable way in preserving judicial independence and impartiality. However, it fails to address the challenges posed to these values by the impact of secrecy on public confidence in the impartial administration of justice, by the erosion of party rights so fundamental to the adversarial system, and by placing judges in the onerous – perhaps untenable – position of assessing the weight and import of untested evidence. Ultimately, the criminal intelligence cases demonstrate that a close focus on the court's decisional independence – as is called for in a Ch. III analysis – overlooks or gives insufficient weight to factors such as perceived independence, the capacities of the judge to act with substantive independence (even where the judge's inherent powers and discretions are preserved), open justice, and fairness to the parties.

Conclusion

Secret evidence compromises procedural fairness. Through a string of cases starting with *Gypsy Jokers* and culminating in *Condon*, the High Court has adopted a clear position on how the tension between secrecy and fairness is resolved. In short, secret evidence is generally permissible in state court proceedings provided that three conditions are met. First, the court must have the capacity to independently determine whether the information had been properly classified. Second, the court must not be forced to take a particular course of action with respect to the secret evidence. Third, the court must retain sufficient discretion to allow it to counteract any potential unfairness resulting from the secret evidence. In achieving this final end, the court may attribute less, or no, weight to the evidence, or order a stay of proceedings for want of fairness.[77]

The challenge that secret evidence poses to procedural fairness should not be underestimated. It is misleading to assert that the Constitution permits no compromise to procedural fairness when, in fact, the threshold for constitutional repugnancy is high, and secret evidence is a generally permissible and increasingly common feature of judicial proceedings. The cases upholding secret 'criminal intelligence' evidence in State court proceedings do not bode well for the development of substantive fair process protections from Ch. III. To say, as Gageler J did, that the existence of exceptions to procedural fairness is 'more apparent than real' seriously understates the impact of secrecy on the fairness of court proceedings or, perhaps, reflects an attempt to extend Ch. III's existing protections for fair process beyond their current scope. In light of the cases discussed, it would seem more appropriate to say that exceptions to procedural fairness are limited, balanced and controlled by an independent judicature; not simply that these exceptions do not exist. A court may have the power to stay proceedings for want of fairness, or to give no weight to secret evidence, but a system that relies on the exercise of these discretions still falls short of the adversarial system of open and fair justice.

This discussion demonstrates that Ch. III of the Constitution is an inadequate tool in the protection of basic fair process rights. The High Court has succeeded in giving relative clarity and certainty to a contentious area of law. It has balanced secrecy and fairness, a balance that will never be beyond criticism. The approach adopted in the criminal intelligence cases overlooks the importance of public confidence in the independent judicature and the close relationship between the separation of judicial power and the rule of law, and overestimates the capacity for the court to effectively ameliorate procedural unfairness.

The High Court's focus on the decisional independence of courts in the cases discussed is unsurprising when one considers the nature of Ch. III, and the absence of any comprehensive, Australian notion of due process. It appears that the Australian Constitution will tolerate considerable erosion of procedural fairness, drawing the line only at provisions that force the judge to permit unfair proceedings. This high bar for constitutional invalidity on fair process grounds risks considerable damage to the independence and impartiality of judges in insidious and subtle, but still vital, ways.

Notes

1 (2013) 87 ALJR 458 (*Condon*).
2 *Condon* (n. 1) 497 [177] (Gageler J).

3 Ibid. [192] (Gageler J).
4 See, for example, *Kable v Director of Public Prosecutions (NSW)* (1996) 189 CLR 51, 106–7 (Gaudron J); *Re Nolan; Ex parte Young* (1991) 172 CLR 460, 496–7 (Gaudron J); *Leeth v Commonwealth* (1992) 174 CLR 455, 487–8 (Deane and Toohey JJ); *Condon* (n. 1) 463 (French CJ), 494 (Hayne, Crennan, Kiefel and Bell JJ), 497 (Gageler J); Will Bateman, 'Procedural Due Process under the Australian Constitution' (2009) 31 *Sydney Law Review* 411; Fiona Wheeler, 'Due Process, Judicial Power and Chapter III in the New High Court' (2004) 32 FLR 205; George Williams and David Hume, *Human Rights Under the Australian Constitution* (2nd ed., Oxford University Press 2013) 325–8.
5 *R v Kirby Ex parte Boilermakers' Society of Australia* (1956) 94 CLR 254, 270 (Dixon CJ, McTiernan, Fullagar and Kitto JJ).
6 *Kable* (n. 4) 103 (Toohey J), 82 (Dawson J).
7 *Kirk v Industrial Relations Commission (NSW)* (2010) 239 CLR 531, 579–81 [95]–[100] (French CJ, Gummow, Hayne, Heydon, Crennan, Kiefel and Bell JJ); *Fardon v Attorney-General (Qld.)* (2004) 223 CLR 575, 591 [15].
8 *Kable* (n. 4).
9 *Forge v Australian Securities and Investments Commission* (2006) 228 CLR 45; see also *Wainohu v New South Wales* (2011) ALJR 746, 208 (French CJ) (*Wainohu*).
10 For explanation and critique, see Wheeler (n. 4); Bateman (n. 4); Rebecca Welsh, 'A Path to Purposive Formalism: Interpreting Chapter III for Judicial Independence and Impartiality' (2013) 39(1) *Monash Law Review*, 66, 78–80.
11 Fiona Wheeler, 'The *Kable* Doctrine and State Legislative Power over State Courts' (2005) 20 *Australian Parliamentary Review* 15, 22; Anthony Mason, 'A New Perspective on Separation of Powers' (1996) 82 *Canberra Bulletin of Public Administration* 1, 2, 5.
12 *Nolan* (n. 4) 496 (Gaudron J), endorsed in, for example, *Fardon* (n. 7) 615 (Gummow J); *Condon* (n. 1) 491 (Hayne, Crennan, Kiefel and Bell JJ).
13 *Condon* (n. 1) 463 (French CJ), quoting A. L. Goodhart, 'What is the Common Law' (1960) 76 *Law Quarterly Review*, 45, 46.
14 Australian Law Reform Commission, *Keeping Secrets: The Protection of Classified and Security Sensitive Information*, Report No. 98 (2004) 10.8.
15 For a valuable discussion of public interest immunity and control order proceedings, see: Greg Martin, 'Outlaw Motorcycle Gangs and Secret Evidence: Reflections on the Use of Criminal Intelligence in the Control of Serious Organised Crime in Australia' (2014) 36 *Sydney Law Review*, 505.
16 (2008) 234 CLR 532 (*K-Generation*).
17 Liquor Licensing At 1997 (SA) s. 4.
18 For discussion of this migration, see Andrew Lynch, 'Control Orders in Australia: A Further Case Study in the Migration of British Counter-Terrorism Law' (2008) 8 *Oxford University Commonwealth Law Journal* 159; Andrew Lynch, Tamara Tulich and Rebecca Welsh, 'Secrecy and Control Orders: The Role and Vulnerability of Constitutional Values in Australia and the United Kingdom' in David Cole, Federico Fabbrini and Arianna Vedaschi (eds.), *Secrecy, National Security, and the Vindication of Constitutional Law* (Edward Elgar 2013) 154; Lisa Burton and George Williams, 'What Future for Australia's Control Order Regime?' (2013) 24 *Public Law Review*, 182; Susan Donkin, *Preventing Terrorism and Controlling Risk: A Comparative Analysis of Control Orders in the UK and Australia* (Springer 2014).
19 Criminal Code Act 1995 (Cth.), s. 104.4 (Commonwealth Criminal Code).
20 Ibid. s. 104.4(1)(b)-(c).
21 (2007) 233 CLR 307 (*Thomas*).
22 See 'A New Coat of Paint: Law and order and the Refurbishment of *Kable*' (2012) 40 *Federal Law Review*, 1.
23 Commonwealth Criminal Code, div. 102.
24 CCOCA, ss. 26–27; SOCCA, s. 14(5), (7).

25 CCOCA, s. 26; SOCCA, s. 22.
26 See Kent Roach, 'The Eroding Distinction Between Intelligence and Evidence in Terrorism Investigations' in Nicola McGarrity, Andrew Lynch and George Williams (eds.), *Counter-Terrorism and Beyond: The Culture of Law and Justice After 9/11* (Routledge 2010) 48.
27 SOCCA, s. 14(1).
28 Ibid. s. 10(1).
29 Ibid. s. 13(1).
30 Ibid. s. 13(2), except to a person conducting a review of the legislation or a person specifically authorised by the Commissioner.
31 Ibid. s. 3.
32 Ibid. s. 21(2)(a).
33 Ibid. s. 15(4).
34 CCOCA, ss. 9, 26–27; SOCCA, ss. 10, 14.
35 CCOCA, s. 28.
36 This distinction is of integral importance in the Australian context, where the strict separation of judicial power prevents the conferral of non-judicial functions, such as the administrative task of declaring an organisation, on courts. Whilst this rule, derived from the Commonwealth Constitution, only prevents *state* courts from undertaking those non-judicial tasks that are incompatible with their independence and integrity, the rule accounts for the parliament's reticence to give the role to a court *per se*. For authority on these principles as they apply in the state and federal contexts, respectively, see *Wainohu* (n. 9); *Wilson v Minister for Aboriginal and Torres Strait Islander Affairs* (1996) 189 CLR 1; *Grollo v Palmer* (1995) 184 CLR 348.
37 See CCOCA, ss. 8–9; *Wainohu* (n. 9) 752, 767, 769–70 (French CJ and Kiefel J).
38 CCOCA, s. 13.
39 Ibid. s. 28.
40 COA, ss. 10, 18.
41 Defined almost identically to existing control order schemes in other states: Ibid. s. 59(1).
42 Ibid. ss. 86, 89, 90.
43 See, for example, *Kable* (n. 4) 106–7 (Gaudron J); *Re Nolan; Ex parte Young* (1991) 172 CLR 460, 496–7 (Gaudron J); *Leeth* (n. 4) 487–8 (Deane and Toohey JJ); *Condon* (n. 1) 463 (French CJ), 494 (Hayne, Crennan, Kiefel and Bell JJ), 497 (Gageler J); Bateman (n. 4); Wheeler (n. 4).
44 (2008) 234 CLR 532 (*Gypsy Jokers*).
45 Corruption and Crime Commission Act 2003 (WA), s. 76(2).
46 *Gypsy Jokers* (n. 44) 560–1 (Gummow, Hayne, Heydon and Kiefel JJ).
47 Ibid. 560 (Gummow, Hayne, Heydon and Kiefel JJ).
48 *K-Generation Pty Limited v Liquor Licensing Court* (2009) 237 CLR 501, 542–3 (Gummow, Hayne, Heydon, Crennan and Kiefel JJ).
49 (2010) 242 CLR 1 (*Totani*).
50 Ibid. 21 (French CJ).
51 *Wainohu* (n. 9).
52 Ibid. 752 (French CJ and Kiefel J), 50 (Gummow, Hayne, Crennan and Bell JJ).
53 *Totani* (n. 49).
54 *Wainohu* (n. 9).
55 *Totani* (n. 49) 61 (Gummow J), 109–10 (Heydon J), 153 (Crennan and Bell JJ); *Wainohu* (n. 9) 194 (French CJ and Kiefel J), 229 (Gummow, Hayne, Crennan and Bell JJ), 233–4 (Heydon J).
56 *Totani* (n. 49) [283] (Heydon J); *Wainohu* (n. 9) 773 [92] (Gummow, Hayne, Crennan and Bell JJ).
57 *Condon* (n. 1) 482 [88] (French CJ).
58 Ibid. 495 [166], see also 495–6 [167], [168].

59 Ibid. 503 (Gageler J).
60 Ibid. 497 [177] (Gageler J).
61 Ibid. 499–500 [192] (Gageler J).
62 Ibid. 500 [194] (Gageler J).
63 On the importance of perceived independence see, for example, Stephen Parker, 'The Independence of the Judiciary' in Fiona Wheeler and Brian Opeskin (eds.), *The Australian Federal Judicial System* (Melbourne University Press 2000) 62, 63; United Nations Office on Drugs and Crime, *Commentary on the Bangalore Principles of Judicial Conduct* (September 2007) 77; HP Lee and Enid Campbell, *The Australian Judiciary* (2nd edn., Cambridge University Press 2012) 6, 308–15; Gerard Brennan, 'The State of the Judicature' (1998) 72 *Australian Law Journal*, 33, 34; Anthony Mason, 'The Courts and Public Opinion' in Geoffrey Lindell (ed.), *The Mason Papers* (The Federation Press 2007) 94.
64 *Nicholas v The Queen* (1998) 193 CLR 173, 256–7 (Kirby J) (*Nicholas*); *Kable* (n. 4) 116 (McHugh J); *International Finance Trust Company Limited v New South Wales Crime Commission* (2009) 240 CLR 319, 354 (French CJ); *Grollo v Palmer* (1995) 184 CLR 348, 365 (Brennan CJ, Deane, Dawson and Toohey JJ).
65 *Nicholas* (n. 64) 197 (Brennan CJ), 275 (Hayne J); cf. the opinions of Gaudron, McHugh and Kirby JJ (two of whom were in dissent) that the court's power to protect its own processes and maintain public confidence in the administration of justice was central to the constitutional conception of judicial power: 209 (Gaudron J), 224, 226 (McHugh J), 258 (Kirby J).
66 *Nicholas* (n. 64).
67 Ibid. 209 (Gaudron J), 224, 226 (McHugh J), 258 (Kirby J).
68 Wendy Lacey, 'Inherent Jurisdiction, Judicial Power and Implied Guarantees under Chapter III of the Constitution' (2003) 31 *Federal Law Review*, 57, 76.
69 *A v United Kingdom* App. No. 3455/05 (ECtHR, 19 February 2009); see also Lynch, Tulich and Welsh (n. 18); Martin (n. 15).
70 Lee and Campbell (n. 63) 5; Cheryl Saunders and Katherine Le Roy, 'Perspectives on the Rule of Law' in Cheryl Saunders and Katherine Le Roy (eds.), *The Rule of Law* (The Federation Press 2003) 1, 2; Denise Meyerson, 'The Rule of Law and the Separation of Powers' (2004) 4 *Macquarie Law Journal*, 1, 2; Mason (n. 11) 2.
71 Fiona Wheeler, 'The *Kable* Doctrine' (n. 11), 22; Mason (n. 11) 2.
72 For further critique on this point see Welsh (n. 10).
73 Fenwick and Phillipson acknowledge that when there is a significant degree of non-disclosure, the role of special advocates becomes 'absolutely critical': Helen Fenwick and Gavin Phillipson, 'Covert Derogations and Judicial Deference: Redefining Liberty and Due Process Rights in Counter-Terrorism Law and Beyond' (2011) 56(4) *McGill Law Journal*, 863, 897.
74 Martin (n. 15) 529; Lynch, Tulich and Welsh (n. 18).
75 On this, see the dissenting judgment of Hayne J in *Thomas* (n. 21) 477–8.
76 Ibid. 477–8 (Hayne J). In a unique step for an independent reviewer of legislation, the Independent National Security Legislation Monitor, Bret Walker SC, adopted this passage and its surrounding text in his report: Australian Government Independent National Security Monitor, *Declassified Annual Report 20th December 2012* (May 2013) 43: '[N]one of these difficulties [identified by Hayne J] is dispelled by the reasoning of the majority. Rather, and with commendable confidence in the Australian judiciary, the outcome opposite to that favoured by Hayne J involved acceptance of the difficulty of the judicial task when a judge is required to determine drastic consequences on the basis of predicted conduct. And none of these difficulties arise when the ordinary judicial processes are applied. On the 'judicialisation of intelligence' brought about by the state control order schemes, see Martin (n. 15) 505.
77 This last option being the only effective option, according to Gageler J.

Part 3

Right to know

Chapter 8

Secrecy, the media and the state

Controlling and managing information about terrorism and security

Lawrence McNamara

Introduction

Information about terrorism offences is, inevitably, tightly controlled by the state, whether it relates to the preparation or commission of offences or to the actions of the authorities tasked with combating terrorism. These are matters of great public interest and the media's fourth-estate role in informing the public is extremely important in terrorism matters. Traditions of media freedom characterise and sustain open, informed public debate – the basis of the public's 'right to know' – and the ability to effectively access and report information is a mainstay of those traditions. It is surprising, then, that journalists' experience of reporting on terrorism has received little attention and has not been the subject of sustained empirical work. Yet, it warrants close attention because, as Cram has noted, 'while some additional degree of restraint is inevitable and justified', limits on media freedom 'constitute a threat to expressive freedom, putting at risk the informed scrutiny of government policy and executive conduct'.[1] The media experience is especially significant as governments increasingly pursue laws that enable information to be kept secret in an ever-widening range of circumstances.[2] The legal changes are accompanied by an acute political caution regarding the release of information.

This chapter examines how practices of information control and access in the United Kingdom affect the media when reporting on terrorism and security. It does so by looking at the experiences of journalists who have covered terrorism matters. It uses journalists' words to convey their experiences and interactions with those who work within legal institutions and with Muslim communities affected where terrorism matters arise, as Muslim communities have increasingly become 'suspect communities' in the post-9/11 landscape. After briefly outlining the research and its methodology, three areas are addressed: first, journalists' access to information in the period following terrorism arrests, but prior to charges being laid; second, access to information once a matter reaches the courts; and third, the ways that journalists may be required to reveal information to the authorities.[3]

It will be suggested that where terrorism and security is in issue, the public right to know about what is happening in our communities and what is being done by our state is neither adequately protected nor appropriately respected. There is no doubt that both institutions and the individuals within them face very difficult challenges and numerous obstacles as they try to carry out their work, but these challenges can and must be met more effectively – and must not be hindered by laws and practices that embed secrecy and distrust as the norm – if democratic accountability is to be pursued.

Methodology and context: the 'Law, Terrorism and the Right to Know' project

The research for this chapter was undertaken as part of the 'Law, Terrorism and the Right to Know' research programme. Running from 2009–13, the programme explored how governments and courts deal with security-related information, and the relationships between the state and the media. It examined matters such as how different parties involved in controlling and communicating information understand and draw connections between principles of open justice, the rule of law, public accountability and national security. It explored how information can be selectively and strategically presented or concealed, how access can be controlled, and what the effects of these processes might be.

The project included around 70 confidential research interviews conducted over 18 months in 2010–12. Interviewees were drawn from the judiciary and courts, government, policing, legal profession, and – most relevantly for this chapter – journalists, media lawyers and editorial decision-makers. Most interviews were UK-orientated, although a small number were conducted in Australia and the United States with individuals from those countries.[4]

Sixteen print and broadcast journalists were interviewed. Some had long experience in reporting on terrorism matters for UK outlets (both national and regional) and some had also reported for international outlets. They included journalists with many years' experience in terrorism and related areas such as crime, home affairs and court reporting. In a few instances, interviewees had covered only one terrorism matter, but had done so in depth.

The political and legal context in which the interviews were conducted is noteworthy. First, the Leveson Inquiry into the Culture, Practice and Ethics of the Press ran for a year from November 2011.[5] Although it dominated the headlines, it was not a significant point of reference in the interviews. As the next section explains, although it provides some information about the issues, for the most part it was not concerned with police–media relationships in the terrorism context. Second, and this was a point of reference in interviews, legislation was being debated that would increase secrecy in civil proceedings. This was occurring against the background of increasing scepticism about the propriety or legality of the ways that authorities have operated in combating terrorism. The archetypal cases were actions against the British government by former Guantanamo Bay detainees returned to the UK without having been charged, but the provisions in the Bill that would become the Justice and Security Act 2013 applied to all civil proceedings. They would overcome the Supreme Court's decision in *Al Rawi v The Security Services*[6] that closed material proceedings could not be used in civil actions. With journalists less willing to accept at face value claims made by the authorities (especially about the actions of the state), and expanding secrecy laws that would prevent scrutiny, the issues under discussion were very much in the minds of interviewees. Consequently, interviewees were often very reflective about both their experiences and what the current debates might mean for the future.

Journalists' access to information after arrests

Terrorism activities come into the media and public eye when arrests are made. Only very occasionally are arrests made after an act of violence has been committed. Most arrests are made when the authorities suspect that individuals possess materials or are engaged in activities that are preparatory to committing a terrorist act. There may be simultaneous arrests in different cities. As such, arrests will not be predictable and it may be unclear for some time exactly who has been arrested and on what basis. As journalists struggle to get a reliable picture of what has happened and what is suspected, they will be heavily reliant in the first instance on information from police. However, that information may be minimal, and journalists will want to test its accuracy and completeness. This, it was explained by interviewees, can be extremely difficult.

To verify information they have been given and to obtain further information not generally available, the 'critical thing' for journalists is 'sources, having their trust so they will talk to you, and then making an assessment of what they tell you'.[7] In terrorism and security matters, both the trust and assessment aspects are difficult because 'journalists are distrusted by police and by the Muslim communities where arrested persons will often live or will have family or other connections'.[8] Media relationships with police and communities are tested in these circumstances, and especially before anyone is charged or where no charges are laid.

Relationships with police and security services

The Leveson Inquiry revealed that around the time of the 7/7 London bombings in 2005,[9] there was a close relationship between police and crime reporters. Police would brief journalists off the record on the basis that there was 'an overwhelming public interest' in conveying to the public any terrorist threat to the UK, but without prejudicing investigations or trials.[10] With one exception, it appears that information about terrorism investigations was never leaked to the media.[11] Rather, information would generally be provided to the media only in order to prevent a report being published that may adversely affect an investigation.[12] As such, even while Leveson was critical of the close relationship between some police and some journalists, and there was much discussion of how unattributable or off the record briefings are problematic, there is nothing in the Leveson Inquiry to suggest that journalists ever found it easy to obtain information about terrorism investigations.

On the whole, the Leveson Inquiry does not tell us a great deal about the media experience of terrorism reporting. What, then, do journalists say about their dealings with the authorities when reporting on terrorism?

All journalists reporting on terrorism matters have interactions and relationships with the police, via both police press offices and individual contacts, but most do not have direct relationships with the security services.[13] When arrests have taken place, the authorities are a key source of information, but journalists are 'entirely vulnerable to being misled and really you have to cultivate contacts who you trust greatly'.[14]

The limited sources of information and vulnerability were regularly raised. One journalist thought there was:

> a huge problem about total reliance on government interpretation of intelligence and evidence presented in the early days of an investigation. . . . [T]he media can quite easily be, and has been, persuaded to follow a particular course of enquiry which has later transpired not to be [correct].[15]

Terrorism cases operated differently. Police contacts were not a fruitful avenue of information because, unlike the general run of criminal matters, including serious crime: 'It's different because ultimately it's controlled by MI5, so even your usual police contacts don't want to say anything. They might claim they don't know anything'.[16] For another: 'We couldn't get out anything out of anyone. The police just locked down like you would not believe. Usually on big stories they do have their protocols in what they can say but they will usually give you something – and we had nothing to go on'.[17] Journalists are aware of the difficult position police may be in and want to maintain ongoing good relationships; while obviously seeking information from police, 'I don't want to compromise them either'.[18]

The information shut-down can be sweeping. One journalist recalled not being able to find out in what street in a regional city some arrests had occurred overnight. There was no information coming in as there usually would be from, for example, neighbours in the street. The police did not arrive with flashing lights and so, even if neighbours had woken up and looked out of the window, they would not have thought much of it; as a result, 'it happened without anyone seeming to know about it' and so the next day was a matter of 'traipsing round, just hoping to stumble across it'.[19] Another described what happens once the street or house is located:

> It wasn't like normally – there was no police line of officers outside in uniform. [But] it was quite obvious. . . . For instance there were a couple of properties in an area which has got a high BME [black, minority and ethnic] population, with a couple of middle class white guys stood outside the door dressed very well. . . . [It] makes everything harder because it is, in one sense, obvious that it's that property. But [the police] won't confirm it. Neighbours are talking, but

> it's hard. You've got to give your readers something, but how do you confirm? Because [the police] won't confirm this, they won't confirm that.[20]

The 'lack of information fuels speculation', which is unnecessary and counter-productive.[21] The police may provide some steer. The following is a typical example:

> [They] will, sort of, give you on a scale of 1-to-10 how serious these arrests are. . . . Police are quite understanding of [our needs]. If it's a biggie, then we are going to need to deploy a satellite truck, producers, camera crews. We're asking, really, because of the logistics involved. We have limited resources. [If] we throw everything up to a raid in Birmingham and it turns out [to be] one bloke with some dodgy DVDs, then it's not worth it. If it's three or four guys building a bomb, then it's going to be major news, it's probably going to lead our bulletins. We need to . . . gauge that. [Arrests] come up on the wires, [my news desk will ask] me, 'Should we send on this?' . . . I need to answer that almost instantly.[22]

There was some very strong criticism of press officers in the counter-terrorism units:

> They release very short on the record statements which may or may not be true. But then what the public and civil society is oblivious to is that then you get all the off the record briefing. And it can [come from] senior cops, and it can be spooks [security services officers]. But actually a lot of the time it's press officers disguised as senior police sources and they use that off the record briefing to twist and slant news coverage beyond what the [on the record] statement has already done.[23]

To that journalist, 'all state sponsored press officers' have a function which 'essentially is kind of a barrier between the people who hold information, the truth if you like and those who are trying to get it out. They are not enablers they are kind of preventers'.[24] Other interviewees did not characterise that so strongly, but there was considerable scepticism of the way that police officers present facts:

> The largest obstacles are officialdom itself, the uneasiness that exists within the relationship between official press officers and the media. There is a default position, there's a complete unwillingness to share information. That means that journalists like myself look elsewhere and we try to forge unofficial relationships as much as possible.[25]

Not all police forces or counter-terrorism units were seen to be the same. One journalist saw some as simply unhelpful, and others, although they perhaps provided more information, were misleading: 'I don't know if I believe anything that [X Police Force] say to me, certainly about counterterrorism operations'.[26] Regardless of the differences across units or forces, the one-sidedness of information at the time of arrests inherently raised great difficulties:

> It is very hard to test information that you are being spoon fed and it is so sensitive by nature that it is almost impossible. [T]here is an acceptance of credibility which you can't afford really to go behind. . . . A bit later on [you] are in a better position to question some of the facts that you were given at the time. This is usually [through] information which emerges through the lawyers working for the suspects and a better picture emerges.[27]

The scepticism is endemic and more acutely felt where the security services are concerned: 'The instinctive position of the security forces is to provide the media with something that they believe will serve their own purposes'.[28] Of course, this is not necessarily any different from the approach taken by anyone dealing with the media; in all circumstances, 'you're kind of constantly aware that [everybody you speak to has] got their own agenda'.[29] Nonetheless, the security services seemed more able than the police to entice journalists into believing what they were told. The way that an experienced journalist searches for words helps to illustrate both the difficulty of obtaining information and the vulnerability to being misled when dealing with the security services:

> If I wasn't sure of something, I would say, 'If I were to say this, would that be accurate?' And they would say, 'Well, it's not a million miles wide of the mark', or something like that. So it's a sort of . . . almost . . . it's not a game, but it's . . . it's a testing process . . . I think it's quite . . . potentially . . . not dangerous but . . . unwise for . . . you know, young reporters who are starting out doing this beat to appreciate what the, you know, what the . . . what the pitfalls are. And they may be more vulnerable to spinner . . . spinnery, which happens, you know, than I would.[30]

One was:

> a bit suspicious of some of my colleagues' closeness to the security services. Some . . . sound like mouth pieces for various agencies. You have to be constantly on your guard at getting too close to these people, about being sucked into their world and feeling like, 'Oh, you know, well I owe him a favour,' and all this, that and the other.[31]

The difference between dealing with the security services and the police was that the former could and would shut people out if they so chose, and there was little or no recourse:

> The police are kind of big enough and ugly enough to have an argument with and fall out with and then you build bridges with them. . . . With MI5, they

> only speak to certain journalists. . . . We haven't had a big falling out yet but I get the feeling that if you piss them off then they cut you off. And I know there are certain journalists that they don't talk to who write about their worlds continually. And to my mind, that's unhelpful because that is not an open or two way kind of thing. I mean, they don't really fucking tell you anything anyway. They tell you what they want to tell you and they have stuff they want to push. But when you go in with a direct question you get, you get almost non-answers really. I find it a quite unsatisfactory relationship.[32]

There were suggestions that the security services should hold open, on the record briefings for journalists. 'If they did,' I asked, 'Could those be trusted?' 'No,' was the response, 'Because you can't trust anything. But at least we know who said it and when'.[33] The scepticism about the agencies' dealings with the media was not a criticism, as such, of the agencies' work. There was acceptance that the security services are managing difficult issues, have had great success in disrupting plots, and often are unable to secure recognition. For example, where a case does not proceed to court and information does not come out – it either ends up in closed proceedings in the Special Immigration Appeals Commission, or a plot is disrupted before there is sufficient evidence to charge a person with an offence – then there is a well-recognised effect on the security services: 'It's a problem for them . . . because they don't, they can't, show any results . . . [But] when they get a result they're very keen to make a big show of it'.[34]

Relationships with Muslim communities

With information from the authorities tending to be minimal and, on occasion, even misleading, there is a great need to supplement, test and verify what is made available by the state. To do that, sources in local communities where arrests have occurred will be crucial. There is now an established literature on British Muslim communities as suspect communities and, within that, documentation of media coverage of those communities and how such coverage is perceived within them.[35] The experience of journalists is consistent with that literature. Journalists frequently engage with Muslim communities, either with families or neighbours of those arrested or at a more representative level through organisations or perhaps someone respected in the community that the defendant calls home. Responses were unequivocal: when engaging with Muslim communities journalists found a 'huge, huge', 'massive' lack of trust of members of the media and thought they were seen by many 'as the enemy'.[36] Faced with the media, Muslim locals would '[shut] up shop or [be] withdrawing into themselves'.[37]

Importantly, journalists were unsurprised by this; in fact, they thought it understandable and justifiable that communities were 'pretty cynical about the media'.[38] Journalists themselves saw the media as having contributed to the environment of distrust through a lack of depth in analysis, knee-jerk reactions and tendencies to sensationalise.[39] 'You can't really blame the Muslim community,' said one. 'They do get an awful kicking and they're rightly suspicious I think'.[40] Said another, 'I think they see the media as part of the prosecution, you know, a part of the Islamophobia that is evident in British society'.[41]

When asked about whether it is possible or appropriate to speak of 'the Muslim community', one respondent argued that it was not because there were differences across ethnic backgrounds, age groups and strands of belief, but that, nevertheless, 'All those communities, I'm pretty sure, feel under the same kind of pressure'.[42]

> You're fighting the mindset, which is really difficult, because the community feels itself under siege, under attack, victimised, stereotyped. I'm not talking about families whose sons are in jail for terrorist offences, I'm talking about the community as a whole.[43]

A raid resulting in arrests will combine with subsequent media presence to fuel community caution and cynicism. First, the police arrive:

> Police raids do have a big impact on the community, especially when [those arrested are] subsequently released when they haven't got the evidence to charge them, but also, the reason why it happens . . . It's . . . disruptive . . . it's to break up the cell. So they know they're being watched.[44]

Next, the media descends:

> It's very difficult to build relationships and trust with people that you just sort of parachute into their neighbourhood for a couple of days and, and bang on every door and have cameras everywhere and then you bugger off to the next circus. People like myself should probably be spending more time investing in people in those communities.[45]

The journalists in the pack are not only from outside the communities, but their relationship with Muslim communities is also 'as white journalists, to be brutally honest' and when a person is charged 'my job would be to look at background and I will go out to that house and knock on the neighbours' doors but you tend to find (a) animosity, (b) mistrust'.[46]

How, then, can journalists build relationships of trust? They need to put in time, just as they would in building any relationship.[47] It is a slow process: '[T]hey weren't prepared to do anything without long conversations about what I was going to do with the information and how I felt the information might be used'.[48] They 'have to go into the community – that is the only way to do it'.[49]

> Gone are the days when you can pick up the phone and speak to people who represent . . . members of [a] Muslim community and expect to get . . . a meaningful answer. You would [now] get a 'no comment' or a platitude that is a summary of what you knew already. You won't get the kind of in-depth analysis or intelligence that perhaps you are looking for. [50]

While 'it's not impossible' to build relationships, whether by 'show[ing] a degree of empathy and understanding' or 'just [being] persuasive', it is:

> more difficult [as] all the tabloids turn up with huge wodges of cash basically saying, 'Let me buy your story.' And it will normally work with the white neighbours next door who've got some stuff to slag off about them. But for the actual Muslim communities – for the kernel of the story – that doesn't work.[51]

One (white British) senior journalist described an approach of not seeking to develop sources directly:

> Getting the contacts within the Muslim community is really, really difficult, because there is an inbuilt mistrust of . . . outsiders, non-Muslims, those who work for [major media]. And there is a natural reluctance to have anything to do with people like me. Not because of who I am or what I've done, but because of what I represent in their eyes.[52]

Instead, contacts and relationships were built by Muslim colleagues, and that was productive:

> They refused to meet me. [Among the reasons], I think they would have been concerned that if I'd interviewed them I would have given them a much, much harder time. But in a way, that's no bad thing. They gave extremely frank, blunt interviews with my colleagues, which they would not have done with me, because I would have had to challenge them, and they would have probably clammed up.[53]

The 'tendency for reporters [to] always work in packs', the dynamic of media presence and competition for stories do not make it easy for journalists to build individual relationships over time. A good example of how news desk demands affect relationship-building was explained by a journalist who had secured an interview against the odds:

> [O]ne guy . . . had spent [two days] outside the mosque being interviewed . . . [Only once] everyone had gone . . . we just started chatting. And I think it was because it was no longer the pack that he kind of opened up . . . [But] if you are in that pack and you are all roaming around the streets looking for quotes, you're always going to find it really, really hard. But the thing is that's what the news desk wants. They don't want to be behind the competition so they will want everyone to kind of work together. They'll be a bit nervous about someone saying, 'Right I'm going off on my own to do my own thing'.[54]

The experience of reporting on terrorism arrests is unlike crime reporting generally. The authorities reveal less information, either formally or informally. What is revealed is less likely to be reliable and, with communities less prepared to provide information to the media, it will be more difficult to test. Few things will be clear or certain; the circumstances do not lend themselves to any other outcome. Once charged, a person will be brought before the courts and then any information obtained and reported will be (hopefully) more reliable.

The legal process: obtaining information after charge

Where a person is charged with terrorism offences in England or Wales, his or her first court appearance is at Westminster Magistrates Court in London.[55] That appearance is the media's first opportunity to see the charge sheet (although there are no systematic processes in place to provide it) and it is also the first time the Crown Prosecution Service (CPS) reveals the allegations. Ideally, the police leading the operation provide a press statement that usually includes a contribution from the CPS. An excellent example was a press release by West Midlands Police in December 2010, which listed the names, ages and addresses of those charged, along with particulars of the offence, and comments from the CPS.[56] That level of information was thought by journalists to be useful and appropriate, but was also said to be the exception rather than the rule.

The first appearance will dispel or confirm pre-charge speculation about the allegations, although reports will inevitably be one-sided. The allegations can be reported and, driven by editorial demands, there may be 'a tendency towards spectacular writing, towards hyperbole'[57] or 'a tendency to go for the hottest line you can and sometimes to ignore inconvenient facts in order to promote the best story'.[58] Defence lawyers will not have a great deal of information and will tend to say little or nothing at all. It would not be unusual for defence lawyers (with no objection from the Crown) to seek reporting restrictions on details regarding their clients. Where a group is arrested and some members are charged and some released, the releases will garner little attention. It is the case against those who are charged that is of interest.

Information will rarely come out until trial. While journalists 'might get the odd leak', they 'don't get anything until [they] hear it in court usually'.[59]

Criminal trials

Trials are about contested versions of events. The Crown has alleged a person has committed criminal offences and the accused person has pleaded not guilty. However, not every issue is contested. On the contrary, much will be uncontested and a 'much more firm' factual picture will emerge:

> Agreed statements, admissions, facts that are just completely indisputable. . . . You get the amounts of money. [You get] the travel patterns – he went here, he went there. [You get] the emails. All of that stuff comes out and that's gold dust really.[60]

The authorities will almost certainly be pleased that this kind of uncontested information is in the public domain, even if it is many months after the arrests. At trials, journalists will 'get to see sensitive material'[61] and will hear first-hand accounts:

> No matter how many miles you walk and no matter how many people you speak [to, at the end of the day] the best stuff always comes out [at trial]. [Y]ou've got the defendant speaking for themselves, or the defendant's mother speaking. You've got the cops speaking. You've got a cop saying, 'Well, I broke down the door and this is what I saw.'[62]

This, for reporters, is a part of democratic public scrutiny: 'That stuff only ever comes out in court and court reporting is so important it is fundamental to our democracy'.[63] With most organisations financially pressed, sitting through a long-running case was described as 'a luxury' and this was worrying because in court: 'Instead of getting the embellished stuff and the spin and the bullshit you get . . . what they have to tell the jury. That's limited to an extent but you do get more facts and I think more reliable information'.[64]

For major trials, including terrorism trials, embargoed media briefings by police and the CPS will also be important, enabling reporters to 'learn more about the background [to the case and] to question about what [investigators] did and what they didn't do and why they did it. And that can be very useful'.[65] That said, these briefings are a way for the state to parade its strengths. The journalist continued:

> [I]f you want to learn more about [what] investigators would like to conceal about their investigations then you really will find it a lot more difficult because you'll be met with, generally, denial, obfuscation, people misleading you, sometimes people threaten you. Trying to learn the truth about that [can be] extraordinarily difficult and certainly . . . one place where you should go is listen to the legal argument that precedes trials in which lawyers try to argue about what will be admissible in evidence. Much of [that] will be heard in camera and it seems to me, from what I know now, that they will be heard in camera effectively to conceal evidence of official wrongdoing. But some of it will come out . . . Sometimes it is possible [to find one or two people there who will indicate to you something of what was said in camera]. But you also have the problem of sometimes people will deliberately leak something to you in order to give you a misleading impression of what's been said in camera.[66]

Reporting the courts

In spite of the value of press and public scrutiny of criminal trials, and even though journalists generally consider the Judicial Communications Office to be a useful point of access to basic information, reporting the courts is not easy.[67] Journalists described feeling unwelcome, and being treated 'as a nuisance'[68] and as 'second class citizens'.[69] They were critical of poor press facilities and a lack of awareness of media needs.[70] There were strong criticisms of the lack of access to materials:

> We are sitting in a court trying to report a case and the entire courtroom will have documents in front of them that they're reading from, which we're not given access to. They will skip through these documents, they'll refer to paragraph seven and they'll flick back to paragraph six. . . . And we won't have any idea what they're talking about.[71]

Most journalists reported little contact with judges, one describing the judiciary as 'invisible' and having no contact 'whatsoever, except when they tell you off'.[72] The criticisms may not be entirely justified, or at least do not present the full picture. First, these perceptions are markedly out of kilter with judicial views of the media's role and reporting on terrorism cases.[73] Generally, the judiciary takes the view that the media has an important and valuable role in reporting on terrorism cases. Judges tended to see themselves as doing their best to accommodate media interests, although they were largely of the view that the courts were not providers of information for the media, but adjudicators where the media may want access to material. They should not be 'entering into the ring to take part in a boxing match'; rather, they should be 'the umpire'.[74]

Second, the media can request material from the Crown and so the judiciary's perception of its role makes some sense in this context. A protocol agreed by the CPS, the Association of Chief Police Officers (ACPO) and media bodies enables the media to request prosecution material.[75] Journalists criticised police selectivity in the material provided. For example, only extracts of terrorist training videos shown in court would be released; parts that suggested the accused were incompetent were not made available.[76] Still, the police and the CPS have been described as 'pretty even-handed'[77] and on the whole the protocols provide a good pathway to accessing prosecution material, even though 'we get a boiled down, cut down version of what we want'.[78] Sitting alongside the protocols are more recent Criminal Procedure Rules that allow access to documents.[79] The courts have held that these rules are important and a fundamental aspect of securing effective open justice.[80]

Relationships with defence lawyers

With scepticism about information supplied by the state, and difficulty in obtaining information through the courts, do defence lawyers play an important role? To some extent, the answer is yes. Not every defence lawyer deals with or is helpful to the media; some 'are great, very helpful and very talkative', while others are 'very unhelpful'.[81] The former can be important sources, even while they work within legal and ethical constraints. They may provide information that is not restricted, but that is not easily accessible. Journalists, however, are still rightly cautious. Some defence lawyers, it was said, have 'sophisticated media strategy plans,

[are] very experienced and know exactly what to say and when to say it'.[82] Some may 'manipulate' journalists.[83] They are 'not stupid' and they are not naive; rather, they 'will talk when it is in their interest'.[84] From one perspective, this makes them no different from the prosecution or the police; whatever the party, 'self-serving documents' will be passed on to the media.[85]

At heart, however, lawyer–journalist relationships are simply professional, each acting with their respective interests in mind. Lawyers are acting for a client and – not without reason – are usually cautious. They can be 'very wary' because 'there is a tendency [and we are guilty of this] to cover the prosecution and not the defence'.[86] The reciprocal position was expressed well by a lawyer who said that it is easy to be on one's guard against 'less friendly elements of the press' and 'more difficult to be guarded with [those you trust a lot]' but:

> still at the back of my mind is, 'You are a journalist. What if I let something slip?' Can I really? [That person] is just going to get this out there. And they are good at their job. They are good at getting stuff out of you even when you don't really think you are saying that much.[87]

Journalists are reporting on matters of public interest and while they may be friendly with lawyers, that does not stop them reporting: 'I just have to make a difficult phone call at 10 o'clock at night and say, you know, "I'm sorry. I'm going to shit all over your client tomorrow."'[88] On both sides, trust is the central issue to the relationship. It is an acceptance that journalists and lawyers have different roles, but that they can co-exist. This was captured well by a journalist who said there are lawyers 'who will not mislead me. They may not be in a position to tell me the whole [story] because they're bound by the court, but they will not mislead me, and will not if possible allow me to mislead myself, to make wrong assumptions'.[89]

While journalists' main challenges will ordinarily lie in obtaining information, they may also be challenged by the legal requirement to disclose to the authorities information they have obtained. This challenge cannot go unremarked upon because the laws are a component part of the state's management and control of information. The fact that it is less visible than the difficulties associated with obtaining information does not render it less important.

The other side of the coin: journalists' obligations to disclose information

Journalists are not immune to or unfamiliar with demands for information. Journalistic materials can be sought using a 'production order' obtained under the Police and Criminal Evidence Act 1984 (UK) (PACE) or, in terrorism matters, under the less demanding provisions of the Terrorism Act 2000 (UK).[90] However, these established procedures are only engaged when the state requests material. There is no general obligation in British law for anyone to provide information to the authorities.

Terrorism legislation changes that general position. Under s. 38B of the Terrorism Act 2000, a person who has information 'which he knows or believes might be of material assistance' in preventing an act of terrorism or apprehending or prosecuting an offender must disclose that information to the authorities. A failure to do so carries a punishment of up to five years' imprisonment. It is a defence if a person has 'a reasonable excuse' for not disclosing, although 'reasonable excuse' is undefined. The offence existed in Northern Ireland from the mid-1970s but it was always controversial.[91] It was not a part of the Terrorism Act 2000 – it was expressly rejected – but was inserted in 2001 after the 9/11 attacks in New York City.[92] The provision is aimed at families, friends and others close to people who are planning or have committed offences, but it can clearly apply to others, including journalists.

The Independent Reviewer of Terrorism Legislation, David Anderson QC, has remarked upon this potential application in his annual reports.[93] In the academic literature, only Clive Walker has paid substantial attention to the laws, also observing the potential application.[94] Anderson concludes that the fears 'have not been realised in practice', noting that there have been no prosecutions of journalists and, although he indicates that the police may tend to give communities 'a firm reminder' of the implications of failing to disclose information, he does not indicate that police approach journalists in this way.[95] He does, however, consider that 'there is no doubt that some journalists have the availability of s. 38B well in mind: whether it has a chilling effect on their activities is something that would repay study'.[96] This chapter cannot accommodate a detailed discussion of s. 38B, but three brief observations may be made.

First, the research interviews – not only with journalists, but also with lawyers – indicated very clearly that this section is having an effect on the media. Although prosecutions to date have only been against family and friends, there is nothing in the legislation or the case law to suggest that a media prosecution is out of the question.[97] It was clear that in-house lawyers, external lawyers and journalists are all acutely aware of the possibility that journalists may be prosecuted. Interviews revealed that at least two journalists had sought legal advice on s. 38B from outside their organisations. I was told nothing which indicated that the police or security services have threatened journalists with prosecution, or even highlighted this particular power, but that should not lead to an inference that prosecution is unlikely. Rather, it is more likely that the authorities know that the media will disclose information. Certainly, the interviews left no doubt that disclosures have been made by media organisations on a number of occasions.

Second, although s. 38B was considered when the CPS drafted guidelines for prosecution of cases likely to affect the media, it is not in the list of offences to which the guidelines apply.[98] Given the media awareness of the issue, the effects it has had, and the judicial statements which make it clear that it is a serious offence, there was and remains a strong case for inclusion.[99] While it may not be 'likely' in the sense that it will be frequently prosecuted, it seems no less likely than some of the other offences in what is quite a long list.

Third, the research interviews strongly suggest that s. 38B is unnecessary where the media is concerned. There is little (if any) doubt that journalists and media organisations would disclose information in the circumstances contemplated by the Terrorism Act 2000. This does not mean an exemption or media-specific defence is appropriate. Instead, repeal of the section would be a better path.

So, can it be said that there is a chilling effect? That is, are journalists changing their behaviour and self-censoring what they write or stepping back from asking investigative questions that may place them in difficult positions? At this stage, no, but if there was a prosecution, then that would almost certainly change. There would be a very high risk that journalism would become more cautious than it needs to be. Unless there were clear grounds and a very strong evidentiary and public interest case for prosecution, a chilling effect would seem inevitable.

Conclusion

Where terrorism and national security are concerned, openness should be the default position. Unless there are good reasons for secrecy, the state should disclose information about terrorism and security. At certain times and in relation to a limited range of issues, secrecy may of course be essential where national security matters are concerned. Even among the most robust proponents of free speech and openness in the UK, and among the most trenchant sceptics of government behaviour, that proposition is widely accepted. But openness should be the presumptive starting point.

However, as this chapter has suggested, the deck is stacked against openness. At formal and informal levels, information remains largely in the control of the state. Within Muslim communities, the mainstream media faces great challenges in building trust, with those challenges, arguably, substantially a product of the media's own making. Journalists – even very experienced journalists with good contacts – find it very difficult to get reliable information and, importantly, to test the information they are given by the authorities. Even if imperfect, the courts are absolutely crucial avenues for obtaining information of great public interest. In terrorism and security matters, where information will be closely guarded by the state, the ability to adequately report court cases is essential if scrutiny of government is to be effective, if the threat of terrorism is to be understood, and if the public is to have confidence in the way that such threats are addressed. Things could and should be improved, but the main struggle at present is to ensure that open justice is not trumped by an all-encompassing – whether necessary or not – national security priority. In the words of a journalist interviewee, 'national security is an easy umbrella to put up to deflect what you think is going to be troublesome rain'.[100]

Are journalists reckless about managing information relating to terrorism and security? The answer is, resoundingly, 'no'. Do journalists view their roles uncritically? Again, clearly, 'no'. An accountable and responsible state should not fear the media where national security or natural justice are at issue. In the practice of journalism, as it emerged in the research interviews, the public interest in openness and the application of open justice principles are of vital importance, but they are ultimately secondary and will yield to primary priorities of natural justice and the public interest in national security. However, state controls over information currently make the gulf between these primary and secondary commitments unacceptably and unhealthily wide. There is still considerable scope to maintain and improve access to information before either natural justice or national security is threatened.

Notes

1 I. Cram, 'Regulating the Media: Some Neglected Freedom of Expression Issues in the United Kingdom's Counter-Terrorism Strategy' (2006) 18 *Terrorism and Political Violence*, 335, 336.
2 Most notable in the UK is the Justice and Security Act 2013. In Australia, the most recent expansion of powers is found in the National Security Legislation Amendment Act (No. 1) 2014.
3 Interviews have been given randomised codes in the format 'LTRK-XXX' and references to interviews are in this form so that the range of interviews drawn upon can be seen. Beyond this, for reasons of confidentiality, interviewees are not identified other than in general terms.
4 For earlier work on the Australian experience, see L. McNamara, 'Closure, Caution and the Question of Chilling: How Have Australian Counter-Terrorism Laws Affected the Media?' (2009) 14 *Media and Arts Law Review*, 1.
5 Lord Justice Leveson, *An Inquiry into the Culture, Practices and Ethics of the Press: Report* (November 2012) vols. 1–4 (Leveson Inquiry).
6 *Al Rawi v The Security Services* [2011] UKSC 34. This sat alongside other litigation that sought to secure the disclosure of executive documents under the *Norwich Pharmacal* principles: see especially *Binyam Mohamed v Secretary of State for Foreign & Commonwealth Affairs* [2010] EWCA Civ. 65, [2010] EWCA Civ. 158.
7 LTRK-129.
8 LTRK-168.
9 On 7 July 2005, four suicide bombers detonated devices in central London; three exploded on the underground and a fourth on a bus. Fifty-two people died and hundreds were injured.
10 Leveson Inquiry, above n. 5, vol. 2, p. 797, para. 2.59 (evidence of former Metropolitan Police Service Assistant Commissioner, Peter Clarke); see also vol. 2, p. 794, para. 2.47 (evidence of journalist, Sandra Laville).
11 The exception was the plot to behead a British soldier. Arrests were made and it appeared that one outlet had advance knowledge, and details of allegations were also subsequently leaked more widely: see, for example, Ian Gallagher, Andy Wilks and Keith Beabey, 'Police Chief's Fury over "Labour Leaks on Beheading Plot"' *Daily Mail* (London, 9 February 2007) 2; Steve Bell, 'Terror Leaks: Both Home Office and Police Implicated' (cartoon), *The Guardian* (London, 25 April 2007) 33. An internal investigation did not uncover the source of the leak: Leveson Inquiry, above n. 5, vol. 2, p. 802, para. 2.80.
12 Leveson Inquiry, above n. 5, vol. 2, pp. 783–5, paras. 2.10–2.18.
13 A useful examination of media and security services relationships can be found in R. Dover and M. Goodman (eds.), *Spinning Intelligence* (Hurst & Co 2009). Among numerous excellent chapters is one by BBC security correspondent, Gordon Corera (pp. 57–70).
14 LTRK-124. See also LTRK-129.

15 LTRK-153.
16 LTRK-163.
17 LTRK-132.
18 LTRK-163.
19 LTRK-181.
20 LTRK-163.
21 Ibid.
22 LTRK-137.
23 LTRK-168. Hopefully this pattern will change following publication of the College of Policing, 'Guidance on Relationships with the Media' (May 2013) <http://www.acpo.police.uk/documents/reports/2013/201305-cop-media-rels.pdf> accessed 22 September 2014. This document sets out to clarify a number of issues, including those relating to on-the-record, non-reportable, and embargoed briefings, as well as when and how unattributable statements may be made.
24 LTRK-168.
25 LTRK-137.
26 LTRK-124.
27 LTRK-153.
28 Ibid.
29 LTRK-126.
30 LTRK-129.
31 LTRK-126.
32 Ibid. (This person also cautioned that their contact with MI5 had been quite limited.)
33 LTRK-168.
34 LTRK-126.
35 See, for example, J. Lewis, P. Mason and K. Moore, 'Images of Islam in the UK: The representation of British Muslims in the National Print Media 2000–2008' in J. Petley and R. Richardson (eds.), *Pointing the Finger: Islam and Muslims in the Contemporary UK Media* (One World 2011) 40–64. For a good example of how communities perceive that coverage, see G. Mythen, S. Walklate and F. Khan, '"I'm a Muslim But I'm Not a Terrorist": Victimisation, Risky Identities and the Performance of Safety' (2009) 49 *British Journal of Criminology* 736, 742–3.
36 LTRK-126; LTRK-129.
37 LTRK-153; see also LTRK-168.
38 LTRK-153.
39 For example, LTRK-126, LTRK-129, LTRK-168, LTRK-131, LTRK-153.
40 LTRK-126.
41 LTRK-153.
42 LTRK-129.
43 Ibid.
44 LTRK-129.
45 LTRK-126.
46 LTRK-157.
47 LTRK-126.
48 LTRK-153.
49 Ibid.
50 Ibid.
51 LTRK-168.
52 LTRK-129.
53 Ibid.
54 LTRK-168.
55 'Protocol on the Management of Terrorism Cases Issued by the President of the Queen's Bench Division' (2nd edn., Courts Service 2007) para. 5.

56 Copy on file with author. For an insight into the CPS perspectives, see S. Hemming, 'The Practical Application of Counter-Terrorism Legislation in England and Wales: A Prosecutor's Perspective' (2010) 86 *International Affairs*, 955.
57 LTRK-168.
58 LTRK-131.
59 LTRK-153.
60 LTRK-126.
61 LTRK-153.
62 LTRK-131.
63 Ibid.
64 LTRK-126.
65 LTRK-124. LTRK-137 commented that these briefings were 'excellent'. This practice was established in 2005 by former Director of Public Prosecutions, Ken Macdonald: Leveson Inquiry, above n. 5, vol. 2, p. 798, para. 2.62.
66 LTRK-124.
67 Journalists and media lawyers generally viewed the England and Wales Judicial Communications Office and the England and Wales courts' approach to media relations as being less helpful and less effective than the far more organised system used in Scotland, although they noted consistently that this was in part a resourcing issue and that the Scottish justice system is far smaller than that of England and Wales.
68 LTRK-137.
69 LTRK-131.
70 LTRK-126, LTRK-131.
71 LTRK-131.
72 LTRK-126.
73 For background to the courts' approach to developing media relations, see generally Select Committee on the Constitution, *Relations between the Executive, the Judiciary and Parliament* (2006–07, HL 151) ch. 4.
74 LTRK-180.
75 CPS, *Protocol for Working Together: Chief Police Officers, Chief Crown Prosecutors and the Media* (October 2005) <www.cps.gov.uk/publications/agencies/mediaprotocol.html> accessed 22 September 2014. See also Association of Chief Police Officers Communication Advisory Group, *Guidance 2010* (November 2011) section 5 <http://www.acpo.presscentre.com/imagelibrary/downloadMedia.ashx?MediaDetailsID=238> accessed 22 September 2014.
76 LTRK-137.
77 LTRK-126.
78 LTRK-137.
79 Criminal Procedure Rules (UK), r. 5.8.
80 *R (on the application of Guardian News and Media) v Westminster Magistrates Court* [2012] EWCA Civ. 420.
81 LTRK-126. See also LTRK-131.
82 LTRK-153.
83 LTRK-124.
84 LTRK-168.
85 LTRK-153.
86 LTRK-137.
87 LTRK-182.
88 LTRK-126.
89 LTRK-124.
90 For a comparative analysis of the Australian and UK positions see L. McNamara, 'Proxies for the Authorities: Using Media Information in the Investigation and Prosecution of Terrorism Offences' in A. Lynch, N. McGarrity and G. Williams,

Counter-Terrorism and Beyond: The Culture of Law & Justice after 9/11 (Routledge 2010) 173–198; L. McNamara and S. McIntosh, 'Confidential Sources and the Legal Rights of Journalists: Re-thinking Australian Approaches to Law Reform' (2010) 32(1) *Australian Journalism Review*, 81. Closed material procedures may soon be available for production order proceedings under PACE: Gill Phillips, 'Another Backdoor Attempt to Restrict Essential Protection', *Media Lawyer* (30 January 2014).

91 See, for example, Lord Lloyd of Berwick, *Inquiry into Legislation against Terrorism* (Cm 3420, 1996) vol. 1, paras. 14.16–14.23, which also summarises previous reviews. The Home Office Consultation Paper, *Legislating Against Terrorism* (Cm 4178, 1998) received 20 responses regarding its proposal to omit the provision from the permanent terrorism legislation that would become the Terrorism Act 2000 (UK). Twelve supported the retention of the offence in permanent legislation and seven said it should be discarded: Home Office, *An Analysis of the Responses to the Government's Consultation Paper* (Cm 4178, 1998) <https://www.gov.uk/government/uploads/system/uploads/attachment_data/file/265689/4178.pdf> accessed 22 September 2014. Prior to 2000, terrorism laws were enacted or revised on four occasions: in 1974, 1976, 1989 and 2000. The Government did not propose the law in 1974 or 1976. The Bill did include it in 1989, albeit as retention of an existing law rather than introduction of a new law.

92 Anti-Terrorism, Crime and Security Act 2001 (UK), s. 117.

93 David Anderson, *Report on the Operation in 2010 of the Terrorism Act 2000 and Part 1 of the Terrorism Act 2006*, July 2011 (The Stationery Office, London) 6.24–6.25; David Anderson, *The Terrorism Acts in 2011: Report of the Independent Reviewer on the Operation of the Terrorism Act 2000 and Part 1 of the Terrorism Act 2006* (June 2012), 6.10, 6.19; David Anderson, *The Terrorism Acts in 2012: Report of the Independent Reviewer on the Operation of the Terrorism Act 2000 and Part 1 of the Terrorism Act 2006* (June 2013), 7.13.

94 Clive Walker, *Terrorism and the Law* (OUP 2011) ch. 3.

95 Anderson, above n. 93, *The Terrorism Acts in 2012*, 7.13–7.14.

96 Anderson, above n. 93, *The Terrorism Acts in 2011*, 6.19.

97 See, for example, *R v Sherif* [2008] EWCA Crim 2653; *R v Girma* [2009] EWCA Crim 912.

98 The CPS put interim guidelines out to consultation and the submission that drew attention to s. 38B was the author's own. While other points in that submission were apparently taken up in preparation of the final guidelines, this one was not. For final guidelines see DPP, 'Guidelines for Prosecutors on Assessing the Public Interest in Cases Affecting the Media' (13 September 2012), with listed offences at Annex A <http://www.cps.gov.uk/legal/d_to_g/guidance_for_prosecutors_on_assessing_the_public_interest_in_cases_affecting_the_media_/> accessed 22 September 2014.

99 *R v Sherif* [2008] EWCA Crim 2653; *R v Girma* [2009] EWCA Crim 912.

100 LTRK-137.

Chapter 9

Secret material and anti-terrorism review in Australia and Canada

Jessie Blackbourn

Introduction

In April 2010, the Australian Commonwealth Parliament enacted a law that established the new office of Independent National Security Legislation Monitor (Independent Monitor).[1] The purpose of the Independent Monitor is to provide an ongoing and holistic review of the operation, effectiveness and implications of Australia's national security and anti-terrorism laws,[2] as well as to consider whether that legislation 'contains appropriate safeguards for protecting the rights of individuals; remains proportionate to any threat of terrorism or threat to national security, or both; and remains necessary'.[3] In effect, the Independent Monitor is tasked to review both the content of the laws and their use by the security and intelligence agencies. To fulfil this function, the Independent National Security Legislation Monitor Act 2010 (Cth.) grants the Independent Monitor substantial coercive information-gathering powers.[4] There is no limitation to these powers. They allow the Independent Monitor to access all relevant classified national security information, including information pertaining to members of the government and the security and intelligence agencies. For example, the Independent Monitor may hold a hearing and summon a person to attend.[5] A witness at a hearing may be required to take an oath or affirmation.[6] The Independent Monitor may also 'request, by written notice, a person: (a) to give the Monitor the information referred to in the notice; or (b) to produce to the Monitor the documents or things referred to in the notice'.[7] Furthermore, the Act imposes penalties for failing to produce a document or thing or for failing to provide any information requested by the Independent Monitor.[8]

These powers are unusual in the anti-terrorism review context; none of the *ad hoc* reviews previously established to examine Australia's national security laws had been granted such extensive powers to access information.[9] However, powers such as these are crucial to the accuracy of any review. Without full access to all of the relevant information, reviews may draw incomplete or unreliable conclusions.[10] Having granted the Independent Monitor powers to access classified material, the Australian Parliament also put in place procedures to regulate the disclosure of such material. The Independent National Security Legislation Monitor Act 2010

(Cth.) prohibits the Independent Monitor from publishing a report that contains material that cannot be disclosed to the public.[11] The Independent Monitor must instead provide a classified private report to the Prime Minister alongside a supplemental declassified public report to be tabled in the parliament.[12] The Act provides a list of potential national security information to assist the Independent Monitor to decide whether material may be publicly disclosed or must be contained within the classified report submitted only to the Prime Minister. For example, the legislation states that the Independent Monitor may not publicly disclose:

> (a) any operationally sensitive information; or (b) any information that would or might prejudice: (i) Australia's national security or the conduct of Australia's foreign relations; or (ii) the performance by a law enforcement or security agency of its functions; or (c) any information that, if included in the report, would or might endanger a person's safety.[13]

This list acts as a guide; the Independent Monitor retains responsibility for determining what information should be included in a classified, declassified or unclassified report. This model of disclosure is unusual. Earlier reviews of Australia's anti-terrorism laws had, for example, been subject to censorship by the Attorney-General prior to the publication of any report.[14] The Independent Monitor is thus granted some unique powers and privileges to conduct the review of Australia's national security laws. However, the office was nearly abolished in early 2014 as part of the Coalition Government's red-tape reduction programme. As part of the repeal process, the Independent National Security Legislation Monitor Repeal Bill 2014 (Cth.) was referred to the Senate Legal and Constitutional Affairs Legislation Committee for inquiry and report. In a submission to the committee's inquiry, the legislation governing the coercive information gathering powers of the Independent Monitor was described by the United Kingdom's Independent Reviewer of Terrorism Legislation (Independent Reviewer) as 'a global benchmark for the independent supervision of counter-terrorist activity'.[15] This chapter examines whether the model of disclosure employed by the Independent Monitor justifies that accolade. It does so from both a domestic and international comparative perspective.

Domestic and international comparisons

Globally, the Independent Monitor is unique. The only directly comparable office, the UK's Independent Reviewer, is not governed by a single regulatory statute.[16] That office has no formal powers to access classified information and there is no official regime regulating the disclosure of any such material[17] – this prevents a comparison of the disclosure regimes of the only two bodies that independently review anti-terrorism laws. In Australia, the Independent Monitor is also unique in terms of its function. No other statutory body provides for the ongoing review of both the content and use by the intelligence and security agencies of Australia's national security and anti-terrorism laws. However, the Inspector-General of Intelligence and Security (IGIS) is tasked to review the activities of Australia's intelligence agencies, including their use of the national security and anti-terrorism laws. Furthermore, the IGIS has powers to access classified material comparable to the Independent Monitor. So, too, do commissioners appointed to conduct inquiries in Canada, which is the system of review that was adopted to investigate the activities of Canada's security and intelligence agencies after the 11 September 2001 terrorist attacks on the United States. Like the Independent Monitor, both the IGIS in Australia and inquiries conducted under the Inquiries Act 1985 (Can.) may require a person to attend before them to provide information.[18] A person who attends before the IGIS or a Canadian inquiry may be required to take an oath.[19] The IGIS and Canadian inquiries may also require a person to produce information or documents.[20] Finally, these powers to access information are coercive; penalties apply for failing to attend or to produce the requested information.[21]

The IGIS and Canadian inquiries thus have powers analogous to the Independent Monitor to access classified material during the conduct of their reviews. However, they offer different models for regulating the disclosure of such information. In Australia, no official framework exists to regulate the public disclosure of information following an inquiry conducted by the IGIS. Although there is no obligation to make reports available to the public, a number of declassified reports have been released. This has occurred in circumstances where there has been a 'significant public interest in the outcomes of this inquiry' and where 'the Prime Minister has agreed to the public release of an abridged version of the report'.[22] These reports have been 'prepared on the basis that they will contain as much information as possible, while satisfying the requirement that they do not prejudice security, the defence of Australia, Australia's relations with other countries, law enforcement operations or the privacy of individuals'.[23] However, there is little information available regarding the process by which material is selected for inclusion in, or exclusion from, a public report, with one exception:

> Where the Inspector-General proposes to set out in a report in relation to an inquiry conducted under this Act opinions that are, either expressly or impliedly, critical of a person, the Inspector-General shall, unless doing so would, in the opinion of the Inspector-General, prejudice security, the defence of Australia or Australia's relations with other countries, give the person a reasonable opportunity to appear before the Inspector-General and to make, either orally or in writing, submissions in relation to the matters that are the subject of the inquiry.[24]

In contrast to the IGIS, the disclosure of information obtained by inquiries conducted under the Inquiries Act 1985 (Can.) is tightly regulated by provisions in the Canada Evidence Act 1985 (Can.). The latter Act restricts the disclosure of information that might engage 'international relations and national defence and national security'.[25] Any person who believes that 'sensitive information or potentially injurious information'[26] might be disclosed during a proceeding must 'notify the Attorney-General of Canada in writing of the possibility of the disclosure, and the nature, date and place of the proceeding'.[27] The Act then prohibits the disclosure of such information[28] unless the Attorney-General authorises it.[29]

The Attorney-General does not have the final say over the question of disclosure. Parties to any proceeding where material has been prohibited from disclosure may apply to the Canadian Federal Court for a determination on whether the disclosure of that information actually 'would be injurious to international relations or national defence or national security'.[30] The judge may either order or refuse the disclosure of the information.[31] In the case that the judge finds that the disclosure of the information 'would be injurious to international relations or national defence or national security but that the public interest in disclosure outweighs in importance the public interest in non-disclosure', then the judge may authorise the disclosure or partial disclosure of the information.[32]

Methodology

While all three bodies have analogous powers to access secret material during the course of their review, the Independent Monitor, IGIS and Canadian inquiries offer three different models of disclosure. In Australia, the Independent Monitor determines what types of material should be publicly disclosed in its annual report, but it is unclear who is responsible for such decisions in inquiries conducted by the IGIS. In Canada, initially it is the Attorney-General who decides whether material should be excluded from public disclosure; however, the courts also play a role, by confirming or rejecting the Attorney-General's decision. These different models of disclosure present an opportunity to examine how classified material accessed during the course of a review or inquiry has been disclosed or has been prevented from disclosure in practice in the national security context in Australia and Canada. The aim of this chapter is to question whether the office of Independent Monitor offers a 'global benchmark' in terms of its disclosure regime, in contrast to other comparable reviewing bodies. To do so, it assesses how effective the Independent Monitor, IGIS and Canadian commissioners have been at dealing with the problems created by their powers to access secret material in the reviewing process, notably the necessity to prevent the disclosure of material that genuinely poses a risk to national security, while also ensuring disclosure of the maximum amount of material possible in order to ensure the validity of the review. A review will be considered to have successfully fulfilled its function if it conforms to the principles of open justice.

Although they are typically used as a benchmark to assess the extent to which the courts act as a check on executive power,[33] the principles of open justice also offer an appropriate framework to assess the conduct of national security reviews. For the purposes of this chapter, the principles of open justice will be considered to have been satisfied if a review or inquiry serves both an educative and a supervisory function; that is, it should inform the government, parliament and the public about the content of the laws and their use by the security and intelligence agencies, as well as scrutinise the content of the laws and the actions of those who use them. This scrutiny function should fulfil the basic requirements of procedural fairness; the review or inquiry should be transparent, free from bias and fair.

This chapter therefore assesses the extent to which the disclosure regimes of the Independent Monitor and IGIS in Australia and commissions of inquiry in Canada have conformed to the principles of open justice as outlined above. It does so through an examination of how those regimes have operated in practice. The chapter assesses two of the Independent Monitor's reports. First, the *Independent National Security Legislation Monitor Declassified Annual Report 2012*. This report was tabled in parliament in May 2013. It examined Australia's control order and preventative detention order legislation, as well as the special powers to question and detain granted to the Australian Security Intelligence Organisation (ASIO). The second report is the *Independent National Security Legislation Monitor Annual Report 2013*. This report was tabled in parliament in December 2013. It examined the laws relating to the financing of terrorism, as well as procedures for dealing with national security information. The chapter looks at two inquiries conducted by the IGIS. The first examined the actions taken by ASIO in respect to Izhar Ul-Haque (the Ul-Haque Inquiry). In particular, the IGIS focused on the 'methods of questioning employed by two ASIO officers' in relation to Ul-Haque. The second looked into the case of Mamdouh Habib (the Habib Inquiry).[34] Habib, a dual Egyptian–Australian citizen, was arrested by Pakistani authorities in late 2001, rendered by the US to Egypt and eventually transferred to the Guantánamo Bay detention camp. The inquiry focused on the role played by ASIO officers in Habib's detention and questioning abroad.[35] The chapter assesses two inquiries that Canada held into aspects of its post-9/11 anti-terrorism regime. First is the *Commission of Inquiry into the Actions of Canadian Officials in Relation to Maher Arar* (the Arar Inquiry), chaired by Dennis O'Connor. In 2002, Maher Arar, a dual Canadian–Syrian citizen, was stopped at New York's John F. Kennedy airport while transiting to Canada. He was rendered to Syria, detained and tortured before being released and returned to Canada after just over a year in detention.[36] The Arar Inquiry's remit was to investigate the extent to which Canadian officials had been involved in Arar's detention, rendition and torture by US and Syrian officials. During the course of its investigation, the Arar Inquiry recommended the creation of a second inquiry to investigate the actions of Canadian officials in the detention and mistreatment of three other Canadian citizens in Syria and Egypt between 2001 and 2004.[37] This second inquiry, the *Internal Inquiry into the Actions of Canadian Officials in Relation to Abdullah Almalki, Ahmad Abou-Elmaati and Muayyed Nureddin* was chaired by Frank Iacobucci (the Iacobucci Inquiry).

The Independent National Security Legislation Monitor

Issues regarding the disclosure of secret material have arisen at two stages in the Independent Monitor's reviews: first, during the course of conducting the review; and second, once the final report was ready for submission. Under the Independent

National Security Legislation Monitor Act 2010 (Cth.), the Independent Monitor may hold a hearing for the purposes of conducting the review.[38] Hearings 'may be held in private if the Independent National Security Legislation Monitor so directs'; however, they '*must* be held in private for any time during which a person is giving evidence that discloses operationally sensitive information'.[39] Otherwise 'a hearing must be held in public'.[40] In the course of the second annual review, the report of which was tabled in parliament as a declassified report with a separate classified report presented to the Prime Minister, the Independent Monitor only held private hearings.[41] This was because hearings were held only with 'officers of relevant Commonwealth departments and agencies' 'for the purposes of considering the legislative provisions for questioning warrants and questioning and detention warrants in Div 3 of Part III of the ASIO Act 1979 (Cth.) and control orders and preventative detention orders in Divs 104–105 of Part 5.3 of the Code'.[42] For the third annual report, tabled in 2013, the Independent Monitor held both public and private hearings. Where a person summoned to attend might have presented evidence 'that discloses operationally sensitive information', the hearing was held in private.[43] Thus, consistent with the previous year's review: 'All hearings held this year with Australian government officials were conducted in private'.[44] However, the Independent Monitor also 'held two public hearings with members of civil society and academia'.[45]

In effect, the Independent Monitor adopted a dual public–private strategy for holding hearings under the terms of the Independent National Security Legislation Monitor Act 2010 (Cth.). Hearings were conducted in public when they were held with members of the public, civil society and academia. In contrast, hearings were held in private when those presenting evidence might be in possession of operationally sensitive information. Private hearings were conducted with members of, among others, relevant government departments, ASIO and the Australian Federal Police.

The Independent National Security Legislation Monitor Act 2010 (Cth.) required the Independent Monitor to hold hearings in private in order to prevent the possible disclosure of operationally sensitive information. However, when it came to the publication stage of the reviewing process, the Independent Monitor was solely responsible for determining whether any of the secret material ascertained from those private hearings could be disclosed to the public in the annual report tabled in parliament. The 2013 report did not contain any secret material. The annual report tabled in parliament was therefore unclassified.[46] In contrast, the 2012 report did contain material that could not be disclosed to the public. A declassified report was thus tabled in parliament and a classified report – which contained the material that could not be disclosed – was submitted to the Prime Minister.[47] In the declassified report, the Independent Monitor outlined the material in the classified report, without stating its contents. For example, having examined all the files for every time a control order was considered or applied for, the Independent Monitor explained:

> More detail of this examination is to be found in classified Appendix CA, which should not be contained in the declassified Annual Report because it

is operationally sensitive information and information that might prejudice the performance by a law enforcement or security agency of its functions.[48]

Again, with ASIO's questioning warrant powers, the Independent Monitor examined the files for every questioning warrant issued and stated:

> The grounds for seeking the QWs [questioning warrants] were considered, the transcripts of the questioning were read and the mandatory reports on the assistance obtained from the questioning were scrutinized. . . . More detail of this exhaustive examination of every actual use of QWs is to be found in classified Appendix CB, which should not be contained in the declassified Annual Report because it is operationally sensitive information and information that might prejudice the performance by a law enforcement or security agency of its functions.[49]

By describing the type of information included in the declassified report, the Independent Monitor made the process of non-disclosure as transparent as possible. The Independent Monitor has also been able to release material into the public domain that was not previously known. Prior to the publication of the 2012 report, there was no public knowledge regarding the number of control orders that had been considered, only those that had been issued. While some of the material – such as names and operational details – was not disclosed, the publication of aspects of this new material has significantly added to the public understanding of the operation of Australia's anti-terrorism laws.

In practice, the Independent Monitor has been able to navigate the problems associated with accessing classified material during the conduct of a review by following the terms of the legislation governing the office. The Independent Monitor did not accept that all of the material heard in secret should remain classified; a number of new pieces of information were disclosed during the publication of the Independent Monitor's reports.

The Inspector-General of Intelligence and Security

The IGIS has a different remit to the Independent Monitor, whose purpose is to evaluate the operation, effectiveness and implications of Australia's national security laws, as well as to review whether those laws remain necessary, proportionate to the threat of terrorism and contain appropriate safeguards for protecting human rights. The Independent Monitor thus looks at a vast range of material, both classified operational material and public contributions, to enable a review which fulfils that specific role. The IGIS, in contrast, is tasked solely to assess the use of powers – including those relating to national security – by the security and intelligence agencies. The vast majority of the material under consideration by the IGIS then comes from those agencies. Because of this, the IGIS has adopted an approach of privacy in conducting inquiries into the potential misuse of the powers by the security and intelligence agencies. Both the Habib and Ul-Haque Inquiries were conducted entirely in private. In each case, the IGIS used the powers under s. 18 of the Inspector-General of Intelligence and Security Act 1986 (Cth.) to compel current or former Commonwealth officers to attend a hearing to produce information.[50] Both the Habib and Ul-Haque Inquiries also requested the production of a vast number of files from ASIO relating to the actions of its officers.[51] In addition, the Habib Inquiry 'inspected files directly at ASIO to look for further relevant documents including further emails, original diaries and legal advice'.[52]

The current IGIS, Vivienne Thom, has argued that conducting an inquiry in private is beneficial to the process of review. In the report of the Habib Inquiry, Thom states:

> These coercive powers [to access information], together with the security with which information is treated by this office and the private nature of the inquiry, mean that the range of evidence available to the IGIS is greater than that which might ordinarily be available to other forms of inquiry.[53]

IGIS inquiries are fully able to assess whether the intelligence and security services have exceeded their powers. However, the IGIS is not necessarily required to publish a report and so the educative effect of the inquiry process may be negated. When reports are published, they are subject to potentially serious censorship by the government and the intelligence and security agencies. For example, where a report by the IGIS contains opinions that are critical of a Commonwealth officer, that person must have reasonable opportunity to appear before the IGIS to make a submission.[54] Similarly, the Inspector-General of Intelligence and Security Act 1986 (Cth.) requires the IGIS to give the heads of relevant agencies an opportunity to comment on the preliminary report, as well as any ministers who are responsible for the agencies.

In the Habib Inquiry, the IGIS informed a number of individuals and six agency heads of preliminary views and invited comment. This process took two months to complete. Once the individuals and agency heads had commented on the preliminary report, the IGIS then wrote to ministers to give them a chance to discuss the report. Only after that stage could the IGIS provide a 'draft report to agency heads for comment'.[55] According to the IGIS: 'These comments were considered in the final report'.[56] However, the final report of the Habib Inquiry, like that of the Ul-Haque Inquiry three years earlier, contained information that could not be disclosed to the public. A classified report was thus presented to the Prime Minister and an abridged report was made public. The IGIS in the Ul-Haque Inquiry took a slightly more transparent approach than the IGIS in the Habib Inquiry regarding the information excluded from the final public report. There is no way to know what information was omitted from the report of the Habib Inquiry. The Ul-Haque Inquiry, however, adopted an approach similar to the Independent Monitor. Two of the attachments in the Ul-Haque Inquiry report remained classified, but the IGIS stated to what they referred: Attachment C described the '[s]trategic and operational environment in ASIO in late 2003' and Attachment D outlined 'ASIO training and procedural matters'.[57]

Canadian inquiries

In contrast to the Independent Monitor, the process for disclosure in Canada is incredibly protracted, even more so than with the IGIS. This is because of the involvement of the government and the courts in determining national security claims. The commissioners in both the Arar and the Iacobucci Inquiries were plagued by national security information concerns during their investigations. However, the two inquiries took very different paths with regards to the issue of disclosure.

In the Arar Inquiry, the presumption was in favour of full public disclosure of material during the investigative stage of the process. In particular, the Inquiry's commissioner was responsible for preventing the 'disclosure of information that, if it were disclosed to the public, would, *in the opinion of the Commissioner*, be injurious to international relations, national defence or national security'.[58] The commission could be directed by the Attorney-General to hold proceedings in camera and *ex parte*, but that was dependent on it being necessary to do so 'in the opinion of the Commissioner'.[59] The terms of reference even provided for some public disclosure of material from in camera and *ex parte* proceedings: '[I]n order to maximize disclosure to the public of relevant information, the Commissioner may release a part or a summary of the information received in camera and shall provide the Attorney-General of Canada with an opportunity to comment prior to its release'.[60]

Commissioner O'Connor made a substantial effort to ensure that the inquiry was conducted, as far as possible, in public. He consistently challenged the Canadian Government's claims of national security confidentiality. However, the Arar Inquiry still held 75 days of in camera hearings, predominantly with members of the Royal Canadian Mounted Police (RCMP) and the Canadian Security Intelligence Service (CSIS).[61] Arar and his counsel were excluded from these hearings, and an independent counsel was appointed to attend on behalf of Arar and test the evidence presented by the government.[62]

The Arar Inquiry also held 45 days of public hearings;[63] it took a number of steps to ensure that as much evidence and testimony as possible was heard in public hearings. For example, 'commission staff prepared binders of all the documents, redacted to take account of the Government's NSC [national security confidentiality] claims that would be entered into evidence'.[64] Despite conducting the inquiry as much as possible in public, O'Connor recognised the limitations of the public inquiry in the context of national security. In recommending that the government should establish an inquiry into the cases of Abdullah Almalki, Ahmed Abou-Elmaati and Muayyed Nureddin, O'Connor proposed that 'the reviews should be done through an independent and credible process that is able to address the integrated nature of the underlying investigations'.[65] However, he did not propose a public inquiry akin to the one he had just conducted. Instead, he stated that 'there are more appropriate ways than a full-scale public inquiry to investigate and report on cases where national security confidentiality must play such a prominent role'.[66]

The Canadian Government adopted O'Connor's proposed scheme when it established the commission of inquiry to investigate the cases of Almalki, Abou-Elmaati and Nureddin. The Iacobucci Inquiry was constituted with fundamentally different terms of reference to the Arar Inquiry. Rather than a public inquiry, the Canadian Government established the commission as an 'internal inquiry'.[67] Commissioner Iacobucci was authorised to 'adopt any procedures and methods that he considers expedient for the proper conduct of the Inquiry, *while taking all steps necessary to ensure that the Inquiry is conducted in private*'.[68] Iacobucci sought clarification on what this meant in practice for the conduct of the inquiry and the Attorney-General submitted the view that:

> [I]n order to determine who may properly attend the hearings conducted 'in private', it is necessary to consider the meaning of that expression. The specific meaning of 'in private' flows from the context in which it is used. 'In private' generally means 'in camera' and may mean '*ex parte*'. A hearing held 'in camera' excludes members of the public in the broadest possible sense, but may include parties to a proceeding; a proceeding *ex parte* excludes the other parties to the proceedings from appearing to make representations.[69]

Having explained these two possible interpretations of 'in private', the Attorney-General submitted that, in this case, '"in private" must be interpreted to mean both in camera and *ex parte*'.[70] A number of other submissions, including those from Almalki, Abou-Elmaati and Nureddin, proposed that the presumption should be in favour of the open court principle, with private hearings only to be held when genuine national security concerns prevented hearings from taking place in public.[71] However, Iacobucci disagreed. In effect, he appears to have accepted the Attorney-General's proposal. He ruled that:

> Although the Terms of Reference admit of a public hearing they emphasize the presumptively private nature of the hearings, among other things to respect national security confidentiality. Unless I specifically direct otherwise, the formal hearings conducted as part of this Inquiry will be conducted in private, a term that I interpret to mean, in this context, *in camera* and *ex parte*.[72]

Commissioner Iacobucci took this understanding of 'in private' seriously. According to Jasminka Kalajdzic, who appeared as counsel for Almalki before the Iacobucci Inquiry,[73] 'over a 22-month period, the Inquiry held only four and a half days of public hearings – three of them on issues of standing and interpretation of the rules of the commission'. During this period, the inquiry 'called no witnesses in public, disclosed no documents and gave the three men in whose name the Inquiry was called no opportunity to test the evidence of government witnesses'.[74]

It was not only during hearings that disclosure issues arose for the two inquiries. The same provisions in the Canada Evidence Act 1985 (Can.) that restrict the disclosure of information during the investigative stages of an inquiry also apply to the disclosure of that material in the published report of an inquiry. In practice, the strict disclosure restrictions available to the Attorney-General under that Act regarding the information that can or cannot be included in the public report have been, to some extent, mitigated by a post-inquiry negotiated process between the commission and the Attorney-General.[75] If, following the end of the negotiations and after the publication of the report, the inquiry still considers that the Attorney-General has over-classified some material that it thinks should be disclosed, it can challenge that decision in the federal court. Roach has argued that 'reviewers should review the classification decisions made by the governments with particular attention to the danger that governments will over-classify information including embarrassing information that reveals inefficiencies and improprieties'.[76] This tendency for the government to over-classify material can be observed in both the Arar and Iacobucci Inquiries.

Following the publication of its final report in 2006, the Arar Inquiry made a number of appeals to the federal court to authorise the disclosure of redacted information.[77] The court rejected some of these applications, but it did authorise the disclosure of some previously classified secret material.[78] That material was published in 2007.[79] The Arar Commission published the relevant pages on which the newly disclosed material appeared and set the previously redacted material in bold. In the original report, redacted material appeared as '[***]'. For the most part, the newly disclosed material consisted of the words 'the CIA' and 'the FBI'.[80] However, it also revealed material that the Canadian Government had attempted to keep classified – not because it was injurious to national security – but because it was embarrassing. One of the new disclosures highlighted that CSIS was aware that the US was engaged in the practice of extraordinary rendition. The new material revealed that during the inquiry's investigation, a CSIS liaison officer 'spoke of a trend they had noted lately that when the CIA or FBI cannot legally hold a terrorist subject, or wish a target questioned in a firm manner, they have them rendered to countries willing to fulfill [sic] that role'.[81] According to Whittaker, '[d]isclosure of these passages has done no harm to national security, but it has caused embarrassment to the government'.[82] He continues: 'Using national security as a cover to avoid embarrassment, however, demeans the legitimate use of secrecy'.[83]

The Iacobucci Inquiry also published supplemental material after the main findings of its report had been released. However, in this case, there was not so much additional information sought for public disclosure. Iacobucci stated that:

'When the public report was submitted, I was satisfied that, with one exception, the information contained in the confidential report but omitted from the public report was properly subject to national security confidentiality'.[84] That one exception included information that Iacobucci 'believed could and should be included in the public report, but which the responsible Minister considered should not be disclosed because its disclosure would be injurious to national defence, national security or international relations'.[85]

Unlike the Arar Inquiry, Iacobucci did not use the official system provided by the Canada Evidence Act 1985 (Can.) to resolve the outstanding issue of disclosure. Instead, the commissioner held 'extensive further discussions' with the Attorney-General in order to secure the disclosure of information that had previously been excluded because of national security confidentiality concerns.[86] The supplemental material related to the actions of CSIS in its correspondence with, and subsequent visit to, Egypt (where Abou-Elmaati was rendered and detained) in 2002.[87] Iacobucci also published his findings in relation to the newly disclosed material. He stated that, in his view, and based on all the evidence available to him, 'Mr Elmaati suffered mistreatment of some form as a consequence of the [Canadian Security Intelligence] Service's interactions with Egyptian authorities'.[88] This material was not injurious to Canada's national security, as was claimed by the minister responsible for preventing its disclosure; rather, it was information that, if it were disclosed, would embarrass the government. It demonstrated Canada's complicity in the US Government's programme of extraordinary rendition. Material was therefore over-classified in both inquiries; however, the commissioners managed to successfully secure the further dissemination of some additional material.

Principles of open justice

There is no doubt that classified material poses significant problems to those who are tasked to review the state's national security laws. However, in order for a review to fulfil its core oversight function, it must conform to the principles of open justice. It must be educative, in terms of informing the government, parliament and the public about the content of the laws and their use by the security and intelligence agencies. Furthermore, it must scrutinise the content of the laws and the actions of those who use them. That scrutiny must be transparent, free from bias and fair. The three case studies in this chapter have demonstrated that each review has struggled to maintain these principles of open justice, but to differing extents.

The educative effect of a review can be assessed in terms of the extent to which it was conducted in public and previously unknown material was publicly disclosed in the final report. The Independent Monitor, IGIS and the two Canadian inquiries differed significantly in terms of the public disclosure of their reviews. The Independent Monitor and the two Canadian inquiries adopted similar practices, albeit to differing extents, to prevent the public disclosure of secret material during the investigative stage of the inquiry process. In essence, where there was the likelihood that secret material would be involved, hearings were held in private. The Arar Inquiry attempted to hold as much of its inquiry as possible in public, but the Iacobucci Inquiry was held almost entirely in private. The Independent Monitor fell somewhere between the two; hearings were held in private when they might contain national security information, but were held in public at all other times. In contrast, both IGIS inquiries were conducted entirely in private.

The educative nature of a review is important, particularly in the national security context where security and intelligence operations are often shrouded in secrecy. Despite a significant portion of the investigations being conducted in private, the reports of the Independent Monitor, IGIS and Canadian inquiries all released a considerable amount of previously unseen and unknown material into the public domain. The Habib Inquiry, for example, provided significant detail about the actions of Commonwealth officers in their dealings with foreign agencies. However, the manner in which the material is obtained is crucial to a review's capacity to properly inform – and thereby educate – the public. This is illustrated by the two Canadian inquiries, which adopted different practices to deal with secret material in the reviewing process. Where Commissioner O'Connor sought to ensure that the Arar Inquiry was conducted as much as possible in public and that the final report of the inquiry disclosed the maximum material possible, Commissioner Iacobucci took the opposite approach. He held his inquiry almost completely in private and his report did not push the boundaries of disclosure. The outcome of these two different approaches was notable. The Arar Inquiry ignited the public imagination in Canada. Arar was awarded 10,000 CAD in compensation from the Canadian Government following the publication of O'Connor's report. He was named 'Canadian of the Year' by Toronto's *Globe and Mail* in 2006.[89] In contrast, there was very little publicity surrounding the Iacobucci Inquiry. Almalki, Abou-Elmaati and Nureddin received no compensation for their ordeals, despite the similarity to Arar's.

A lack of public disclosure during both the investigative and reporting stages of an inquiry not only prevents a review from performing its educative function, but also calls into question the capacity of that review to provide scrutiny that is transparent, free from bias and fair. If a review cannot be held in public for reasons of national security, then transparency – in terms of who decides what material may be disclosed and how that decision is made – becomes important. In Australia, the office of the Independent Monitor retains responsibility for testing the government's national security claims, and may publish any material – even if that material has been classified – it considers may be publicly disclosed. However, it is not known how the IGIS determines which material should be disclosed, or even if it is the IGIS who makes that decision. Disclosure issues have also troubled the inquiry process in Canada. A significant amount of secret material was over-classified by the government, and the only recourse was to apply to the federal court to force its disclosure by the Attorney-General. These subsequent disclosures occurred long after the inquiry had published its primary report, when the public's – and the government's – focus had transferred elsewhere.

In national security reviews or inquiries, where the public is unable to judge any non-disclosed material on its own merits, procedures need to be put in place to ensure that the review is free from bias. The person appointed to carry out the review, the way in which that appointment is made, and the independence of the reviewer from the government and the organisations subject to review then become important. Both Australia and Canada have adopted appointment processes to ensure that the person conducting the inquiry or review is entirely independent from the government and the security and intelligence agencies. Canada has appointed either retired or serving judges to head its commissions of inquiry. Judges, even retired judges, are, by their very nature, independent from the government. The public should, therefore, be able to trust that inquiries held by judges, or former judges, have not been subject to undue influence from the government subject to review. Australia adopted a more formal approach to its appointment process. Both the Independent Monitor and the IGIS are appointed by the Governor-General on the recommendation of the Prime Minister, who must have consulted with the leader of the opposition in the House of Representatives.[90] The government therefore does not have free reign to appoint anyone it would like. This process should prevent the appointment of a person overtly biased towards the government of the day. This is particularly important in reviews conducted by the Independent Monitor, because it is the person appointed to the office who is responsible for assessing which material can and cannot be disclosed.

In order for a review to be fair, it must have full access to all the relevant secret material. This prevents it from being unduly influenced into making a particular decision. Powers to access secret material are imperative in reviews of anti-terrorism laws. However, there is one situation in which reviews may fail to access secret material, despite the existence of substantial information-gathering powers: in cases where reviews need to access material from external sources. Both Canadian inquiries had difficulty accessing secret material across jurisdictional boundaries. The Arar and Iacobucci Inquiries dealt with the treatment of Canadian citizens at the hands of external authorities (the US, Syria, Egypt and Malaysia) as well as by the RCMP and Canadian Government. The coercive information-gathering powers granted to Canadian inquiries only apply inside the state. They are unable to compel information from external organisations. The Iacobucci Inquiry stated that it 'sent letters to the appropriate authorities in the United States, Syria, Egypt and Malaysia, requesting that they participate in the Inquiry's activities. Regrettably authorities in the United States, Egypt and Malaysia did not respond to the Inquiry's initial or follow-up requests'.[91] Syria initially responded by asking for further information into the subjects of the inquiry, but did not subsequently provide any of the information requested.[92] Likewise, the Arar Inquiry invited authorities outside of Canada to participate in the inquiry process. The report of the Arar Inquiry states:

> The governments of the United States, Jordan and Syria declined my invitation to give evidence or otherwise participate in the hearings. Despite their

> failure to participate, I have for the most part been able to determine what actually happened and reach the conclusions required by the mandate. In a few instances, however, I have been hampered by the lack of evidence of officials of these other countries.[93]

While the inability to access information from outside sources did not, according to each of the inquiries, prohibit them from ascertaining the facts of the situation, it does raise worrying concerns for future reviewing processes. In a counter-terrorism era increasingly characterised by co-operation across borders, the quality of future reviews may suffer at the hands of jurisdictional restrictions on access to information.

Conclusions

This chapter has examined how access to, and the disclosure of, secret material has been regulated in three types of review in Australia and Canada: the Independent Monitor, IGIS and commissions of inquiry. It sought to assess whether the Independent Monitor – an office established to review the content and use of Australia's anti-terrorism laws – is uniquely suited to performing that function because of its disclosure regime. There is no doubt that the Independent Monitor has managed to perform the function of review in conformity to the principles of open justice. The office has been granted substantial coercive information-gathering powers, which allow it to access all relevant secret material, as have the IGIS and Canadian inquiries. The appointment process in the Independent National Security Legislation Monitor Act 2010 (Cth.) ensures that the person who performs the role of Independent Monitor is independent from the government and is not subject to undue influence. However, this is not a unique feature of the office of Independent Monitor. The IGIS is also appointed in an independent procedure and the Canadian Government has appointed independent judges to head their inquiries.

Where the Independent Monitor perhaps excels over the IGIS and Canadian inquiries is in terms of transparency. While some of the Independent Monitor's powers require hearings to be held in private, ultimately, it is the Independent Monitor who determines – based on government guidelines – whether any of that secret material may then be disclosed to the public. Such disclosure is time-limited; the Independent Monitor reports annually to the Prime Minister, who must table those reports in parliament. In contrast, the process for determining what information may be disclosed in inquiries by the IGIS is unknown, and in Canada both the government and the courts play a significant role in determining national security information claims. This creates a protracted process; information may be disclosed long after the final report of an inquiry – particularly in the Canadian case – has been published. The Independent Monitor therefore offers a model for the review of the content and use of the anti-terrorism laws in Australia which, for the most part, conforms to the principles of open justice. The Independent

Monitor's reviews have, to date, performed the function of educating the government, parliament and the public, while also providing meaningful and effective scrutiny of the anti-terrorism laws.

It is not a model that will be suitable in all situations; however, it currently ensures that Australia's national security laws, and the agencies using those laws, are subject to rigorous oversight. Given parliament's recent enactment of a range of new anti-terrorism laws to deal with the threat posed by the conflict in Syria and Iraq,[94] it is essential that the Independent Monitor continues to have full access to classified material and may disclose that material where it is necessary and appropriate to do so.

Notes

1 Independent National Security Legislation Monitor Act 2010 (Cth.).
2 Ibid. s. 6(1)(a).
3 Ibid. s. 6(1)(b).
4 Ibid. ss. 21–5.
5 Ibid. s. 22.
6 Ibid. s. 23.
7 Ibid. s. 24(1).
8 Ibid. s. 25.
9 Jessie Blackbourn, 'Power without Responsibility?' in Daniel Baldino (ed.), *Spooked: The Truth about Intelligence in Australia* (UNSW Press 2013) 270–1, 281–3.
10 Jessie Blackbourn, 'Anti-Terrorism Law Reform: Now or Never?' (2014) 25 *Public Law Review*, 3, 3–7.
11 Independent National Security Legislation Monitor Act 2010 (Cth.), s. 29(2A).
12 Ibid. s. 29(2A).
13 Ibid. s. 29(3).
14 See, for example, Security Legislation Review Committee, *Report of the Security Legislation Review Committee* (June 2006), 19.
15 David Anderson, *Independent National Security Legislation Monitor Repeal Bill 2014 Submission to the Senate Legal and Constitutional Affairs Committee by David Anderson QC, UK Independent Reviewer of Terrorism Legislation* (28 April 2014), 4.
16 Jessie Blackbourn, 'Independent Reviewers as Alternative: An Empirical Study from Australia and the UK' in Fergal F. Davis and Fiona De Londras (eds.), *Critical Debates on Counter-Terrorism Judicial Review* (Cambridge University Press 2014) 169.
17 Ibid. 170.
18 Inspector-General of Intelligence and Security Act 1986 (Cth.), s. 18(3) (IGIS Act 1986); Inquiries Act 1985 (Can.), s. 4(a).
19 IGIS Act 1986, s. 18(4); Inquiries Act 1985 (Can.), s. 4(a).
20 IGIS Act 1986, s. 18(1); Inquiries Act 1985 (Can.), s. 4(b).
21 IGIS Act 1986, s. 18(7); Inquiries Act 1985 (Can.), s. 5.
22 IGIS, 'Public Reports' <http://www.igis.gov.au/inquiries/index.cfm> accessed 22 September 2014.
23 Ibid.
24 IGIS Act 1986, s. 18(7); Inquiries Act 1985 (Can.), s. 17(5).
25 Canada Evidence Act 1985 (Can.), s. 38.
26 'Sensitive information' is defined in the Canada Evidence Act 1985 (Can.), s. 38 as 'information relating to international relations or national defence or national security

that is in the possession of the Government of Canada, whether originating from inside or outside Canada, and is of a type that the Government of Canada is taking measures to safeguard'. 'Potentially injurious information' is defined in the Act as 'information of a type that, if it were disclosed to the public, could injure international relations or national defence or national security'.

27 Ibid. ss. 38.01(1)–38.01(4).
28 Ibid. s. 38.02.
29 Ibid. s. 38.03(1).
30 Ibid. s. 38.04(2).
31 Ibid. s. 38.06(1).
32 Ibid. s. 38.06(2).
33 See, for example, chs. 5 and 7 in this volume.
34 IGIS, *Report of Inquiry into the Actions Taken by ASIO in 2003 in Respect of Mr Izhar Ul-Haque and Related Matters* (2008).
35 Vivienne Thom, *Inquiry into the Actions of Australian Government Agencies in Relation to the Arrest and Detention Overseas of Mr Mamdouh Habib from 2001 to 2005* (Inspector-General of Intelligence and Security 2011).
36 Kent Roach, 'Review and Oversight of National Security Activities and some Reflections on Canada's Arar Inquiry' (2007) 29 *Cardozo Law Review*, 53, 55.
37 Jasminka Kalajdzic, 'Outsiders: The Sources and Impact of Secrecy at the Iacobucci Inquiry' (2010) 36 *Queen's Law Journal*, 161, 165–8.
38 Independent National Security Legislation Monitor Act 2010 (Cth.), s. 21.
39 Ibid. s. 21(2) (emphasis added).
40 Ibid.
41 Bret Walker, *Independent National Security Legislation Monitor Declassified Annual Report* (Commonwealth of Australia 2012) 131.
42 Ibid.
43 Ibid. 165.
44 Ibid.
45 Ibid.
46 Ibid.
47 'Independent National Security Legislation Monitor' (*Australian Government Officer of the Prime Minister and Cabinet*, 18 June 2004) <http://www.dpmc.gov.au/INSLM/index.cfm> accessed 22 September 2014.
48 Walker (n. 41) 12–13.
49 Ibid. 68.
50 Thom (n. 35) 16–17; IGIS (n. 34) 4–5.
51 Thom (n. 35) 14–16; IGIS (n. 34) 3–4.
52 Thom (n. 35) 6.
53 Ibid. 18.
54 Ibid. 19.
55 Ibid.
56 Ibid.
57 IGIS (n. 34) index.
58 'Terms of Reference for the Commission of Inquiry into the Actions of Canadian Officials in Relation to Maher Arar' (5 February 2004) <http://epe.lac-bac.gc.ca/100/206/301/pco-bcp/commissions/maher_arar/07-09-13/www.ararcommission.ca/eng/Terms_of_Reference.pdf> accessed 22 September 2014 (emphasis added).
59 Ibid.
60 Ibid.
61 Commission of Inquiry into the Actions of Canadian Officials in Relation to Maher Arar, *Report of the Events Relating to Maher Arar: Analysis and Recommendations* (2006) 295.

62 Ibid. 304.
63 Ibid. 295.
64 Ibid. 298.
65 Ibid. 278.
66 Ibid. 277–8.
67 Internal Inquiry into the Actions of Canadian Officials in Relation to Abdullah Almalki, Ahmed Abou-Elmaati and Muayyed Nureddin, 'Terms of Reference' (11 December 2006, amendments 2008) <http://epe.lac-bac.gc.ca/100/206/301/pco-bcp/commissions/internal_inquiry/2010–03–09/www.iacobucciinquiry.ca/en/terms-of-reference/index.htm> accessed 22 September 2014.
68 Ibid. (emphasis added).
69 Internal Inquiry into the Actions of Canadian Officials in Relation to Abdullah Almalki, Ahmed Abou-Elmaati and Muayyed Nureddin, *Outline of Submissions of the Attorney-General of Canada on the Terms of Reference and Draft Rules of Procedure and Practice* (2007) 7.
70 Ibid.
71 For all submissions to the Iacobucci Inquiry see 'Documents: List of Submissions for Hearing on Procedure (22 February 2011) <http://epe.lac-bac.gc.ca/100/206/301/pco-bcp/commissions/internal_inquiry/2010–03–09/www.iacobucciinquiry.ca/en/documents/2007–04–12.htm> accessed 22 September 2014.
72 Internal Inquiry into the Actions of Canadian Officials in Relation to Abdullah Almalki, Ahmed Abou-Elmaati and Muayyed Nureddin, *Ruling on Terms of Reference and Procedure* (2007) 26.
73 Kalajdzic (n. 37) 161.
74 Ibid. 163.
75 Internal Inquiry into the Actions of Canadian Officials in Relation to Abdullah Almalki, Ahmed Abou-Elmaati and Muayyed Nureddin, *Supplement to Public Report* (2010) 4.
76 Roach (n. 36) 73.
77 Commission of Inquiry into the Actions of Canadian Officials in Relation to Maher Arar, 'Rulings' (12 December 2006) <http://epe.lac-bac.gc.ca/100/206/301/pco-bcp/commissions/maher_arar/07–09–13/www.ararcommission.ca/eng/11g.htm> accessed 22 September 2014.
78 Commission of Inquiry into the Actions of Canadian Officials in Relation to Maher Arar, 'Arar Commission Will Not Appeal Federal Court Decision on the Release of Public Information' (Press release, 2007).
79 Commission of Inquiry into the Actions of Canadian Officials in Relation to Maher Arar, *Report of the Events Relating to Maher Arar: Factual Background Volume I, II, and Analysis & Recommendations – Addendum* (2007).
80 Ibid.
81 Ibid. 245.
82 Reg Whittaker, 'Arar: The Affair, the Inquiry, the Aftermath' (2008) 9(1) *IRPP Policy Matters*, 1, 14.
83 Ibid.
84 Internal Inquiry into the Actions of Canadian Officials in Relation to Abdullah Almalki, Ahmed Abou-Elmaati and Muayyed Nureddin (n. 75).
85 Ibid.
86 Ibid. 3–5.
87 Ibid. 6–12.
88 Ibid. 11.
89 Rod Mickleburgh, 'Sgt Patrick Tower and Maher Arar, 2006', *Globe and Mail* (30 December 2006) <http://www.theglobeandmail.com/news/national/sgt-patrick-tower-and-maher-arar-2006/article4392154/?page=all> accessed 22 September 2014.

90 Independent National Security Legislation Monitor Act 2010 (Cth.), ss. 11(1) and (2); IGIS Act 1986, s. 6.
91 Frank Iacobucci, *Internal Inquiry into the Actions of Canadian Officials in Relation to Abdullah Almalki, Ahmed Abou-El Maati and Muayyed Nureddin* (2008) 31.
92 Ibid.
93 Commission of Inquiry into the Actions of Canadian Officials in Relation to Maher Arar (n. 61) 11.
94 National Security Legislation Amendment Bill (No. 1) 2014 (Cth.); Counter-Terrorism Legislation Amendment (Foreign Fighters) Bill 2014 (Cth.).

Chapter 10

Secret policing

Boundaries of undercover evidence

Miiko Kumar

Introduction

There has been a notable increase in the type of proactive policing that employs deceptive techniques to obtain evidence.[1] This chapter considers the issues that arise from the use of evidence obtained from undercover policing. In particular, it looks at the regulation and control of undercover operatives within Australia. Issues that arise in respect of an undercover officer's oral evidence will also be considered, specifically the use of public interest immunity and applications for suppression/non-publication orders to protect the police operative and/or the disclosure of confidential police methods. The chapter asks whether secrecy orders are justified and will then examine the admissibility of evidence obtained by covert means. The admissibility of admissions elicited by covert means are considered in light of the shift in the High Court of Australia's decisions from *R v Swaffield; Pavic v The Queen*[2] to *Em v The Queen*.[3] Finally, the chapter examines possible reform to the rules of evidence in the Uniform Evidence Acts,[4] inquiring whether the law should require admissions obtained by undercover operatives to be recorded in order for such admissions to be used as evidence in court proceedings.

Legality of undercover operations

Police methodology can involve the use of tricks, deceit and secrecy in the investigation of crime. Issues regarding the admissibility of the resulting evidence have arisen when police officers have acted illegally or improperly in the course of police work.[5] In Australia, undercover operatives and some types of operations are regulated by legislation.[6]

Australia's highest court's decision of *Ridgeway v The Queen*[7] prompted legislative schemes to legalise controlled drug operations which frequently utilise undercover operatives.[8] The *Ridgeway* case involved a police informer importing heroin from Malaysia with the assistance of the Australian Federal Police (AFP) for the purpose of apprehending Ridgeway in Australia with possession of heroin. Ridgeway's subsequent appeal against conviction succeeded on the basis of the illegally obtained evidence that formed proof of the crime against him. The court held that the importation by police was illegal and hence ought to have been inadmissible evidence on public policy grounds.[9] Subsequent to the High Court's decision in *Ridgeway*, piecemeal legislation was enacted in each jurisdiction in Australia to make controlled operations legal and to protect police operatives from criminal or civil liability in relation to activities engaged in while undercover. The legislation was unsuccessfully challenged in the High Court of Australia on the basis that it constituted an improper interference with the separation of the judicial power under Ch. III of the Australian Constitution.[10]

Prior to the introduction of specific legislation, there was an informal practice where police were liable to be charged with criminal offences, but relied on other police and prosecutors not charging them. It has been observed that the decision not to charge or prosecute took 'account of all the circumstances surrounding the offences and weigh[ed] up the public interest in pursuing a prosecution . . . [s] imilarly, the courts needed to be persuaded to allow the evidence gathered during the operation to be used in the trial against the accused person'.[11]

The Australian scheme

At the federal level, the Crimes Act 1914 (Cth.) deals with undercover operations.[12] Part IAC of that Act covers assumed identities, while pt. IAB concerns controlled operations and major controlled operations (the latter including undercover operations). Pursuant to s. 15LD(1), the AFP must produce an annual report dealing with assumed identities. The report consists of a single page with basic information regarding how many authorisations for assumed identities were granted in the year (100 in 2012–13[13] and 52 in 2011–12).[14] The annual report also provides a general description of the activities undertaken by authorised civilians and authorised law enforcement officers when using assumed identities and whether or not any fraud or other unlawful activity was identified by an audit during the year.

At the state level, there are separate statutes dealing with various aspects of undercover operations. In 2003, the Leaders' Summit on Terrorism and Multi-Jurisdictional Crime developed Australian model laws for powers for cross-border investigations covering controlled operations (covert investigations), assumed identities legislation, surveillance devices, and witness anonymity. The Australian Capital Territory (ACT),[15] New South Wales (NSW),[16] Queensland (Qld.),[17] Victoria (Vic.),[18] Tasmania (Tas.)[19] and Western Australia (WA)[20] have all enacted legislation that, to a greater or lesser extent, adopts the model laws.[21] South Australia (SA) does not appear to have followed the model laws. The situation in the Northern Territory (NT) is unclear.[22]

Undercover operatives can be used in any investigation; however, they are commonly deployed in particular types of investigations, such as for drug offences.[23] All the legislation (except the SA Act)[24] provides that it is not intended to limit a court's discretion either to admit or exclude evidence, or to stay criminal proceedings, in the interests of justice.[25] However, these provisions do attempt to circumvent *Ridgeway* by directing the court to disregard criminal activity on the part of undercover operatives in determining whether evidence will or will not be admitted, since the conduct is deemed to be lawful. For example, s. 15GA(2) of the Crimes Act 1914 (Cth.) states that when determining the admissibility of the evidence, the fact that it was obtained as a result of a person engaging in criminal activity is to be disregarded if either: (a) the person was part of, and the criminal activity constituted, a 'controlled operation' (explained below); or (b) the person was acting as part of a 'controlled operation' authorised under state legislation, and the criminal activity constituted an offence for which he or she would ordinarily be criminally responsible, but for an exculpatory section of the Act. The court can still choose to exclude the evidence on the basis of unfairness to the accused or prejudicial effect outweighing probative value.

Definition of 'controlled operation'

Under the Crimes Act 1914 (Cth.) s. 15GD(1), a 'controlled operation' is defined as an operation involving the participation of law enforcement officers for the purpose of obtaining evidence that may lead to the prosecution of a person for certain offences. A 'major controlled operation' is a controlled operation of a certain magnitude. It must involve the infiltration of one or more undercover officers in an organised criminal group for more than seven days, continue for more than three months, or target suspected criminal activity that includes a threat to human life. The controlled operation commences when authorised; an urgent authority can be granted orally.[26]

The NSW Act defines a 'controlled operation' as an operation conducted to frustrate or obtain evidence of criminal activity or corruption, or to arrest a person involved in such activity. It also includes any activity involving 'controlled conduct' (conduct that would be a crime but for an exculpatory section of the Act) that is reasonably necessary to achieve any of the above purposes.[27]

This definition is largely the same as the corresponding state and territory Acts,[28] the key elements being that: the purpose of participating in the controlled operation or undertaking the controlled activity is to gather evidence for the purpose of law enforcement (prosecution); and the activity would be a crime but for an exculpatory section of the Act.

The states and territories also have legislation governing assumed (that is, undercover) identities to protect the true identity of the operative.[29] The legislation permits the lawful acquisition and use of assumed identities. The effect of an authority for an assumed identity protects the undercover operative from liability since 'anything done by an authorised person (whether in this jurisdiction or elsewhere) in the course of acquiring or using an assumed identity is not unlawful'[30] and the operative is indemnified by the law enforcement agency for any liability incurred for something done in the course of using an assumed identity.[31] The legislation can also protect the true identity from being disclosed by providing the power to make non-publication/suppression orders and order in camera hearings.[32]

The decision to conduct a controlled operation

The legislation specifies who is competent to authorise undercover investigations. Under the Commonwealth Act, a major controlled operation may only be authorised by the commissioner or a deputy commissioner of the AFP.[33] A controlled operation may be authorised additionally by an authorised officer of the AFP, the Australian Crime Commission or the Australian Commission for Law Enforcement Integrity.[34] Under the state Acts, authorisation can be granted by the chief officer of the law enforcement agency (or in SA a 'senior police officer')[35] who may also authorise the use of an assumed identity. In Queensland, the chief officer must refer to a committee, though he or she is not obliged to follow the committee's advice.[36]

The criterion for obtaining authorisation to conduct a controlled operation is that the authorising officer must be satisfied on reasonable grounds that it is necessary. In particular, he or she must be satisfied that a 'relevant offence' has been, is being, or is likely to be committed.[37] A 'relevant offence' is generally defined in the Acts as one punishable by three or more years of imprisonment.[38] New South Wales and Queensland adopt a broader definition, which refers simply to 'criminal activity' (and in NSW also to 'corrupt conduct').[39]

Authorisations may be either standard or urgent. A standard application should be in writing; an urgent application may be made by phone, in person or by radio (but rendered into writing as soon as possible). Under the NSW and WA Acts, a retrospective authorisation can also be made; it must generally be applied for within 24 hours of the conduct being engaged in.[40]

If granted, the authorisation (whether standard or urgent) must contain certain information identifying the operation, the participants (by number or code name, if applicable), the controlled activities they may engage in, and the period for which the authorisation is to remain in force.[41] The authorisation is generally subject to a limit. Authorities for controlled operations can generally not remain in force for more than three, six or twelve months, or a period of days for an urgent authority (for example, 72 hours). Authorities may be renewed subject to certain conditions and can be cancelled at any time.[42] There is nothing provided for regarding the continuation of controlled activities beyond the prescribed term, although there are exemptions for operatives who are unaware of the variation or cancellation of an authority to be protected from liability. The authority for an assumed identity, once granted, generally remains in force until cancelled.[43]

The activities that are not authorised during controlled operations are:[44]

- anything that is not authorised by the authority that has been granted for the controlled operation;
- anything that is likely to cause death or serious injury to a person;
- anything that involves the commission of a sexual offence against a person;[45]
- anything that induces or encourages another person to engage in criminal activity that he or she would not reasonably have been expected to engage in otherwise.

These exceptions do not apply in SA, which provides a blanket immunity.[46] The other states, however, provide that as long as the (otherwise criminal) activity was authorised, the participant will not be held criminally responsible.[47]

Participants are also not criminally liable under the assumed identities legislation and are indemnified for civil liability arising from it.[48] The legislation contains an exemption for something that would not be an offence if the assumed identity were the person's real identity.[49] It is an offence to disclose information about a controlled operation or the identity of an undercover operative.[50]

Secrecy in the adducing of evidence from undercover operatives

Anonymous witnesses

When an undercover officer testifies in court proceedings, he or she will usually give evidence anonymously. This means that the witness may give evidence under a pseudonym, possibly in closed court, with non-publication orders and suppression orders in place to protect his or her identity and, in some cases, the witness may be screened from the accused or give evidence via video link. The protection of the identity of the operative is based on protecting the safety of the officer, ensuring his or her future use in undercover operations, and may also be intended to ensure that other officers are not deterred from becoming undercover operatives in the future.[51] The development of Australian law in respect of anonymous witnesses has not received the same level of scrutiny as it has in countries such as the United Kingdom,[52] New Zealand[53] and the United States.[54] There is not a unified approach in Australian common law as to when anonymous testimony can be used.[55] Furthermore, Australian law has not developed to devise safeguards (or requirements) for when anonymous testimony can be used.[56]

The leading case in NSW on anonymous witnesses is *R v Ngo*,[57] where two witnesses were called to identify the accused. The accused was on trial for the murder of a politician; the accused was also involved in politics. Both witnesses gave evidence under a pseudonym and via video link. The accused was prevented from seeing the faces of the witnesses. The trial judge ordered that the testimony be adduced via video link as he was satisfied that 'the fears of the witnesses were genuine and that they would probably not give evidence if required to do so in the courtroom in the presence of the accused. He concluded that it was in the interests of the administration of justice to make the order'.[58]

One of the grounds of appeal relied on by Mr Ngo was that 'since issues of identity were involved, [he] should be entitled to see the witnesses because otherwise he would not have the opportunity to properly contest that evidence'.[59] Mr Ngo argued that as he was:

> prevented from seeing the witnesses' faces, he could not instruct counsel as to whether he recognised them; and if he did, whether there were any matters

> which might affect their reliability or credibility. This was all the more so because the jury believed that the appellant could see the witnesses. The jury would assess the reliability of the witnesses on the assumption that there was no basis to challenge their credibility.[60]

The NSW Court of Criminal Appeal dismissed the appeal and found that the trial judge was entitled to conclude that the witnesses had genuine fears for their own safety and that of their family, which would 'prevent or impede them from giving adequate evidence in court'.[61] Furthermore, they 'would probably not give evidence if required to do so face to face with the appellant in the courtroom'.[62] Surprisingly, the decision does not consider specifically the accused's right to confrontation. In fact, the issue has not been considered by the High Court.

However, the right to confrontation was considered by the NSW Court of Criminal Appeal in *BUSB v The Queen*,[63] where Australian Security Intelligence Organisation (ASIO) undercover operatives sought to give evidence under pseudonym in closed court and in a way that meant they could not be seen by the accused. The accused argued that the screening order prevented full and effective cross-examination. The court found that the trial judge had exercised his discretion correctly in granting the screening order by considering the risk to national security if the accused viewed the witnesses' faces and the impact of the orders on the accused's fair trial. The court considered that the accused's inability to see the ASIO witnesses for the purpose of cross-examination was not significant.[64] The right to a fair trial was not impinged by the law enforcement officers giving evidence anonymously as their evidence was corroborative, rather than critical, and each case will vary depending on its circumstances.[65] Furthermore, the test of necessity was met because if the order were not made, there would be a risk to ASIO officers and to national security.[66] Significantly, the court did not consider the common law power to make anonymity orders as the accused conceded that the court had the power to make such orders.

The issue has been the subject of two differing approaches in two other Australian states (Queensland and Victoria). In a Queensland decision, the court held that undercover police officers could not give evidence under pseudonym. There was no common law principle to permit the use of pseudonym or power to close the court, and 'it was a basic right of an accused person to know the true identity of his accuser'.[67] However, in Victoria, the court held that evidence from two undercover police officers could be given anonymously, based on the extension of the principles of public interest immunity, as undercover officers were analogous to informers. Justice Brooking, who wrote the lead judgment in the Victorian decision, held that a 'claim to immunity should not be confined to undercover police operatives and that it extends to other witnesses whose personal safety may be endangered by the disclosure of their identity'.[68] The correctness of Brooking J's reasoning has been doubted due to the fact that the informer rule has only protected the anonymity of non-testifying informers.[59] The Victorian approach is considered to be the leading Australian authority in its field.[70]

Most jurisdictions in Australia have legislation enabling law enforcement officers to give evidence anonymously.[71] The main type of witnesses who fall within this category are undercover or surveillance law enforcement officers.[72] For example, pt. IACA of the Crimes Act 1914 (Cth.) concerns witness identity protection for undercover operatives. A witness identity protection certificate may be granted permitting the operative to give evidence under another name.[73] No witness in the proceeding, including the undercover operative, can be asked a question or can give an answer (without leave) that may lead to the disclosure of the operative's identity or where they live.[74] In addition, the court, the parties and the lawyers involved in the proceeding cannot make a statement (without leave) that may disclose these matters.[75] The court may also make a suppression order concerning details that could lead to the identification of the operative.[76] The issue to be tested in the Australian context is the extent to which the use of anonymous witnesses impedes the accused's right to a fair trial. Such a right is recognised by the common law, as opposed to being set out clearly in a bill of rights. In addition, there is no specific legislation, like the United Kingdom's legislation, to deal with witnesses who wish to give evidence anonymously, especially in circumstances where they are fearful or intimidated.[77]

Confidential police methods

The extent to which the defence can cross-examine an undercover operative on confidential police methods is subject to the doctrine of public interest immunity. Law enforcement and the preservation of effective policing is recognised as a category of information, which the courts have accepted may, if disclosed, harm the public interest.[78] Public interest immunity has prevented the disclosure of confidentiality of police methodology where its disclosure could harm future policing.[79]

Suppression and non-publication orders

A court has power to make non-publication orders to protect the public interest.[80] However, disclosure of the information must be against the public interest and 'the test of necessity requires at least that there be identified some substantial detriment or risk of detriment to the administration of justice that would, in a significant way, be alleviated by suppression of the information'.[81] Suppression and non-publication orders are now dealt with in NSW by statute. The Court Suppression and Non-Publication Orders Act 2010 (NSW) provides a statutory basis for protective orders to protect the public interest. The government (or an agency of the government) of the Commonwealth or of a state has the standing to seek orders under the Act. Section 8(1) states that the grounds for making an order are: 'the order is necessary to prevent prejudice to the proper administration of justice'; 'the order is necessary to prevent prejudice to the interests of the Commonwealth or a State or Territory in relation to national or international security'; 'the order is necessary to protect the safety of any person'; 'the order is necessary to avoid causing undue distress or embarrassment to a party to or witness in criminal proceedings involving an offence of a sexual nature (including an act of indecency)'; and/or 'it is otherwise necessary in the public interest for the order to be made and that public interest significantly outweighs the public interest in open justice'. The orders are justified due to the protection of the operative and the effectiveness of future investigations.

The boundaries of admissibility

Making the target speak after exercising the right to silence is out of bounds

Many of the cases involving the admissibility of admissions elicited by undercover officers turn on whether the target has previously exercised his or her right not to speak to the police. In *R v Swaffield; Pavic v The Queen*,[82] Swaffield was initially charged with two offences of breaking and entering and one arson charge. He refused to speak to the investigating police officers. No evidence was led against him at the committal hearing and he was discharged. An undercover officer was deployed and admissions in relation to the fire were elicited from Swaffield. Fresh charges were then laid for all offences. At trial, a question arose as to the admissibility of the admissions made to the undercover operative due to the fact that Swaffield was not cautioned. The High Court held that the admissions were elicited in clear breach of Swaffield's right to choose whether or not to speak.[83]

In the same judgment, the High Court also determined the appeal of *Pavic*. The police interviewed Pavic during their investigation of a murder. At the start of the interview, Pavic was cautioned, then upon advice from his solicitor he refused to speak to the police. The police subsequently took a statement from a friend of Pavic's, Clancy, who provided evidence against Pavic. Clancy later wore a recording device during a conversation with Pavic at the time Pavic made admissions. The question for the High Court was the admissibility of the recorded conversation. The High Court found that the conversation was admissible.[84] The majority of Toohey, Gaudron and Gummow JJ concluded that 'unfairness' would include obtaining a confession through trickery after the accused had exercised his or her right to silence.[85] A key difference between *Swaffield* and *Pavic* was the extent to which the accused's freedom to choose to speak to the police had been impugned.[86] In *Swaffield*, the admissions were actively elicited by the undercover officer,[87] whereas in *Pavic*, the admissions were volunteered by Pavic, rather than elicited by Clancy.[88] In addition, *Swaffield* had shown that he wished to remain silent by refusing to speak to the police.

In *Western Australia v May*,[89] May was charged with murder. He took part in two police interviews in which no admissions were made. After he was refused bail, he was placed in a cell with an undercover operative. The operative repeatedly engaged him in conversation, and partial admissions were recorded. At trial, the accused objected to this evidence. It was found that May would not have spoken to the operative about the murder if the operative had not brought up the subject and used techniques such as pointed and 'bundled' questions. The evidence was elicited in violation of May's decision to say nothing more to the police. It was, in substance, an interrogation, but it was not fair. The common law discretion to exclude was exercised in May's favour.

In a Queensland case of *R v Belford*,[90] the appellants were convicted of murder. The second appellant, Bound, stated he did not wish to speak to the police without first receiving legal advice. He was then placed in a watch house with two covert police operatives. Over the course of some hours, they had a recorded conversation in which Bound made admissions. The trial judge refused to exclude the evidence. On appeal, the court found that the evidence ought to have been excluded. It was unfair to admit it in circumstances in which the police had deliberately and improperly sought to overcome Bound's expected exercise of his right to silence. Significantly, the police knew that Bound was unlikely to co-operate if a further interview was conducted, as Bound had told an operative that his lawyer had told him not to say anything.[91] The trial judge erred in not considering the issue of unfairness from the perspective of the police impropriety in circumventing Bound's rights.[92] It was also necessary to consider specifically whether the use of subterfuge to undermine Bound's right to silence, which police believed (correctly) that he would exercise, would offend community standards.[93]

Along similar lines, in a case in NSW, Cooney was charged with multiple counts of armed robbery and motor vehicle stealing, and was arrested.[94] He was put into a cell with an undercover operative. No admissions were made. That operative was substituted by a second operative, who offered to provide Cooney with a barrister. Cooney then made admissions. Minutes before those admissions were made, an actual barrister, organised by Cooney's brother, called the station to attempt to speak with Cooney. Cooney was not made aware of this in a timely fashion, as was required by statute. The trial judge excluded the admissions pursuant to s. 90 of the Evidence Act 1995 (NSW). Section 90 provides that an admission may be excluded by the court 'having regard to the circumstances in which the admission was made, it would be unfair to a defendant to use the evidence'. On appeal by the Crown, it was held that the trial judge had improperly side-stepped s. 138 (the discretion to exclude improperly or illegally obtained evidence) in favour of exclusive reliance on s. 90.

Taking advantage of stupidity and ignorance is within bounds

In *Em v The Queen*,[95] the accused refused a recorded interview at the police station. The police (not working undercover) took advantage of Em's ignorance or stupidity and took him to a park for a conversation. Em thought that the police could only use anything he said if it was recorded. He was under the misapprehension that his conversation to police was not being recorded and also that the police could not give evidence about it. The High Court allowed the admissions and did not exclude them pursuant to s. 90 of the Evidence Act 1995 (NSW). Gummow and Hayne JJ held that s. 90 is a safety net provision that only applies when all relevant sections have been considered.[96] Furthermore, that reliability is largely irrelevant under s. 90 because it is considered under s. 85.[97] In addition, they rejected the argument that it was unfair to admit evidence because of improper police conduct as that is dealt with in s. 138.[98] *Em* demonstrates that police can take advantage of ignorance or stupidity. Police could exploit the accused's incorrect view of the law by cautioning Em that he did not have to speak, but they did not administer the second part of the caution, namely that anything he said to police could be used against him.

Investigative police technique is within bounds

An investigative technique that was imported from Canada and dealt with by the High Court in *Tofilau v The Queen; Marks v The Queen; Hill v The Queen; Clarke v the Queen*[99] was found to be within the bounds of legality. In this case, four appellants, in four separate appeals, had each been convicted of murder by undercover officers eliciting admissions by creating false set-ups. The challenge by the four appellants to the admissibility of the admissions was that they were not voluntary. The High Court determined that they were.[100] Even though there was a considerable degree of 'trickery' involved, this did not warrant exclusion of the admissions. Furthermore, each of the appellants had not previously exercised his right to silence. Andrew Palmer has observed that this case shows that 'if the crime is serious enough, and the evidence important enough, it may be acceptable for investigators to circumvent or undermine the rights of suspects, including the right to silence'.[101] The seriousness of the crime was a factor in favour of admissibility in each case.[102]

In *Lauchlan v State of Western Australia*,[103] Lauchlan was convicted of murder. He denied involvement in the murder when questioned by police. An undercover operation using the technique[104] that was 'almost identically utilised' in *Tofilau* was found to be permissible.[105] During an interview with an undercover operative, Lauchlan initially denied involvement and the operative stressed that Lauchlan did not have to participate further in the discussion. Lauchlan then explained how he had killed the deceased.[106] The trial judge admitted these admissions into evidence. It was held on appeal that there was no compulsion that would deny 'basal voluntaries' – there was 'no sustained or undue insistence or pressure, no duress or intimidation . . . [and] no unlawful conduct on the part of [the operative]'.[107] Furthermore, there was no basis for its exclusion due to several factors, including: the seriousness of the crime; the lack of an available alternative; that the right to silence was not circumvented; and that the operative did not prey on special characteristics of Lauchlan (such as his education or health).[108] *Lauchlan* was, 'in all material respects, indistinguishable from that of *Tofilau*'.[109]

This technique has been criticised for producing false confessions[110] and violating human rights.[111] The technique has been the subject of two recent Canadian Supreme Court decisions in the latter part of 2014. In *R v Hart*,[112] Hart's twin daughters drowned and he was a murder suspect. Undercover officers interrogated Hart about the deaths; Hart confessed. He later took an undercover officer to the scene, explaining how he had acted. The court expressed concern about the risk of unreliable confessions, prejudice to the accused, and the risk of unacceptable police tactics.[113] As a result, the court developed a new test for the admissibility of such confessions, being concerned that the admissions were reliable and that the bad character evidence did not outweigh the probative value of the admissions. It developed a rule that admissions elicited through this technique are presumptively inadmissible unless the Crown can establish that their probative value outweighs their prejudicial effect, and are to be excluded if the defence establishes an abuse of process[114] (for example, if the confession was obtained by violence or the threat of violence).[115]

The second Canadian Supreme Court decision is *R v Mack*.[116] Mack was convicted of the first degree murder of his room-mate. The investigation of Mack involved, in part, a covert operation that lasted four months, during which time Mack twice admitted committing the murder to undercover police officers. He also took an undercover officer to a fire-pit on his father's property and, when they were there, said that he had removed the ashes and there was 'nothing left' of his room-mate.[117] The police later found the deceased's remains, and shell casings from a rifle in Mack's apartment, in the fire-pit.[118] The courts below did not have the benefit of the recent *R v Hart* decision, but it was found on appeal that the admissions were admissible under the '*Hart* framework'.[119] It was correct to have admitted the admissions into evidence. Their probative value was very high due to substantial corroborative evidence and there was confirmatory evidence in abundance. Furthermore, their prejudicial effect was limited, as it did not reveal unsavoury facts about Mack or any former participation in violent scenarios. The court also considered that there was no impropriety on the part of the officers, and Mack had not been coerced.[120] It was also held that the directions to the jury, regarding reliability and prejudice, were sufficient. The court held that there was 'no magical incantation that must be read' and 'the nature and extent of the instructions required will vary from case to case'.[121] However, the court discussed the necessary content of directions involving cases using this particular technique, and any bad character evidence that is admitted along with any admission.[122] The admissions were determined to be admissible.

This technique has also been successfully used in New Zealand. Cameron was convicted of murder, whereby Cameron met with 'Tony', an undercover operative. The subsequent conversation was recorded on video camera, and Cameron made several admissions about the murder. Prior to trial, Cameron unsuccessfully objected to the admission into evidence of the statements made to 'Tony'. It was found on appeal that: the scenario did not provide a context or incentive for Cameron to make a false confession to murder; there was no evidence that the things Cameron said were out of 'bravado' or puffery; and Cameron's admissions suggested that the 'burden of guilt' weighed heavily on him.[123] There was no reason to doubt its reliability or voluntariness and no indication of overbearing questioning or intimidation.[124] It is noted that the technique has not generated case law in the United Kingdom[125] or the United States.

The technique was recently used in Queensland to successfully convict Brett Cowan for the murder of a 13-year-old boy, Daniel Morcombe.[126] Police did not have a crime scene, nor had they located Daniel Morcombe's body. Daniel Morcombe had disappeared in 2003; Cowan was formally interviewed in 2006. In 2010, police performed a cold case review and commenced the covert operation that led to the conviction. The court refused Cowan's application to exclude the evidence of confessions made by him to police. The facts bore 'striking similarities' to those in *Tofilau*.[127] Undercover police[128] obtained confessions from Cowan that he had abducted and killed Daniel Morcombe,[129] and he later made subsequent confessions to other operatives[130] that ultimately led to Cowan taking the undercover operatives to Daniel Morcombe's remains, at which time he was arrested. Cowan sought to exclude all the admissions that he had made to the undercover operatives on the basis that they were involuntary and/or it would be unfair to admit them. The reliability of the confessions was conceded by the accused. The court found, applying *Tofilau*, that they were voluntary and that the police methods were not improper or unfair. It has been reported that Cowan will appeal his conviction based on the recent Canadian decisions.[131]

The bounds of illegally obtained evidence

There have been cases where an accused has objected to the admissibility of admissions based on the illegal or improper acts of undercover police. Such objections are usually unsuccessful. In the NSW case of *R v Mallah*,[132] the accused was charged with terrorist offences. Mallah applied to exclude evidence from an undercover police officer on the basis that the officer's conduct was not authorised as part of a 'controlled operation' under the Crimes Act 1914 (Cth.) and was thus unlawful. It was held that, while some illegality occurred, the officer did not intentionally induce Mallah to do anything (whether it amounted to an offence or not) that he would not otherwise have intended to do.[133] Mallah had formulated his intentions before speaking to the officer, and was actively looking to enlist someone to further his plan.[134]

Sections 90 and 138 of the Evidence Act 1995 (NSW) both supported the admission of the evidence. It was noted that different considerations apply in relation to s. 90, depending on whether the undercover operation occurred pre- or post-arrest, as the latter is designed to derogate from the fundamental right of silence and the privilege against self-incrimination.[135]

In a South Australian case, Harvey was convicted of using a motor vehicle without consent. He happened upon a car parked with its keys in the door. He started the engine. The car had been modified as part of a police operation to stop car theft. A plain-clothed policeman disengaged the ignition by remote control and Harvey was trapped inside until his arrest. Harvey argued on appeal that because the operation had not been authorised pursuant to the Criminal Law (Undercover

Operations) Act 1995 (SA), the evidence was improperly obtained. This argument was rejected. It was held that the lack of authorisation did not invalidate the operation because the effect of the Act was to establish a mechanism for the approval of undercover operations and provide immunity to police. The Act did not require the approval of all undercover operations. The lack of approval simply meant no police immunity. Therefore, the Act applied without consequence. The conduct of the police was not illegal, and the evidence was not illegally or improperly obtained.[136]

In another case, Stubbs was charged with offences of communicating via the Internet with a person he believed to be under 16 years of age, with the intention of procuring sexual activity. The defence argued that a police detective based in New Zealand, who used a false identity and represented himself to be a 14-year-old girl and then liaised with the Australian police to then charge Stubbs, was 'improper' and required authorisation for a 'controlled operation' or an 'assumed identity' under the legislation. The court held that authorisation was unnecessary because the detective's interaction with Stubbs was not unlawful.[137] The evidence was not excluded because, unlike *Ridgeway*, there was no demonstrated impropriety or breach of Australian law that enlivened s. 138.[138] The police conduct was not entrapment. It was analogous to *Robinson v Woolworths*.[139] The court noted that an authorised 'controlled operation' could still engage s. 138 if it was entrapment or otherwise an improper inducement to commit the offence.[140] However, even if the present facts had involved such inducement, the evidence would still have been admitted under s. 138 due to the nature of the offence and the investigation.[141]

It came the attention of police that Diamond had been making inquiries about having her former partner (who was also the father of her young son) murdered.[142] An undercover operative had electronically recorded conversations with her about what she was seeking to have done to him. Diamond expressed her preference for a drug overdose. The operative attempted on numerous occasions to have Diamond explicitly commit to what she was engaging him to do. She withstood those attempts and asked him if he was recording the conversation, which he denied.[143] After the second conversation, in which a deal was struck, she was immediately arrested for conspiracy to murder.[144] The court reversed the trial judge's finding that the evidence was unlawfully obtained, and thus found that there was no need to consider s. 138 of the Evidence Act 1995 (NSW).[145] The essential finding of fact, that the operative actively encouraged or induced Diamond to engage in the crime of solicit to murder, was not sustained by the evidence.[146]

Finally, in another NSW case, a police informant supplied Dowe with cocaine as part of a 'controlled operation' authorised by the Law Enforcement (Controlled Operations) Act 1997 (NSW) (COA (NSW)). Dowe then supplied it to syndicate members. Following Dowe's conviction, the High Court found, in separate proceedings, that the COA (NSW) authorities were ultra vires and that the supply to Dowe had been unlawful. Dowe appealed his conviction on the grounds that the High Court decision meant that his trial involved a miscarriage of justice and the admissibility of all of the evidence had to be reconsidered. This argument was rejected.[147] There was no miscarriage of justice. *Dowe* was distinguished from *Ridgeway* on numerous grounds, including that, here, the officers believed a valid authority was in place and Dowe was not procured or entrapped into committing an offence.[148] It was open to the court to determine whether the evidence should be admitted, notwithstanding the invalidity of the authority.[149] On the present facts, the s. 138 discretion would still be exercised in favour of its admission.[150]

Taking advantage of impairment is out of bounds

Gallagher was charged with murder.[151] She suffered from brain damage, epilepsy, alcohol dependence and resultant cognitive impairment. The police were aware of her psychological condition but continued contact between her and an undercover operative in an operation that lasted over a year. As Gallagher initially made no admissions to the operative, the operative and the manager of the operation met with a psychologist to discuss how the operative could build a stronger relationship with the accused.[152] Gallagher eventually made admissions to a second operative that were excluded. Although the court found that the police conduct was not illegal or improper,[153] the admissions were excluded because 'having regard to the circumstances in which the admission[s] were made, it would be unfair' to use the admissions against her, given that her mental state and other considerations rendered them unreliable.[154] Her mental state was said to distinguish the case from *Tofilau*.[155]

Considerations for reform

Should admissions elicited from undercover operatives be inadmissible unless they are sound recorded?

The common law does not require that admissions made to police officers be recorded. The common law provides that where the prosecution relies on police testimony of an admission then the jury should be warned that it is dangerous to rely on uncorroborated testimony.[156] Various statutes require recording of admissions in order that they be admissible. The various statutes dealing with the taping of admissions specifically exclude undercover officers from the requirement to tape admissions.[157] The purpose of taping admissions is to prevent verballing and to ensure the reliability of the evidence. The requirement only applies to admissions obtained in the course of official questioning. For example, s. 281 of the Criminal Procedure Act 1986 (NSW) requires recording of admissions made in the course of 'official questioning' by an 'investigating official'. The definition of 'investigating official' in s. 281(4) specifically excludes 'a police officer who is engaged in covert investigations'. If an unrecorded admission is made to police not in the 'course of official questioning' then it is admissible: this is clear from the leading authority of *Kelly v The Queen*[158] and see further *R v Naa*.[159] Unrecorded admissions were admissible to undercover police in *Tofilau v The Queen*.

Should admissions elicited from undercover operatives be required to satisfy the test of reliability?

The definition of 'investigating official' under the uniform evidence legislation excludes undercover officers.[160] Admissions by defendants in criminal proceedings to or in the presence of an 'investigating official' investigating the commission of an offence, or a person the defendant thought could influence his or her prosecution, are not admissible unless it is unlikely that the truth of the admission was adversely affected.[161] The court is to consider the circumstances in which the admission was made, including characteristics of the defendant (such as age, any disabilities, education levels), whether it was made in response to questioning, and the nature of any question, threat, promise or other inducement that elicited the admission.

Conclusion

Covert police operations are essential to successful policing. However, a balance must be achieved between the goals of obtaining probative evidence to convict those who are guilty and ensuring that law enforcement remains with the bounds of legality. After the dramatic decision in *Ridgeway*, Australian legislature acted swiftly to ensure that police operations used to gather evidence, were legal. The lawful boundaries of covert operations are assured by the passage of legislation that gives legal protection by way of immunities to police and informers engaged in controlled operations. This is a positive development in the law. Furthermore, the secrecy measures used when undercover officers give evidence in court are justified to protect the safety of the officer, and to ensure anonymity for further covert work. The extent to which undercover operatives are at risk of death and injury cannot be underestimated. Such work, by its very nature, is dangerous.

Deceptive methodology used in covert operations to elicit admissions from an accused has been the basis for the exclusion of admissions. However, as Brennan CJ said in *Swaffield*:

> The investigation of crime is not a game governed by a sportsman's code of fair play. Fairness to those suspected of crime is not the giving of a sporting opportunity to escape the consequences of any legitimate and proper investigation or the giving of a sufficient opportunity 'to invent plausible falsehoods'.[162]

The cases discussed in this chapter demonstrate that the operation of the rules of evidence in the trial exclude admissions that impugn the accused's right to choose to speak to the police. The trial allows judicial control of police methods by the application of the rules of evidence. The cases demonstrate that the rules of evidence respond to the dangers that exist in obtaining evidence by deception. In particular, a court will exclude a confession made in clear breach of the accused's choice to be silent. A key factor in determining the admissibility of evidence obtained by deception is based on its reliability and any unfairness that is caused to the accused by its tender. Trickery is permissible, as the cases discussed show.

As to reform, it is concluded that the exclusion of undercover operatives from the requirement for the taping of admissions is justified. A remaining issue is whether Australian law should develop a more principled approach, such as the Canadian framework in *Hart*, to regulate the admissibility of admissions by specific consideration of reliability and prejudice.

Notes

1 See Simon Bronitt, 'The Law in Undercover Policing: A Comparative Study of Entrapment and Covert Interviewing in Australia, Canada and Europe' (2004) 33 *Common Law World Review*, 46, citing the seminal work of G. Marx, *Undercover – Police Surveillance in America*, University of California Press 1988. See also Elizabeth E. Joh, 'Breaking the Law to Enforce It: Undercover Police Participation in Crime' (2009) 62 *Stanford Law Review*, 155; Edwin W. Kruisbergen, Deborah de Jong and Edward R. Kleemans, 'Undercover Policing: Assumptions and Empirical Evidence' (2011) 51 *British Journal of Criminology*, 394.

2 (1998) 192 CLR 159.

3 (2007) 232 CLR 67.

4 The Uniform Evidence Acts comprise: Evidence Act 1995 (Cth.); Evidence Act 2004 (NI); Evidence Act 1995 (NSW); Evidence (National Uniform Legislation) Act 2011 (NT); Evidence Act 2001 (Tas.); Evidence Act 2008 (Vic.).

5 *Ridgeway v The Queen* (1995) 184 CLR 19 (*Ridgeway*).

6 Crimes Act 1914 (Cth.) (Crimes Act (Cth.)); Crimes (Controlled Operations) Act 2008 (ACT) (COA (ACT)); Crimes (Assumed Identities) Act 2009 (ACT) (AIA (ACT)); Crimes (Protection of Witness Identity) Act 2011 (ACT); Law Enforcement (Controlled Operations) Act 1997 (NSW) (COA (NSW)); Law Enforcement and National Security (Assumed Identities) Act 2010 (NSW) (AIA (NSW)); Police Powers and Responsibilities Act 2000 (Qld.) (PPRA (Qld.)); Criminal Investigation (Covert Operations) Act 2009 (SA) (COA (SA)); Police Powers (Controlled Operations) Act 2006 (Tas.) (COA (Tas.)); Police Powers (Assumed Identities) Act 2006 (Tas.) (AIA (Tas.)); Witness (Identity Protection) Act 2006 (Tas.); Crimes (Controlled Operations) Act 2004 (Vic.) (COA (Vic.)); Crimes (Assumed Identities) Act 2004 (Vic.) (AIA (Vic.)); Criminal Investigation (Covert Powers) Act 2012 (WA) (CPA (WA)). Also note that specific aspects of undercover work can require compliance with statutory provisions, such as the use of surveillance and listening devices: see, for example, Surveillance Devices Act 2007 (NSW).

7 *Ridgeway* (n. 5).

8 See references in (n. 6).

9 The public interest in admitting the illegally obtained evidence was outweighed by the public interest in not admitting the evidence: *Bunning v Cross* (1978) 141 CLR 54. Accordingly, Ridgeway's conviction was quashed and his prosecution was permanently stayed, as without that evidence there was insufficient evidence to convict.

10 *Nicholas v The Queen* (1998) 193 CLR 173.

11 Explanatory Statement to the Crimes (Controlled Operations) Bill (ACT), 2 (now the COA (ACT)).

12 Crimes Act (Cth.), pt. IAB.

13 Australian Federal Police, *Assumed Identities Annual Report 2012–13*, 2013.

14 Australian Federal Police, *Assumed Identities Annual Report 2011–12*, 2012.

15 AIA (ACT); COA (ACT); Crimes (Surveillance Devices) Act 2010 (ACT); Crimes (Protection of Witness Identity) Act 2011 (ACT).
16 AIA (NSW) (this replaced the Law Enforcement and National Security (Assumed Identities) Act 1998); COA (NSW).
17 PPRA (Qld.). Chapter 12 of this Act deals with assumed identities; ch. 11 (ss. 228–231) deals with controlled operations. The Act was amended by the Cross-Border Law Enforcement Legislation Amendment Act 2005 (Qld.) to largely incorporate the provisions of the Model Laws. See also Crime and Misconduct Act 2001 (Qld.) (pt. 7, dealing with covert searches); Criminal Organisation Act 2009 (Qld.).
18 AIA (Vic.); COA (Vic.); see also Terrorism (Community Protection) Act 2003 (Vic.) (pt. 2, dealing with covert search warrants); Public Interest Monitor Act 2011 (Vic.); Criminal Organisations Control Act 2012 (Vic.); Crimes Act 1958 (Vic.); Freedom of Information Act 1982 (Vic.) (s. 31 exempts law enforcement documents).
19 COA (Tas.); AIA (Tas.); Witness (Identity Protection) Act 2006 (Tas.).
20 CPA (WA); see also Surveillance Devices Act 1998 (WA); Royal Commission (Police) Act 2002 (WA).
21 Model Laws have been disseminated, which are intended to harmonise the laws throughout Australia: Standing Committee of Attorneys-General and Australasian Police Ministers Council Joint Working Group on National Investigation Powers, *Cross-border Investigative Powers for Law Enforcement Report* (2003).
22 The Explanatory Statement to the Surveillance Devices Act 2007 (NT) states that this Act is intended to implement the national model legislation; however, no mention is made of controlled operations or assumed identities. The Explanatory Memorandum to the Criminal Investigation (Covert Powers) Bill (2011) in Western WA omits the NT (and also SA) from the list of participating jurisdictions (p. 14).
23 For example, *Sinkovich v The Queen* [2011] NSWCCA 90.
24 COA (SA).
25 Crimes Act (Cth.) s. 15GA (s. 15HZ provides that an authority is admissible in legal proceedings); COA (ACT) s. 7; COA (NSW) s. 3A; PPRA (Qld.) s. 10; COA (Tas.) s. 7; COA (Vic.) s. 4; CPA (WA) s. 8.
26 Crimes Act (Cth.) s. 15GN.
27 COA (NSW) s. 3.
28 COA (ACT) s. 3; PPRA (Qld.) ss. 229; COA (SA) s. 3 ('undercover operations'); COA (Tas.) s. 4; COA (Vic.) ss. 6–7; CPA (WA) s. 5.
29 AIA (ACT); AIA (NSW); PPRA (Qld.) ch. 12; AIA (Tas.); AIA (Vic.); CPA (WA) pt. 3.
30 See, for example, AIA (NSW) s. 22.
31 Ibid. s. 23.
32 Ibid. s. 34; *Dodds v The Queen* (2009) 194 A Crim R 408 [54].
33 Crimes Act (Cth.) s. 15GF(1)(a).
34 Ibid. s. 15GF.
35 COA (ACT) s. 9; COA (NSW) s. 5; COA (SA) s. 4; COA (Tas.) s. 9; COA (Vic.) s. 12; CPA (WA) s. 10.
36 PPRA (Qld.) ss. 224, 229, 235, 239, 240.
37 COA (ACT) s. 10; COA (SA) s. 4; COA (Tas.) s. 10; COA (Vic.) s. 15; CPA (WA) s. 12.
38 COA (ACT) s. 3; COA (SA) s. 3 (referring to 'serious criminal behaviour'); COA (Tas.) s. 4; COA (Vic.) s. 3; CPA (WA) s. 5.
39 COA (NSW) ss. 3, 6; PPRA (Qld.) ss. 229, 240.
40 COA (NSW) s. 14; CPA (WA) s. 25.
41 For example, COA (NSW) s. 8.
42 COA (ACT) ss. 13, 15; COA (NSW) ss. 10, 12; PPRA (Qld.) ss. 247, 255; COA (SA) s. 4(5); COA (Tas.) ss. 13, 15; COA (Vic.) ss. 20, 25; CPA (WA) ss. 17–18, 22.
43 AIA (ACT) s. 13; AIA (NSW) s. 8; PPRA (Qld.) s. 285; COA (SA) s. 9; AIA (Tas.) s. 8; AIA (Vic.) s. 7; CPA (WA) s. 50.

44 COA (ACT) s. 18; COA (NSW) s. 7; PPRA (Qld.) s. 258(3); COA (Tas.) s. 18; COA (Vic.) s. 28; CPA (WA) s. 27.
45 Note, however, a possible inconsistency with the assumed identities legislation, which generally provides that (for example, in the AIA (NSW) s. 22(c)), an act is not unlawful if 'doing the thing would not be unlawful or constitute an offence or corrupt conduct if the assumed identity were the person's real identity'. Thus, presumably, the commission of a sexual offence based on deception would be protected (despite, for example, Crimes Act 1900 (NSW) s. 61HA(5)(a) providing that mistake as to identity negates consent).
46 COA (SA) s. 5, which provides '[d]espite any other law, an authorised participant in approved undercover operations incurs no criminal liability by taking part in undercover operations in accordance with the terms of the approval'.
47 COA (ACT) s. 18; COA (NSW) s. 16; PPRA (Qld.) s. 258; COA (Tas.) s. 18; COA (Vic.) s. 28; CPA (WA) s. 27.
48 AIA (ACT) ss. 27–28; AIA (NSW) ss. 22–23; PPRA (Qld.) ss. 303–304; COA (SA) ss. 19–20; AIA (Tas.) ss. 22–23; AIA (Vic.) ss. 20–21; CPA (WA) ss. 65–66.
49 AIA (ACT) s. 27; AIA (NSW) s. 22; PPRA (Qld.) s. 303; COA (SA) s. 19; AIA (Tas.) s. 22; AIA (Vic.) s. 20; CPA (WA) s. 65.
50 Crimes Act (Cth.) ss. 15HK, 15HL; COA (ACT) s. 26; AIA (ACT) s. 37; COA (NSW) s. 20R; AIA (NSW) s. 33; PPRA (Qld.) ss. 266, 313; COA (SA) s. 26; COA (Tas.) s. 26; AIA (Tas.) s. 32; COA (Vic.) s. 36; AIA (Vic.) s. 30; CPA (WA) s. 35.
51 This is based on the argument used in *Jarvie v the Magistrates Court of Victoria at Brunswick* [1995] 1 VR 84, 99: see later in this chapter.
52 In *R v Davis* [2008] UKHL 36, the House of Lords overturned a conviction on the basis that the sole and decisive evidence to prove the conviction was from three anonymous witnesses. The legislature responded to this decision with a statutory framework to permit anonymous witnesses.
53 In *R v Hughes* [1986] 2 NZLR 129, the New Zealand Court of Appeal held that the right of the accused to know the true identity of undercover police witnesses was so fundamental to the criminal trial that it could not be dispensed with. The government responded with legislation to permit undercover officers to testify under an assumed name, provided that the police commissioner provides a certificate that the officer has no criminal convictions, and notice must be given of any adverse comments about the officer's credibility made in other proceedings: s. 13A of the Evidence Act 1908 (NZ).
54 In *Alvarado v Superior Court (People)*, 60 Cal Rptr 2d 854 (1997), the Supreme Court of California concluded that the identities of the witnesses had to be disclosed to ensure effective investigation and cross-examination of the witnesses. The Confrontation clause was relied on.
55 David Lusty, 'Anonymous Accusers: An Historical and Comparative Analysis of Secret Witnesses in Criminal Trials' (2002) 24 *Sydney Law Review*, 361, 404.
56 Such as exist in Scotland: see Criminal Procedure Scotland Act 1995 s. 271R.
57 (2003) 57 NSWLR 55.
58 Ibid. [58].
59 Ibid. [60].
60 Ibid. [69].
61 Ibid. [106].
62 Ibid. [106].
63 (2011) 80 NSWLR 170.
64 Ibid. [81].
65 Ibid. [82]–[83].
66 Ibid. [57]–[62].
67 *R v Stipendiary Magistrate at Southport; Ex parte Gibson* [1993] 2 Qd R 687, 692 (Williams J).
68 *Jarvie* (n. 51) 99.

69 Lusty, 'Anonymous Accusers: An Historical and Comparative Analysis of Secret Witnesses in Criminal Trials' (n. 55) 406.
70 David Lusty, 'House of Lords Rejects Anonymous Witnesses in Criminal Trials' (2008) 32 *Criminal Law Journal*, 316, 319.
71 For example: Crimes Act (Cth.) s. 15YV; Crimes (Protection of Witness Identity) Act 2011 (ACT); AIA (NSW); COA (SA) pt. 4; Witness (Identity Protection) Act 2006 (Tas.) pt. 2; CPA (WA) pt. 4.
72 In *Dodds* (n. 32), McClellan CJ at CL (Simpson and Harrison JJ concurring) held in consideration of the NSW provision for assumed identities (s. 14) at [54]:

> Section 14 is provided for the obvious purpose of protecting the identity of relevant law enforcement officers. That their identities should be protected could not be in doubt. Both the safety of the officer and that person's continuing capacity to operate as an effective 'undercover' officer are at risk if the true identity of the officer becomes known. Although there are many categories of information which in the public interest require protection, but which may be disclosed to counsel with appropriate undertakings, the true identity of an 'undercover' officer has a particular sensitivity.

73 Crimes Act (Cth.) s. 15MJ.
74 Ibid. ss. 15MJ, 15MM.
75 Ibid. ss. 15MJ, 15 MM.
76 Ibid. s. 15MK.
77 Of course, there are witness protection programmes, but they have limitations.
78 *Young v Quin* (1985) 4 FCR 483; *Attorney-General for NSW v Stuart* (1994) 34 NSWLR 667; *S v State of New South Wales (No. 3)* [2009] NSWCA 248 [7]; *Commissioner of Police New South Wales v Nationwide News Pty Ltd* (2007) 70 NSWLR 643, 648 [35]; *McCausland v State of NSW* [2010] NSWSC 1562 [19]–[20] (Latham J).
79 *Young* (n. 78) 494 (Beaumont J, citing *D v National Society for the Prevention of Cruelty to Children* [1978] AC 171, 232–233); *S* (n. 78) [7]; *Commissioner of Police New South Wales* (n. 78) 648 [35]; *McCausland* (n. 78) [20]; *Smith* (1996) 86 A Crim R 308, 311.
80 *S* (n. 78); *Commissioner of Police New South Wales* (n. 78).
81 *Attorney-General for NSW v Nationwide News Pty Limited* (2007) 73 NSWLR 635 [39] (Hodgson JA, Hislop and Latham JJ agreeing).
82 *R v Swaffield* (n. 2).
83 Ibid. [93]–[98].
84 Ibid. [99]–[103].
85 Ibid. [80]–[92].
86 Ibid. [91].
87 Ibid. [33] (Brennan CJ); [98] (Toohey, Gaudron and Gummow JJ); [165] (Kirby J).
88 Ibid. [35] (Brennan CJ); [101]–[103] (Toohey, Gaudron and Gummow JJ).
89 [2011] WASC 365.
90 [2011] QCA 43.
91 *R v Belford* [2011] QCA 43 [61].
92 Ibid. [63].
93 Ibid.
94 *R v Cooney* [2013] NSWCCA 312.
95 (2007) 232 CLR 67.
96 Ibid. [109].
97 Ibid. [112].
98 Ibid. [121]–[122].
99 (2007) 231 CLR 396. See also *R v Favata* [2004] VSC 7 (23 January 2004).
100 (2007) 231 CLR 396.
101 Andrew Palmer, 'Applying Swaffield Part II: Fake Gangs and Induced Confessions' (2005) 29(2) *Criminal Law Journal*, 111, 115.

102 (2007) 231 CLR 396, 432 (Gummow and Hayne JJ), 527 (Callinan, Heydon and Crennan JJ).
103 [2008] WASCA 227.
104 *Lauchlan v State of Western Australia* [2008] WASCA 227, [16]–[17].
105 Ibid. [62].
106 Ibid. [18]–[23].
107 Ibid. [73].
108 Ibid. [76].
109 Ibid. [97].
110 Timothy E. Moore, Peter Copeland and Regina A. Schuller, 'Deceit, Betrayal and the Search for Truth: Legal and Psychological Perspectives on the "Mr Big" Strategy' (2009–2010) 55 *Criminal Law Quarterly*, 348, 351.
111 Violation of the right to remain silent and other violations of s. 7 of the Canadian Charter can be used to exclude the evidence procured by the technique. This has resulted in a 6.5 per cent success rate as analysed by Kate Puddister and Tory Riddell, 'The RCMP's "Mr Big" Sting Operation: A Case Study in Police Independence, Accountability and Oversight' (2012) 55(3) *Canadian Public Administration*, 385, 393.
112 2014 SCC 52.
113 Ibid.
114 Ibid. [84]–[86].
115 Ibid. [115]–[118].
116 2014 SCC 58.
117 Ibid. [13].
118 Ibid. [15].
119 Ibid. [32].
120 Ibid. [33]–[36].
121 Ibid. [50].
122 Ibid. [51]–[61].
123 *R v Cameron* [2009] NZCA 87 [29]–[31].
124 Ibid. [33]–[43].
125 However, in *R v Christou* [1992] 4 All ER 559 (CA), undercover operatives set up a fake jewellery shop to attract stolen goods.
126 He was convicted for unlawfully and indecently dealing with a child, murder and improperly dealing with his body.
127 *R v Cowan* [2013] QSC 337 [31].
128 Ibid. [129].
129 Ibid. [148]–[150].
130 Ibid. [155].
131 Clare Colley, 'Daniel Morcombe's Father Bruce is Confident the Australian Legal System Will Prevail over Murderer's Appeal' *Sydney Morning Herald* (online, 30 October 2014) <http://www.smh.com.au/national/daniel-morcombes-father-bruce-is-confident-the-australian-legal-system-will-prevail-over-murderers-appeal-20141030–11e7ch.html> accessed 9 November 2011.
132 [2005] NSWSC 358.
133 Ibid. [91]; [139].
134 Ibid. [92].
135 Ibid. [114].
136 *Harvey v Police* [2006] SASC 222.
137 *R v Stubbs* [2009] ACTSC 63 [63].
138 Ibid. [66].
139 (2005) 64 NSWLR 612; *R v Stubbs* [59].
140 Ibid. [50].
141 Ibid. [67]–[72].

142 *R v Diamond* [2013] NSWCCA 337.
143 Ibid. [25].
144 Ibid. [33].
145 Ibid. [46]–[48].
146 Ibid. [44].
147 *Dowe v The Queen* [2009] NSWCCA 23 [102].
148 Ibid. [78]; [97].
149 Ibid. [103].
150 Ibid. [104].
151 *R v Gallagher* [2013] NSWSC 1102.
152 Ibid. [62].
153 For the purpose of s. 138 of the Evidence Act 1995 (NSW): *R v Gallagher* (n. 152) [204]–[205].
154 *R v Gallagher* (n. 151) [233]–[242]. The admissions were excluded under s. 90 of the Evidence Act 1995 (NSW).
155 *R v Gallagher* (n. 151) [221].
156 *McKinney v The Queen* (1991) 171 CLR 468. Now, s. 165 of the Uniform Evidence Acts provides for a warning if the court considers that the evidence is unreliable. However, there is no requirement for a corroboration warning: s. 164.
157 For example, s. 281 of the Criminal Procedure Act 1986 (NSW).
158 (2004) 218 CLR 216.
159 (2009) 76 NSWLR 271.
160 The Dictionary to the Uniform Evidence Acts provides 'investigating official' means:

(a) a police officer (other than a police officer who is engaged in covert investigations under the orders of a superior), or
(b) a person appointed by or under an Australian law (other than a person who is engaged in covert investigations under the orders of a superior) whose functions include functions in respect of the prevention or investigation of offences.

161 Section 85 of the Uniform Evidence Acts.
162 *R v Swaffield* (n. 2) [35].

Chapter 11

Anonymity and defamation

David Rolph

Introduction

An anonymous plaintiff in a defamation proceeding seems like an anomaly, a curiosity, an oxymoron. Although ordinarily considered to be part of private law, defamation is, in many ways, indelibly public. The plaintiff has recourse to a public forum in order to have alleged damage to his or her reputation adjudicated. That public forum is a repository of public power. In each case, damage done to the plaintiff's reputation needs to occur in public, at least to some degree.[1] The interest protected by defamation law, reputation, is essentially the public self of the plaintiff – what other people think of the plaintiff.[2] Of course, it is always open to potential plaintiffs to elect not to sue at all, thereby preserving their anonymity but receiving no redress, or to settle proceedings prior to trial, thereby potentially minimising the encroachment upon their anonymity. However, there are cases in which plaintiffs have persisted with their defamation claims and sought to have their anonymity preserved. In some of those cases, the plaintiffs have even succeeded in having their identities suppressed.

The concept of an anonymous plaintiff in a defamation trial is challenging for a number of reasons. The common law's longstanding commitment to the principle of open justice seems to be firmly set against the notion of a defamation plaintiff being able to be anonymous. Moreover, the nature of the interest protected by the tort of defamation and the purposes of a defamation proceeding, principal among which is the vindication of the plaintiff's reputation, reinforce the common law's disposition towards publicity. However, there are certain developments that may support anonymity for those defamation plaintiffs who desire it. There has been recent concern about the incidence of suppression and non-publication orders, which can be a substantial derogation from the principle of open justice.[3] More importantly, there is a reconceptualisation of reputation underway in United Kingdom law as a result of the introduction of the European Convention on Human Rights (ECHR) into domestic law. The treatment of reputation as one aspect of the right to a private life under art. 8 of the ECHR is likely to have profound consequences for United Kingdom defamation law, not all of which are fully appreciated yet. This reconceptualisation of reputation arguably permits claims for anonymity in defamation claims to be entertained more readily and to be treated more favourably.

The legal blurring of reputation and privacy is not the only contributing factor. The rapid rise of social media, and consequently litigation based on social media publications, help explain why applications for anonymity are being raised in some defamation cases. Social media publications do not respect the taxonomical distinctions imposed by law, often implicating both a plaintiff's reputation and privacy, among other interests. In addition, although social media publications are sufficiently public for the purposes of defamation law, suing upon them gives even greater publicity to them. The defamation trial as the forum for providing a remedy to a damaged reputation might be a disproportionate response to the harm initially inflicted and, in fact, might cause greater harm.

Concerns about anonymity in defamation proceedings have tended to focus on anonymous defendants. In a number of jurisdictions, in Australia and overseas, there have been attempts, sometimes successful, to compel Internet intermediaries in particular to disclose the true identities of anonymous potential defendants.[4] Rather than focus on anonymous defendants in defamation proceedings, this chapter focuses on anonymous plaintiffs. It analyses the factors supporting and opposing a plaintiff being able to claim anonymity. It canvasses applications for anonymity in defamation claims as determined by English, Australian and Canadian courts. It argues that the principle of open justice and factors particular to defamation litigation, most notably the concept of reputation, properly understood, and the need for vindication, militate significantly, if not decisively, against allowing plaintiffs in defamation proceedings to be anonymous. To the extent that this practice is allowed, it should be closely circumscribed. This chapter acknowledges, however, that the greater legal recognition of privacy, and the confluence of reputation and privacy, pose conceptual and practical challenges to this position. Ultimately, it questions the efficacy of the defamation trial as a forum in which to vindicate and protect all reputations.

The principle of open justice

The starting point for a consideration of anonymity in defamation is necessarily the principle of open justice. The common law has a longstanding commitment to this principle.[5] Presumptively, court proceedings are conducted in public. Courtrooms are physically open to members of the public to attend. The identities of litigants and witnesses are publicly known. Fair and accurate reports of court proceedings can be made, as a corollary to the principle of open justice.[6] The reasons for the common law's commitment to the principle of open justice are well-known. It furthers the proper administration of justice. It seeks to ensure, not only that justice is done, but that it is seen to be done.[7] It is essential to promoting public confidence in the judicial system. It is an integral aspect of the rule of law.[8] It helps to keep judges accountable, to ensure that they act with integrity and propriety, and to exercise a check on the arbitrary exercise of power. The openness of court proceedings is considered to be an essential attribute of judicial, as opposed to executive, power.[9]

Although the common law takes the position that the proper administration of justice is facilitated by the principle of open justice, it does not treat it as absolute. There can be departures from the principle of open justice so long as they are necessary to protect the administration of justice. Given the importance of open justice, the exceptions to it are narrowly circumscribed.[10] The common law test for derogating from the principle of open justice is a strict one based on necessity.[11] Just because the ventilation of a matter in open court is embarrassing or intrusive upon privacy or damaging to reputations is an insufficient basis upon which to depart from the principle of open justice.[12] Thus, if a plaintiff wants to sue for defamation, the matter is presumptively heard in open court. The publicity of the trial, and the publicity the trial might attract, could actually increase the harm to the plaintiff's reputation. It is ultimately a matter for the plaintiff as to whether he or she wishes to sue for defamation, knowing the risks of the publicity of the proceedings.

Importantly, however, there are certain categories of claims in which derogations from the principle of open justice are readily recognised.[13] The most relevant one for present purposes relates to the willingness of courts to derogate from the principle of open justice in claims involving confidential information. Courts are more disposed to derogate from the principle of open justice in such cases because the failure to do so is likely to deprive the confidential information of its confidential quality, thereby destroying the subject matter of the litigation before it can be litigated.[14] Given that English courts have developed a tort of misuse of private information through an adaptation of the existing equitable cause of action for breach of confidence,[15] and that there are dicta suggesting that superior courts in Australia are most comfortable with developing direct privacy protection in a similar way,[16] this well-established derogation from the principle of open justice will assume greater importance. The complex, evolving relationship between reputation, privacy and confidentiality will present some difficulty for the proper application of the principle of open justice in claims implicating two or more of these interests. Nevertheless, it is clear that the orthodox application of the principle of open justice to defamation proceedings means that ordinarily there will be no grounds for departing from full publicity of the proceedings.

The role of vindication in defamation law

There is an additional reason, particular to defamation law, for favouring publicity. The plaintiff's reputation – what other people think of him or her – is the principal interest protected by the tort of defamation.[17] The most significant purpose of defamation law is to vindicate the plaintiff's damaged reputation.[18] Defamation law proceeds on the basis that the plaintiff's public self was publicly harmed. In order to provide adequate redress, then, there needs to be a public vindication of the plaintiff's reputation.[19] The fact of the verdict in favour of the plaintiff,[20] the award of damages and especially the quantum of damages,[21] the reasons given (if any) in support of the award of damages,[22] and the publicity of the trial[23] and its outcome are considered to be important to securing the vindication of the plaintiff's reputation. The nature of the interest protected by, and the principal purpose of, defamation law reinforces the common law's strong predisposition to publicity.

The suggestion, then, that a defamation plaintiff might be anonymous seems incompatible not only with the principle of open justice, but more fundamentally with defamation law itself. An obvious question arises as to how a plaintiff's reputation can be vindicated if the public is unable to know the plaintiff's identity. It is instructive to examine how Australian, Canadian and English courts have dealt with applications for anonymity in defamation cases.

Australian case law

Periodically, there have been attempts by plaintiffs in Australian defamation cases to proceed anonymously. The results have been mixed, from a plaintiff's perspective. Two recent decisions of the Supreme Court of Western Australia illustrate unsuccessful attempts by plaintiffs in Australian defamation proceedings to secure anonymity orders. In *Ives v State of Western Australia*,[24] the plaintiff sued upon statements allegedly made by a police sergeant when executing a search on the plaintiff's former residence. Benjamin Ives was subject to an interim restraining order, preventing him from approaching or contacting his ex-girlfriend, Joyce Lim. In late December 2009, Lim attended Perth police station and complained that Ives had been sending her threatening emails in breach of the interim restraining order. Ives alleged that, when the police attended his last-known residential address, the police gratuitously repeated these untested allegations to the occupants and to the neighbours. He further alleged that the police also defamed him to the couple caring for his child and the plaintiff's doctor, as well as a number of other people. In his statement of claim, Ives complained, not only about the damage done to his reputation, but also the 'disregard for the plaintiff's privacy'. Ives later added a complaint that the police had encouraged Lim to publish material about the restraining order against Ives in her publicly accessible blog.[25] Ultimately, after a protracted procedural history, Ives' defamation claim was dismissed, as the Western Australia Police were able to establish a defence of common law qualified privilege.[26]

During the proceedings, Ives applied to have the names of all the people involved in the trial referred to only by their initials and to have Lim's Internet alias suppressed.[27] He relied upon a practice direction that provided for limitations on the publication of identifying information in fraud and defamation cases.[28] The practice direction allows a person who reasonably expects to be identified in a judgment in a fraud or a defamation case to apply to the court for an order that the publicly available version not identify him or her, or, if that were not practicable, an order that the reasons are not to be made publicly available. In dealing with such an application, the court was to have regard to the fundamental principle of open justice. Ives claimed that the publication of the reasons for the decision on the Internet was likely to do him greater damage than the original publication upon which he sued.[29] In determining Ives' application, Le Miere J observed that:

> [t]he court should do what it can to avoid unnecessary harm to a party or other persons by the publication of reasons for judgment. In a defamation case, the court should formulate its reasons for judgment in such a way as to avoid unnecessarily repeating the defamatory material of which the plaintiff complains. However, it may be necessary to expose some of the matters of which the plaintiff complains in order to adequately disclose the court's reasoning.[30]

His Honour found that he had repeated the defamatory matter only to the extent that it was reasonably necessary to explain his reasons for decision and had not gratuitously identified non-parties. He was satisfied that Ives had not established a sufficient reason to suppress his identity.

More recently, in *McJannett v Daley*,[31] the Supreme Court of Western Australia again had to deal with an application brought by a plaintiff for the suppression of reasons for judgment with a view to minimising the damage to his reputation. Robert McJannett and Leanne Daley were involved in a child custody dispute in the Family Court of Western Australia. McJannett claimed various documents in and related to the proceedings were defamatory of him, so he commenced separate defamation proceedings in the Supreme Court of Western Australia. Le Miere J struck out the proceedings in relation to two of the five publications – an affidavit and a letter seeking permission to file an application in the Family Court proceedings – on the basis that they were clearly covered by absolute privilege. Subsequently, McJannett applied for a suppression order in relation to the judgments already handed down in the defamation proceedings. He claimed the judgments repeated untrue statements about him, thereby aggravating the damage to his reputation.

Le Miere J found that the principle of open justice should prevail in the circumstances. As with Ives, McJannett claimed that the publication of the reasons for decision was likely to do more damage to his reputation than the original publications.[32] His Honour found that suppressing the judgments was not necessary to ensure that the proceedings were fair. He acknowledged that the publication of the judgments might be embarrassing to McJannett and might harm his reputation, but that was not a sufficient reason to make the orders sought.[33] To the extent that the judgments repeated the defamatory matter, it was necessary in order to set out the court's reasoning. In any event, the judgments made it clear that McJannett was firmly of the view that the allegations were false.[34] McJannett had failed to establish a sufficient reason for the making of the suppression orders.[35]

In both of these cases, then, the plaintiffs were unsuccessful in their attempts to assert a need for their anonymity in defamation proceedings. Tellingly, in neither case was it necessary for the judge to have recourse to the role of vindication in defamation proceedings. The principle of open justice was sufficient to reject the applications. The fact that the publications in both cases were made to a limited audience and, in *McJannett v Daley*, that there was a child indirectly involved in the defamation proceedings, were not sufficient grounds to allow the plaintiffs to be anonymous or otherwise to suppress the judgments in the proceedings.

Although exceptional, anonymity orders have been made in Australian defamation cases but their basis is not always clear. There are two District Court of New South Wales decisions in which anonymous plaintiffs have been awarded damages. In *RJ v JC*,[36] the parties were the grandparents of a toddler. Since his birth, the boy had been the subject of court proceedings about access. At an access handover in early July 2007, the defendant told the plaintiff's daughter that her father was a paedophile. Gibson DCJ found that this allegation was defamatory, not mere vulgar abuse.[37] In the absence of any viable defence, her Honour proceeded to assess the damages. She emphasised the importance of hurt feelings in the present case,[38] noting later in the judgment the need for the plaintiff's reputation to be vindicated.[39] In rejecting the submission that the damages should be low, given the limited extent of the publication, Gibson DCJ pointed out that the defamation was literally directed towards the plaintiff 'where he lives'. Her Honour also noted the seriousness of the allegation as another factor supporting an award of substantial damages.[40] In mitigation and the avoidance of aggravated damages, the defendant had apologised to the plaintiff and ensured that the apology was communicated to the people to whom the original publication was made.[41] Ultimately, Gibson DCJ awarded RJ 30,000 AUD damages.[42] The judgment does not make clear the basis for the anonymity orders, but one might surmise that the Family Court proceedings being on foot and the involvement of a child were significant factors in support of such orders.

In *PK v BV (No 2)*,[43] the plaintiffs sued a former family friend and business associate over statements made to two other people on two separate occasions, in a private home and in a schoolyard, to the effect that the plaintiffs were thieves and fraudsters and were generally untrustworthy.[44] The first plaintiff was described as 'the Chief Executive Officer of a company which was considering a public float in the future',[45] which suggests that he might have had some public profile, at least in business circles. Gibson DCJ explained the anonymity of the parties at the outset of judgment thus:

> [A]t the request of the parties, their names and all identifying factors have been removed from this judgment. The reasons for this were explained to me by counsel for the plaintiff, and in my view, it is appropriate that such orders should be made, particularly having regard to the distress caused to the plaintiff's children.[46]

There was no further analysis of the issue and no express engagement with the principle of open justice. Gibson DCJ had no difficulty finding that the defamatory imputations had been conveyed. In the absence of any defence and, indeed, any appearance by the defendant,[47] her Honour proceeded to assess damages. Notwithstanding the limited nature of the publication, there were factors clearly supporting an award of substantial damages, namely the repetition of the defamatory publications and the adverse impact this had upon the plaintiff's children.[48] Furthermore, her Honour found that an award of aggravated damages was appropriate, given the baseless pursuit of a defence of justification[49] and the making of a belated, inadequate apology.[50] Ultimately, Gibson DCJ awarded the plaintiffs 50,000 AUD damages each.[51] The emphasis in the judgment is on the plaintiffs' hurt feelings, with no mention being made whatsoever of the vindication of their reputations.

There are some older, isolated instances of damages being awarded for defamation where the plaintiff remained anonymous. For example, in *W v R*,[52] the defendant published a number of statements to a limited number of people, alleging that the plaintiff was promiscuous and was involved in prostitution and drug dealing.[53] The defendant did not defend the proceedings, preferring to 'go to slot for 10 years rather than pay a cent',[54] so all that remained for Brettingham-Moore J to do was to assess the damages payable. His Honour awarded 3,000 AUD compensatory damages, as well as granting a permanent injunction against R.[55]

In *Xx and Yy v Pan Macmillan Australia Pty Ltd*,[56] the plaintiffs sought an injunction to restrain the publication of the controversial non-fiction book, *The First Stone*, by Helen Garner. The book concerned sexual harassment allegations brought against the master of Ormond College, a residential college at the University of Melbourne.[57] Beach J refused the relief because the plaintiffs could not establish that they had reasonable cause to believe that defamatory matter was to be published about them, as they had not seen the manuscript.[58] More importantly, his Honour was of the view that freedom of speech should prevail over the plaintiffs' right to protect their reputations.[59] Beach J's view was reinforced by the fact that the plaintiffs had had their anonymity preserved.[60]

More recently, in *YZ v Amazon*,[61] McCallum J made an order suppressing the identity of a plaintiff in defamation proceedings, pursuant to the Court Suppression and Non-Publications Orders Act 2010 (NSW), s. 7. The plaintiff sued Amazon over the publication of an electronic book.[62] The book and the defamation proceedings touched upon Family Court proceedings in which YZ was involved.[63] Under the Family Law Act 1975 (Cth.), s. 121, it is an offence to publish material that identifies or tends to identify persons involved in Family Court proceedings. McCallum J granted the order suppressing the plaintiff's identity to preserve YZ's statutory entitlement to anonymity under the Family Law Act 1975 (Cth.).[64] For pleading deficiencies, however, YZ being self-represented, YZ's statement of claim was struck out with leave to replead granted.[65]

The issue of anonymity for a plaintiff has also arisen in cases where defamation has been pleaded concurrently with other causes of action. For instance, in *Y and Z v W*,[66] W was granted an interlocutory injunction to restrain Y from filing an affidavit containing scandalous material in proceedings that Y and Z had brought against W's ex-husband, X. Y threatened to file the affidavit unless W intervened to secure the settlement proceedings. The trial judge, Brereton J, granted the injunctive relief on the basis of defamation and contempt of court. On appeal, the New South Wales Court of Appeal found that contempt of court alone would have been sufficient to support the orders made.[67] The grant of injunctive relief was not an impermissible attempt to avoid the restrictive approach to such orders in defamation.[68] It also suggested that, in any event, W's case for injunctive relief in defamation would have been strong.[69] An important reason for granting the injunction, and presumably the suppression orders, was because, as Giles JA observed, Y's conduct was clearly an attempt at blackmail.[70] As the English case law demonstrates, courts are especially willing to suppress plaintiffs' real identities where they are the subject of attempted blackmail.

Anonymity orders have also been made in cases that are analogous to defamation. For instance, in *PW v MS [No. 3]*,[71] PW sued his former *de facto* spouse, M, and her mother, S, for injurious falsehood. PW alleged that M and S had accused him of physically and sexually abusing his child, P. At the time the statements were made, PW and M were involved in acrimonious Family Court proceedings. Le Miere J found that the statements had been published,[72] were false[73] and were actuated by malice.[74] However, the claim failed because PW had failed to establish that the statements had caused him actual damage, either in the form of economic loss or psychiatric harm.[75] Given the nature of the allegations and their relationship to Family Court proceedings, the identities of the parties were suppressed. It is not apparent from the judgment why PW did not frame his claim in defamation, which has the benefit of a presumption of damage. A clue might be found in the fact that both parties were self-represented. The grant of suppression orders in quasi-defamation proceedings, however, was not controversial.

Canadian case law

The tension between the principle of open justice and the nature of defamation proceedings, on the one hand, and the vulnerability of children and the right to privacy, on the other, arose starkly in the Canadian decision of *AB v Bragg Communications Inc.*[76] It is noteworthy that this case concerns a social media publication. AB was a 15-year-old girl who discovered that an unknown person had created a fake Facebook profile of her. The profile included a photograph of AB and was accompanied by commentary about her physical appearance, her weight and her alleged sexual conduct. AB wished to commence defamation proceedings against the person responsible for the fake Facebook profile. In the Supreme Court of Nova Scotia, she sought an order that Bragg Communications disclose the identity of the holder of the IP address provided by Facebook as being the one linked to the fake Facebook profile. In addition, she sought a pseudonym order and a partial publication ban. At first instance, LeBlanc J ordered the disclosure but refused the other relief sought.[77]

AB appealed the decision all the way to the Supreme Court of Canada. The judgments of the Nova Scotia Court of Appeal and the Supreme Court of Canada illuminate the tension between the competing interests in this type of case. In the Nova Scotia Court of Appeal, Saunders JA, with whom MacDonald CJNS and Oland JA agreed, characterised the tension as one between a teenager's claim to privacy and freedom of the press in the context of a planned defamation action.[78] The trial judge's decision had become known to local media outlets, Halifax Herald Ltd and Global Television, which intervened on appeal to oppose AB's application for an anonymity order and a publication ban.[79] Saunders JA emphasised that the trial judge's decision was discretionary and should not lightly be set aside.[80] His Lordship further emphasised the principle of open justice and the narrowly circumscribed departures from it. He did not accept that the trial judge had erred in failing to exercise his *parens patriae* jurisdiction to protect a vulnerable child, noting that such jurisdiction had not been invoked before the trial judge.[81] Saunders JA did not accept that protections of children's identities in criminal law and family law proceedings and in civil claims relating to child sexual abuse meant that there was a more general presumption of special harm to children involved in all forms of litigation, such that there was a general presumption of anonymity for children in court cases.[82] In the absence of any direct evidence of the harm likely to be suffered by this particular plaintiff, his Lordship was unwilling to infer such harm as a consequence of a refusal to grant the anonymity order and the publication ban. He gave the greatest weight then to the principle of open justice and the related, constitutionally protected freedom of the press.[83] In addition, Saunders JA ascribed significance to the nature of defamation law, observing that:

> Defamation is a claim that one's reputation has been lowered in the eyes of the public. To initiate an action for defamation, one must present oneself and the alleged defamatory statements before a jury and in open court. To be able to proceed with a defamation claim under a cloak of secrecy, strikes me as being contrary to the quintessential features of defamation law. AB would wish to have her identity shielded from the public, and the fake Facebook profile banned, apparently as a protection from further embarrassment and public scrutiny. But, when AB chose to avail herself of the court process in the pursuit of damages for defamation, she submitted to whatever public scrutiny attaches to civil litigation and must accept the attendant diminished expectation of privacy.[84]

Thus, his Lordship emphasised: the publicity of the proceedings and the important public interests at play supporting open justice;[85] that the plaintiff had voluntarily elected to sue for defamation in full knowledge of the principle of open justice;[86] that secrecy 'would be anathema to an action in defamation';[87] and that embarrassment was an unfortunate but often inevitable by-product of defamation litigation[88] and that a court should not determine departures from the principle of open justice guided by evidence of a particular plaintiff's subjective feelings.[89] Saunders JA was not convinced that the refusal to grant an anonymity order and a publication ban would act as a disincentive to potential litigants complaining about cyber-bullying, describing such a view as speculative. His Lordship surmised that:

> [o]ne could just as easily imagine a salutary result in being required to pursue an action in defamation, by name and in public. Such will serve the public interest by both alerting social networking players to the inherent risk of sharing very personal information among 'friends', while at the same time deterring would-be bullies with the threat of retribution once unmasked.[90]

The contrast between the reasoning of the Nova Scotia Court of Appeal and the Supreme Court of Canada is stark. Giving the judgment of the Supreme Court, Abella J made no reference at all to the particular nature of defamation proceedings supporting the need for openness. Instead, her Ladyship characterised the tension as one purely between the plaintiff's right to privacy – specifically her right to 'privacy from the relentlessly intrusive humiliation of sexualised online bullying'[91] – and the principle of open justice.[92] Abella J observed that the principle of open justice had been well-explored in the court's jurisprudence so that the focus instead needed to be on the child's right to privacy and the child's right to be protected from cyber-bullying.[93] Her Ladyship found that the courts below had failed to give appropriate weight to the 'objectively discernable harm' to the plaintiff.[94] Abella J noted that Canadian law, in a number of contexts, such as criminal law and child welfare, recognised 'the *inherent* vulnerability of children'.[95]

Her Ladyship then considered a recent report on cyber-bullying, released after the decision in the Nova Scotia Court of Appeal had been handed down.[96] In light of this report, Abella J was satisfied that the failure to provide anonymity to victims of cyber-bullying would be a significant disincentive to them seeking help,[97] contrary to the reasoning of Saunders JA in the court below. Drawing an analogy with victims of sexual offences, where there has been a long-standing protection of victims' identities, her Ladyship found that the reporting of the name of the victim of cyber-bullying was relatively unimportant.[98] Balancing the competing interests in this case clearly favoured the grant of an anonymity order.[99] Having protected AB in this way, the publication ban became an unnecessary intrusion upon the principle of open justice.[100]

English case law

The issue of anonymity in defamation claims has also arisen recently in the English decision in *ZAM v CFW*.[101] In this case, the claimant brought defamation proceedings against his brother-in-law.[102] The defendant published and threatened to publish further defamatory matter about the claimant with a view to increasing his own nuclear family's portion of distributions from family trusts.[103] CFW published material on the Internet and in a fax to the school at which ZAM served on the board of governors, as well as repeating the allegations to ZAM's employer.[104] The allegations related to financial mismanagement and paedophilia.[105]

The anonymity orders were initially made because the publications were an attempt at blackmail, a recognised category in which derogation from the principle of open justice is permitted.[106] ZAM sought to make the anonymity order permanent.[107] He pointed to the limited circulation of the publications and the seriousness of the allegations.[108] He submitted that the orthodox position at common law, that the award of damages and the vindication of the plaintiff's reputation at the end of the trial was an adequate remedy, was 'too blunt'. More specifically, given that reputation is part of the right to a private life under art. 8 of the ECHR, he argued that the orthodox position at common law was incompatible with the ECHR and did not provide him with an effective remedy.[109] Tugendhat J observed that:

> [m]ost libel claimants are unlikely to want an anonymity order. If the libel has been widely published, the claimant will want a judgment that is equally widely published, to demonstrate that he has cleared his name. It is in cases where the libel has been published to small numbers of publishees that the question of anonymity is likely to arise in a defamation action. In many cases, a publication to a single publishee may not be sufficiently serious to merit a defamation action at all. But in some cases, such as where the publication is to an employer or prospective employer, a single publication can be more damaging than a publication to the world at large.[110]

Tugendhat J decided to grant ZAM anonymity on a permanent basis because of CFW's attempted blackmail.[111] His Lordship wanted to make clear that the court 'does not provide encouragement or assistance to blackmailers, and does not deter victims of blackmail from seeking justice from the courts'.[112] Tugendhat J noted that anonymity orders in defamation claims were unusual, but not unknown.[113] His Lordship stated that, '[a]s a matter of principle, there is no reason why an anonymity order should not be made in a defamation action'[114] and cited other defamation cases in which plaintiffs had proceeded anonymously.[115] In this context, Tugendhat J made no reference to the particular, public features of defamation law and its vindicatory purpose.

In the absence of any viable defence, Tugendhat J proceeded to assess ZAM's damages. His Lordship noted vindication as the primary purpose of an award of damages for defamation.[116] He stated that, in relation to an allegation as serious as paedophilia, 'even the most categorical vindication does not prevent a person so accused of having his name permanently linked with the allegation'.[117] Ultimately, Tugendhat J awarded ZAM 100,000 GBP damages for defamation and 20,000 GBP damages for harassment.[118]

Anonymity should have an impact on the assessment of damages for defamation. The plaintiff's anonymity already serves as a measure of protection of his or her reputation. This is illustrated by *KC v MGN Ltd.*[119] KC was the birth father of Baby P, a child who was killed by his mother and two other men. The death of Baby P caused a public outcry, due not only to the heinous nature of the crime but also to the failure of health and social services to prevent it. It also attracted considerable media attention. *The People* newspaper published an article falsely accusing KC of being a convicted sex offender. The publisher, MGN Ltd, apologised and offered to pay damages. At first instance, KC was awarded 75,000 GBP damages. Bean J's assessment emphasised the large circulation and readership of *The People*.[120] On appeal, the Court of Appeal found that the trial judge had erred by failing to give adequate weight to the plaintiff's anonymity.[121] The plaintiff's anonymity had the effect that the nature and extent of the publication was 'very limited', thus the damage to KC's reputation was reduced.[122] The Court of Appeal thus reduced KC's damages to 50,000 GBP. This case suggests that plaintiffs can proceed anonymously but they would have to anticipate a reduced level of damages, as their anonymity itself already confers a level of reputational protection.

Anonymity and defamation

It is likely that anonymity orders will continue to be rare in defamation cases but there are indications that they might become relatively less so. There are certain categories of defamation claims in which an anonymity order might more readily be granted. Cases involving children are a clear example. Courts are more readily disposed to derogate from the principle of open justice to protect the interests of children.[123] Indeed, in many jurisdictions, there are statutory provisions suppressing material identifying or tending to identify children involved in court proceedings.[124] As *ZAM v CFW* demonstrates, defamation claims involving blackmail will also cause a court to be disposed to grant an anonymity order. As the review of the authorities in Tugendhat J's judgment indicates, there is a surprising incidence of these claims in English courts,[125] in contrast to the position in Australia and Canada.

One feature of a defamation claim, which might make a court disposed to grant an anonymity order, is that the publication was made only to a limited audience. Historically, this was not a reason for a plaintiff's anonymity in a defamation claim. Indeed, many important defamation cases involve publications with a limited audience (and a much greater audience in legal posterity, due to their inclusion in the law reports).[126] It did not occur to the plaintiffs to seek to protect their anonymity. By suing for defamation, they must have been aware of the publicity of the proceedings. Countenancing an anonymity order in a contemporary defamation case is possible because a more critical and more realistic approach to the efficacy of defamation law in practice has developed among judges and academics. At the level of principle, a formal approach is adopted by defamation law. An award of damages at the end of the defamation trial vindicates a successful plaintiff's reputation.[127] It is right to be critical of this position: it is difficult to accept in practice that defamation law can compel others not to believe the falsehoods they have been told about the plaintiff. Indeed, judges have often remarked that an award of damages is an imperfect remedy,[128] but historically it is the only real one available.[129]

Fundamentally, reputation is a dynamic, not a static, interest. In principle, defamation law might assume that reputations, once vindicated by an award of damages, should stay vindicated. The reality is more complex than that. Indeed, the defamation trial itself can become part of the plaintiff's reputation. The openness of defamation proceedings here becomes problematic. It is paradoxical that a defamation trial, which is intended as the forum in which the plaintiff's reputation is to be vindicated, can, through its openness, increase the damage to the plaintiff's reputation by giving the defamatory matter publicity. This is particularly acute when the defamatory matter was initially of limited circulation. Suing for defamation on such a publication then potentially means that the collateral damage done to the plaintiff's reputation in the defamation proceedings designed to vindicate the plaintiff's reputation is disproportionately greater than the damage inflicted by the original publication. Allowing a plaintiff in such a case to proceed anonymously is a means of seeking to limit the actual damage to the plaintiff's reputation. Such cases are predicated on a more realistic understanding of the efficacy of defamation law and the impact of the openness of a defamation trial than the formal principles of defamation law suggest. It is unsurprising that cases allowing for the anonymisation of plaintiffs omit reference to or de-emphasise vindication as a purpose of a defamation claim or posit a more nuanced and more realistic account of defamation law.

Limited publication alone is not sufficient for a court to grant a plaintiff anonymity in defamation proceedings, as *Ives v State of Western Australia* and *McJannett v Daley* attest. Part of the impetus for a more sophisticated account of defamation law in practice and the need for a plaintiff's anonymity has been the development of Internet technologies, as *AB v Bragg Communications* and *ZAM v CFW* demonstrate. Social media publications are challenging because they have features that can be characterised as ephemeral and permanent. For complex historical reasons, defamation law developed a differential treatment for oral or transient publications – slander – and for written or permanent publications – libel.[130] This distinction has now been abolished,[131] but it broadly worked in the sense that cases of slander were less likely to be damaging to a person's reputation than cases of libel, so, in all but exceptional cases, plaintiffs suing for slander had to prove actual damage, whereas damage to reputation was presumed when plaintiffs sued for libel.[132] In relation to social media publications, courts have been willing to recognise that people treated social media as an instantaneous, ephemeral form, akin to speech, and consequently are more uninhibited when expressing themselves using it. The actual audience to which a social media publication is directed or which in fact consumes it is often small or circumscribed. This suggests that social media publications are somewhat like slander. On the other hand, a social media publication is in a permanent form, able to be searched and retrieved long after the original publication.[133] It is unsurprising, then, that social media publications have been at the centre of encouraging judges to rethink the relationship between anonymity and defamation.

The final noteworthy feature of these cases is the role of privacy, as distinct from reputation. In Australia, where it is still accurate to state that there is no general, direct protection of privacy at common law,[134] concerns about privacy are not given weight in deciding applications for anonymity in defamation cases. *AB v Bragg Communications* suggests a blurring of the distinction between reputation and privacy in Canadian law. In lay terms, reputation and privacy might be treated as different but not distinct aspects of an individual's persona. In legal terms, however, the common law has drawn a sharp distinction between reputation and privacy. For centuries, through the tort of defamation, the common law has provided substantial, direct protection to reputation but has not protected privacy directly at all. Over the last two decades, in particular, common law countries have been developing direct privacy protection, in varying ways and to varying degrees. The most significant development has occurred in United Kingdom law, the impetus being the introduction of the ECHR into that country's domestic law, requiring United Kingdom law to accommodate the right to a private life under art. 8 of the ECHR. In order to provide an effective remedy for litigants' right to a private life, as United Kingdom courts are obliged to do under the ECHR, United Kingdom courts have readily granted litigants anonymity orders in such claims.[135]

There has been another development in United Kingdom law, which has had and will continue to have a profound effect on the evolution of the law of defamation and privacy. The European Court of Human Rights has increasingly treated reputation as an aspect of the right to a private life.[136] The United Kingdom Supreme Court has recognised this as part of domestic law in that country.[137] The consequences of this recognition have not yet been fully explored. It involves a complete inversion of the relationship between reputation and privacy in United Kingdom law. Whereas, previously, reputation was protected highly and privacy not at all, now reputation is treated as a subsidiary part of the right to a private life. Concurrent claims for libel and misuse of private information are increasingly brought before United Kingdom courts.[138] In terms of anonymity in defamation, if United Kingdom courts recognise reputation as part of the right to a private life and are more disposed to grant anonymity in such claims, cases like *ZAM v CFW* will not be isolated instances in the future.

Conclusion

To a common lawyer, the idea of an anonymous plaintiff in a defamation case seems unusual. The tort appears fundamentally antithetical to anonymity, premised upon public harm to a public self and the need for vindication of reputation. To allow a plaintiff to proceed with such a claim under a cloak of secrecy seems contrary to basic features of defamation law, as well as the common law's strong commitment to the principle of open justice.

Yet, the practice of granting anonymity to those who seek it appears to be increasing. Recent reformulations of the right to privacy in English courts, incorporating reputation, arguably permit claims for anonymity in defamation to be entertained. Moreover, certain categories of claim lend themselves more readily to anonymity. Tellingly, the basis for such orders is not always clear. The emerging differences between jurisdictions highlight the tensions inherent within allowing such a claim and the need for further consideration and reflection. Most important, then, may be cases involving social media, which provide an impetus for judges to rethink the relationship between anonymity and defamation. Such cases readily expose the paradox of the defamation trial as a forum in which to vindicate and protect reputation, yet which, through its openness, can increase the damage done by giving the matter publicity. Allowing a plaintiff in such a case to proceed anonymously is thus a means to limit actual damage, predicated on a more nuanced and realistic account of defamation law than the formal principles suggest.

Notes

1 In order for the tort of defamation to be established, there must be publication of defamatory matter to at least one person other than the plaintiff: see *Webb v Bloch* (1928) 41 CLR 331, 363 (Isaacs J); *Consolidated Trust Co Ltd v Browne* (1948) 49 SR(NSW) 86, 88 (Jordan CJ); *Dow Jones & Co Inc v Gutnick* (2002) 210 CLR 575, 600 (Gleeson CJ, McHugh, Gummow and Hayne JJ); [2002] HCA 56.

2 *Plato Films Ltd v Speidel* [1961] AC 1090, 1138 (Lord Denning); David Rolph, *Reputation, Celebrity and Defamation Law* (Ashgate 2008) 5–6; Kenneth H Craik, *Reputation: A Network Interpretation* (Oxford University Press 2009) xvii.

3 Andrew Kenyon, 'Not Seeing Justice Done: Suppression Orders in Australian Law and Practice' (2006) 27 *Adelaide Law Review*, 279, 280–1; Jason Bosland and Ashleigh Bagnall, 'An Empirical Analysis of Suppression Orders in Victorian Courts: 2008–12' (2013) 35 *Sydney Law Review*, 671, 671–2.

4 Tony Wright, 'Cyber Poison-Penner Hunted Down and Sued' *The Sydney Morning Herald* (Sydney, 25 February 2010); AAP, 'Google Ordered to Reveal Bloggers' Identities' *Australian Financial Review* (Sydney, 15 January 2013). As to the position in the United Kingdom, see, for example, *Applause Stores Productions Ltd v Raphael* [2008] EWHC 1781 (QB) [10] (Richard Parkes QC). However, see also *Clift v Clarke* [2011] EWHC 1164 (QB). See also *G & G v Wikimedia Foundation* [2009] EWHC 3148 (QB). As to the position in the United States, see *Dendrite International Inc v Doe*, 775 A 2d 756 (NJ 2001); *Doe v Cahill*, 884 A 2d 451 (Del 2005); *Mobilisa Inc v Doe*, 170 P 3d 712 (Az 2007); *Cohen v Google Inc*, 25 Misc 3d 945, 887 NYS 2d 424 (NY 2009); *Yelp, Inc v Hadeed Carpet Cleaning, Inc*, 62 Va App 678 (2014).

5 *Scott v Scott* [1913] AC 417; *Dickason v Dickason* (1913) 17 CLR 50. As to the importance of the principle of open justice, see generally Peter Wright, 'The Open Court: The Hallmark of the Judicial Proceedings' (1947) 25 *Canadian Bar Review*, 721; Garth Nettheim, 'The Principle of Open Justice' (1984) 8 *University of Tasmania Law Review*, 25; Chief Justice Spigelman, 'Seen to be Done: The Principle of Open Justice – Part I' (2000) 74 *Australian Law Journal*, 290; Chief Justice Spigelman, 'Seen to be Done: The Principle of Open Justice – Part II' (2000) 74 *Australian Law Journal* 378; Joseph Jaconelli, *Open Justice: A Critique of the Public Trial* (Oxford University Press 2002). For a more critical approach to the principle of open justice, see Colleen Davis, 'The Injustice of Open Justice' (2001) 8 *James Cook University Law Review*, 92.

6 *Kimber v Press Association Ltd* [1893] 1 QB 65, 68–70 (Lord Esher MR), 73 (Lopes LJ), 75 (Kay LJ); *John Fairfax & Sons Ltd v Police Tribunal of New South Wales* (1986) 5 NSWLR 465, 476–7 (McHugh JA); *Hogan v Hinch* (2011) 243 CLR 506, 532; [2011] HCA 4, [22] (French CJ).

7 As to the origin of this phrase, see Chief Justice Spigelman, 'Seen to be Done: The Principle of Open Justice – Part I' (2000) 74 *Australian Law Journal*, 290, 290–2.
8 *Re S (A Child)* [2005] 1 AC 593, 607–8 (Lord Steyn).
9 *Russell v Russell* (1976) 134 CLR 495, 520 (Gibbs J).
10 *John Fairfax Publications Pty Ltd v District Court of New South Wales* (2004) 61 NSWLR 344, 353 (Spigelman CJ).
11 *Scott v Scott* [1913] AC 417, 436–7; *John Fairfax & Sons* (n. 6) 476–7 (McHugh JA).
12 *Scott* (n. 11) 435, 485 (Lord Shaw of Dumfermline); *John Fairfax Publications Pty Ltd v Local Court of New South Wales* (1991) 26 NSWLR 131, 142–3 (Kirby P); *Herald & Weekly Times Ltd v Medical Practitioners Board of Victoria* [1999] 1 VR 267, 294–5 (Hedigan J).
13 For example, blackmail, national security, police informers, wards of the state and the mentally ill. See, for example, *Scott* (n. 11) 437 (Viscount Haldane LC); *Hogan* (n. 6) 531–2 (French CJ).
14 *Australian Broadcasting Commission v Parish* (1980) 43 FLR 129, 132.
15 *Campbell v MGN Ltd* [2004] 2 AC 457, 465 (Lord Nicholls of Birkenhead). The United Kingdom jurisprudence on the tort of misuse of private information is now substantial. As to some of the leading authorities, see *Douglas v Hello! Ltd* [2006] QB 125; *OBG Ltd v Allan* [2008] 1 AC 1; *McKennitt v Ash* [2008] QB 73.
16 *Giller v Procopets* (2008) 24 VR 1, 35–6 (Ashley JA), 106 (Neave JA). See also *Australian Broadcasting Corporation v Lenah Game Meats Pty Ltd* (2001) 208 CLR 199, 223–7 (Gleeson CJ). Inferior courts in Australia have been more willing to recognise a free-standing tort of invasion of privacy: see *Grosse v Purvis* (2003) Aust Torts Reports ¶81–706; *Doe v Australian Broadcasting Corporation* [2007] VCC 281.
17 *Lange v Australian Broadcasting Corporation* (1997) 189 CLR 520, 568 (*per curiam*); *Dow Jones* (n. 1) 599 (Gleeson CJ, McHugh, Gummow and Hayne JJ).
18 *Coyne v Citizen Finance Ltd* (1991) 172 CLR 211, 240 (McHugh J).
19 *Uren v John Fairfax & Sons Pty Ltd* (1966) 117 CLR 118, 150 (Windeyer J); *Carson v John Fairfax & Sons Ltd* (1993) 178 CLR 44, 60 (Mason CJ, Deane, Dawson and Gaudron JJ).
20 *Kiam v MGN Ltd* [2003] QB 281, 303 (Sedley LJ).
21 *Broome v Cassell & Co Ltd* [1972] AC 1027, 1071 (Lord Hailsham of St Marylebone LC); *John Fairfax & Sons Ltd v Kelly* (1987) 8 NSWLR 131, 139 (Samuels JA); *Carson* (n. 19) 66 (Mason CJ, Deane, Dawson and Gaudron JJ), 69–70 (Brennan J); *The Gleaner Co Ltd v Abrahams* [2004] 1 AC 628, 647 (PC).
22 *Applause Store Productions* (n. 4) [76] (Richard Parkes QC).
23 *Ballina Shire Council v Ringland* (1994) 33 NSWLR 680, 699 (Kirby P).
24 [2010] WASC 178.
25 *Ives v State of Western Australia* [2010] WASC 339.
26 *Ives v State of Western Australia (No 8)* [2013] WASC 277.
27 *Ives v State of Western Australia (No 2)* [2010] WASC 221.
28 Consolidated Practice Direction 8.2.1.
29 *Ives* (n. 27) [9] (Le Miere J).
30 Ibid. [7].
31 [2012] WASC 217 (S).
32 *McJannett v Daley (No. 2)* [2012] WASC (S), [6].
33 Ibid. [7].
34 Ibid. [10].
35 Ibid. [11], [13].
36 [2008] NSWDC 217.
37 Ibid. [23]–[25].
38 Ibid. [47].
39 Ibid. [63].
40 Ibid. [48].
41 Ibid. [55], [57].

42 Ibid. [64].
43 [2008] NSWDC 297.
44 Ibid. [2]–[3].
45 Ibid. [12].
46 Ibid. [6].
47 Ibid. [4].
48 Ibid. [27].
49 Ibid. [32]–[33].
50 Ibid. [34].
51 Ibid. [41].
52 [1985] Tas. R 178; [1985] TASSC 27.
53 Ibid. [1] (Brettingham-Moore J).
54 Ibid. [2].
55 Ibid. [10], [12], [14]–[15].
56 [1995] VSC 64.
57 Ibid. [1] (Beach J). For the final version of the book, see Helen Garner, *The First Stone: Some Questions About Sex and Power* (Picador 1995). For a critique of this book, see Jenna Mead (ed.), *Bodyjamming* (Vintage 1997).
58 *Xx and Yy* (n. 56) [8].
59 Ibid. [13]–[14].
60 Ibid. [13].
61 [2013] NSWSC 1522.
62 Ibid. [1].
63 Ibid. [2].
64 Ibid. [2], [4].
65 Ibid. [20]–[35].
66 (2007) 70 NSWLR 377.
67 Ibid.
68 Ibid. 379 (Spigelman CJ).
69 Ibid. 387.
70 Ibid. 381.
71 [2014] WASC 202.
72 Ibid. [46], [59].
73 Ibid. [51], [61]
74 Ibid. [67], [68].
75 Ibid. [81], [84].
76 As to the decision of the Supreme Court of Canada in this case, see *AB v Bragg Communications Inc* 2012 SCC 46; [2012] 2 SCR 567; (2012) 350 DLR (4th) 519. As to the decisions at lower level, see *AB v Bragg Communications Inc* 2010 NSSC 215; *AB v Bragg Communications Inc* [2011] NSCA 26.
77 2010 NSSC 215.
78 2011 NSCA 26, [1].
79 Ibid. [14].
80 Ibid. [31]–[33].
81 Ibid. [55]–[56].
82 Ibid. [65]–[70].
83 Ibid. [76]–[78].
84 Ibid. [80].
85 Ibid. [85].
86 Ibid. [83], [85].
87 Ibid. [84].
88 Ibid. [84].
89 Ibid. [83].

90 Ibid. [99].
91 2012 SCC 46; [2012] 2 SCR 567; (2012) 350 DLR (4th) 519 [10]–[11], [14].
92 Ibid. [10].
93 Ibid. [13].
94 Ibid. [9].
95 Ibid. [17] (emphasis in original).
96 Ibid. [20]–[22].
97 Ibid. [23]–[24], [26]–[27].
98 Ibid. [25], [29].
99 Ibid. [28]–[29].
100 Ibid. [30].
101 [2013] EWHC 662 (QB).
102 Ibid. [4].
103 Ibid. [5].
104 Ibid. [12]–[13].
105 Ibid. [15].
106 Ibid. [24].
107 Ibid. [26].
108 Ibid. [27]–[28].
109 Ibid. [28].
110 Ibid. [31].
111 Ibid. [39].
112 Ibid. [44].
113 Ibid. [47].
114 Ibid. [48].
115 Ibid., citing *C v Mirror Group Newspapers* [1997] 1 WLR 131; *S v Newham LBC* [1998] EMLR 583; *H v Tomlinson* [2008] EWCA Civ. 1258; and *KC v MGN Ltd (sub nom Cairns v Modi)* [2013] 1 WLR 1015; [2012] EWCA Civ. 1382.
116 *ZAM v CFW* (n. 97) [53]–[54], [72].
117 Ibid. [117].
118 Ibid. [122].
119 *C v MGN Ltd (sub nom Cairns v Modi)* [2013] 1 WLR 1015; [2012] EWCA Civ. 1382.
120 *KC v MGN Ltd* [2012] EWHC 483 (QB) [41].
121 *KC v MGN Ltd* (n. 111) 1029 [48].
122 Ibid.
123 See, for example, *X (A Woman Formerly Known as Mary Bell) and Y v O'Brien* [2003] EWHC 1101 (QB); *Tomlinson* (n. 111); *CVB v MGN Ltd* [2012] EWHC 1148 (QB) [67] (Tugendhat J).
124 See, for example, *Children (Criminal Proceedings) Act 1987* (NSW) s. 15A; *Children and Young Persons (Care and Protection) Act 1998* (NSW) s. 105; *Young Offenders Act 1997* (NSW) s. 65; *Crimes (Domestic and Personal Violence) Act 2007* (NSW) s. 45. There are analogous provisions in all other Australian states and territories.
125 See, for example, *ADG v GSA* [2009] EWCA Civ. 1574 [1]–[3] (Waller LJ); *DFT v TFD* [2010] EWHC 2335 (QB); *AMM v HXW* [2010] EWHC 2457 (QB); *SKA v CRH* [2012] EWHC 2236 (QB).
126 See, for example, *Duke of Brunswick v Harmer* (1849) 117 ER 75; *Sim v Stretch* [1936] 2 All ER 1237; *Byrne v Deane* [1937] 1 KB 818; *Consolidated Trust Co* (n. 1).
127 *Dingle v Associated Newspapers Ltd* [1964] AC 371, 396 (Lord Radcliffe); *Jameel v Wall Street Journal Europe SprL* [2007] 1 AC 359, 375 (Lord Bingham of Cornhill).
128 *Plato Films* (n. 2) 1125 (Viscount Simonds); *Broome* (n. 21) 1071 (Lord Hailsham of St Marylebone LC).
129 John G. Fleming, 'Retraction and Reply: Alternative Remedies to Defamation' (1978) 12 *University of British Columbia Law Review*, 15, 15. See also *John Fairfax & Sons Ltd v*

Carson (1991) 24 NSWLR 259, 300 (Mahoney JA); *Ballina Shire Council* (n. 23) 699 (Kirby P); *Cerutti v Crestside Pty Ltd* [2014] QCA 33, [35]–[36] (Applegarth J).

130 J. M. Kaye, 'Libel and Slander – Two Torts or One?' (1975) 91 *Law Quarterly Review*, 524; J. H. Baker, *An Introduction to English Legal History* (Butterworths LexisNexis 2002) 445–6.

131 See *Defamation Act 2005* (NSW) s. 7 and equivalent provisions in the other states and territories.

132 See, for example, *Wainer v Rippon* [1980] VR 129, 134 (O'Bryan J).

133 See, for example, *Cairns v Modi* [2013] 1 WLR 1015, 1024; [2012] EWCA Civ. 1382; *Mickle v Farley* [2013] NSWDC 295, [21] (Elkaim DCJ); see generally Jacob Rowbottom, 'To Rant, Vent and Converse: Protecting Low Level Digital Speech' (2012) 71 *Cambridge Law Journal*, 355.

134 Australian Law Reform Commission, *Serious Invasions of Privacy in the Digital Era* (Discussion Paper No. 80, 2014) [3.52]–[3.60].

135 As to the relevant principles, see *JIH v News Group Newspapers Ltd* [2011] 2 All ER 324, 331–2; [2011] 1 WLR 1645 (Lord Neuberger MR).

136 See, for example, *Radio France v France* (2005) 40 EHRR 29, 729 [31]; *Chauvy v France* (2005) 41 EHRR 29, 629–30 [70]; *Cumpana v Romania* (2005) 41 EHRR 14, 220 [91]; *Pfeifer v Austria* (2009) 48 EHRR 8, 182–3 [35]; *Karako v Hungary* (2011) 52 EHRR 36, 45–6 [22]–[23].

137 *Re Guardian News and Media Ltd* [2010] 2 AC 697, 717–18, [2010] UKSC 1 [37]–[42] (Lord Rodger of Earlsferry JSC).

138 See, for example, *Tomlinson* (n. 111); *Applause Store Productions* (n. 4); *Cooper v Turrell* [2011] EWHC 3269 (QB).

Part 4

Secrecy and society

Chapter 12

Strategy for public interest leaking

Brian Martin

Introduction

Speaking out in the public interest – being a whistleblower – can be risky. The classic example is an employee who learns about corruption, abuse or dangers to the public and tells the boss. Such employees are often subject to reprisals, including reprimands, harassment, ostracism, assignment to onerous duties, assignment to trivial duties, referral to psychiatrists, demotion, dismissal and blacklisting. These are all-too-common responses to whistleblowing.[1] Sometimes whistleblowing is welcome; for example, when it exposes a problem that can be fixed to the organisation's benefit. But when senior managers are implicated in the problem, whistleblowers may be treated as traitors.

Many whistleblowers start by informing their bosses of the problem. Indeed, many do not even think of themselves as whistleblowers, rather as workers just doing their jobs. After receiving an inadequate response or experiencing reprisals, many then take their message to other audiences, usually watchdog bodies such as ombudsmen, auditors-general and anti-corruption agencies. Although these bodies sometimes help, a great deal of the time they do not.[2] Whistleblowers then sometimes go to the media, which provide a powerful avenue for exposing problems, although whistleblowers themselves may still pay a serious price for their actions.

Not only do whistleblowers often suffer reprisals, but in most cases speaking out does not fix the problem. Employers and agencies orient attention towards the whistleblower. During the months and years that the whistleblower makes complaints to various agencies, the original problem remains unaddressed. Furthermore, as soon as a whistleblower speaks out, managers can take action to hide evidence of the problem or of their own complicity in it.

There are, thus, quite a number of reasons why whistleblowing can be a poor strategy for addressing problems: it leads to reprisals, it alerts management so responsibility can be avoided, and it delays fostering the wider awareness that is often the only lever powerful enough to bring about change.

In this context, there are advantages to a slightly different strategy, which can be called 'anonymous whistleblowing' or 'public interest leaking'. Instead of making his or her identity known, the employee remains anonymous, providing information and documents to outsiders. This has the great advantage of avoiding reprisals, at least so long as anonymity is maintained. Another advantage of anonymity is that the focus is more on the leaks than the leaker; in contrast, non-anonymous whistleblowers are often the centre of attention, rather than their disclosures. Finally, anonymous whistleblowers can remain on the job and continue to gather and leak information, whereas whistleblowers who reveal their identity are often immediately cut off from sources of information and are sometimes dismissed.

Public interest leaking has gained tremendous visibility due to WikiLeaks. The spectacular releases by WikiLeaks – especially the 'collateral murder' video, the Afghanistan and Iraq war logs, and the US diplomatic cables – have attracted widespread media coverage, overshadowing WikiLeaks exposés on other topics, such as Guantánamo detention camp procedures and elite corruption in Kenya. Public interest leaking drew further attention after revelations of the US National Security Agency's (NSA's) vast surveillance operations, based on documents leaked by NSA contractor Edward Snowden to *The Guardian* in 2013. However, public interest leaking is not new. The most famous pre-internet public interest leaker is Daniel Ellsberg, who leaked the Pentagon Papers, a history of US military involvement in the Vietnam War, to *The New York Times*.[3] There are many other cases, but few of them are documented, precisely because the leakers have remained anonymous and their personal stories have never been told.

The focus here is on leaking in the public interest. However, most leaking, by politicians and government officials, is to serve private interests or advance political goals. For example, politicians will tell journalists about party room discussions in order to hurt rivals, support allies or affect the public agenda. Politicians or senior bureaucrats will tell business executives about government plans to give advantages to favoured companies, sometimes reaping a political favour or pay-off. Senior bureaucrats may leak plans for new policies to test public reaction. Leaking in the public interest, in contrast, is usually by lower-level employees and serves neither the personal interests of the leaker nor the agendas of politicians and top bureaucrats.[4]

Surprisingly, there are very few studies of public interest leaking. Kathryn Flynn tells of a group of Australian government employees concerned about fraud in the national health insurance system who, knowing that their concerns would not be acted upon by senior officials or politicians, regularly leaked information to the media, generating pressure for action.[5] Her study is a reminder that leaking is not always a solo activity, but can be collective and well organised.

In the next section, five common tactics used by managers and other opponents of whistleblowing are described. Only some of these tactics are easily applied to leakers. This analysis of tactics reveals the many advantages, as well as a few weaknesses, of leaking. This analysis is then applied to the experience of WikiLeaks, showing ways in which the operation has been effective and ways in which it has been targeted, with some suggestions for an improved strategy. Following that, the experience of Edward Snowden is examined similarly. The conclusion sums up lessons for public interest leakers and their supporters.

Tactics against whistleblowers

Many whistleblowers are conscientious employees who see something that might be a problem and report it in good faith to 'higher-ups', assuming the issue will be investigated and, if necessary, fixed. However, instead of addressing the complaint, all too often management shoots the messenger, visiting reprisals against the employee. From the point of view of outsiders, there are two potential injustices involved. The first is the corruption, abuse or public hazard about which the whistleblower speaks out; the second is the reprisals against the whistleblower, which often seem unfair.

When powerful groups do something that others see as unjust – for example, censorship, bullying, massacres of peaceful protesters, torture or genocide – the perpetrators often act in ways that reduce public outrage.[6] Five tactics are commonly used:

1 covering up the action;
2 devaluing the target;
3 reinterpreting what happened by lying, minimising the consequences, blaming others or reframing the perspective;
4 using official channels to give an appearance of justice;
5 intimidating people involved.

For example, these five methods were used by the US Government to reduce outrage from the torture and abuse of prisoners by US guards at Abu Ghraib prison in Iraq, revealed to the world in 2004. Before the exposure, the action by the guards was covered up. The prisoners were devalued by being labelled criminals and terrorists, so what was done to them seemed more acceptable. After the exposure, US officials downplayed the seriousness of the treatment, calling it 'abuse' rather than 'torture', and the media went along with this framing. The prison guards were blamed so higher officials could escape responsibility. The official charges against some of the guards gave the appearance of justice, while policies and responsible senior officials were left untouched. Some of those who helped to reveal the abuse were ostracised and threatened.[7]

It is plausible that these same five methods will be used against whistleblowers and their supporters, to reduce outrage over both the activities exposed by the whistleblower – corruption, abuse or hazards – and the reprisals taken against the whistleblower.

Cover-up is the first method.[8] Wrongdoers usually keep their activities hidden. This is precisely why whistleblowing is such a threat. In addition, some reprisals, such as ostracism and petty harassment, are subtle, difficult to document and therefore hidden from wider audiences. Other reprisals are more obvious, such as reprimands at meetings, and are intended to send a warning to other employees. Leakers, if they remain anonymous, avoid reprisals, so there are no reprisals to be covered up.

The second method is devaluation. Whistleblowers are commonly labelled as traitors, troublemakers or difficult personalities. Management may encourage spreading of rumours that a whistleblower is a poor worker, thief or sexual deviant, among other derogatory allegations. Whistleblowers are often referred to psychiatrists, serving to cause humiliation and devaluation. When whistleblowers are anonymous, general negative labels, like 'traitor' or 'troublemaker', can be applied, but making specific allegations is less credible. Maintaining anonymity reduces the potency of devaluation.

Reinterpretation is the process of changing the meaning of actions. For example, corruption can be reinterpreted as acceptable business practice that does not hurt anyone, or it can be blamed on low-level operatives. Reinterpretation is commonly applied to reprisals against whistleblowers – for example, by denying that reprisals have occurred (in other words, lying), minimising their significance or blaming someone else. Disclosures by leakers are subject to the usual array of reinterpretations, for instance by claiming that what was revealed was an unusual occurrence, was actually an instance of best practice, or was due to a mistake. When there is an investigation to discover the identity of a leaker, this is commonly said to be motivated by a concern for privacy, confidentiality, proper procedures, security or public safety – anything except a desire to exact reprisals and prevent further disclosures.

Most whistleblowers report problems through official channels, typically to their bosses, senior management or watchdog agencies, such as ombudsmen. When they suffer reprisals, they often complain to the same sorts of agencies. Unfortunately, many whistleblowers find that official channels do not help. In one key study, whistleblowers reported that 90 per cent of their approaches to agencies did not help; moreover, some approaches made things worse.[9] Official channels, including whistleblower protection laws, give the appearance of dealing with these problems, but often do not. Furthermore, most official processes are slow, focus on procedural technicalities and rely on experts such as lawyers, all of which serve to reduce the potential for public outrage. One of the unanticipated consequences of whistleblower protection laws is that they encourage workers to report concerns and reveal their identity, opening them to reprisals, rather than publicising their concerns. In many cases, most of the attention is on dealing with claims about reprisals, so that the original issue – corruption, abuse or hazards – remains unaddressed.

The alternative for whistleblowers is to take their concerns to wider audiences, for example, by going to the media. Leaking as a strategy typically avoids the traps inherent in official channels and takes the message directly to outsiders.

The fifth method commonly used against whistleblowers is intimidation. This is most obvious in the reprisals taken against whistleblowers. The threat of reprisals serves to deter other workers from speaking out about the original issue or openly supporting the whistleblower. Leakers, if they remain anonymous, can avoid reprisals. However, witch-hunts for leakers, and reprisals visited on those who are identified, can serve as a powerful deterrent to others. That said, in some cases the unfairness of reprisals can operate to inspire action by witnesses. Leaking probably has a greater potential for encouraging emulation, because a leaker's success provides a model to others, whereas the fate of non-anonymous whistleblowers is something co-workers seek to avoid.

In summary, employers have many more opportunities to exact reprisals when the identity of the whistleblower is known. Leaking, by this analysis, has many advantages. However, it is important to note several circumstances that make anonymity inadvisable or unfeasible.[10] First, in many cases, an employee is already known for speaking out, and thus is an obvious suspect when a leak occurs. This is the situation for many who do not initially think of themselves as whistleblowers: they raise an issue of concern, expecting it to be investigated and addressed, and discover to their dismay that they have become the target of attack. These are employees who thought they were just doing their job and inadvertently discovered or exposed something highly sensitive.

Second, if inside information is known only to a few individuals, leaking is risky because the source of the leak can be readily identified. Third, some individuals are not suited for covert operations. Being an effective leaker requires a capacity to keep a secret, cover one's tracks, disguise one's emotions, and sometimes to lie (in a good cause). If this causes great discomfort or is exceedingly difficult to carry out and maintain, then leaking may not be a suitable option. Fourth, some individuals are well protected from reprisals, so it may be better to speak openly and gain the extra credibility this sometimes entails. Often, this means they have obtained a new job in safe circumstances. Having a new job also means there are no further opportunities for leaking in the previous one. In such circumstances, the advantages of leaking are fewer and the benefits of being open can be greater.

These considerations suggest that leaking is unlikely to become the prime option for more than a minority of whistleblowers. Nevertheless, because it is such a potent method, with the possibility of ongoing action, it has the potential for much greater impact. With this background on the tactics relevant to leaking, it is useful to examine the experience of WikiLeaks, to show the relevance of this analysis to the world's most prominent formal system for public interest leaking.

WikiLeaks tactics

WikiLeaks was the first, and remains the most prominent, system for anonymous whistleblowing through a web interface. It is important to distinguish between leakers (who submit items to WikiLeaks) and WikiLeaks itself, which is more akin to a traditional editor and publisher.[11] Julian Assange, who set up WikiLeaks and is its most visible figure, is not himself a whistleblower. The most well-known person who has leaked information via WikiLeaks is Chelsea Manning (formerly Bradley Manning), whose identity became known not via WikiLeaks, but via another person, and who has received both condemnation and praise.

Analysing the tactics used in relation to WikiLeaks involves looking at methods used for and against Manning, Assange and the WikiLeaks operation. The five methods for reducing outrage from injustice are cover-up, devaluation, reinterpretation, official channels and intimidation. It is useful to begin with intimidation because it has played such an important role in the story.

Manning has been subject to the most ferocious reprisals, including arrest, imprisonment and torture via solitary confinement and suicide-watch procedures.[12] As well as serving as punishment of Manning for her acts against the US state, these reprisals serve two other important functions. First, they send a signal to other potential leakers about the fate that awaits them. Second, they distract attention from the information that Manning revealed, including the 'collateral murder' video that exposed the casual killing of Iraqi civilians and the vast archives of war logs and diplomatic cables.[13] In the extensive media coverage of Manning's arrest, imprisonment and trial, the information exposed often is secondary to Manning's own story.

Assange is alleged to have committed rape in Sweden, and has been threatened with arrest and criminal prosecution in the US, with some US politicians calling for him to be assassinated. Then, there are the attacks on WikiLeaks as an operation. Internet service providers, including Amazon, withdrew services for WikiLeaks, and financial institutions – including Visa, Mastercard, PayPal and Bank of America – denied services to WikiLeaks, thereby making it difficult for members of the public to financially support WikiLeaks, a not-for-profit organisation largely funded by donations.[14] The US Department of Justice issued subpoenas to Twitter for all records concerning several people associated with WikiLeaks.[15]

Intimidation is a tool of direct attack and a method of reducing the expression of outrage over acts that might be considered unfair. In the case of WikiLeaks, some US Government intimidation has discouraged the expression of outrage. For example, financial institutions such as Visa seem to have been deterred from speaking out. On the other hand, intimidation itself can be a source of outrage, and this has been the case especially in the case of Manning, who has become a martyr in the eyes of many supporters.

Cover-up is a tactic commonly used to reduce outrage over injustice: if people do not know about something, they will not be upset about it. It is a primary means of curtailing awareness of criminal or disreputable US military and diplomatic activities. Cover-up commonly operates in layers, with a few core individuals having full information, others knowing less and yet others, further away from the core, knowing little or nothing or believing falsities. The outer layers normally rely on mass media coverage, so if the information is restricted to specialist outlets, a significant level of cover-up is achieved.[16]

In relation to stories broken by WikiLeaks, based on leaks by Manning, the US Government was unsuccessful in cover-up: the collateral murder video, war logs and the diplomatic cables were widely publicised via mass media collaborating with WikiLeaks. It is reasonable to presume that US agencies covertly pursued a wide range of methods of disrupting or shutting down the WikiLeaks operation. Overall, the role of cover-up in the attack on WikiLeaks was variable: some methods of attack were hidden, some were known in limited circles and some became more widely known.

Next is the tactic of devaluation: when a person or organisation is seen as low status, disreputable, criminal or deviant, then actions taken against the person or organisation do not seem as serious as they might otherwise. Although in principle 'murder is murder', most people are more upset by the murder of a respected physician than the murder of a paedophile. Therefore, the devaluation of targets of attack is predictable.

Devaluation is the most obvious tactic used against Manning, Assange and WikiLeaks. Manning has been called a traitor; Assange has been called a terrorist. As well as the outpouring of words by opponents of Manning and Assange, actions taken against them have served to demean and discredit them. Manning, by being held in a high-security prison, is implicitly portrayed as a terrorist; by being treated as suicidal, she was portrayed as unstable. Assange was devalued by the rape claims made against him; although his sexual activities in Sweden had no significant connection with his work with WikiLeaks, the allegations served to discredit him as a person.

Reinterpretation is a process of creating or fostering meanings, in this case to make the actions taken against Manning, Assange and WikiLeaks seem understandable, even virtuous. Four important methods of reinterpretation are: lying about what happened; minimising the impact of actions taken; blaming others; and framing events in a favourable manner. An example of lying is the claim that Manning's treatment in prison was for her own safety. An example of minimising was the claim by US officials that the treatment of Manning in prison did not amount to abuse or torture. The most important framing process was to present leaking, and the publishing of leaks, as a threat to national security and as putting named individuals in danger. All of these types of reinterpretation challenged or weakened the alternative interpretation – that WikiLeaks is a valuable contribution to society because of its exposure of corruption, abuse and government perfidy.

Official channels, such as grievance procedures, ombudsmen and courts, are supposed to be fair. People expect them to provide justice. However, when powerful groups are transgressors, official channels often give only the appearance of justice, with little or no substance.[17] Therefore, they can serve to dampen public outrage with minimal impact on the status quo. Whistleblowers commonly seek action via official channels, often trying one after the other, usually with little success.

In the case of WikiLeaks, no substantive action was taken about the problems revealed, for example by the collateral murder video. Outrage apparently was not great enough to stimulate official inquiries into the abuses revealed. Instead, official channels were used as a means of attack; Manning received a 35-year sentence, and Assange was sought for extradition over a rape claim. These actions would have had little credibility if not for their status as operations of the criminal justice system. Manning and Assange were treated as criminals, while the actions they exposed were exempted from proceedings. Official channels in this case gave the stamp of approval for processes of devaluation and intimidation.

To summarise this case study, the US Government and its allies, in their campaign against WikiLeaks, used all five methods of reducing outrage. Although the full extent of cover-up remains to be revealed, it is plausible that covert methods have been used. Devaluation has been a prominent technique, with attempts to discredit Manning, Assange and WikiLeaks more generally. The technique of reinterpretation, including lying, minimising, blaming and framing, has been used to suggest WikiLeaks revelations are a source of danger (for example, to individuals named in leaked documents), thereby diverting attention from the crimes revealed by the leaks. One of the most significant achievements of the anti-WikiLeaks campaign has been to frame the issue around WikiLeaks itself, rather than around the matters exposed by the group; many members of the public hear more about Assange and WikiLeaks than about the documents hosted on the site. Official channels, especially the courts, have been used to make the attacks on WikiLeaks seem more justified. Finally, Manning, Assange and others involved in WikiLeaks have experienced serious intimidation.

The attack on WikiLeaks should not be seen in isolation. There is, after all, a long history of reprisals against whistleblowers, as well as pressures against media outlets considering reporting on government crimes, often due to leaks. Highlights of this history include Ellsberg's leaking of the Pentagon Papers, delayed for many months by media timidity; reprisals against A. Ernest Fitzgerald, a US Defense Department employee who exposed billion-dollar cost overruns;[18] and a recent upsurge in whistleblowing by current and former employees of the US national security apparatus.[19] The attack on WikiLeaks has been accompanied by plans to deal with the 'insider threat' – namely to track down public interest leakers.[20]

Manning, Assange and WikiLeaks supporters have many ways to respond to attacks. To better understand the dynamics of outrage management, it is useful to classify responses into five categories:

1 expose attacks (countering cover-up);
2 validate the target (countering devaluation);
3 interpret the attacks as unfair (countering reinterpretation);
4 avoid or discredit official channels – instead, mobilise support (countering official channels);
5 resist intimidation.

Expose attacks

The attacks on WikiLeaks have been widely publicised. For example, the blocking of funding for WikiLeaks was revealed in various media accounts.

Validate the target

Manning and Assange have received endorsements from numerous journalists and prominent individuals, not to mention thousands of bloggers. Indeed, the attempt to discredit them seems to have triggered a counter-movement to portray them as martyrs to a noble cause. Demonising or glorifying them may not provide an accurate representation of Manning and Assange as individuals, but these responses do reflect the struggle over the value of their acts, cast as evil by detractors and, in defence, as justified and needed by supporters. Underlying the attention to the worthiness or otherwise of Manning and Assange is the more basic issue of the value of WikiLeaks and other online leaking operations.

Interpret the attacks as unfair

In the face of the reinterpretation techniques of lying, minimising, blaming and framing, WikiLeaks supporters have emphasised the unfairness of shooting the messenger, namely attacking leakers and WikiLeaks rather than addressing the problems they have exposed.

Avoid or discredit official channels – instead, mobilise support

The official channels involved in the attacks, which give greater legitimacy to them, have received considerable criticism. The best example is the sceptical reception given to the Swedish legal system by Assange supporters, with many commentators seeing the claims about rape as a process being misused for political purposes. This has made many people sympathetic to Assange's refusal to go to Sweden to face questioning. Normally, a legal system in a well-respected liberal democracy is assumed to function fairly; the discrediting of the Swedish legal system is thus a sign of the power of the campaign to support Assange.

There is ample evidence for outpourings of support for Manning, Assange and WikiLeaks. Where this campaign has a weakness is in not providing an easy opportunity for more direct challenge to the laws and techniques used against WikiLeaks. An analogy would be the McLibel campaign challenging legal action against authors of the leaflet 'What's wrong with McDonald's?'. Supporters distributed the leaflet, itself an action that directly challenged the McDonald's defamation action, vastly increasing the circulation of the information the company was trying to suppress.[21] A possible parallel action in support of WikiLeaks would be for numerous employees in a company all to leak the same document. However, there is no immediately obvious action like this that members of the public can join.

Resist intimidation

Manning, Assange and WikiLeaks supporters have resisted, each in their own way. Manning's calm and considered defence of her actions, in the face of charges against her, revealed thoughtfulness and courage that can be an inspiration to others, although few would be willing to make equivalent sacrifices. The hacker movement Anonymous responded by attacking companies that withdrew credit facilities from WikiLeaks. The actions of Anonymous certainly show a willingness to resist, but most members of the public can only be second-hand witnesses to hacking exploits. Anonymous operates as a vanguard network, undertaking actions in which participation is impossible for most, and thus is not a model for a wider campaign that can involve a broad cross-section of the population in forms of resistance.

Julian Assange, as the founder and public face of WikiLeaks, has received extraordinary visibility. Whether he has used his support to maximum advantage is another question. As is well known, he refused to go to Sweden to be questioned over rape allegations, first fighting the extradition order in court and then seeking asylum in the Ecuadorian Embassy in the UK. Another option would have been for Assange to go to Sweden and take the risk of being extradited to the US to face charges. If this had happened, he could have become even more of a cause celébrè, generating enormous sympathy and support. A case against him in the US would have been a contemporary equivalent to the possibility of charges against Daniel Ellsberg, who leaked the Pentagon Papers 40 years earlier. Ellsberg could have been charged and gone to prison, but he was so prominent that he was left alone. On a global scale, Assange is even more well-known than Ellsberg ever was; a case against him on the grounds of running a leaking operation could possibly backfire on the US Government, just as the McLibel case backfired on McDonald's. This assessment is hypothetical, of course. The point is that actions taken by key players can open or foreclose opportunities for support actions. Leakers and their supporters need to keep this in mind.

The Snowden story

In June 2013, Edward Snowden, a contractor for the NSA, leaked a massive trove of top secret NSA documents to *The Guardian*.[22] These documents revealed that the NSA, for years, had been undertaking widespread surveillance of electronic communications around the world. The ongoing revelations from the leaked documents caused a worldwide furore. It could be said that Snowden is the world's most successful public interest leaker. Therefore, it is worth examining Snowden's experience to see whether and how he and his supporters avoided or countered the tactics used to reduce outrage over the abuses revealed by his disclosures.

Snowden, like Manning, had great technical skills that he used to obtain, order and explain NSA documents. However, in some ways this was not the greatest challenge he faced. He sought a media outlet that would give his material the visibility he believed it deserved and that would not capitulate to the US Government. Therefore, he did not approach mainstream US media giants, such as *The New York Times*, instead choosing the UK-based *Guardian*, which has a small US operation.

Snowden did not approach just anybody: he wanted to make contact with Glenn Greenwald, a *Guardian* freelance columnist who had taken strong stands critical of US Government surveillance. Snowden initially sent anonymous emails to Greenwald using secure channels, asking him to install encryption software, but Greenwald was too busy to make this a priority. So Snowden tried an indirect route, approaching journalist Laura Poitras, a fierce critic of the US security state, and a victim of it, who worked closely with Greenwald.

By initially sending a few NSA documents as 'tasters', Snowden captured the interest of Poitras and then Greenwald, enough to entice them, as part of a *Guardian* team, to a meeting in a Hong Kong hotel. Snowden took extraordinary precautions to maintain security, for example, having *The Guardian* visitors put their phones in the freezer, in case they were bugged. Snowden proceeded to pass over the documents and provide an informed explanation of what they meant, given that many were highly technical.

The Guardian decided to go ahead and, in the usual fashion, asked for comment from US officials, who responded with a combination of blandishments and threats. United States media probably would have pulled back at this point, but *The Guardian* went ahead with publication, causing a storm on mainstream and social media throughout the world. After obtaining and leaking the NSA files, Snowden did not want to remain anonymous. A few days after the first *Guardian* stories, he revealed his identity, providing calm explanations of why he had leaked the NSA documents. In going public, Snowden gave greater credibility to the material.

The tactics involved in the Snowden saga fit the same pattern as with WikiLeaks. First, consider the methods used by the US Government to reduce outrage over the NSA's massive surveillance operation. Prior to Snowden's leaks, the NSA's primary tactic had been cover-up: relatively few members of the public knew much about the surveillance, and the mass media did little to pursue the story. Those who tried to expose the problem were devalued: attempts were made to discredit Snowden – for example, calling him variously a 'shithead', traitor, narcissist and Chinese agent.[23] The government reinterpreted its spying operation as protection of the population against terrorism, and attempted to shift attention to Snowden and away from his disclosures. The official channels for addressing the problem were only a facade; the secret court that assessed NSA requests was a rubber stamp. Finally, there is the tactic of intimidation. Under the Obama administration, treatment of state security whistleblowers was especially harsh,[24] as Manning's experience revealed to Snowden.[25]

The same sorts of tactics were used to reduce outrage over methods used to pursue Snowden. There is an overlap here between methods to reduce outrage over NSA surveillance and those to reduce outrage over pursuit of Snowden because, obviously, Snowden provided information to expose the surveillance.

First, cover-up: the US Government used a range of means to snare Snowden, but most of these were unknown to the general public. For example, US officials applied pressure on the Hong Kong and Chinese governments to relinquish Snowden. Later, after Snowden was in Moscow, the US Government induced European governments to refuse permission for an aircraft carrying Bolivian president Evo Morales to use their airspace because of an incorrect suspicion that Snowden was on board. This extraordinary use of power received little media attention. Most of the public knew little about the sustained efforts of US officials to hunt down and capture Snowden.[26]

Second, devaluation: politicians, government officials and media commentators made various derogatory comments about Snowden. Glenn Greenwald, a key media interpreter of Snowden's disclosures, was also subject to sustained denunciation.[27]

Third, reinterpretation: US officials tried to frame the issue as Snowden violating the confidentiality agreements he had signed, and being disloyal, rather than recognising him as a whistleblower.

Fourth, US Secretary of State John Kerry, among others, said Snowden should return to the US and let the courts deal with him, in other words, to trust in official channels.[28] This was an appeal in principle to official channels, rather than an actual use of them.

Fifth and finally, intimidation: Snowden could predict, from what happened to Manning, his likely fate. In the prospect of torture (through sensory deprivation) and a lengthy jail sentence, there was a combination of techniques. United States officials had partially hidden the harsh treatment of Manning, which blunted public awareness. Snowden knew very well what he faced, yet many members of the public did not, and might have been taken in by US Government statements (using techniques of reinterpretation, including lying and framing) about obtaining a fair trial.

Despite all this, Snowden was highly effective, arguably the most effective leaker in history. The actual impact of his disclosures on policy remains to be seen,[29] and will be limited by various processes, but in terms of popular awareness, the leaks had a tremendous impact. So what did Snowden do to make this possible? First is the tactic of exposure. Of course, this is the essence of whistleblowing, but Snowden sought disclosure to the public via journalists, rather than using internal paths as most whistleblowers do. Second is validation: Snowden calmly and carefully explained his motivations, showing himself to be a sober, socially concerned person. He had no obvious skeletons in his past that could be used to discredit him, and he recruited *The Guardian*, and through it other media outlets, adding credibility to his claims. Third is reinterpretation: Snowden and *The Guardian* stayed on message about the importance of addressing threats to privacy and freedom. Fourth is avoiding official channels and instead mobilising support: Snowden did not pursue formal processes within the NSA, but instead aimed at bringing on board first the journalists Laura Poitras and Glenn Greenwald, then additional *Guardian* workers, and through them a wider constituency. Fifth is standing up to intimidation: Snowden knew his opponents and the risks he faced, yet he continued with calm and courageous commitment to his principles.

In summary, the Snowden saga reveals the usual set of tactics and countertactics found in most struggles between employers and whistleblowers. In this highly unequal struggle between the US Government and a single individual, Snowden fared remarkably well, getting his message to huge audiences around the world. In doing this, he used the tactics of exposure, validation, interpretation, mobilising support (and avoiding official channels) and resisting intimidation. However, it is important to recognise that Snowden did not do all this on his own. Mobilising support implies others playing a role and taking risks. Many individuals working for *The Guardian* were ingenious in gathering and verifying the stories and courageous in standing up to intimidation; others in media outlets, government departments and elsewhere played crucial roles in protecting Snowden and ensuring his revelations received the publicity they did.[30] The message here is that, just as secrecy is multilayered, challenging secrecy requires a multilayered effort.

Conclusion

Most whistleblowers speak out without taking any precautions against reprisals. Many do not think of themselves as whistleblowers: they are employees just doing their jobs. Others trust in the system, and therefore initially make reports to bosses, senior management and outside watchdog agencies, such as ombudsmen. For too many whistleblowers, this approach is disastrous. They are subject to reprisals and little or nothing is done about the matters they raise. Indeed, by reporting matters internally, they alert wrongdoers to the need to cover their tracks, for example, by destroying evidence and creating false stories. By revealing their identity, whistleblowers make it possible for perpetrators to initiate reprisals and prevent access to any more incriminating information.

Anonymous whistleblowing – leaking in the public interest – is often a far more effective option. It reduces the risk of reprisals, keeps attention on the information leaked rather than on the person revealing it, and enables the whistleblower to remain on the job, collect more information and leak again. Public interest leaking has been occurring for decades, but has had far less visibility than conventional non-anonymous whistleblowing, in part because most news stories based on public interest leaking focus on the information, not on the person who has revealed it. Journalists, who are prime recipients of leaks, often make extraordinary efforts to avoid revealing their sources, sometimes even going to jail rather than acquiescing to court orders.

The attention on Chelsea Manning, Julian Assange and WikiLeaks has served, among other things, as a distraction from the documents that WikiLeaks has enabled to become public, including both those leaked by Manning and by others from around the world. The crimes exposed through WikiLeaks should be the centre of attention, but few of them are known to the public.

Even so, the attack on WikiLeaks has had a significant positive impact: it has made leaking far more prominent as an option for whistleblowers. Leaking directly to WikiLeaks is a possibility, but for most whistleblowers there are other leaking options, often more effective, most commonly through contact with local journalists (professional or citizen journalists) or action groups or by directly circulating or posting information anonymously. Edward Snowden took the route of leaking to journalists he carefully selected as recipients, thereby amplifying the impact of his disclosures.

In some ways, then, WikiLeaks need not exist as an actual operation to provide an inspiration for more leaking. Others can set up operations similar to WikiLeaks, learning from the experience of WikiLeaks to be more effective in defending against attack, liaising with mass media and providing a service to whistleblowers. For employees who observe wrongdoing and want to do something about it, the WikiLeaks story is a pointer to a different option: remaining anonymous.

The lessons from the experiences of whistleblowers, WikiLeaks and Snowden are straightforward:

- If possible, keep your identity secret.
- Win allies for publicising leaked material, such as the media and action groups.
- Be very careful about what is leaked, to prevent damage to others, to communicate well to outsiders and to minimise the risk of detection.
- Be prepared for a witch-hunt for the leaker.

Finally, there is a certain irony in recommending anonymity – a type of secrecy – in order to be more effective in exposing secrets.

Notes

1 C. Fred Alford, *Whistleblowers: Broken Lives and Organizational Power* (Cornell University Press 2001); David W. Ewing, *Freedom Inside the Organization: Bringing Civil Liberties to the Workplace* (Dutton 1977); Myron Peretz Glazer and Penina Migdal Glazer, *The Whistleblowers: Exposing Corruption in Government and Industry* (Basic Books 1989); Geoffrey Hunt (ed.), *Whistleblowing in the Health Service: Accountability, Law and Professional Practice* (Edward Arnold 1995); Geoffrey Hunt (ed.), *Whistleblowing in the Social Services: Public Accountability and Professional Practice* (Edward Arnold 1998); Nicholas Lampert, *Whistleblowing in the Soviet Union: Complaints and Abuses under State Socialism* (Macmillan 1985); Marcia P. Miceli, Janet P. Near and Terry Morehead Dworkin, *Whistle-blowing in Organizations* (Routledge 2008); Terance D. Miethe, *Whistleblowing at Work: Tough Choices in Exposing Fraud, Waste, and Abuse on the Job* (Westview 1999).

2 William De Maria, *Deadly Disclosures: Whistleblowing and the Ethical Meltdown of Australia* (Wakefield Press 1999); William De Maria and Cyrelle Jan, 'Behold the Shut-eyed Sentry! Whistleblower Perspectives on Government Failure to Correct Wrongdoing' [1996] 24 *Crime, Law & Social Change*, 151.

3 For his own account, see Daniel Ellsberg, *Secrets: A Memoir of Vietnam and the Pentagon Papers* (Viking 2002).

4 David E. Pozen, 'The Leaky Leviathan: Why the Government Condemns and Condones Unlawful Disclosures of Information' [2013] 127 *Harvard Law Review*, 512 provides evidence of government tolerance of high-level leaking, namely leaking by those who do not think of themselves as whistleblowers. Pozen's analysis is restricted to the US federal government, and national security issues in particular; he notes the different response to what is called in this chapter 'public interest leaking'.

5 Kathryn Flynn, 'Covert Disclosures: Unauthorized Leaking, Public Officials and the Public Sphere' [2006] 7 *Journalism Studies*, 256; see also Kathryn Flynn, 'The Practice and Politics of Leaking' [2011] 30 *Social Alternatives*, 24. Other treatments include *The Art of Anonymous Activism: Serving the Public While Surviving Public Service* (Project on Government Oversight; Government Accountability Project; Public Employees for Environmental Responsibility 2002) especially 7–16; Nicky Hager and Bob Burton, *Secrets and Lies: The Anatomy of an Anti-environmental PR Campaign* (Craig Potton 1999) 240–7.

6 Brian Martin, *Justice Ignited: The Dynamics of Backfire* (Rowman & Littlefield 2007). For many other sources see 'Backfire Materials' <http://www.bmartin.cc/pubs/backfire.html> accessed 14 September 2014.

7 Truda Gray and Brian Martin, 'Abu Ghraib' in Brian Martin, *Justice Ignited: The Dynamics of Backfire* (Rowman & Littlefield 2007).

8 Cover-up is closely related to secrecy, and indeed these terms can be used as synonyms. 'Cover-up' in this context suggests hiding information about wrongdoing as opposed to a general system of secrecy, which can apply to a range of activities.
9 De Maria (n. 2).
10 Brian Martin, *Whistleblowing: A Practical Guide* (Irene Publishing 2013) 133–5.
11 On the relationship between WikiLeaks and mainstream media – which themselves are in rapid transition – see Charlie Beckett with James Ball, *WikiLeaks: News in the Networked Era* (Polity 2012).
12 Chase Madar, *The Passion of Bradley Manning* (OR Books 2012).
13 Dawn L. Rothe and Kevin F. Steinmetz, 'The Case of Bradley Manning: State Victimization, Realpolitik and WikiLeaks' [2013] 16 *Contemporary Justice Review*, 280.
14 It is uncertain whether these companies were responding to pressure from the US Government or acting on their own to please the government.
15 See, for example, 'Note on the Various Attempts to Persecute WikiLeaks and People Associated with It' in Julian Assange with Jacob Appelbaum, Andy Müller-Maguhn and Jérémie Zimmermann, *Cypherpunks: Freedom and the Future of the Internet* (OR Books 2012) 13–19.
16 The idea of layers of secrecy is addressed by David E. Pozen, 'Deep Secrecy' [2010] 62 *Stanford Law Review*, 257, who elaborates on the distinction between shallow secrets, in which the existence of a secret is known but not its content, and deep secrets, in which the existence of a secret is unknown to wider audiences. A similar idea, related to the tactics for reducing outrage outlined here, is censorship of censorship; that is, reducing awareness that censorship has occurred: see Sue Curry Jansen and Brian Martin, 'Making Censorship Backfire' [2003] 7(3) *Counterpoise*, 5. For a related concept, see Thomas Mathiesen, *Silently Silenced: Essays on the Creation of Acquiescence in Modern Society* (Waterside Press 2004).
17 For the case of the US legal system, see Thane Rosenbaum, *The Myth of Moral Justice: Why Our Legal System Fails to Do What's Right* (HarperCollins 2004).
18 A. Ernest Fitzgerald, *The High Priests of Waste* (Norton 1972).
19 For one account, see Sibel Edmonds, *Classified Woman: The Sibel Edmonds Story. A Memoir* (Sibel Edmonds 2012).
20 Andy Greenberg, *This Machine Kills Secrets: How WikiLeakers, Cypherpunks, and Hacktivists Aim to Free the World's Information* (Dutton 2012) 176–225.
21 John Vidal, *McLibel* (Macmillan 1997); see also Fiona J. L. Donson, *Legal Intimidation: A SLAPP in the Face of Democracy* (Free Association Books 2000).
22 For informative accounts, see Glenn Greenwald, *No Place to Hide: Edward Snowden, the NSA and the Surveillance State* (Hamish Hamilton 2014); Michael Gurnow, *The Edward Snowden Affair: Exposing the Politics and Media Behind the NSA Scandal* (Blue River Press 2014); Luke Harding, *The Snowden Files: The Inside Story of the World's Most Wanted Man* (Guardian Books 2014).
23 Greenwald (n. 22) 222–6; Gurnow (n. 22) 76–7; Harding (n. 22) 317.
24 Edmonds (n. 19).
25 Harding (n. 22) 147.
26 Gurnow (n. 22) gives considerable detail.
27 Greenwald (n. 22) 210–22.
28 For the contrary view, see Daniel Ellsberg, 'Snowden Would Not Get a Fair Trial – and Kerry is Wrong' *The Guardian* (London, 30 May 2014) <http://www.theguardian.com/commentisfree/2014/may/30/daniel-ellsberg-snowden-fair-trial-kerry-espionage-act> accessed 14 September 2014.
29 For one account, see Simon Davies (ed.), *Security Services Reform: Sound and Fury, Signifying Nothing? A Global Analysis of the Impact of the Snowden Revelations* (Privacy Surgeon 5 June 2014).
30 Harding (n. 22).

Chapter 13

Open secrets, open justice

Katherine Biber

Introduction

What happens to intimate and criminal secrets in a regime of open justice? This chapter addresses this question and will argue that, in some instances, the law ought to guard the secrets disclosed in criminal proceedings. The principles of open justice demand that the law's work be conducted in public. Open justice is 'one of the most pervasive axioms of the administration of justice',[1] 'the best means of winning . . . public confidence and respect' for the administration of justice;[2] it takes seriously Bentham's aphorism that 'publicity is the very soul of justice'.[3] In order to be accountable, the law must be transparent – it must be seen to be done. Law occurs in public. Bringing disputes to the law, or being brought before the law, is to surrender to publicity what might otherwise not have been disclosed. Law already has the capacity to protect some disclosures on the grounds that they may be private, personal, sensitive, privileged, confidential or secret. This chapter is about whether and how the law might make an exception to open justice, keeping some criminal secrets hidden from our view.

To explain how the law could keep these secrets, this chapter puts forward a 'jurisprudence of sensitivity'. Public spaces, including court rooms, are frequently the sites of acts and disclosures that might be personal, humiliating, intimate or secret. A jurisprudence of sensitivity enables the law to assume responsibility for these secrets. Criminal lawyers recognise that criminal conduct is usually characterised by its clandestine nature.[4] These hidden facts, once they form the basis for criminal charges, are resolved in public, in the court room; they become open secrets. But criminal lawyers also recognise that, in revealing criminal secrets, additional harm might be done – to defendants and others – and a jurisprudence of sensitivity aims to address this.

This chapter is structured in four parts. The first uses a photographic series, 'Kōen/The Park' to illustrate the illicit pleasures and dangers of viewing criminal images. These photographs (which were never used in criminal proceedings) and other artworks made from candid photography open up a discussion about the sensitivities and ethics involved in seeing someone's intimate secrets. These images show us that, when we are spectators to an event that was never intended to be seen, special responsibilities are conferred upon us. The chapter then sets out the meaning of 'jurisprudence of sensitivity', and goes on to explore some cultural and theoretical approaches to secrecy, in the context of intimate secrets. Finally, the chapter explores another photographic series, the photo books tendered at the committal proceedings against Adrian Bayley, charged with the murder and sexual assault of Jill Meagher in Melbourne, Australia, in 2012. The images were released by the court following a media application. In that final part, the chapter examines those proceedings to show what it might mean to be sensitive about the secrets contained in criminal evidence.

'Kōen/The Park'

In the early 1970s in Tokyo, a young photographer walked through Chuo Park in Shinjuku with a colleague at night. He saw a couple having sex on the veranda of a model home, and several men furtively watching them from a short distance. The photographer returned to the park, and visited other Tokyo parks, several times; enough to learn that many couples frequented these parks for sex, and that many men visited those parks to watch the couples, and sometimes to touch them. The photographer learned to take photographs in the dark and began to capture images of this activity.

These are photographs about looking, specifically an illicit kind of looking: looking without permission, looking for pleasure, looking secretly. The series 'Kōen/The Park' was first exhibited at a small gallery in Tokyo in 1979 and the photographer used the pseudonym 'Kohei Yoshiyuki'. The images were blown up to life size, the gallery was in complete darkness, and visitors were given a torch. Despite the exhibition's success, afterwards, for reasons that are not clear, the prints were destroyed.[5] New attention was drawn to his work in 2006,[6] after which Yoshiyuki, whose real name has never been revealed, was contacted by a New York gallery owner. Yoshiyuki agreed to reprint photographs from the remaining negatives.[7] Between April and September 2007, images from the series had been acquired for the collections of major public galleries,[8] and these were then exhibited in New York at the Yossi Milo Gallery, attracting considerable interest from the media, the arts world and the public. The photographs were celebrated for their audacity, for their surprising content, and for their representation of a world otherwise unfamiliar to American art audiences: public sex in Japan.

One striking feature of these illicit images is the absence of the police. In Japan at that time these acts were crimes, but they were largely unpoliced. Under the Japanese criminal code, it was, and remains, a criminal offence to have public sex, to photograph people having public sex, and to display images of these acts in a public context.[9] Yoshiyuki's photographs constitute the only surviving evidence of transgressions that eluded the law. As such, they document intimate secrets, but they cannot be properly labelled as 'crimes'. While looking at these images now might be titillating, fascinating, perhaps even shocking, special sensitivities are not demanded from their display. Instead, different critical responses to intimate secrets are required when the law *is* engaged. If these images were to be used in criminal prosecutions, different sensitivities would arise. This chapter does not argue that artworks made from criminal facts are benign, nor that when artists capture secrets illicitly, that their practice is unproblematic. However, all of these artworks teach us about both the pleasures and ethics of looking at secretive acts.

Kohei Yoshiyuki was interviewed in 1979 by Nobuyoshi Araki, another photographic provocateur. In their conversation, Araki said that the photographs 'are powerful enough to thrill anyone who comes to see them'.[10] A curator at the Museum of Contemporary Photography in Chicago, Karen Irvine, said that 'our appetite for observing people in extremely personal circumstances doesn't seem to wane'.[11] Artists and art critics draw upon a haphazard range of legal terms, loosely grasped, when talking about capturing intimate secrets in photography, and some of them do not refer to the law at all. Looking at Yoshiyuki's photographs, Benjamin Genocchio described as 'naughty, clandestine' the effect of looking at these images.[12] The curators of the 'Exposed' exhibition at the Tate Modern in 2010, in which some of Yoshiyuki's photographs were included, said the images pose 'difficult questions' about whether or not we should collude with their capture.[13] Naomi Cass, who curated 'In Camera and in Public', a 2011 exhibition of candid and surveillance art in Melbourne, also showed some images from 'Kōen' and wrote that, in candid photography of this kind, 'the contract between the photographer and subject has been broken'.[14] She pointed out the two diverging consequences of candid photography: it has taught us things we might never have known (it is evidentiary), and it has also 'hurt, harmed and destroyed people'.[15]

The artist, Cherine Fahd, who has also worked in the candid tradition, said: 'I never considered asking anyone if I could take their photo. It would have defeated the whole point. People change when they know there is a camera present, better to let them be'.[16] She explained that she stopped taking candid photographs because 'audiences became obsessed with whether I had permission to photograph people. . . . The moral dilemmas engulfing candid photography are not something I am interested in addressing in my work'.[17] Luc Delahaye, describing his art practice, wrote: 'I stole these photographs between '95 and '97 in the Paris metro. "Stole" because it is against the law to take them, it's forbidden'.[18] While, initially, he was talking about the proscription against taking a photograph without seeking the subject's permission, he added, 'There's another rule, that non-aggression pact we all subscribe to: the prohibition against looking at others. Apart from the odd illicit glance, you keep staring at the wall. We are very much alone in these public places and there's violence in this calm acceptance of a closed world'.[19] Here, Delahaye was defending his art practice, reliant upon his process of looking without permission, as a kind of pro-social gift. It is as if glancing, peeping or outright voyeurism gives – to the furtively looked-at subject – a value; by looking at them, even if unlawfully, we have gifted them with recognition and inclusion, we have transformed them into social subjects. While Delahaye does not photograph people engaged in transgressive acts, his images nevertheless convey some of the intrusion he has perpetrated in capturing them. A similar sense emerges from Mark Wallinger's 2010 series 'Unconscious', in which he photographed people, including children, who had fallen asleep on public transport. While they were sleeping in a public space, which is neither transgressive nor necessarily humiliating, there is something insensitive about his creation of a permanent record of an act that was never intended to be represented.

New York artist, Arne Svenson, sat at his apartment window holding a camera with a telephoto lens and captured photographs of his neighbours, immersed in the photogenic details of their private lives as visible through their windows, or through gaps in their curtains. When his series 'The Neighbors' opened in Los Angeles in 2013, his neighbours' attention was first drawn to his work, and they responded with predictable anger and indignation. Svenson was reported to be 'surprised and upset' by their reactions, stating: 'I was looking for the most quiet moments, the most human moments. . . . People get crazed by the concept and don't see the art'.[20]

All of these photographs fit into a tradition of artists whose work relies, for its power, upon the intimacy of its subjects. Where that work derives from sources that might be transgressive or secret, the image's power becomes more forceful, given the significant heft of illicit or covert capture. Not all covert imagery is illicit, and with ever-reaching technological capabilities, we don't yet have fully formed ethical or jurisprudential responses to covertly made images. While there is a great deal more that can be said about the relationship between technology, intimacy and secrecy,[21] these issues need not be canvassed in this chapter. However, in the conflation of technological innovation and the hitherto unimagined intrusion into hidden spaces, new intimate media are inaugurated, posing new challenges for the capture and disclosure of secrets. This new visibility, the ability to see secrets, demands a sensitive response. For Roland Barthes, the hidden photographer was the perfect operator; the subjects of the photograph unknowingly 'perform' for him, and his photographs – if they are good – will 'surprise' them.[22] Barthes wrote:

> I imagine . . . that the essential gesture of the Operator is to surprise something or someone (through the little hole of the camera), and that this gesture is therefore perfect when it is performed unbeknownst to the subject being photographed. From this gesture derive all photographs whose principle (or better, whose alibi) is 'shock'; for the photographic 'shock' (quite different from the punctum) consists less in traumatizing than in revealing what was so well hidden that the actor himself was unaware or unconscious of it.[23]

The photographer Diane Arbus said that 'a photograph is a secret about a secret'.[24] Part of Arbus' artistic objective was to find a medium in which to represent individuals who operated outside of society's visual register – 'freaks' – and although some of her subjects were vulnerable, she never carried a hidden camera. When Arbus spoke about photographic secrets, she was talking about the camera's ability to simultaneously capture and liberate something that was hidden. As has been discussed elsewhere, in the context of surveillance cameras:

> The photograph seems the ideal place to conceal a secret, given its confident manipulation of darkness and light. Both darkness and light rely upon each other for their existence, and the photograph is the zone in which one yields to the other. . . . And the photograph taken by a hidden camera . . . reminds us that photographic secrets are produced constantly, autonomously, and in unverifiably large numbers.[25]

We now have an apparently limitless capacity to make images from secrets, creating a permanent record of events that were intended to be ephemeral. And we now have new media enabling us to view images that were never intended to be seen by a wider audience of strangers. Given the nature and quantity of this imagery, we now must ask ourselves: Do I need to see this?

A jurisprudence of sensitivity

The purpose of proposing a jurisprudence of sensitivity is to provide some conceptual framework for thinking through difficult questions of judgment where hurt, harm, humiliation or danger might result from the operation of the principles of open justice. A jurisprudence of sensitivity might provide robust justifications for why, in some circumstances, criminal facts and criminal evidence ought *not* to be released to the public. This is termed here a 'jurisprudence of sensitivity', to take advantage of the existing recognition in law of the category 'sensitive'. Particularly in areas of law regulating information management, the concept 'sensitive' already operates as a justification for non-disclosure. Information management principles recognise a range of reasons why information might not, in certain circumstances, be released, including privacy, personal information, health records, protected confidences, trade secrets, disclosures against the public interest or matters of national security. 'Sensitive information' is distinct from 'personal information'. For example, under the Australian Privacy Principles, 'sensitive information' is personal information that is *also* information or an opinion about an individual's: racial or ethnic origin; political opinions; membership of a political association; religious beliefs or affiliations; philosophical beliefs; membership of a professional or trade association; membership of a trade union; sexual orientation or practices; criminal record; or health information; genetic information; biometric information or biometric templates.[26]

There are other examples of legal instruments defining 'sensitive' in order to manage or protect information,[27] as well as many that use the term 'sensitive' without defining it,[28] and while none of them capture the kinds of harm that criminal disclosures might provoke, they offer a promising starting point. None of them recognises 'sensitivity' in any way that demands a sensory response. However, it has been proposed that the legal recognition of sensitivity demands recognition of the senses:

> Listing what is 'sensitive' is an intellectual undertaking; recognizing what is 'sensitive' demands *feeling something*. A jurisprudence of sensitivity recognizes sensibilities, emotions and harm. It acknowledges the special susceptibility of some individuals, especially those whose context or experience makes them vulnerable in some circumstances. It recognizes that certain materials require special care, delicate handling, tact.[29]

This does not accord with Jaconelli's view that privacy considerations, which he sometimes conflates with sensitivity, are 'capable of objective determination'.[30] Jaconelli asks rhetorically: 'Should the courts defer to the needs of the person of above-average sensitivity? Or should the standard be objective? How, in any event, are the courts to gauge whether or not the particular individual . . . reaches the applicable standard?'[31] Rather, the language of objectivity and standards is antithetical to being sensitive. A jurisprudence of sensitivity would help us to respond to criminal evidence, and the context in which it is collected, displayed and received, in a manner that combines openness and secrecy, exposure and sanctuary, disclosure and tact.

Open secrets

In his work on 'the closet' in the context of gay and queer identity, Miller used the term 'open secret' to capture the tension between knowledge and discretion.[32] The open secret seems to encapsulate something of the 'sensitivity' described in this chapter, in trying to articulate a space for guarding secrets within a regime of transparency. In an anthropological discourse, Michael Taussig used the 'public secret' to describe the double power of the secret: first, that it *is* a secret and will not be disclosed, but second, that its existence is publicly acknowledged as a secret.[33] In her writing about spectatorship in some contemporary art practice, Alison Young shows how the concept of the secret-in-public operates to provoke the spectator to recognise the public secret and also to actually see public spaces as public zones of secrecy. These artworks, Young argues, enable us to see secrets that are hiding in plain sight.[34] In cultural and legal scholarship, there is an evident conflation of secrecy, privacy and intimacy,[35] each of which is tethered to decisions about disclosure or non-disclosure: to 'not-telling', 'not-showing' and 'not-looking'.

Berlant invoked the term 'intimacy' for its capacity to unsettle the distinction between the public and the private. Berlant and Warner use the term 'counterpublic' to describe spaces that might be ephemeral or 'secret' sites,[36] and which Berlant has broadly theorised as the 'intimate public sphere'.[37] Berlant and Warner call for a queer refusal of the public/private distinction, arguing that the privatisation of sex, and of representations of sex acts, renders unnoticed the heterosexual hegemony at work in the demonisation of certain practices (as perverted, obscene, exploitative, criminal).[38] Berlant and Warner's work might be drawn into a much wider discourse in which the 'private' sphere is a zone of intimidation, exclusion, invisibility and violence, and so joins with writers from MacKinnon to Califia and Phelan, who call for a radical visibility of otherwise-hidden individuals, groups and practices. That scholarship is not rejected here, but the argument in this chapter is that within criminal proceedings, and for the artefacts they leave behind, there are times where we might legitimately be told: 'You don't need to see this'.

The term 'secret sex' has been used to describe sex acts that occur in public spaces but that are not meant to be seen or permanently recorded.[39] That term was motivated by an artwork named *Tearoom* (1962/2007) by William E. Jones, a Los Angeles artist with a partially archive-based practice, much of whose work portrays gay sexuality. *Tearoom* is made from 55 minutes of film footage taken by police officers in 1962 in a men's public toilet in Mansfield, Ohio. The footage was captured secretly by a police officer hiding behind a two-way mirror, and caught men engaged in illicit homosexual sex acts; at least 31 men were convicted of sodomy as a result of the footage, serving mandatory minimum prison terms of 12 months. After a process written about elsewhere,[40] Jones acquired the film, re-arranged some of the footage, and gave it the title of *Tearoom*, a term which in archaic American gay argot means a public place where men meet for illicit, anonymous sex. In writing about Jones' work, the word 'secret' conveyed some of the inadequacy of the term 'private' for illicit conduct that occurs in a public space. Bennett and Grant draw a distinction between 'privacy as an intrinsic or aesthetic value' and 'privacy as an instrumental or "strategic" value'.[41] *Tearoom* seemed to capture this distinction, as many of the work's critics argued that it breached the privacy of the film's subjects, a charge Jones both defended and denied. The discomfort of many of the film's viewers arose because the notions of aesthetic privacy (illicit, risky, hidden sex) and strategic privacy (safe, lawful, bounded space) were incompatible with tearoom sex. In either event, United States privacy jurisprudence demonstrated that privacy – whether as a right or a privilege – is incoherent, undefinable and usually incapable of protection.[42] Instead, privacy was more likely to be framed as this aesthetic affinity, an aspiration for secret spaces in which to live out hidden desires.

Having proposed 'secrecy' as an alternative space to the public and the private, this chapter will explore the possibilities and limits of secrecy as a jurisprudential and a critical concept, specifically the way in which secrets demand sensitivity. Mark Fenster is a legal scholar who accepts that secrecy harbours a paradox: if secrecy represents the boundary between those who are permitted to know and those who are not, then the secret must be communicated by those inside the boundary in order for the secret to be identified, and also for the boundary to be perceived.[43] Fenster writes that a secrecy regime 'commands an organization's members both to practice control and silence around outsiders and demands that they share, discuss, and obsess over information among those within the organization'.[44] In Jacques Derrida's writing on the secret, the same paradox is evident. For

Derrida, the secret must, by its nature, be shared because we must identify what is secret in order for the secret to come into being. Thus, the secret begins to be lost as soon as it appears.[45]

Secrecy, Derrida demonstrated, is not something that is concealed by a single individual, but a shared cultural, religious and – significantly for Derrida – now a technological phenomenon. Democracy, for Derrida, had proven damaging to notions of privacy and secrecy and he argued that 'if a right to the secret is not maintained, we are in a totalitarian space'.[46] In his book *A Taste for the Secret*, Derrida argued that transparency – 'the demand that everything be paraded in the public square and that there be no internal forum' – exposes the 'totalitarianisation of democracy'.[47] This fear of a 'totalitarian public' can, Jeremy Gilbert cautions, be taken too far: 'Not to put too fine a point on it: no-one has a taste for the secret like Monsanto or Microsoft, so perhaps it isn't a taste we should be too relaxed about cultivating'.[48]

Instead, Gilbert notices that postmodern political discourse has been transformed by secrets; we have lost our traditional and open public sphere, and with it a robust sense of what is 'private' or separate from it. We now live with the realisation that in the space where that public sphere once was 'we now find ourselves inhabiting a culture constituted by moments of (often sensational) disclosure',[49] noting that these disclosures are often 'discursive[ly] constitut[ed] *as secrets*'.[50] For Gilbert, we are faced with a new challenge: not only do we now need to recognise these 'gestures of disclosure' as an inherent feature of modern public life; we also need to find ways of distinguishing 'mere telling of secrets' from 'real acts of . . . "publicity"'.[51] Gilbert says we need to retain '*respect* for the secret' without becoming '*addicted* to it'.[52] He worries that 'it might be that all that remains is the endless and fragmentary production of pieces of knowledge whose legitimacy is partially guaranteed by their discursive constitution as secrets, always on the verge of disclosure or having only-just-been-disclosed'.[53]

Secrecy can be a strategy. For a secret to retain its power, we must remain within the logic of the secret, and its necessary paradox: it is known *and* hidden, released *but* guarded. Perhaps this is crucial to law's management of criminal secrets. Within the regime of open justice, justice must be seen to be done, but the disclosure of the secret demands that somebody is there to see it. Gatekeepers of law generally function with cold efficiency, effectively excluding all those who cannot speak the language of law, access its domain, or decode its secrets. A considerable amount of recent work focuses upon instances of striking, and sometimes shocking, disclosures – where one of law's secrets has fallen out of place, resulting in harm or humiliation. However, we also need to concede that, most of the time, law's secrets are safe from discovery, because nobody has bothered to seek them out.

Law has developed a range of terms and principles that might guard secrets against disclosure, and these principles emerge from the recognition that sometimes disclosure is harmful, and sometimes knowledge is distributed according to a hierarchy of interests, where one party's interest in disclosure is measured against another party's interest in non-disclosure. There are many contexts in which disclosure is – or feels – wrong. The law attempts to protect these feelings, recognising that some information or relationships might be private, personal, confidential, privileged, intimate, sensitive or secret. Not all of these feelings have consistent and coherent legal definitions, and not all of them are protected by law all of the time. Sometimes, the law will recognise the feeling but say that it is outweighed by a greater interest in disclosure. Sometimes, the law will recognise the feeling and regret that it cannot be protected – that it is too late, too soon, or too hard. Sometimes, these feelings are protected through a legal doctrine that recognises autonomy, or control over the secret, or ownership of the secret, or responsibility for the secret. Legal remedies might flow where the secret has been taken without permission, or distributed without consent or by accident, or where harm has been done – to the person or to another – by the disclosure, or where a law has been violated by the disclosure. However, it is often the case that there is another competing legal principle that is satisfied through the disclosure: the disclosure might be evidentiary, it might be lawful or it might be in the public interest.

Fenster argues that legal mechanisms for regulating secrets are doomed to fail, and that the more effective techniques for keeping secrets are likely to be political or ethical. In addition, he argues that the binary opposition between secrecy and disclosure cannot be sustained and, since secrecy is implausible, we would be better to focus our efforts onto more effective management of disclosure.[54] This is the point at which a jurisprudence of sensitivity might be engaged, in the *sensitive* management of intimate and criminal secrets.

Jill Meagher's grave

In early 2013 in the Melbourne Magistrates Court, a group of media agencies sought access to a wide range of documents, including photographs, tendered against Adrian Bayley, who was being committed to trial for the murder and sexual assault of Jill Meagher. Meagher's disappearance and the subsequent discovery of her body had galvanised intense and widespread public interest and concern, which was matched – or possibly fed – by persistent media reportage. In announcing that there was a media application before the court, Deputy Chief Magistrate Felicity Broughton acknowledged that the principles of open justice would guide her decision, but she also articulated sensitivity to some of the visual evidence:

> So I raise [the media application] now as an issue that will need to be considered. In the appropriate and dignified manner in which these proceedings need to take place, be very mindful of having some fruitful discussions as to how [the media application] might be managed in accordance with the principles of open justice, but having regard to what I already anticipate are some extremely distressing and sensitive materials which certainly, on the face of it, without having made any final decision in relation to that that, certainly give me some concern.[55]

As the proceedings unfolded, she twice interrupted counsel for the media to correct him about the degree of sensitivity involved:

Mr Cashen: I understand there has also been an indication from Your Honour that there is some sensitive material . . .
Her Honour: *Extremely* sensitive material.
Mr Cashen: I should say from the outset my client certainly doesn't seek any of that sensitive material. We are obviously in the invidious position of not knowing what's in the brief. It is often the case that there is some material that's sensitive . . .
Her Honour: . . . *Very* sensitive and *very* distressing.[56]

Later in the proceedings, Broughton DCM revealed where the greatest sensitivities arose for her: 'I'm talking about the scene of the grave',[57] images of Meagher's partially naked body buried in a shallow grave. Her Honour appeared to recognise a sensory concept of sensitivity, although she did not attempt to provide any legal framework for her feelings. It was clear, from the audio recording of the proceedings released by the court, that she *felt* there was something wrong with showing these images, and that everyone in the courtroom also felt it. This could be an example of how a jurisprudence of sensitivity might start, but there needs to be something more to make it clear that while everyone in the courtroom feels something, the wheels of justice are actually turning.

In the Melbourne courtroom, the term 'sensitive' operated flexibly, protecting a disparate range of values and individuals at different moments. Sometimes, it referred to the dignity of Meagher, at other times it was used when protecting her family from distress. At times, it appeared to protect the sensibilities of strangers – casual consumers of the news media. And on at least one occasion, it referred to Bayley, as the release of this material could cause unfair prejudice to him at a future trial, given that the media application was made and resolved before he had been committed to stand trial.

Significantly, and worthy of further study, is the issue of sensitive jurisprudence as a form of labour; it demands effort, time and care in a courtroom that is already busy and under pressure. In Bayley's committal, the labour of sensitivity is apparent, although the court lacks a language for valuing it as a jurisprudential technique. Counsel for three media agencies, Jean-Paul Cashen, acknowledged the effort that would be required to sort the distressing/sensitive/excluded materials from those that could be released. Broughton DCM replied: 'Well, we all agree that the principles of open justice are paramount. So I don't think we need to go any further in terms of the effort that needs to be made'. Here, the court made clear that open justice, moderated with sensitivity, is worth the effort. Meanwhile, Bayley's counsel, Helen Spowart, wanted to take care to go through the hand-up brief and the tendered witness statements to ensure that any inadmissible or controversial material was not released to the media. Her Honour had asked for 'considered submissions' and Spowart, who had not had advance notice of the media application, offered to have written submissions before the court at 9.30 the following morning. Her Honour responded that she wanted to release some materials today; while the defence counsel wanted to work carefully, the court wanted to work quickly. Her Honour offered the parties a short adjournment in order for them to identify the materials that would not be released, and to provide some legal justification for the non-disclosure. When they returned, the order was made.

The next morning, as a result of the media application in the Melbourne Magistrates Court, visitors to the *Herald Sun*, *The Age* and the Australian Broadcasting Commission websites could look inside Meagher's handbag since photographs of her handbag and its contents were included in the police photo books released to the media in the name of open justice. While, of course, Broughton DCM was concerned about disclosures that would have been worse, it is not clear that opening Meagher's handbag is an act of open justice.[58] Looking inside a woman's handbag is a recognised transgression of a boundary;[59] that her violent rape and murder by a stranger might erase the transgression and produce a right to rummage in her bag seems to pervert the objects of open justice. During the proceedings, Her Honour said, 'I think it's pretty clear, obviously some of the traumatic and distressing material, I think we're all on common ground that there's no public interest in that'.[60] However, it is difficult to identify the public interest in the images that *were* disclosed: while tendered, they were not the subject of any submissions or arguments before the court; while published, they were not the basis for any reporting or analysis. The images appeared on at least three media websites in the form of a 'slideshow', without any commentary and sometimes without captions, doing nothing other than driving traffic onto these sites.

There is jurisprudential uncertainty about whether media access of this kind is required by the principles of open justice. Whereas Lord Halsbury LC said in 1889 that 'such publication is merely enlarging the area of the court',[61] more recently, Mahoney JA stated that 'the principle that the courts are to be open and that the media may publish what is done in them is not an end in itself. The principle is adopted because it is judged to be the means by which other and more fundamental goods will be achieved'.[62]

While the release of the handbag photographs may not promote the objectives of open justice,[63] it is not clear where the line might be drawn. Why is it not permissible to see photographs of Meagher's dead, naked body in a shallow grave? We can see photographs of a squalid suburban home, taken after the discovery of the bodies of twin toddlers, starved to death as a result of parental neglect and dysfunction.[64] We can watch a video captured by a traffic camera that shows a man being killed by a drunk driver.[65] We can watch footage of the final moments of a woman's life, as her fiancé drags her into their apartment, his hand pressed hard across her mouth, her eyes recording her abject terror just before he throws her off a balcony to her death.[66] Are we entitled to examine images of a victim's most wretched humiliation? Should we share the final despairing moments in the lives of these strangers? Can we poke through their personal effects, inspect the contents of their bedroom, their lounge room, their laundry, their car?[67] If these people had secrets, does their arbitrary encounter with criminal proceedings disentitle them to keep those secrets? The answers to these questions are probably moral and not legal ones, but contemporary judicial practices of open justice force us to ask these questions, and sometimes, given the nature of online media, they are graphically answered before we have had the opportunity to reflect upon whether we need to see these evidentiary images.

In November 2013, media reports revealed that a Victoria police detective had shown one of the photographs of Meagher's dead body, when it was found, to a civilian audience during a fundraising presentation, and there was a brief public outrage about this – 'shock', 'sadness', 'sickening', 'error of judgment' – defended robustly by the Victoria police association.[68] The next day, the detective said he had shown the image with the support of Meagher's parents, and that it was 'never, ever intended to demean the victim', and that the image was visible to the audience for 'one second'.[69] Given the prurient nature of so many of these disclosures, and the courts' willingness to surrender such intimate secrets in the purported pursuit of open justice, how might we reclaim a space for sensitivity?

Conclusion

For Sissela Bok, secrecy is the intentional concealment of information.[70] Secrecy is a withholding, not an outright refusal to disclose. The secret might be revealed reluctantly, it might be revealed only to certain others, it might be redacted, or we might get a quick peek at it before it is snatched from view. The withholding might be to protect something that is vulnerable, or to protect something that is powerful, or the withholding might itself be a source of pleasure. It reminds us that disclosure is both a thing and a practice: the secret and its revelation. Sensitivity applies to both. The disclosures we make, and the *way* that we make them, demand sensitivity because disclosures, once made, cannot be taken back, and the effects of disclosure operate upon a cohort who had taken refuge in a secret.

In the case of Yoshiyuki's photographs, as with other secret photography, special sensitivities might arise because his subjects were not even conscious that they were taking refuge in a secret. As Yoshiyuki said to Araki, 'at that time, nobody ever dreamed they'd be photographed'.[71] The subjects of all of these images failed to anticipate the technological innovations that, when paired with the motivations of their makers, enabled their capture. The circumstances of secret capture might create an ethical obligation upon those of us who look at them. These might include ethical constraints upon our motivations for looking. For example, looking might be restricted to purposes relating to the investigation of unlawful conduct, or the calculation of probative value. Looking for pleasure might exceed these ethical limits. A jurisprudence of sensitivity needs to recognise that disclosures will have multiple effects, not always predictable or governable, and not capable of being ranked in a pre-formed hierarchy. Therefore, a jurisprudence of sensitivity also needs to retain a space for regret: for the disclosure that, upon reflection, should *not* have been made.

Where evidence is tendered in criminal proceedings, laws operate to protect the accused from most of the unfair consequences of the evidence, and victims from some of the effects of giving evidence. But the law does not control every consequence, nor does it control the effects of the evidence upon other people. Fenster, writing about information management, said that 'information is akin to liquid – capable of flowing from the place it is stored in directions and at a speed that are not capable of being fully controlled'.[72] Nevertheless, Fenster does not argue that information must therefore be tightly locked away. Likewise, this chapter does not argue that the solution to excessive openness is closure. Instead, it proposes a jurisprudence of sensitivity for its capacity to respond to harms that are unpredictable, unknowable or uncontrollable. It might do so by working slowly, by asking questions, consulting widely, deliberating, acting and then reflecting, and maybe then re-thinking, articulating concerns, regrets, and new ways forward.

While evidence is adduced in order to disclose the hidden crimes of the accused, it might also make further disclosures that demand sensitivity towards the accused and towards others. Separately from (although not necessarily after) the criminal trial, historians, artists, curators, scholars and journalists come to this evidence with fresh new questions, sometimes unconnected with the guilt of the accused. A jurisprudence of sensitivity would respond to the effects of these extra-legal projects. It would not aim to prevent this work from being done. It favours negotiation over censorship, but it demands an active engagement with the unforeseen consequences of disclosing criminal secrets in an open justice regime.

Notes

1 J. J. Spigelman, 'The Principle of Open Justice: A Comparative Perspective' (2006) 29(2) *University of New South Wales Law Journal*, 147, 150.
2 *Rinehart v Welker* [2011] NSWCA 403 [32] (Bathurst CJ and McColl JA, citing *Scott v Scott* [1913] AC 417, 463).
3 *Scott v Scott* [1913] AC 417, 477 (Shaw LJ citing Jeremy Bentham). An excellent synthesis of open justice principles is Emma Cunliffe, 'Open Justice: Concepts and Judicial Approaches' (2012) 40 *Federal Law Reports*, 385.
4 See, for example, Peter Rush, *Criminal Law* (Butterworths 1997) 235; Yifat Hachamovitch, 'The Dummy: An Essay on Malice Prepensed' in P. Rush, S. MacVeigh and A. Young (eds.), *Criminal Legal Doctrine* (Aldershot 1992); both cited in Alison Young, 'The Art of Public Secrecy' (2011) 35 *Australian Feminist Law Journal*, 57, 57 fn. 1.
5 Philip Gefter, 'Sex in the Park, and its Sneaky Spectators' *New York Times* (New York, 23 September 2007) AR 37.
6 With the publication in 2006 of Martin Parr's *The Photobook: A History – Volume 2* (Phaidon 2004), in which Yoshiyuki was briefly mentioned as a 'little-known innovator'.
7 In Rachel Wolff, 'A Lost Voyeur's Paradise: Images from Tokyo's Furtive Sex Life, Brought to Life Again' *New York Magazine* (New York, 24 August 2007) <http://nymag.com/guides/fallpreview/2007/art/36605/> accessed 23 September 2014.
8 Including the New York Museum of Modern Art, The Museum of Contemporary Art in Chicago, the Museum of Fine Arts in Houston, and the San Francisco Museum of Modern Art.

9 See Milton Diamond and Ayako Uchiyama, 'Pornography, Rape and Sex Crimes in Japan' (1999) 22 *International Journal of Law and Psychiatry*, 1; see also Mark McLelland, *Queer Japan: From the Pacific War to the Internet Age* (Rowman and Littlefield 2005).
10 Araki Nobuyoshi, 'Down in The Park: Yoshiyuki Kohei's Noctures' (tr.) (2007) 188 *Aperture*, 74, 76. Originally published in Japanese in *Weekend Super*, described in *Aperture* as a 'porn magazine', in 1979.
11 Gefter (n. 5) AR 38.
12 Benjamin Genocchio, 'Kohei Yoshiyuki: The Park' *New York Times* (New York, 7 September 2007) E 21.
13 *Exposed: Voyeurism, Surveillance and the Camera*, Tate Modern (London, 28 May–3 October 2010), 'Exhibition guide' <http://www.tate.org.uk/whats-on/tate-modern/exhibition/exposed/exposed-voyeurism-surveillance-and-camera-exhibition-guide-2> accessed 23 September 2014.
14 Naomi Cass, *In Camera and in Public* (Centre for Contemporary Photography, Melbourne, Exhibition catalogue, 2011) 2.
15 Ibid.
16 Cherine Fahd, artist statement in Cass (n. 14) 9.
17 Ibid.
18 Cass (n. 14) 13, extracting Luc Delahaye, *L'autre* (Phaidon 1999).
19 Ibid.
20 Raffi Khatchadourian, 'Stakeout' *The New Yorker* (27 May 2013) 24, 25.
21 There is a considerable body of literature, but a selection of pertinent references includes: David Cohen, 'Peeking in on the Social Set' *The New York Sun* (New York, 6 September 2007) Arts & Letters 15; Bill Henson, artist statement, in Cass (n. 14) 6; Cass (n. 14) 13, extracting Luc Delahaye, *L'autre* (Phaidon 1999); Jacques Derrida, *Of Hospitality* (Stanford University Press 2000) 47, 61; Leslie J. Moran and Derek McGhee, 'Perverting London: The Cartographic Practices of Law' (1998) IX *Law and Critique*, 207; David Bell, 'Bodies, Technologies, Spaces: On "Dogging"' (2006) 9 *Sexualities*, 387; Phil Hubbard, 'Sex Zones: Intimacy, Citizenship and Public Space' (2001) 4 *Sexualities*, 51; Derek E. Bambauer, 'Exposed' (2013) 98 *Minnesota Law Review*, 2025; Kenneth Tam, 'Disappearing in Plain Sight, or How We Used to have Casual Sex before Craigslist' (MFA thesis, University of Southern California 2010); Steven Maynard, 'Through a Hole in the Lavatory Wall: Homosexual Subcultures, Police Surveillance and the Dialectics of Discovery, Toronto 1890–1930' (1994) 5 *Journal of the History of Sexuality*, 207; Kevin Walby and André Smith, 'Sex and Sexuality under Surveillance: Lenses and Binary Frames' in Paul Johnson and Derek Dalton (eds.), *Policing Sex* (Routledge 2012); Melissa Miles, 'Photography, Privacy and the Public' (19 January 2012) *Law, Culture and the Humanities* <http://lch.sagepub.com/content/early/2012/01/06/1743872111430277.abstract> accessed 23 September 2014; Herman Tavani, 'Philosophical Theories of Privacy: Implications for an Adequate Online Privacy Policy' (2007) 38 *Metaphilosophy*, 1.
22 Roland Barthes, *Camera Lucida: Reflections on Photography* (Hill & Wang 1981) 32.
23 Ibid.
24 Susan Sontag, *Styles of Radical Will* (Farrar, Straus & Giroux 1976) 111.
25 Katherine Biber, 'The Spectre of Crime: Photography, Law and Ethics' (2006) 16 *Social Semiotics*, 133, 141.
26 Privacy Act 1998 (Cth.) sch. 3.
27 See, for example, Australian Government, *Information Security Management Guidelines*, v. 1.1 (18 July 2011) <http://www.protectivesecurity.gov.au/informationsecurity/Documents/Australian%20Government%20classification%20system.pdf> accessed 23 September 2014. See also Health Records and Information Privacy Act 2002 (NSW), Guideline 4.4(d); Information and Privacy Commission New South Wales, *NSW Data Protection Principles*, Principle 11; Information Act 2002 (NT), Information Privacy Principle 10;

Office of the Information Commissioner of the Northern Territory, *Information Privacy Principles*, IPP10 'Sensitive information' <http://www.infocomm.nt.gov.au/privacy/ipp.htm> accessed 9 October 2014; Information Privacy Act 2009 (Qld.), sch. 4, adopting National Privacy Principle 9; Personal Information Protection Act 2004 (Tas.), sch. 1 s. 10, containing Personal Information Protection Principles; Information Privacy Act 2000 (Vic.), sch. 1, esp. IPP 10. The Australian Law Reform Commission has various reports pertaining to 'sensitive information', including 'Review of Measures Designed to Protect Classified and Security Sensitive Information in the Course of Investigations and Proceedings' (2003) Background Paper 8; 'Protecting Classified and Security Sensitive Information' (2004) Discussion Paper 67; 'Keeping Secrets: The Protection of Classified and Security Sensitive Information' (2004) Report 98. The South African Law Reform Commission distinguishes between 'critical' information and 'sensitive' information: 'Privacy and Data Protection' (2005) Discussion Paper 109, Project 124, [3.6.5], [3.6.10], [3.6.11], [3.6.18], [4.2.149]. In the United Kingdom, 'sensitive personal data' is defined in the Data Protection Act 1998 (UK), s. 2. Schedule 3 of that Act provides specifically for 'sensitive personal data' and includes provisions as consent (which must be explicit), processing (where required for the administration of justice, among other specifics), and medically necessary processing. In the United States, 'sensitive information' is defined in 5 USCA §552a; see also 18 USC §1905. Canada has opted for a model of sensitivity relying, in part, on context: see National Standards of Canada Model Code for the Protection of Personal Information, SC 2000, C 5, s. 5 [4.3.4], enacted in part in Personal Information and Electronic Documents Act (2000) (Can.). For more on this, see Teresa Scassa, 'Text and Context: Making Sense of Canada's New Personal Information Protection Legislation' (2000–01) 32 *Ottawa Law Review*, 1. For the contextual approach to privacy more broadly, see Helen Nissenbaum, *Privacy in Context: Technology, Policy, and the Integrity of Social Life* (Stanford Law Books 2010). See also Daniel Solove, *Understanding Privacy* (Harvard University Press 2008).

28 Under the OECD Guidelines on the Protection of Privacy and Transborder Flows of Personal Data, the Expert Group concluded that 'it is probably not possible to identify a set of data which are universally regarded as sensitive': Guideline 19(a) <http://www.oecd.org/internet/ieconomy/oecdguidelinesontheprotectionofprivacyandtransborderflowsofpersonaldata.htm> accessed 9 October 2014. Subsection B of the guidelines acknowledges a culturally specific understanding of 'sensitive' and defers to individual countries in deciding the specific level of protection afforded to certain information: see Explanatory Memorandum, s. B, [3], [7] <http://www.oecd.org/internet/ieconomy/oecdguidelinesontheprotectionofprivacyandtransborderflowsofpersonaldata.htm> accessed 9 October 2014. Note that these guidelines were updated in 2013 at <http://www.oecd.org/sti/ieconomy/2013-oecd-privacy-guidelines.pdf>. Under the European Union's Data Protection Directive (Council Directive 95/46/EC of the European Parliament and of the Council of 24 October 1995 on the protection of individuals with regard to the processing of personal data and on the free movement of such data [1995] OJ L281/31), seven principles from the OECD guidelines were incorporated: see art. 8. Note that, on 25 January 2012, the EU proposed an updated comprehensive data protection regime, recognising the particular 'sensitive' nature of some personal data. See European Commission, Proposal for a Regulation of the European Parliament and of the Council on the Protection of Individuals with Regard to the Processing of Personal Data and on the Free Movement of Such Data (General Data Protection Regulation), 2012/0011 (COD), [41]–[42] <http://ec.europa.eu/justice/data-protection/document/review2012/com_2012_11_en.pdf> accessed 9 October 2014.

29 Katherine Biber, 'In Crime's Archive: The Cultural Afterlife of Criminal Evidence' (2013) 53 *British Journal of Criminology* 1033, 1043 (emphasis in original). Definition derived in part from *Oxford English Dictionary* (Oxford University Press 2000) <http://www.oed.com/> accessed 24 September 2014.

30 Joseph Jaconelli, *Open Justice: A Critique of the Public Trial* (Oxford University Press 2002) 169.
31 Ibid.
32 Cited in Eve Kosofsky Sedgwick, 'Epistemology of the Closet' in H. Abelove, M. A. Barale and D. M. Halperin (eds.), *The Lesbian and Gay Studies Reader* (Routledge 1993) 45–6.
33 Michael Taussig, *Defacement: Public Secrecy and the Labor of the Negative* (Stanford University Press 1999).
34 Young (n. 4).
35 See, for example, Maryanne Dever, 'The Private in the Public Archive' in Margherita Carucci (ed.), *Revealing Privacy: Debating the Understandings of Privacy* (Peter Lang 2012); Christian Fuchs, 'Towards an Alternative Concept of Privacy' (2011) 9 *Journal of Information, Communication & Ethics in Society*, 220; Agnes Ku, 'Boundary Politics in the Public Sphere: Openness, Secrecy and Leak' (1998) 16 *Sociological Theory*, 172; Stephen Margulis, 'Privacy as a Social Issue and Behavioral Concept' (2003) 59 *Journal of Social Issues*, 243; Adam Moore, 'Privacy: Its Meaning and Value' (2003) 40 *American Philosophical Quarterly*, 215; Jill Lepore, 'The Prism: Privacy in an Age of Publicity' *The New Yorker* (24 June 2013) <http://www.newyorker.com/magazine/2013/06/24/the-prism> accessed 24 September 2014.
36 Lauren Berlant and Michael Warner, 'Sex in Public' (1998) 24 *Critical Inquiry*, 547.
37 Lauren Berlant, *The Queen of America Goes to Washington City: Essays on Sex and Citizenship* (Duke University Press 1997); Lauren Berlant, *The Female Complaint: The Unfinished Business of Sentimentality in American Culture* (Duke University Press 2008).
38 Berlant and Warner (n. 36) 550.
39 Katherine Biber and Derek Dalton, 'Making Art from Evidence: Secret Sex and Police Surveillance in the Tearoom' (2009) 5 *Crime Media Culture*, 243.
40 Ibid. 245–7.
41 C. Bennett and R. Grant (eds.), *Visions of Privacy: Policy Choices for the Digital Age* (Toronto University Press 1999) 4.
42 For a wider-ranging critique of US privacy jurisprudence generally, see Lawrence M. Friedman, *Guarding Life's Dark Secrets: Legal and Social Controls over Reputation, Propriety, and Privacy* (Stanford University Press 2007).
43 Mark Fenster, 'The Implausibility of Secrecy' (2013) 65 *Hastings Law Journal*, 309. Other examples of legal scholarship about secrecy (excluding scholarship on national secrecy) include Claire Grant, 'Secret Laws' (2012) 25 *Ratio Juris*, 301; Dina Siegel, 'Secrecy, Betrayal and Crime' (2011) 7 *Utrecht Law Review*, 107.
44 Fenster (n. 43) 321.
45 Jacques Derrida, 'How to Avoid Speaking: Denials' in Sanford Budick and Wolfgang Iser (eds.), *Languages of the Unsayable: The Play of Negativity in Literature and Literary Theory* (Stanford University Press 1996) 25.
46 Jacques Derrida, *A Taste for the Secret* (Polity 2001) 59. See also Joseph Masco, '"Sensitive but Unclassified": Secrecy and the Counterterrorist State' (2010) 22 *Public Culture*, 433.
47 Derrida (n. 46) 59.
48 Jeremy Gilbert, 'Public Secrets: "Being-with" in an Era of Perpetual Disclosure' (2007) 21 *Cultural Studies*, 22, 36.
49 Ibid. 37.
50 Ibid. 24 (emphasis in original). See also the special issue on 'Secrecy and Transparency' in (2011) 28(7–8) *Theory, Culture and Society*, and particularly Claire Birchall, 'Introduction to "Secrecy and Transparency": The Politics of Opacity and Openness' (2011) 28 *Theory, Culture and Society*, 7. See also the special issue, 'The Secret Issue' (2007) 21 *Cultural Studies*.
51 Gilbert (n. 48) 38.
52 Ibid. 40 (emphasis in original).

53 Ibid. 23.
54 Fenster (n. 43) 359–62. See also Paul Kockelman, 'Enclosure and Disclosure' (2007) 19 *Public Culture*, 303.
55 *Victoria Police v Bayley* (Melbourne Magistrates Court (Criminal) 12 March 2013), transcript made from audio recording released to the author by the court.
56 Ibid. (emphasis added).
57 Ibid.
58 Katherine Biber, Peter Doyle and Kate Rossmanith, 'Perving at Crime Scenes: A Conversation' (2013) 22(3) *Griffith Law Review*, 804.
59 'They [handbags] suggest womb, heart, breast, and psyche. They are worn or carried in the body's most private zone. They are a small extension of the self that goes forth into the world while maintaining an utterly private dimension': Barbara Hagerty, *Handbags: A Peek Inside a Woman's Most Trusted Accessory* (Running Press 2002) 10.
60 *Victoria Police v Bayley* (n. 55).
61 *McDougall v Knight* (1889) 14 App. Cas. 194, 200.
62 *John Fairfax Group Pty Ltd v The Local Court of New South Wales* (1991) 26 NSWLR 131, 164.
63 Katherine Biber, 'Inside Jill Meagher's Handbag: Looking at Open Justice' (2014) 39 *The Alternative Law Journal*, 73.
64 See, for example, Brooke Baskin, 'Images Released of Home in Which Starved Twins Died in Brisbane's Sunnybank Hills' *The Courier-Mail* (Brisbane, 7 August 2013) <http://www.couriermail.com.au/news/queensland/images-released-of-home-in-which-starved-twins-died-in-brisbane8217s-sunnybank-hills/story-fnihsrf2–1226692083452> accessed 24 September 2014.
65 Brendan Roberts, 'CCTV Captures Drunk Driver's Deadly Crash' (*7News*, 12 November 2013) <http://au.news.yahoo.com/vic/a/19795075/cctv-captures-drunk-drivers-deadly-crash/> accessed 24 September 2014.
66 Emma Partridge, 'Video Reveal the Moments before Lisa Harnum Died and What Simon Gittany Did Next' *Sydney Morning Herald* (Sydney, 1 November 2013) <http://www.smh.com.au/nsw/video-reveals-the-moments-before-lisa-harnum-died-and-what-simon-gittany-did-next-20131101–2wq4h.html> accessed 24 September 2014.
67 Apart from the handbag and laneway photographs, most of the photographs released to the media in Adrian Bayley's committal were taken in his car and in the home he shared with his partner.
68 See, for example, Nino Bucci, 'Senior Detective Shows Graphic Meagher Photos at Fundraiser' *The Age* (Melbourne, 27 November 2013) <http://www.theage.com.au/victoria/senior-detective-shows-graphic-meagher-photos-at-fundraiser-20131127–2yanc.html> accessed 24 September 2014.
69 Kristian Silva, 'Detective Senior Sergeant Ron Iddles Sorry for Showing Jill Meagher Photos' *The Age* (Melbourne, 28 November 2013) <http://www.theage.com.au/national/detective-senior-sergeant-ron-iddles-sorry-for-showing-jill-meagher-photos-20131128–2yblz.html> accessed 24 July 2014.
70 Sissela Bok, *Secrets: On the Ethics of Concealment and Revelation* (Pantheon Books 1983) 5–6.
71 Nobuyoshi (n. 10) 78.
72 Fenster (n. 43) 329.

Chapter 14

Secret isle? Making sense of the Jersey child abuse scandal

Greg Martin and Rebecca Scott Bray

Introduction

> No man is an *Iland*, intire of it selfe; every man is a peece of the *Continent*, a part of the *maine*.[1]

On the face of it, the Channel Island of Jersey is an idyllic and tranquil place to live. It is home to the late Gerald Durrell's famous zoo, specialising in the protection of endangered species, and was the setting for the BBC police drama, *Bergerac*, a fictional portrayal of law enforcement on the island, which belied Jersey as comparatively crime-free. However, in early 2008, Jersey became the focus of a major police investigation into allegations that widespread child abuse had occurred for many years in a range of care institutions on the island. At the heart of the inquiry were suspicions that children had been sexually abused and even murdered at the former children's home of Haut de la Garenne.

Controversy surrounded the inquiry when it was claimed that child abuse allegations had been covered up for decades. Some of the more extravagant claims linked the concealment of child abuse on the island to Freemasonry, the island's occupation by the Nazis during World War II and its status as an offshore tax haven harbouring financial secrets, which was seen by some as a metaphor for Jersey's reputed 'secrecy culture'. In some cases, it was believed that satanism was to blame for the torture and abuse of children on the island, as has been claimed elsewhere.[2] Paedophile politicians, businessmen, civil servants and care workers were all implicated in both the child abuse and its cover-up. The Jersey child abuse case was also linked eventually to the Jimmy Savile scandal over institutionalised child sexual abuse on the British mainland.

Rather than simply explicating the secrecy surrounding child abuse on Jersey in terms of the peculiarities of island life or as an outcome of a particular set of cultural traits, this chapter places the Jersey child abuse case in a broader context, and, by so doing, it strives to make some criminological and sociological sense of it. Accordingly, the chapter applies to the Jersey case research on crime in small rural communities where a premium is placed on privacy, as well as arguments about how modern conceptions of privacy provide spaces where abuse of the kind that occurred on Jersey can take place with relative impunity. Comparing the Jersey case to that of Josef Fritzl in Austria, the chapter also shows how avoidance of some of the more uncomfortable aspects of German occupation may offer insights into the operation of privacy – and, hence, secrecy – on the island.

The chapter then moves on to argue that the reportedly disproportionate internment of children and young people in state care facilities on Jersey is indicative of how societies that stress social cohesion, homogeneity and conformity to ensure paradisiacal qualities do so via excessive punishment for minor crimes and misdemeanours. Arguably, too, in those societies where the moral order is reasserted and affirmed by visibly sanctioning transgressors, deviance is more likely than not to be privatised and thus kept secret. The chapter then explores the possibility that financial secrecy born of Jersey's tax haven status could be part of a wider 'culture of secrecy' on the island, of which the child abuse case is symptomatic. Finally, the chapter considers some of the lessons that may be learned in light of what happened on Jersey, including a need for outside intervention to provide independent assessment and monitoring of child protection services on the island. Analysis of the Jersey child abuse case also highlights that there is a critical role to be played by a robust news media, which should be willing not only to question police tactics, but also to challenge those in authority and the establishment.

The Jersey child abuse case

On 23 February 2008, what was thought to be a fragment of a child's skull was found under a thick concrete floor at Haut de la Garenne, a former children's home on the Channel Island of Jersey. After it closed as a children's home in 1986, Haut de la Garenne became a youth hostel and, in a twist of fate, it featured as a police station in the 1980s BBC detective series, *Bergerac*,[3] where it was used for a graveyard scene in one episode, which police later thought might help explain the 'hotspots' they found indicating possible burial sites.[4] In the days and weeks after the initial discovery of the skull fragment, police found what they believed to be a bricked-up cellar, four secret underground 'punishment rooms',[5] spots of blood in a concrete bath in a cellar, bloodstained objects in underground chambers, and children's teeth and bone fragments. The investigation, and the publicity it attracted, renewed claims that longstanding allegations of child abuse had not been taken seriously by Jersey authorities, including allegations of abuse at the Sea Cadets Corp, which had been investigated more than a year earlier.[6]

The Jersey child abuse inquiry, which was conducted covertly for 12 months, began in November 2006 when police discovered that victims of paedophiles at the Sea Cadets Corp had also been assaulted elsewhere.[7] Many of the Sea Cadets who had alleged abuse had been in care at Haut de la Garenne.[8] While police apparently saw links between the suspects in the Sea Cadets case and a number of institutions on Jersey, including Haut de la Garenne, Deputy Police Chief and head of the child abuse inquiry, Lenny Harper, said there was 'no evidence of a cover-up'.[9] However, this was more likely to be a public relations façade rather than Harper's own view, since he had already begun to make connections between the alleged abuse at the Sea Cadets and other institutions in early 2007 after discovering the care files on which a member of Jersey police's family protection team, Brian Carter, had worked. Carter had since retired, but in 2004 he:

> noticed an unusually high incidence of suicide among men who had passed through Haut de la Garenne. Reviewing the records of 950 former residents, he discovered that a significant number had complained of sexual and physical abuse, describing similar acts and perpetrators, going back to the 50s. Shockingly, even though supervisors at the homes had dutifully noted the complaints, none had been properly investigated.[10]

Such claims indicate, at best, institutional incompetence and, at worst, a cover-up. Although there had been reports of children who may have gone missing over the past four decades, many of them were identified only by a first name or a nickname.[11] Moreover, while an inquest was conducted into the death of one boy who had hanged himself in 1966, it was unclear whether there had been any other inquests into deaths of children at Haut de la Garenne.[12] The comments of one victim who was resident at the home in the 1960s highlighted concern that the alleged suicides were shrouded in secrecy: 'The thing that I could never understand was there was never any police, there was [sic] never any ambulances. If you asked a member of staff what was going on, they would just tell you it had been dealt with'.[13]

During his inquiries, Carter sought out victims and took statements in which they detailed how they had been beaten and raped by older children and staff, and also by Sea Cadet officers, St John Ambulance volunteers and at least one local politician.[14] Yet, when he delivered his dossier to Jersey CID in April 2006, nothing happened.[15] Disillusioned, Carter quit the force later that year, but Harper took up the mantle and alerted his superior, Graham Power, to the dossier. Power then contacted the Association of Chief Police Officers on the British mainland, which launched an independent inquiry, and he gave Harper the go-ahead to launch a full-scale child abuse investigation, with Carter redeployed as a civilian investigator.[16]

However, many, including Harper himself, doubted that justice would be delivered on a small island where conflicts of interest are rife, and where an investigation of this type may be subject to political interference.[17] Such concerns prompted politicians in the United Kingdom and Jersey to call for the then UK justice minister, Jack Straw, to intervene in the investigation to ensure that prosecutions be heard on the mainland.[18] At the same time, Labour MP, Austin Mitchell, tabled a House of Commons motion requesting that an independent inquiry into the child abuse allegations on Jersey be carried out by a member of the British judiciary, while Jersey senator, Stuart Syvret, and British Liberal Democrat MP, John Hemming, called for a judicial review of the five cases where people suspected of abuse had not been charged.[19]

In the face of claims that the matter would become politicised, and others that Jersey's judicial system could not cope with the scale and intricacy of a case such as Haut de la Garenne, the island's Attorney-General, William Bailhache QC, said he was confident that Jersey's legal system could deliver justice. He added that the delivery of justice is an objective process, that the island's judiciary had been delivering justice for centuries, and there was no reason to believe that it would be any different in the Haut de la Garenne case.[20] He stated: 'It is difficult for people outside to understand that in a small place you are particularly aware of the need to behave properly, behave appropriately, to have the integrity to take decisions which need to be taken'.[21] He added that, as an independent appointee, he was in a position to make 'fearless' decisions.[22]

Contrary to the view of Bailhache (whose brother, Sir Philip Bailhache, was the then Jersey Bailiff – the highest officer and senior judge on the island who also acts as the speaker in the States of Jersey, which is Jersey's parliament),[23] Harper claimed his inquiries were constantly hampered, stating that, unlike other similar investigations in which he had been involved, what made this one significant was the degree of political hostility it engendered.[24] Hence, in order to counteract the risk of interference from elements of Jersey's political elite, as well as to reassure witnesses and encourage others to come forward, when something was first found at Haut de la Garenne that a forensic anthropologist cautiously identified as part of a child's skull, Harper adopted a 'strategy of openness', announcing on 23 February 2008 that 'what appears to be partial remains of a child' had been discovered under the stairwell of the former children's home.[25] Harper's vagueness here was deliberate, since he did not want details to be released and picked up by newspapers and recycled by any future witnesses.[26] However, what he admitted was a high-risk strategy of openness also backfired to the extent that it provided some in the press with licence to embellish and sensationalise the story,[27] describing Haut de la Garenne as 'a "kiddies' Colditz" (*Star*), a "fortress of fear" (*Mirror*) and the "home of horrors" (*Mail*)'.[28]

Unsurprisingly, the bad publicity did not go down well on the island. In his annual speech, in May 2008, to mark the liberation of the Channel Islands from German occupation during World War II, Bailiff Bailhache complained 'that many journalists continued to write about the island's "so-called abuse scandal. All child abuse . . . is scandalous, but it is unjustified and remorseless denigration of Jersey and her people that is the real scandal"'.[29] On the other hand, the island's only newspaper, the *Jersey Evening Post*, was accused of aiding and abetting attempts at thwarting the child abuse investigation and being 'more concerned with protecting the island's reputation than the victims of child abuse'.[30] Moreover, in January 2012, the Care Leavers' Association complained to the island's Health and Social Services Department, after a *Jersey Evening Post* journalist appeared to disparage the compensation scheme that was soon to be announced for the victims, writing: 'By the way, you're about to pay out millions upon millions to abuse victims in civil compensation claims. That'll do wonders for the island's image, right?'[31]

Early on in the Haut de la Garenne investigation, Jersey Tourism recognised the negative impact that the case would have on the tourist industry, initially withdrawing 'all its newspaper and television advertising while the Haute de la Garenne investigation continued',[32] and only resuming the marketing campaign on 11 April 2008.[33] Indeed, tourism officials 'spent a great deal of time and money finding out whether Harper's investigation would sour the island's reputation as a holiday resort (or investment destination) forever'.[34] As if to confirm those fears, reportage on a knife attack – where a family was stabbed to death – that occurred on the island in August 2011 portrayed Jersey as a place with a reputation for crime, suggesting the island's image had been tarnished ever since the 'botched' child abuse investigation into Haut de la Garenne.[35]

In August 2008, Harper retired to Ayrshire, but he was unrelenting in his criticism of the Jersey legal system, which, he said, gave him the feeling 'the goalposts were being moved' and had *ad hoc* decision-making processes that appeared to be 'whenever, wherever', having, for example, subjected his gathering of victims' statements to 'inexplicable delays'.[36] Above all, according to Harper, those working in Jersey's legal system 'are held in contempt by the vast majority of victims'.[37] Nevertheless, in early November 2008, States of Jersey Police announced there was no evidence that any children had been murdered at Haut de la Garenne, nor that bodies had been destroyed; the underground chambers were mere holes in the floor; the bath was not, in fact, bloodstained; and the shackles that had been found were just pieces of rusty metal.[38] Furthermore:

> Of the 170 bone fragments found there, burnt or not, the majority were from animals, and were uncovered in a place belonging to the 'Victorian era'. Only three of these fragments were possibly human – two of them thought to date 'from 1400 to the 1600[s]'. The original skull fragment is neither human nor animal: most probably a piece of Victorian coconut.[39]

While approximately 160 people claimed they had been abused over a 40-year period at Haut de la Garenne and other institutions on Jersey,[40] and at one time police had more than 40 suspects – most of whom had worked at Haut de la Garenne, but some were prominent Jersey establishment figures[41] – the Jersey child abuse investigation yielded only seven convictions; although police did say they had gathered evidence that could have led to the prosecution of a further 30 people who had died before any case could be made against them.[42] In the month before the final two convictions, Jersey's Chief Minister, Terry Le Sueur, issued an unreserved apology in the States of Jersey to all of the children who had suffered abuse at Haut de la Garenne, whether or not the abuse had resulted in a criminal conviction.[43] And, in 2012, a compensation scheme (the Historic Abuse Redress Scheme) was opened for around 90 victims of abuse, who will receive up to 60,000 GBP, after Jersey's Chief Minister at that time, Ian Gorst, acknowledged 'that the care system that operated historically in the island of Jersey failed some children in the States' residential care in a serious way'.[44] In the immediate aftermath of the Haut de la Garenne case, Jersey also introduced its first sex offenders register.[45]

However, child victims were not the only casualties of the Jersey child abuse inquiry. Former Jersey Health and Social Services Minister, Stuart Syvret, claimed he was sacked for whistleblowing after highlighting the ill-treatment that had gone on for decades in Jersey's care homes, as well as in the island's elite independent school for boys, Victoria College. Syvret claimed that abuse had carried on for years at the college, and that some senior staff and school governors (which included Bailiff Bailhache) not only failed to deal with it, but took steps to intimidate boys who had made allegations into withdrawing them.[46] In the event, the boys did not withdraw their allegations and, consequently, the head of mathematics was jailed for four years in April 1999 after admitting to a number of indecent assaults.[47] Speaking on UK national radio soon after the Haut de le Garenne investigation went public, Syvret said people should not be distracted by what was happening there, 'because the real issue here is we are looking at multiple examples of abuse at multiple institutions over a period of decades and decades'.[48] For Syvret, the Haut de la Garenne case was 'the latest example of "a culture of cover-up and concealment"'.[49]

Nearly two years after the Haut de la Garenne investigation had prosecuted its final offender in early 2011, Syvret was convicted of data protection offences for refusing to take down articles on his blog that made allegations against people on Jersey, including that a nurse may have killed some of his patients.[50] None of the four people named on Syvret's blogs attempted to sue for defamation; instead, Jersey's data protection commissioner prosecuted Syvret under the island's data protection legislation. In an unusual move, the commissioner argued that Syvret was the 'data controller' of his blog (a position normally held by large corporations), and that he had no right to name and shame people, whether or not the information he presented was correct.[51] UK Liberal Democrat MP, John Hemming, a supporter of Syvret, said that Syvret had been prosecuted unfairly for revealing information that was in the public interest, and that the Jersey judiciary had behaved oppressively by misusing the Data Protection (Jersey) Law 2005 to silence critics. Meanwhile, Syvret referred to himself as a political prisoner.[52]

Jersey's 'secrecy culture' and links to other institutional child sexual abuse scandals

A culture of secrecy on Jersey was reputedly behind the suspension of Jersey police chief, Graham Power, on 12 November 2008. Although he was reportedly suspended for showing a lack of competence in running the historic abuse inquiry and, in particular, for failing to exercise proper oversight of his deputy, Lenny Harper, in the Haut de la Garenne investigation, Jersey States' Members voted to keep secret the transcript of their debate into whether the minister responsible for Power's removal from office had misled the States over the reasons for his suspension.[53]

While he was conscious of the special challenges posed to policing on a small island, and that conflicts of interest due to school and family connections, for instance, could occur in any small community, Power believed he was suspended (until his retirement in July 2010) by an establishment riddled with conflicts of interest, stating: 'I was suspended by the very government whose institutions were being investigated. You cannot get much more conflicted than that'.[54] Deputy Mike Higgins, who called for the States' debate into Power's suspension, went further, saying:

> In my opinion, Mr Power's original suspension resembled a *coup d'etat* engineered by a small group of powerful people who denied him natural justice and have attempted since then to thwart enquiries, investigations and scrutiny into this affair and the original child abuse investigations. They have been aided and abetted by a politicised civil service, compliant media and other well meaning but naïve politicians.[55]

As if to underscore the whiff of conspiracy, Sir Philip Bailhache, who became an elected politician in the States of Jersey two years after retiring from the office of Bailiff in June 2009, was one of 19 Members who had voted against holding an *in camera* debate on whether the Home Affairs Minister had misled the States over Power's suspension, and was known also to have opposed the committee of inquiry set up to investigate how so many children in the care of Jersey authorities were abused.[56] Adding to suspicion of a cover-up was the fact that, at the height of the child abuse investigation, the two key posts of Attorney-General and Bailiff were held, respectively, by brothers, William and Sir Philip Bailhache, who are 'members of one of the oldest and most powerful families on Jersey'.[57]

There are elements of the Jersey child abuse case that make it at once strange yet uncomfortably familiar. Not least, there are those ingredients that make it inherently newsworthy and ripe for conspiracy theories, implicating 'Masons, paedophile rings, corrupt national or local politicians, civil servants and businessmen'.[58] Add to the mix ideas connecting the case of Haut de la Garenne to Jersey's reputation as a tax haven where financial secrets are kept and privacy is safely guarded, as well as the island's Nazi past,[59] and it is not hard to see why the case had irresistible journalistic appeal. However, there are also aspects of the Jersey case that are all too familiar. Most obvious are the similarities it has with historic abuse cases in children's homes across the UK, and in care institutions in Ireland and Nova Scotia, Canada.[60] As a consequence of these and a succession of scandals since the 1980s exposing sexual abuse in private schools and religions institutions, which forced the issue of institutionalised abuse onto the political agenda, it has been said that 'it is no longer possible for British society to deny knowledge of child sexual abuse in institutional settings'.[61]

Nonetheless, a culture of secrecy combined with institutional failure and denial has been a hallmark of all of these examples. The most extraordinary case in recent times is the Jimmy Savile scandal, which is linked to the Haut de la Garenne case, as it is believed Savile could have been involved in indecent assaults that occurred at the home during the 1970s.[62] There are also similarities in the cases insofar as some of the most prolific sexual predators in the Jersey case, like Savile, died before anything could be done about their crimes. And, rather disturbingly, some of those people were identified by victims in the Carter dossier, discussed above.[63]

The Jersey and Savile cases also display similar dynamics, each having key phases through which many institutional child sexual abuse scandals pass.[64] Greer and McLaughlin show how the Savile case shifted 'from a latent and slow-burning child sexual abuse scandal to an activated and rapidly amplifying scandal that retrofitted Sir Jimmy Savile as a prolific sexual predator and the BBC as a mendacious institution that knowingly connived at his offences'.[65] The Jersey case followed a similar pattern, particularly by connecting allegations of child abuse to institutional failure and cover-up.

Hence, the Jersey scandal lay dormant until it was 'activated', when Lenny Harper made public the discovery of what he believed to be the partial remains of a child on 23 February 2008. Furthermore, in the Jersey case, as described above, we see the hallmarks of the activated phase, where news organisations 'not only [knew] about the alleged sexual abuse, but decide[d] to report it and, crucially, to name the alleged abuser(s)'.[66] In an era where powerful individuals and institutions may sue for defamation or libel if allegations are made on the basis of unreliable or unsubstantiated evidence, scandal activation is not inevitable.[67] However, in the Jersey case, there appeared to be sufficient evidence, initially at least, corroborated by witness and victim accounts of abuse, to enable activation by the media.

According to Greer and McLaughlin, 'public denial drives and animates an activated institutional child sexual abuse scandal'.[68] Here, the typical institutional reaction is one of 'institutional narcissism',[69] the purpose of which 'is to prioritise at any cost the protection of the institution's reputation from negative publicity'. We see this clearly in the reaction of Jersey's political elite, which, concerned about how the Haut de la Garenne affair might affect the island's tourism industry and its reputation as an attractive place for financial investment, not only sacked whistleblower, Stuart Syvret, but went further, prosecuting him for arguably spurious data protection offences. A similar argument might be put in respect of the controversial suspension of the police chief, Graham Power.

Greer and McLaughlin argue that the 'primary techniques of reputation management, seemingly woven into the fabric of powerful institutions accused of child sexual abuse, are concerted ignorance and public denial of wrongdoing'.[70] Although public denial of wrongdoing was not as strong in the Jersey case as it had been with the BBC in the Savile scandal, Jersey authorities nevertheless appear to have ranged from being wantonly indifferent to wilfully blind about the child abuse that had been perpetrated in its care facilities over many years. Certainly, however, the Jersey story entered an amplification phase, when the transgressions of individuals were connected to 'institutional failure'.[71] Indeed, this was highlighted early on in the scandal when Syvret claimed that '[t]here has been a long-running systematic failure of child protection on the island'.[72] Moreover, as with other cases of institutional child sexual abuse, during this amplified period, talk of cultures of denial, cover-up and impunity were not limited to a single institution, but were applied to a range of institutions,[73] including, in the Jersey case, the Sea Cadets, St John Ambulance, private schools and other care facilities.

Finally, the 'justice' stage of an institutional child sexual abuse scandal comprises, among other things, repetition of initial allegations, disclosure of new transgressions, and public confessions and apologies by those involved or implicated.[74] It can also result in conviction for criminal offences. Hence, as we have seen, systemic failures in the case of Haut de la Garenne resulted not only in revelations about procedural incompetence and mismanagement,[75] but also in criminal convictions. Furthermore, as we have also seen, when faced with the veritable mountain of evidence pointing to institutional failure, Jersey's Chief Minister at the time, Terry Le Sueur, proffered an unreserved apology to victims, who can now claim compensation from the Historic Abuse Redress Scheme, so long as they are able 'to prove they were abused while in the island's full-time residential care at any time between 9 May 1945, the day Jersey was liberated from its Nazi occupation, and 31 December 1994'.[76]

However, there is one significant way in which the Jersey case differed from the Savile scandal (which resulted in the resignation of the Director-General of the BBC, along with organisational reform of its news reporting, and numerous inquiries into its failings as a corporation before and after the scandal's activation).[77] While the Jersey case saw some of the perpetrators caught and convicted, victims provided with a compensation fund and a sex offender register introduced, ultimately, it claimed no establishment figures, but instead claimed dissident officials, Syvret and Power.

It is probable that the scandal would have claimed Lenny Harper too, had he not retired early in the piece. Indeed, when some forensic experts began to cast doubt on the initial discovery of putative human remains, thinking them likely to be pieces of wood or coconut rather than bone, many locals blamed Harper for bringing shame on the island by divulging prematurely what his team had found, and one senator in the States of Jersey even accused him of misrepresenting the facts.[78] While Harper's experience fell short of being a 'trial by media' in which he would have been 'tried and sentenced in the "court of public opinion"',[79] his can be seen as another case in which senior police officers, 'subject to intense and critical journalistic scrutiny' in the 24/7 global news mediasphere,[80] might just as easily be built up as have their reputation and credibility knocked down.[81] Therefore, although the Jersey case has its idiosyncrasies, it also has elements in common with other cases of institutional child sexual abuse, such as the Savile scandal – which has itself been connected to a broader 'culture of secrecy' that persists across British society, and some of its key institutions,[82] as evidenced by, for instance, the police cover-up over the doctoring of evidence in the wake of the Hillsborough disaster,[83] and the phone-hacking scandal.[84]

Problems with privacy in small communities

As noted earlier, Jersey chief of police, Graham Power, was cognisant of some of the particular challenges faced in policing a small island, which, he said, could apply to any small community.[85] While life in small communities may appear to be (and in fact be) idyllic, criminological literature reveals there is also a dark side to communal life. For example, in *Policing the Rural Crisis*, Hogg and Carrington[86] show how Robert Putnam's[87] research in Italy debunked the romantic myth of pacific *Gemeinschaft* communities in the south of that country, which were actually violent, fearful, low-trust communities. Conversely, Putnam found the highly urbanised, impersonal and politically and legally sophisticated communities of northern and central Italy to be more egalitarian, stable and non-violent.[88] Similarly, Hogg and Carrington show how some family and community spaces have remained relatively less pacified compared to those of densely settled urban environments, where there has been a more concerted interpenetration of social, private and familial worlds. Accordingly, there is a sense in which rural communities are marked by a mentality of keeping up appearances:

> The more tightly-bound family and community structures that characterise the architecture of rural life tends [sic] to render them less receptive to forms of social intervention that might threaten projected images of self-reliance, family respectability and responsibility and stoicism in the face of adversity.[89]

Linked to this is the notion of the home as one's castle, an attitude born of the dense patterns of interaction that occur in small communities which, while strengthening interpersonal and communal bonds, also 'require special efforts if some privacy is to be achieved in the face of the highly visible nature of daily life'.[90] Hogg and Carrington go on to note that the careful management of everyday privacy is one factor that can contribute to a more ready recourse to violence in interpersonal relationships and encounters in many rural contexts. While the police are expected to rigorously enforce the norms of public order and laws safeguarding the sanctity of the private realm, greater circumspection is appropriate in respect of the policing of matters defined as 'private'. For example, attempts to police domestic and sexual violence fail largely because interventions by professionals and police officers are regarded as unwanted and unnecessary 'meddling' in matters regarded as 'private'.[91] Hogg and Carrington's analysis of the role of privacy in small communities may help to explain why, for so long, institutional child abuse remained unexposed on the island of Jersey.

As stated earlier, when faced with the criticism that Jersey's legal system could not cope with a case of the scale and intricacy of Haut de la Garenne, the Attorney-General, William Bailhache QC, said that outsiders might find it difficult to understand how things operate on a small island, where there is the upmost need for integrity.[92] Indeed, it has been observed that while Jersey has one of the highest per capita incomes on the planet, by far the most valuable asset on the island is discretion:

> The most cursory conversation with islanders will reveal how much they cherish their privacy. When the Dean of Jersey, the Very Rev Robert Key, held a service after the skull was found, it included the words: 'From over-inquisitiveness, false sensationalism and prurient curiosity, good Lord, deliver us'.[93]

On the face of it, this is an unremarkable statement, which reinforces Hogg and Carrington's findings. However, if it is read in the context of some of the more outlandish claims connecting Jersey's occupation by the Nazis to the secrecy surrounding historic child abuse on the island,[94] there is an interesting parallel with the case of Josef Fritzl, the 73-year-old man from the small Austrian town of Amstetten who, it was discovered in 2008, had imprisoned his daughter in a cellar under his family home for 24 years, subjecting her to abuse of various kinds and fathering her seven children. In 2009, Fritzl's trial was held behind closed doors, which was seen as indicative of 'Austria's obsession with privacy'.[95] According to some commentators, 'this culture of secrecy that enabled Fritzl to get away with his crimes for so long . . . has its roots in Nazi-era Austria'.[96] In this respect, there are stark similarities with the Jersey example:

> Austria's preoccupation with privacy is a throwback to the Nazi era, when Hitler was enthusiastically welcomed into towns like Amstetten, where a young Josef Fritzl sat on his father's shoulders and cheered the Fuhrer. Collaborators were encouraged to inform on neighbours who did not embrace the Nazi agenda, who were then taken away to a nearby concentration camp. After the war, Austria was desperate to hush up its complicity in the Holocaust: three out of every four death camp commandants was Austrian. Hence the instinct, which exists to this day, to cover up the unsavoury and discourage the sort of curtain-twitching that was rife during the war.[97]

Similarly, although the Channel Islands profit from 'dark tourism' associated with the Nazi occupation, Lennon and Foley argue that the view presented by the islands 'is sanitized and avoids elements which might compromise the islanders' self-history'.[98] Accordingly, 'aspects of the occupation such as collaboration, fraternization and compromise are in most cases avoided', as holidaymakers are encouraged simply 'to combine tourism with wartime reminiscences'.[99] Islanders' own interpretation of the German occupation focuses almost exclusively on liberation, and there is a kind of collective amnesia about some of the less palatable aspects of the occupation, such as the mass killings that occurred in forced labour camps on the islands.[100]

While the Fritzl case is extreme, it is not a one-off in Austria: 'Natascha Kampusch escaped her captor in 2006 after eight years in a bunker; three children were rescued from a cellar in Linz in 2007 after being locked up for seven years by their mother'.[101] Hence, Fritzl is seen as symptomatic of a broader malaise in Austrian society, as intimated by a protestor outside the court in which Fritzl was tried:

> We have a society where child abuse is hushed up and trivialised. People who report cases of abuse are often ignored or even intimidated by the authorities. The golden rule, which starts with bureaucrats and filters down through society, is that you shouldn't pry into people's private lives.[102]

On the other hand, it could be that the response to Fritzl and, in turn, the Jersey case, can be explained in more prosaic terms as simply reflecting modern notions of privacy. In his study of serial killing as a quintessentially modern phenomenon, Haggerty shows how the modern conception of 'a private sphere free from the prying eyes of officials and neighbours provides a space where serial killers can operate comparatively freely'.[103] If we extend the analogy to Fritzl and the cases of institutional child abuse on Jersey, we may find a similar explanation as to why the abuse apparently went unnoticed for so long:

> [P]eople who discover they have been living close to a serial killer mimic western neighbourly dynamics more generally in that they often profess to have known their murderous neighbour in only the most perfunctory fashion, and frequently appeal to notions of privacy to justify why they have failed to investigate the blatantly bizarre behaviour that was often demonstrated by the killer next door.[104]

A dark side to paradise

Criminological research into the ways in which moral regulation occurs in societies via the use of criminal sanctions also provides some useful insights that could help explain some of what happened on Jersey. New Zealand offers an interesting reference point. John Pratt has shown how New Zealand's cultural values may explain the unlikely paradox that New Zealand projects a self-image as an open, friendly and welcoming place, but in fact has high rates of imprisonment, especially for petty crime.[105] In short, says Pratt, New Zealand has 'a level of punitiveness out of proportion to the level of crime problems'.[106] Using a Durkheimian frame,[107] Pratt argues that punishment and imprisonment function to reinforce social cohesion, homogeneity, security and conformity, and to ensure New Zealand's paradisiacal qualities, which are 'reasserted and affirmed by sanctioning the transgressors'.[108]

Pratt goes on to state that '[t]hroughout the history of New Zealand, the famed qualities of friendliness and openness have been denied to those who were outside its narrow parameters of acceptability'.[109] In recent times, intolerance to those who threaten social cohesion, and excessive punitiveness in reactions to criminal behaviour have been underlain by:

> a new ethnic toxicity . . . 50 per cent of the prison population are indigenous Maori, even though they make up only 15 per cent of the population – in

> 1950, they constituted only 18 per cent of the prison population. The Maori rate of imprisonment is 350 per 100,000 of the population; that for Europeans is 100 per 100,000.[110]

Parallels between New Zealand and Jersey may be made, beginning with the notion that, like New Zealand, Jersey is a relatively pacific place to live, where people feel safe and secure, and where there is no real crime problem to speak of:

> Just 4,554 crimes were recorded in 2010 – a below-average number for a population of 92,500, and 9% down on 2009 . . . Only 6% of people said they were very worried that they might become a victim of violent crime, compared with 13% of UK respondents to the British Crime Survey in England and Wales.[111]

However, while in New Zealand it is the Maori population that bears the brunt of intolerance and excessive punitiveness, in Jersey it appears young people are most likely to be affected by the strictures of conformity, as evidenced by reports that, for example, 'four times more children, proportionately, are imprisoned in Jersey than in its nearest neighbour, France'.[112] Some support for applying Pratt's arguments about New Zealand to Jersey can also be found in a confidential report that was produced by two visiting social workers, David Lambert and Elizabeth Wilkinson, following the death in Jersey in 1979 of a two-year-old child at the hands of a foster parent.[113] The report looked more broadly at Jersey society, concluding that:

> while the island was reinventing itself as a haunt for jetsetters, there was a neglected group afflicted by a 'high incidence of marital breakdown, heavy drinking, alcoholism and psychiatric illness'. These problems were exacerbated by a small island mentality that demanded everyone 'conform to acceptable public standards'.[114]

The report also confirmed Pratt's analysis, following Durkheim, that societies placing excessive stress on social cohesion and conformity have equally exaggerated responses to threats posed to the *conscience collective*, evident in the high incidence of punishment for low-level crimes:

> Children rebelled in small ways: dropping litter, swearing, facing down the police, having parties on the beach. On Jersey, all of these 'offences' were, according to Lambert and Wilkinson, often sufficient to get a child into serious trouble. And once children had come to the attention of the police, it was almost inevitable that they would enter Jersey's care home system. Without any provision for children to be bailed, most were incarcerated on remand, placed alongside children taken from their families, often for such reasons as 'giving the mother a break'. In this rural backwater, one in 10 children had been in care, a ratio far higher than on the mainland.[115]

The idea that there is an oft-forgotten inconvenient underside to island life in Jersey beyond the picture-postcard image and its reputation as a playground for the rich was also a point made in the midst of the Haut de la Garenne investigation by a former island resident who grew up there but left in the late 1990s to pursue higher education on the UK mainland.[116] Scratch the surface, he said, and 'one discovers a prejudice-ridden isolationist mentality on an island with high walls and closed eyes'.[117] When he was growing up in Jersey, underprivileged children on the island – of which, he said, there were many – had few places to hide, and 'invariably fell into a "safety" net of questionable borstal-style homes or, if old enough, La Moye prison. As islands within islands, they were quickly forgotten'.[118]

An island set apart

A final set of explanations for the secrecy surrounding the Jersey child sexual abuse scandal relates to the island's status as an offshore tax haven, harbouring financial secrets,[119] which is seen by some as a metaphor for the wider culture of secrecy on the island.[120] In his book, *Treasure Islands*,[121] Nicholas Shaxson makes such a connection, observing that 'the ethos of the Jersey establishment derives ultimately from the offshore industries and their onshore controllers, not from innate island character'.[122] Shaxson describes the experience of John Christensen, a native of Jersey, who, after being appointed as an economic adviser upon his return to the island in the mid-1980s, encountered not only 'extremist right-wing offshore attitudes', but also 'elite, secretive insider networks, typically linked to the financial sector'.[123] He found that:

> many people who came to see him wanted him to join their Masonic lodge, and gave him the secret signal. 'Their thinking is very much of the old-boy network – you are either one of us or you are against us', he continued. 'It means they can trust you to do the right thing without having to be told – an insidious meaning of the word "trust"'.[124]

Equally, Shaxson says, '[t]here is something about island life that stifles dissent', which means islands are 'especially hospitable to offshore finance, reassuring international financiers that local establishments can be trusted not to allow democratic politics to interfere in the business of making money'.[125] Shaxson shows how this has been borne out by the experience of Stuart Syvret, who described Jersey as 'a society with no checks and balances, run by an oligarchy', in which a 'climate of fear' prohibits people from expressing 'anti-Jersey' sentiments.[126]

However, the term 'tax haven' is something of a misnomer, because rather than being solely about tax, what offshore entities primarily sell is escape 'from the laws, rules and taxes of jurisdictions elsewhere, usually with secrecy as their prime offering'.[127] Despite having their own elected parliament and being responsible for their own finances, as the name indicates, British Crown dependencies such as Jersey are only semi-autonomous of the UK.[128] Indeed, they have a somewhat ambiguous relationship with Britain, which:

> goes to great lengths to hide its control . . . Jersey's most senior public sector officials are appointed in London; its laws are all approved by the Privy Council in London, and Britain handles Jersey's foreign relations and defence, and the lieutenant governor represents the Queen.[129]

The special relationship between Britain and the island runs deep and is truly heartfelt, as is evidenced by Winston Churchill's comment in his speech marking the unconditional surrender of German forces in Europe on 8 May 1945 that, 'our dear Channel Islands are also to be freed today'. Translating that sentiment into financial terms, Jersey Finance sees the island as 'an extension of the City of London'.[130] Hence, it forms part of the 'secretive financial web' that has the City of London at its heart, surrounded by Crown dependences and overseas territories, where:

> hi-tech global finance melds into ancient rites and customs that underline its separateness and power with mystifying pomp. Among the City's 108 livery companies, or trade associations, you will find the Worshipful Companies of Loriners (concerned with stirrups and other harnesses for horses) and Fletchers (arrow-makers) as well as the Worshipful Company of Tax Advisers, among whose four prime aims is 'to support the Lord Mayor and the City of London Corporation', and the Worshipful Company of International Bankers, whose heraldic 'supporters' are the griffins, guardians of treasure.[131]

The 'elsewhere' status of offshore tax havens, and ambiguous position of the City of London, are reminiscent of the Vatican City's spurious claim to statehood that originates in the Lateran Treaty of 1929, which is relied upon by Britain even though it is a pact, not a treaty, to which Britain is not a party.[132] Furthermore, it has been observed that this claim to statehood was central to the crisis that enveloped the Catholic Church when it emerged it had covered up the sexual abuse of children by paedophile priests, who were dealt with under the secrecy of the Vatican's own canon law and procedures rather than local criminal law.[133]

Like the Jersey child abuse case, this arrangement nurtured feelings of secrecy, conspiracy and corruption,[134] which is why, as in the case of Savile,[135] it was suggested that an independent inquiry be set up to determine what happened on Jersey.[136] There have also been calls for UK authorities to conduct a thorough analysis of the child protection system in Jersey, where, it has been said, there is a 'need to attract new and experienced staff'.[137] Indeed, apart from Stuart Syvret, all of the main players in the child abuse investigation on Jersey were outsiders, who assembled a team that included police officers and support staff from the British mainland.[138]

However, the treatment of both insiders and outsiders before, during and after the child abuse inquiry would appear indicative of the Jersey establishment's instinct to close ranks. As recently as 2007, UK social worker, Simon Bellwood, claimed he had been sacked for blowing the whistle on the practice of holding children as young as 11 in solitary confinement in a children's home on the island.[139] And in 2012, an American author and journalist, Leah McGrath Goodman, claimed she had been barred from entering the UK and Channel Islands after authorities discovered she was writing a book about the historic child abuse inquiry focusing on Haut de la Garenne.[140] As a former Tier-1 visa holder with a spotless record, Goodman said she was surprised by the UK Border Agency's statement that she had been refused entry because it was 'not satisfied she was genuinely seeking entry as a visitor for the limited period she claimed', and that 'she attempted to mislead the Border Force officer about her travel plans and the reason she required entry to the UK'.[141]

Although the Jersey child abuse case indicates strongly that there is a need in any small and relatively closed society for independent assessment and monitoring of child protection services, amidst the furore over Haut de la Garenne, one outsider, Malcolm Johnson, leapt to the defence of those he had worked with on Jersey for more than seven years as an adviser on ageing, stating he was 'constantly struck' by the 'openness to constructive criticism' of 'the island's civil servants, professionals and many of its politicians'.[142] These comments were made in response to what Johnson saw as some of the gratuitous observations of journalist, Helen Pidd,[143] linking the child abuse case at Haut de la Garenne to Jersey's status as a tax haven and its Nazi past, which, in Johnson's view, unfairly denigrated the entire island.

This leads to a final point about media reporting of the crimes that allegedly occurred at Haut de la Garenne. Although Lenny Harper's initial vagueness as to the nature of the discoveries at the children's home and his openness were tactics adopted with the intention of protecting the police investigation and any future prosecutions, as well as providing an environment in which victims and witnesses would feel safe in coming forward, they also left a 'news vacuum' that, as shown above, was filled by some rather lurid newspaper headlines.[144] For some more vociferous critics, this provided yet another example of the media's commercial predilection for producing sensationalist stories, regardless of their veracity.[145] For others, it highlighted the failure of journalists to challenge police statements at press conferences.[146] Other commentators suggested that child abuse on Jersey had been unexamined for so long, not only because of the indifference of relevant authorities, but also because of the absence of a robust local press,[147] which did not perform its public watchdog role.[148]

Conclusion

This chapter has sought to explicate the secrecy surrounding child abuse in Jersey by reference to a confluence of specific factors unique to Jersey, including the alleged collective amnesia associated with the island's occupation by the Nazis during World War II, as well as the island's status as a tax haven harbouring financial secrets. However, the chapter has also looked at the Jersey case according to more generalised ideas about the operation of privacy and moral regulation in small communities. Although such communities often appear idyllic and paradisiacal, a sinister or dark side to life in these places sometimes comes to light when scandals like the concealment of systemic child abuse arise. Furthermore, the sequence of events in the Jersey case suggests that there are common dynamics in cases of institutional child abuse involving secrecy and alleged cover-up. The presence of institutional failure in such cases points to the need for independent and external assessment, and monitoring and review of child protection services, not only in small communities, but in general, as well as the need for news media to play a critical public interest role in scrutinising police and political authority.

Notes

1 John Donne, Meditation XVII, *Devotions Upon Emergent Occasions* (Anthony Raspa (ed.), Oxford University Press 1987) 87.
2 For example, a satanic day care moral panic was triggered in the United States in the 1980s by the McMartin Preschool case, where 369 current and past enrolees 'named not only seven McMartin day care providers as their satanic abusers, but local businesspeople and city officials, world leaders, television and film stars, and even their own family members': Mary deYoung, 'Another Look at Moral Panics: The Case of Satanic Day Care Centers' (1998) 19(3) *Deviant Behaviour*, 257, 261.
3 Helen Pidd and Steven Morris, 'Six More Bodies Feared Buried in Jersey Home' *The Guardian* (London, 25 February 2008) <http://www.theguardian.com/uk/2008/feb/25/jersey.child.bodies> accessed 5 October 2014.
4 Anil Dawar, 'Police to Review Bergerac Episode in Jersey Investigation' *The Guardian* (London, 5 March 2008) <http://www.theguardian.com/news/2008/mar/04/ukcrime.childprotection> accessed 5 October 2014.
5 Claire Truscott, 'Police Find Two More Jersey "Punishment Rooms"' *The Guardian* (online, 26 March 2008) <http://www.theguardian.com/uk/2008/mar/25/hautdelagarenne.jersey.childabuse> accessed 5 October 2014.
6 Haroon Siddique and David Batty, 'Police Investigate Jersey "Failures" over Abuse Claims' *The Guardian* (London, 26 February 2008) <http://www.theguardian.com/society/2008/feb/25/childprotection.ukcrime> accessed 5 October 2014.
7 Ian Cobain, 'Cellar Police Sift through Past for Abuse Secrets' *The Guardian* (London, 1 March 2008) <http://www.theguardian.com/uk/2008/mar/01/childabuse.jersey> accessed 5 October 2014.
8 Cathy Scott-Clark, 'Home to Something Evil' *The Guardian* (London, 14 March 2009) <http://www.theguardian.com/society/2009/mar/14/haut-de-la-garenne> accessed 5 October 2014.
9 Siddique and Batty (n. 6).
10 Scott-Clark (n. 8).
11 Ian Cobain, 'Police Look into Claim of Secret Suicides at Jersey Home' *The Guardian* (London, 4 March 2008) <http://www.theguardian.com/uk/2008/mar/04/ukcrime.children> accessed 5 October 2014.
12 Ibid.
13 Ibid.
14 Scott-Clark (n. 8).
15 Ibid.
16 Ibid.
17 Anil Dawar, 'We Can Cope with Child Abuse Inquiry, Says Jersey Law Boss' *The Guardian* (London, 1 August 2008) <http://www.theguardian.com/uk/2008/aug/01/ukcrime.jerseyisland> accessed 5 October 2014.

18 Ibid.; see also Helen Pidd, 'House of Horrors' *The Guardian* (London, 2 August 2008) <http://www.theguardian.com/uk/2008/aug/02/jerseyisland.ukcrime> accessed 5 October 2014.
19 Dawar (n. 17); Pidd (n. 18).
20 Dawar (n. 17).
21 Ibid.; cf. Malcolm Johnson, 'Don't Let the Haut de la Garenne Horrors Demonise an Entire Island' *The Guardian* (London, 8 August 2008) <http://www.theguardian.com/commentisfree/2008/aug/08/jerseyisland.childprotection> accessed 5 October 2014.
22 Dawar (n. 17).
23 David Batty, 'Jersey to Get First Sex Offenders Register' *The Guardian* (London, 3 June 2008) <http://www.theguardian.com/news/2008/jun/02/jerseyisland.childprotection> accessed 5 October 2014; see also Pidd (n. 18).
24 Dawar (n. 17).
25 Nick Davies, '"It Started with a Piece of Bone" – and a Dog' *The Guardian* (London, 5 May 2008) <http://www.theguardian.com/media/2008/may/05/pressandpublishing.childprotection> accessed 5 October 2014.
26 Ibid.
27 Ibid.
28 Brian Cathcart, 'Jersey Child Abuse Case' *New Statesman* (London, 6 March 2008) <http://www.newstatesman.com/media/2008/03/child-abuse-jersey-police> accessed 5 October 2014.
29 Pidd (n. 18).
30 Helen Pidd, 'Jersey's "Secrecy Culture" Led to My Suspension, Says Former Police Chief' *The Guardian* (London, 29 June 2012) <http://www.theguardian.com/uk/2012/jun/28/jersey-secrecy-culture> accessed 5 October 2014.
31 Ibid.
32 Dawar (n. 4).
33 Pidd (n. 18).
34 Ibid.
35 Helen Pidd, 'Jersey Knife Attacks Add to Island's Reputation for Crime' *The Guardian* (London, 16 August 2011) <http://www.theguardian.com/uk/2011/aug/15/jersey-knife-attacks-crime> accessed 5 October 2014.
36 James Orr, 'Former Head of Jersey Inquiry Attacks Island's Legal System' *The Guardian* (London, 22 August 2008) <http://www.theguardian.com/uk/2008/aug/22/jerseyisland> accessed 5 October 2014.
37 Ibid.
38 Catherine Bennett, 'Baby P Exposes Our Need to Believe in the Perfect Parent' *The Observer* (London, 16 November 2008) <http://www.theguardian.com/commentisfree/2008/nov/16/child-protection-babyp-catherine-bennett> accessed 5 October 2014; see also Peter Wilby, 'Murder, They Wrote' *The Guardian* (London, 1 December 2008) <http://www.theguardian.com/media/2008/dec/01/jersey-children-home-haut-garenne> accessed 5 October 2014.
39 Bennett (n. 38).
40 David Batty, 'Children "Also Abused on Guernsey"' *The Guardian* (London, 5 March 2008) <http://www.theguardian.com/society/2008/mar/05/childprotection> accessed 5 October 2014.
41 Scott-Clark (n. 8); see also Siddique and Batty (n. 6).
42 Ian Cobain, 'Jersey: Haut de la Garenne Children's Home Abuse Scandal Ends with One Last Conviction' *The Guardian* (London, 7 January 2011) <http://www.theguardian.com/uk/2011/jan/06/jersey-childrens-home-scandal-ends> accessed 5 October 2014.

43 Ibid.
44 Helen Pidd, 'Jersey Child Abuse Victims to Receive Compensation' *The Guardian* (London, 30 March 2012) <http://www.theguardian.com/uk/2012/mar/29/jersey-child-abuse-victims-compensation> accessed 5 October 2014; see also Clare Dyer, 'Lawyers Want Special Board to Deal with Jersey Abuse Victims' Claims' *The Guardian* (London, 9 June 2008) <http://www.theguardian.com/uk/2008/jun/09/law.ukcrime> accessed 5 October 2014.
45 Batty (n. 23).
46 Haroon Siddique, 'Jersey Care Homes "Covered up Abuses"' *The Guardian* (London, 27 February 2008) <http://www.theguardian.com/uk/2008/feb/26/ukcrime.childprotection1> accessed 5 October 2014; see also Scott-Clark (n. 8).
47 Cobain (n. 7).
48 Siddique (n. 46).
49 Ibid.
50 Helen Pidd, 'Former Jersey Minister Stuart Syvret to be Jailed over Blog Allegations' *The Guardian* (London, 5 November 2013) <http://www.theguardian.com/uk-news/2013/nov/04/jersey-stuart-syvret-jailed-blog-allegations> accessed 5 October 2014.
51 Ibid.
52 Ibid.
53 Pidd (n. 30).
54 Ibid.
55 Ibid.
56 Ibid.
57 Scott-Clark (n. 8).
58 David Wilson, 'Waifs and Strays' *The Guardian* (London, 29 February 2008) <http://www.theguardian.com/commentisfree/2008/feb/29/waifsandstrays> accessed 5 October 2014.
59 See, for example, Cathcart (n. 28); Pidd (n. 18).
60 See, for example, Cathcart (n. 28); Davies (n. 25); Dyer (n. 44); Pidd (n. 18); Wilby (n. 38); Wilson (n. 58).
61 Chris Greer and Eugene McLaughlin, 'The Sir Jimmy Savile Scandal: Child Sexual Abuse and Institutional Denial at the BBC' (2013) 9(3) *Crime Media Culture*, 243, 245.
62 Josh Halliday, Katharine Viner and Lisa O'Carroll, 'Jimmy Savile Linked with Haut de la Garenne Children's Home Scandal' *The Guardian* (London, 9 October 2012) <http://www.theguardian.com/media/2012/oct/08/jimmy-savile-jersey-childrens-home> accessed 5 October 2014; Sandra Laville and Josh Halliday, 'Report Reveals Jimmy Savile Assaulted Children as Young as 10' *The Guardian* (London, 11 January 2013) <http://www.theguardian.com/media/2013/jan/10/jimmy-savile-abuse-inquiry-published> accessed 5 October 2014.
63 Scott-Clark (n. 8).
64 Greer and McLaughlin (n. 61).
65 Ibid. 259.
66 Ibid. 246.
67 Ibid.
68 Ibid.
69 Fiona Gardner, 'Defence Processes and Deception: An Analysis of the Response of the Institutional Church to Disclosures of Child Sexual Abuse' (2012) 28 *British Journal of Psychotherapy*, 98.
70 Greer and McLaughlin (n. 61) 246.
71 Ibid.
72 Pidd and Morris (n. 3).

73 Greer and McLaughlin (n. 61) 247.
74 Ibid.
75 Alleged abusers were either moved into other care roles on the island or, as in the case of former Haut de la Garenne headmaster, Colin Tilbrook, moved to the British mainland, having never been investigated by Jersey social services: Scott-Clark (n. 8).
76 Pidd (n. 44).
77 Greer and McLaughlin (n. 61) 260.
78 Pidd (n. 18).
79 Chris Greer and Eugene McLaughlin, '"Trial by Media": Policing, the 24–7 News Mediasphere and the "Politics of Outrage"' (2011) 15(1) *Theoretical Criminology*, 23, 27.
80 Chris Greer and Eugene McLaughlin, 'Trial by Media: Phone-hacking, Riots, Looting, Gangs and Police Chiefs' in Jill Peay and Tim Newburn (eds.), *Policing, Politics, Culture and Control: Essays in Honour of Robert Reiner* (Hart 2012) 137.
81 Ibid. 136.
82 David Vincent, *The Culture of Secrecy: Britain, 1832–1998* (Oxford University Press 1998).
83 On 15 April 1989, the Hillsborough football disaster resulted in the deaths of 96 people caught in a fatal crush at Hillsborough stadium, Sheffield, England. The 2012 Hillsborough Independent Panel report discredited the official version of events, and outlined numerous failings, including police alteration of statements: see <http://hillsborough.independent.gov.uk/> accessed 5 October 2014. The Independent Police Complaints Commission is now investigating alleged police criminality regarding the Hillsborough disaster: see <http://www.ipcc.gov.uk/hillsborough/the-investigation> accessed 5 October 2014. See also Rebecca Scott Bray, 'Paradoxical Justice: The Case of Ian Tomlinson' (2013) 21 *Journal of Law and Medicine*, 447, 447–8; Greg Martin and Rebecca Scott Bray, 'Discolouring Democracy? Policing, Sensitive Evidence, and Contentious Deaths in the United Kingdom' (2013) 40(4) *Journal of Law and Society*, 624, 626.
84 Allegations of phone hacking by the British press first emerged in 2005, and further erupted when investigations revealed systematic phone hacking targeting celebrities, politicians and victims of crime, including the hacking of murdered teenager Milly Dowler's phone, by employees of the *News of the World* newspaper. The scandal led to the closure of *News of the World*, the Leveson Inquiry into the culture, practices and ethics of the British press, and criminal convictions. See George Eaton, 'Tom Watson Accuses May of "a Cover-up" Over Child Abuse Claims' *New Statesman* (London, 6 November 2012) <http://www.newstatesman.com/politics/2012/11/tom-watson-accuses-may-cover-over-child-abuse-claims> accessed 5 October 2014.
85 Pidd (n. 30).
86 Russell Hogg and Kerry Carrington, *Policing the Rural Crisis* (The Federation Press 2006).
87 Robert Putnam, *Making Democracy Work: Civic Traditions in Modern Italy* (Princeton University Press 1993).
88 Hogg and Carrington (n. 86) 196.
89 Ibid. 188.
90 Ibid. 190.
91 Ibid. 191.
92 cf. Johnson (n. 21).
93 Cobain (n. 7); see also Cathcart (n. 28).
94 See, for example, Pidd (n. 18); cf. Cathcart (n. 28); Johnson (n. 21).
95 Gordon Rayner, 'Culture of Secrecy That Allowed Austria to Look the Other Way over Josef Fritzl' *The Telegraph* (London, 17 March 2009) <http://www.telegraph.co.uk/comment/5008054/Culture-of-secrecy-that-allowed-Austria-to-look-the-other-way-over-Josef-Fritzl.html> accessed 5 October 2014.

96 Ibid.; see also Ian Traynor, 'After Josef Fritzl: A Time for Introspection or Looking the Other Way?' *The Guardian* (London, 20 March 2009) <http://www.theguardian.com/world/2009/mar/19/josef-fritzl-austria-society> accessed 5 October 2014.
97 Rayner (n. 95).
98 John Lennon and Malcolm Foley, *Dark Tourism: The Attraction of Death and Disaster* (Thomson 2004) 67.
99 Ibid.
100 Ibid. 69–73.
101 Rayner (n. 95).
102 Ibid.
103 Kevin Haggerty, 'Modern Serial Killers' (2009) 5(2) *Crime Media Culture*, 168, 176.
104 Ibid.
105 John Pratt, 'The Dark Side of Paradise: Explaining New Zealand's History of High Imprisonment' (2006) 46(4) *British Journal of Criminology*, 541, 541.
106 Ibid.
107 Emile Durkheim, *The Division of Labour in Modern Society* (first published 1893, Macmillan 1991).
108 Pratt (n. 105) 545.
109 Ibid. 553.
110 Ibid. 542.
111 Pidd (n. 35).
112 Scott-Clark (n. 8).
113 Ibid.
114 Ibid.
115 Ibid.
116 Ryan Thompson, 'Siege: An Island Mentality' *The Guardian* (London, 27 February 2008) <http://www.theguardian.com/commentisfree/2008/feb/26/siegeanislandmentality> accessed 5 October 2014.
117 Ibid.
118 Ibid.
119 Sophie McBain, 'Why Britain is a World Leader in Financial Secrets' *New Statesman* (London, 7 November 2013 <http://www.newstatesman.com/tax-and-spending/2013/11/why-britain-world-leader-financial-secrecy> accessed 5 October 2014.
120 Pidd (n. 18); cf. Cathcart (n. 28); Johnson (n. 21).
121 Nicholas Shaxson, *Treasure Islands: Tax Havens and the Men who Stole the World* (Bodley Head 2011).
122 Nicholas Shaxson, 'The Truth about Tax Havens' *The Guardian* (London, 8 January 2011) <http://www.theguardian.com/theguardian/2011/jan/08/jersey-tax-haven-nicholas-shaxson> accessed 5 October 2014.
123 Ibid.
124 Ibid.
125 Ibid.
126 Ibid.
127 Nicolas Shaxson, 'The Tax Haven in the Heart of Britain' *New Statesman* (London, 24 February 2011) <http://www.newstatesman.com/economy/2011/02/london-corporation-city> accessed 5 October 2014.
128 Simon Bowers, 'Roots of Channel Islands' Uncertain Relationship with UK Go Back to 1066' *The Guardian* (London, 27 June 2012) <http://www.theguardian.com/uk/2012/jun/27/channel-islands-uncertain-relationship-uk> accessed 5 October 2014.
129 Nicholas Shaxson, 'The Truth about Tax Havens: Part 2' *The Guardian* (London, 10 January 2011 <http://www.theguardian.com/business/2011/jan/09/truth-about-tax-havens-two> accessed 5 October 2014.
130 Shaxson (n. 127).

131 Ibid.
132 Geoffrey Robertson, 'The Case against Vatican Power' *New Statesman* (London, 8 September 2010) <http://www.newstatesman.com/law-and-reform/2010/09/vatican-rights-state-italy> accessed 5 October 2014.
133 Ibid; Matthew Kneale, 'Pope Francis's Mission to Cleanse the Catholic Church of Luxury' *New Statesman* (London, 24 October 2013) <http://www.newstatesman.com/2013/10/austerity-pope> accessed 5 October 2014; Cristina Odone, 'The New Intolerance: Will We Regret Pushing Christians out of Public Life?' *New Statesman* (London, 14 January 2014) <http://www.newstatesman.com/2014/01/new-intolerance> accessed 5 October 2014.
134 Kneale (n. 133).
135 Greer and McLaughlin (n. 61) 258–9.
136 Dawar (n. 17); Pidd (n. 18).
137 Liz Davies, 'We Must Support the Jersey Survivors' *The Guardian* (London, 1 August 2008) <http://www.theguardian.com/society/2008/aug/01/childprotection.jersey-island> accessed 5 October 2014.
138 Cobain (n. 7).
139 Davies (n. 137).
140 Pidd (n. 30)
141 Ibid.
142 Johnson (n. 21).
143 Pidd (n. 18).
144 Cathcart (n. 28).
145 Davies (n. 25).
146 Wilby (n. 38).
147 Michael White, 'Does Fleet Street Treat the Police Fairly?' *The Guardian* (London, 5 March 2008) <http://www.theguardian.com/politics/blog/2008/mar/05/michaelwhitespoliticalblog94> accessed 5 October 2014.
148 See Greer and McLaughlin (n. 61) 260.

Index

For Product Safety Concerns and Information please contact our EU representative GPSR@taylorandfrancis.com
Taylor & Francis Verlag GmbH, Kaufingerstraße 24, 80331 München, Germany

www.ingramcontent.com/pod-product-compliance
Ingram Content Group UK Ltd.
Pitfield, Milton Keynes, MK11 3LW, UK
UKHW010956180926
475701UK00004B/398

* 9 7 8 0 4 1 5 7 9 2 2 5 7 *